Summer 1998 Vol. XVIII, no. 2
ISSN: 0276-0045 ISBN: 1-56478-191-7

THE RE[illegible] CONTEMPOR[illegible]N

 Address all correspondence to:
The Review of Contemporary Fiction,
ISU Campus Box 4241, Normal, IL 61790-4241 USA.

visit our website: www.cas.ilstu.edu/english/dalkey/dalkey.html

The Review of Contemporary Fiction is published three times a year (February, June, October) by The Review of Contemporary Fiction, Inc., a nonprofit organization located at ISU Campus Box 4241, Normal, IL 61790-4241. ISSN 0276-0045. Subscription prices are as follows:

Single volume (three issues):
Individuals: $17.00; foreign, add $3.50;
Institutions: $26.00; foreign, add $3.50.

DISTRIBUTION. Bookstores should send orders to:

Dalkey Archive Press, ISU Campus Box 4241, Normal, IL. 61790-4241. Phone 309-438-7555; fax 309-438-7422.

This issue is partially supported by a grant from the Illinois Arts Council, a state agency.

Indexed in *American Humanities Index, International Bibliography of Periodical Literature, International Bibliography of Book Reviews, MLA Bibliography,* and *Book Review Index.* Abstracted in *Abstracts of English Studies.*

The Review of Contemporary Fiction is also available in 16mm microfilm, 35mm microfilm, and 105mm microfiche from University Microfilms International, 300 North Zeeb Road, Ann Arbor, MI 48106-1346.

visit our website: www.cas.ilstu.edu/english/dalkey/dalkey.html

The Review of Contemporary Fiction

Future issues devoted to: Rikki Ducornet, Curtis White, Milorad Pavić, Richard Powers, Ed Sanders, and postmodern Japanese fiction.

Back Issues

Back issues are still available for the following numbers of the *Review of Contemporary Fiction* ($8 each unless otherwise noted):

Douglas Woolf / Wallace Markfield
William Eastlake / Aidan Higgins
Alexander Theroux / Paul West
Camilo José Cela
Claude Simon ($15)
Chandler Brossard
Samuel Beckett
Claude Ollier / Carlos Fuentes
John Barth / David Markson
Donald Barthelme / Toby Olson
Paul Bowles / Coleman Dowell
Brigid Brophy / Robert Creeley / Osman Lins
William T. Vollmann / Susan Daitch / David Foster Wallace
William H. Gass / Manuel Puig
Robert Walser
José Donoso / Jerome Charyn
Georges Perec / Felipe Alfau
Joseph McElroy
Djuna Barnes
Angela Carter / Tadeusz Konwicki
Stanley Elkin / Alasdair Gray
Edmund White / Samuel R. Delany
Mario Vargas Llosa / Josef Skvorecky
Wilson Harris / Alan Burns
Raymond Queneau / Carole Maso

Novelist as Critic: Essays by Garrett, Barth, Sorrentino, Wallace, Ollier, Brooke-Rose, Creeley, Mathews, Kelly, Abbott, West, McCourt, McGonigle, and McCarthy
New Finnish Fiction: Fiction by Eskelinen, Jäntti, Kontio, Krohn, Paltto, Sairanen, Selo, Siekkinen, Sund, Valkeapää
New Italian Fiction: Interviews and fiction by Malerba, Tabucchi, Zanotto, Ferrucci, Busi, Corti, Rasy, Cherchi, Balduino, Ceresa, Capriolo, Carrera, Valesio, and Gramigna
Grove Press Number: Contributions by Allen, Beckett, Corso, Ferlinghetti, Jordan, McClure, Rechy, Rosset, Selby, Sorrentino, and others
New Danish Fiction: Fiction by Brøgger, Høeg, Andersen, Grøndahl, Holst, Jensen, Thorup, Michael, Sibast, Ryum, Lynggaard, Grønfeldt, Willumsen, and Holm
The Future of Fiction: Essays by Birkerts, Caponegro, Franzen, Galloway, Maso, Morrow, Vollmann, White, and others

Individuals receive a 10% discount on orders of one issue and a 20% discount on orders of two or more issues. To place an order, use the form on the last page of this issue.

contents

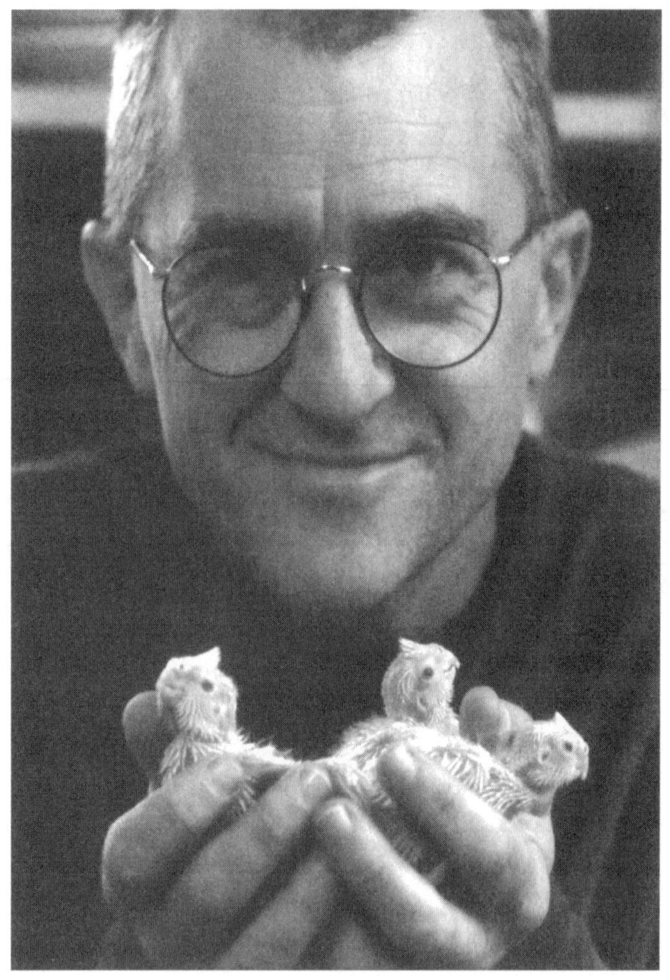

Curtis White

Photograph by Georganne Rundblad

Dream for Us a Different World: Introducing Curtis White

Robert L. McLaughlin

I think of Curtis White as the model of the child-of-the-sixties as writer. Born in 1951 and raised in San Lorenzo, California, in a postwar, prefabricated housing development, White came of age in the political turbulence of the late sixties, as activism veered from passive civil disobedience to the increasingly violent, in the countercultural climate of San Francisco, and in the anything-goes literary heyday of High Postmodernism. These contexts are important in understanding the shapes of White's subsequent careers—as theorist, teacher, publisher, and writer. As a theorist, he has pursued a social critique of the ways culture, especially pop culture, can serve and subvert the ideological status quo. (A collection of White's essays—*Monstrous Possibility*—has just been published.) As a teacher of literature and creative writing, he seeks to educate students as to the roles they play in the maintenance and reproduction of the dominant ideology and the potential they have to challenge it. As a publisher—White is the long-time co-director of FC2—he seeks to make available to a reading audience the most avant of the avant-garde, fiction that breaks all the rules and challenges all social, cultural, and personal assumptions. I find it strikingly fitting that, as I write this, White is leading the Illinois State University faculty fight against administrative attempts to curtail faculty involvement in the running of the university; the issue is what we now call shared governance and what we used to call participatory democracy.

But for the purposes of this essay, I want to consider White as a writer of fiction. Like many of the authors I admire—Thomas Pynchon, William Gaddis, Richard Powers—White is able to create fiction that recognizes the poststructural challenges to the ability of narrative to function as a meaning-conveying vehicle and at the same time gives the inescapable impression that its author cares deeply about many things and believes in fiction's ability to have an impact on the world. This seeming contradiction is mirrored in concerns that are evident in all five of his books. They all embrace a wide social and historical landscape, yet they seek to explore the individual psyche. They all establish the artist as detached witness of social atrocity and folly, yet they argue for the social activism of art. They all critique the way pop culture serves the needs of power, yet they find in pop culture liberatory potential. In one of White's early stories, "The Heretical Singing of Pietro Carnesecchi," the title character—corrupt monk, accused heretic, but visionary storyteller—has a dream in which a large group of people come to him, saying, "We've all decided that we're tired of this life. We feel that we need another," and they ask him, "Dream for us a different world and impose it on this one" (*Heretical Songs* 108). This idea is developed into the shortest chapter in *The Idea of Home*, "Remember John Lennon":

> Everybody of my generation has the same memory. We were twelve or thirteen or we were twenty-one, for that matter, and we were going to be veterinarians or we were, like Ringo, going to own a hairdresser's parlor. We walked into the record store and saw the cover of *Sgt. Pepper's Lonely Hearts Club Band*. We thought together, "Life can be other than it has been."
>
> This experience is the phenomenal moment of our generation's Ought. The fact that yippies became yuppies changes that Ought no whit. Every generation has similar opportunities. Our cumulative failure to understand and claim our opportunities is the large part of our poverty. (156)

This articulates a good way of thinking about White's mission as an artist: to inspire his readers to recognize the poverty of existence in contemporary America and to offer the opportunity to discover new possibilities for being.

Considering what we now know about White's mission, the subject matter for his first book seems odd in that it is so far removed from contemporary society and its problems. White has said that when he began writing, rather than immersing himself in the life he had lived so far, he wanted to get as far away from it as he could; so he explored instead worlds that were unfamiliar to him but worlds that through research and imagination he could make his own. The result was *Heretical Songs* (1980), a collection of stories that focus on writers, artists, and musicians, all European, from time periods ranging from the sixteenth century to the end of the nineteenth century. Taken together, these stories explore ideas about the production of art, the interpretation of art, the power of art to imagine new worlds, and the power of the state to maintain the status quo.

The stories connect art and sex in that both potentially can create new worlds, but this connection is saved from cliché and made problematic both by the humorous and graphic nature of its presentation and by the difficulty of realizing the promise of those new worlds. In "Mahler's Last Symphony," written through a description of Mahler's Fourth Symphony, Rotthamus Angelicus Krisper, the narrator, describes showing Mahler his latest work: "I then led him to my dim closet and presented a pile of crumpled and thoroughly soiled drafts. Mahler backed away in horror and disgust. 'Krisper's Symphony #4 in G minor. Take a look.' The last pages and calamitous finale were still moist with creation. 'This, Mahler, is what the works of man are worth' " (3). The story follows this conflict between Mahler's transcendent and Krisper's earthy ideas of creation. Krisper seems intent on dispelling notions of the transcendent in art, arguing instead that art is about what is, not what could be: "We understand that life is as it happens, but that it is never inaccessible or impenetrable to those of us capable of casting a cold eye on it. Simple life yields its secrets and substance after only the most rudimentary prodding. Meaning is simple. 'Why?' obvious" (9). Similarly, for him, sex is simple and biological, as we see in his description of Mahler, his wife Alma, and their infidelities: "Mahler requires a certain sexual variety and so goes to Anna. Alma, feeling a little left out, dabbles in some of the same with the dapper, articulate Rott. There is no anxiety because the participants understand that it is all just something between us animals" (9). But Krisper's position is undercut when Mahler comes upon the bound Alma. He loosens her and tenderly hugs her, but then the two are apparently shot by Krisper, intent on dragging them, their act, and their art back into the earth. But the love, the violence, and the description of the music overlap to create a transcendent world and even to conjure up children (a choir): "Mahler, in those fading seconds, hit upon the choral arrangement he sought for the conclusion to his last work. And that rack of children no doubt sang like a thousand angels and lifted the two with frightful hosannas to God's promised song of bliss" (10).

Many of the stories here set their artist characters in the tension between the mundane phenomenal world and a possible transcendence made possible through art. In "Claude" title character Claude Debussy's faith in the possibilities of transcendence through sex and art leads to his dismissal of the phenomenal world as unreal. At the end of a London affair, his English lover offers a revelation: "a beautiful ring at her thigh, two inches of bare feminine flesh between stockings and frilly knickers. Her skin gave off a pale but beautiful light" (59). This sight offers Claude a kind of revelation that convinces him "that the world was a vast contrivance and that he was the only real person in it. The rest of humanity with its outrageous improbabilities was fictitious" (59). Back in Paris Claude is swept up in the rebellion of the avant-garde, who shout, "We do not like this life!" (64). His intercourse with Mona, the leader of the rebellion, which is seen in silhouette by all the rebels and thus becomes a piece of art, should offer the opportunity to create a world to replace this one:

> At the vertiginous moment of his orgasm, Claude had a vision. He saw from afar, as in a milky empyrion, once again the bright slowly turning ring of flesh from high-up the thigh of a woman because of whom one thought the world might change. On it he managed to read, in an incredibly subtle hand, the musical notation of a single continuous theme, which nothing interrupted, which never returned upon itself. It meant for Claude everything and nothing. Was this beauty? Paradise? He asked his God in that childish, mindless moment. (65)

But this vision, instead of inspiring a new world, reveals the illusory nature of the transcendent world Claude had sought and recalls him to the reality of the phenomenal world he had tried to dismiss: "But then (and one might have expected this) he woke to the hard light of the true and single world. . . . Claude turned to Mona morosely. 'You see then, *ma cherie*, that after all it was nothing. We were but shades, shadows. Our act was an illusion *la plus bete*. . . .' Poor Mona. How ludicrous she looked, standing naked among all these people only a fraction of whom she knew. He began to pick out blemishes and protruding veins on what had seemed a matchless body" (65). The two inches of thigh, which had promised the possibility of a new world, becomes instead a fetish, a symbol of the objectification of love and art in this world, when Claude cuts two inches of skin from the thigh of his lover, Gaby. This victory of the mundane becomes clear as Claude, near death while World War I rages, "reached unwillingly to his side (life's last inspiration) where he pinched at his little sack (which itself contained a soft ring of would-be flesh, though not so bright, what was not good enough for the dream of flesh, or, perhaps, what was flesh's undoing, this was flesh failed, just as his own flesh would soon fail) and laughed miserably to think that what had often seemed so beautifully involved should be so brutally simple" (69).

Claude's end reveals another difficulty: Is the transcendent world that art offers—the world Claude seeks and Mahler apparently achieves—something that artists should be seeking? Does it answer the demands of the rebels who are tired of the world they inhabit and who want a new one? In seeking the transcendent, are artists betraying the here-and-now of the world they inhabit? In "The Heretical Singing of Pietro Carnesecchi" Lorenzo, a lutenist whose wife has been abducted (or, perhaps, has eloped), seeks not transcendence but a reworking of his reality. He tells a Boccaccian story to accompany his masturbation, so that the two, sex and art, are intertwined in a fantasy. But his failure to create a world is underscored, when, later, an attempt to rescue his wife fails because he mistakes her portrait for her: "Lorenzo now realized that the Lucrezia he had seen across the room was a portrait, and that her smiling, entreating look—which smiled and enticed still—was for another moment. Was in a completely different world. Was linked hook-and-eye with a series of gestures, light touches, spoken words completely indifferent to his own wishes" (105). Lorenzo has been unable to create a world where he and his wife can be together and is alienated from the world she now inhabits.

This idea about the difficulty of finding and sharing a place where love can occur is at the heart of "Rossetti's Blessed Lady." Narrator Dante Gabriel Rossetti freely equates art and sex as he alternately paints and seduces his models, but his relationship with Nora Guggums increases the complexity of the ideas of art, sex, love, and habitation. The two seem to want to use their art to create a place, a world, where their love can exist. They first live together as celibate artists, each creating, both in love, but living "the illusion of life" (28). In a telling moment, after Nora has taken laudanum and assumed a corpselike appearance, Dante admits, "I loved as much at that moment as I would ever love again" (30). This love is pure but dead, incapable of offering a world beyond the present one. They marry finally and have sex, but instead of creating a new world, marriage, Dante realizes, is "a different way of being the same" (38). The main difference is that instead of existing in the pure death of art, they exist in the death of the physical world. Both are frequently ill, Nora is delivered of a dead child, and Nora finally kills herself. In "The Blessed Damozel" Dante imagines a place in heaven, a transcendent place where their love can finally exist, but in White's story Dante, in a chloral-induced fantasy, sees heaven as a failed place too: "I was deceived when I imagined that she would find it in her heart to wait for me here, at God's railing. I can see now that any such possibility was only the most mystical sort of imagining. She's wandered off. Bored no doubt. Unless she's with someone else, loving in a cloudy undergrowth" (52). Heaven, it seems, is just more of the same. If art's purpose is to imagine new worlds where love can exist, this purpose is made problematic, perhaps impossible, by art—like sex—existing in the tension between mundane physical reality and an ideal but unreachable transcendent world.

The difficulty art faces in remaking the world is further complicated by the role of the reader. In *Heretical Songs* White continually associates the reader with the critic. "The Poet's Sister" is narrated by a critic who, in making sense of the Richard and Madelyn

Stanhope (apparently stand-ins for William and Dorothy Wordsworth), is constantly defending them against other critics, who, he says, have maliciously misread their texts so as to conclude that the two had an incestuous relationship. He gripes,

> Unfortunately, some writers of more recent times, times less conscious of professional propriety, less concerned with a man's right to his good name even after death, have made much of the information found in the diary. Let it be clear, however, that there is nothing in Miss Stanhope's diary (and I have read and studied it from its first to its last pages) that suggests any indecency or corruption in her personal life. . . . But the sensationalist scribblers of our own depraved (I call it so!) time load Madelyn's words with their own saccharescent bile, tinge her musings with their own ill-thought and contemptible yellowings. (13)

But as he writes, this unnamed scholar becomes less and less convinced of his ability to discern the truth and sees himself not as different from but as just like the critics he had previously attacked:

> to tell you the truth, I'm a little tired of my opinions. . . . Originally a bright flame, my idea seems now only a guttering "position" to be defended among my "colleagues". . . . I worry that I've created a hateful thing: a palimpsest, perhaps, which holds beneath its thin outer tissue a mirror (not an impress in believable clay), a mirror reflecting whatever extravagance, whatever shameless conceit critics are capable of. It might be that what there is of truth in my observations is the direct result of private passions I have nowhere mentioned. (19-20)

We are left wondering to what extent art's ability to create new worlds is limited by readers' or viewers' inability to get beyond themselves and what they already know in interpreting it.

This problem is compounded when what readers already know is connected to the power of the state. In two stories here interpreters of texts or critics are associated with state officials who have the power to enforce the laws that maintain the status quo. In "Claude" Debussy dreams of creating "a kind of music free from themes and motives, or formed on a continuous theme, which nothing interrupts and which never returns upon itself. It shall mean everything and be nothing" (57). But to this idea of art without laws, Beranger, the protector of public morals, responds, "You find our laws restricting and so do I! But that does not mean no laws, *cher coeur,* it means an infinity of laws, more, more sweet laws" (67). The laws that critics devise to govern the way texts mean are equated with the laws society devises to impose order and control and to maintain power. In the final story Pietro Carnesecchi is executed because Duke Cosimo of Florence thought the monk's story lacked credibility, stretched his willingness to suspend disbelief, and because the monk insists on the truth of his tale. As a bishop explains at the moment of execution:

> "You should have confessed that you made it up! The Duke would have understood! He'd have laughed and congratulated you. He's a practical man himself and aware of the value of a well told lie. No one knew more intimately than you how farcical your 'Tragedy' was at heart. It was nothing. A fart in the wind. And yet how eager you were to believe that somehow, mysteriously, *it was all true*. Suddenly in your headachy fantasy you were willing to see a 'true' self (perhaps even the peculiar fate of our civilization) brilliantly appear. Dangerous, deluded, pathetic man. For this, you've been judged harshly. It's for your delusions that you will die." (120)

Art that is nothing but lies and that seeks nothing but to entertain is not a threat to the state and perhaps can help support it; but art that claims the truth for the worlds it creates is dangerous and must be suppressed. The book ends with Carnesecchi's burning body and books magically re-creating the story he has just sung for us, suggesting that art's power is stronger than the state's. But beyond this hint of hope, the book leaves us with a mission for art but also with thoroughly complicated, problematic, and discouraging means for enacting it.

Metaphysics in the Midwest (1988), White's second collection of stories, is in many ways different from *Heretical Songs*. The stories are less obviously connected in content, treatment, and style, and they are somewhat closer to home: though mostly set in the past, the stories are set in the midwest, many of them in downstate Illinois, where White was—and still is—living. The language here is less stylized, frequently dropping into a conversational intimacy. In these stories White is still concerned with the power of the state and the power of art, with how art functions in a state that seeks infinitely to extend its control, though here the issue becomes less the ability of art to provide a means to a transcendent other world and more about how art can enact possibilities for an alternate reality.

One of the concerns of this volume is the way people are conditioned to accept the social world—as it has been defined by the power elite's ideology of control—as the only possible reality, even though this reality fails to serve and works against the interests of the great majority of us. In "A Disciplined Life" Daniel Campabruno, the narrator, who with his wife and child has emigrated to the United States to escape fascist Italy, happily participates in his own repression by the state, never realizing that his new home is a disguised version of the totalitarian society he has fled. Not long after arriving in a small central Illinois town, Daniel is arrested for vaguely understood crimes: "I had in dismaying ignorance violated principles (understood by everyone but myself) of propriety, decorum, decency. I had trespassed, caused material loss, breach of faith, personal trauma and—in cases that haunt and amaze me even now—bodily pain" (51). Not having been interpellated into this society, he has apparently broken various social codes of which he had no knowledge. He pleads, "I want to say to my readers, especially my American readers, that I have nothing against corrections or the officers thereof. But I would suggest that they (the corrections, the adjustments) be made *before* a well-meaning, misfortuned man like myself is allowed to join the life in progress and make a muck of things. There can be better screening and perhaps a brief program for us on arrival" (52). To his surprise, when Daniel is taken to his cell, it doesn't appear to be a cell at all: "There in an imperturbably bright light was no European gaol, but a home, a little home. . . . There were side tables and a beautiful scrolled wicker chair, a bed with a quilt cover, pictures on the walls, flowers in vases, even a good Catholic corner with a cross clean as Volterran alabaster" (55, 57). Hearing a rumor that his wife and daughter have become sexual slaves at the home of one of the corrections officials, Daniel, in his one rebellious act, escapes from prison and rushes to the official's house. But looking through the window, he sees a scene not unlike his cell: " 'Cella sat in a large, comfortable chair, buried in its generosity of cushions, a well-adjusted reading lamp above her, and a copy of LIFE in her lap. On the other side of the room was Trisha (hardly emaciated, a solid five pounds happier) in the lap of Anderson Smyth. On her head was a baseball cap; on the RCA radio were the New York Yankees playing the Chicago White Sox; on Smyth's lips were patient explanations of the rules of the great American game" (64). In Althusserian terms, while Daniel has been the victim of repressive state apparatuses, his family has been subject to ideological state apparatuses. The result is that all of them learn to live within the intellectual and social prison created by "the rules of the great American game." Daniel docilely returns to his prison, and, at the end of the story, he demonstrates his complete submission to the authority of the state by volunteering for an apparently life-threatening experiment involving a disease-carrying mosquito.

This process of interpellation, so effective with a naive newcomer such as Daniel, makes controllable subjects out of even those who most wish to rebel. In "More Crimes against the People of Illinois"

Jeannette, who seeks to organize the women workers of Sears and Roebuck to demand salaries equal to men's, is undercut in her feminism and her socialism by the social conditioning she has undergone. The narrator observes, "Surely you too have met women like this, women who can hold forth over lunch about the rights of women and the cruel stereotypes fostered by men, and then for the rest of the afternoon hound you about whether or not their waist is thick, their hair dull, or their complexion rough. Well, such a subtle dupe was Jeannette. All that she knew not to be was for her utterly real" (78-79). When Jeannette is fired for her activities—but with the charge of prostitution as the excuse—she undresses and stands topless as company security men come to remove her from the building. There is a moment of sympathy between her and the other women workers, a moment of potential rebellion that remains unrealized:

> Now, if every one of those women had turned then to every other woman in proximity, why—Lord!—rebellion would have multiplied like a strange new kind of wealth. They might have all followed her lead. Imagine a thousand breasts instantly smiling above the brilliant typewriters!
>
> Well, I saw dozens of agitated fingers trembling around necklines. Of course, as soon as this became conscious it was translated up the neck into a frantic pulling and scraping. Someone complained of the heat, another actually fainted. And of course, Jeannette was left alone. The moment had passed. (85)

Jeannette is betrayed and her cause fails because her co-workers have been subject to the same socialization as she, with its respect for propriety and its fear of authority.

White pays special attention in this book to the contradictory role pop culture plays in this socialization process. Pop culture can be seen as serving the needs of cultural conditioning, providing the discourses with which people articulate and know their positions in their society, as in "You've Changed," where the narrator, a nightclub singer, understands her every experience through the lyrics of thirties' and forties' ballads. In "Howdy Doody Is Dead" *The Howdy Doody Show* serves to socialize children into the America they will grow up to live in, but the America it presents, a vision of America necessary for the maintenance and reproduction of the ideological status quo, is clearly an illusion, an America that has never existed except in pop culture. Here, all children are innocent, all parents are nurturing, cowboys are noble and brave, and so on. But in this story pop culture can also explode this illusory America, as on one of Howdy's rival shows, *Andy's Gang*, where Froggy the Gremlin subverts each of host Andy Devine's messages about children's proper behavior: as a result, "The kids would lift from their ordinary lives and begin to storm" (116). Similarly, when Howdy's evil twin takes over his program, instead of perpetuating the illusory America, he exposes the decay and corruption it seeks to mask. In a final showdown between the good and evil Howdys, the illusory America is destroyed when the evil one stabs the good one: "it was only seconds before we realized that this wound was like puncturing the bag of the world. A bubble in which we had long found our comfort had been perforated. A terrible sucking force ripped the smiles from our faces" (126).

This idea of innocence masking something spoiled or even evil recurs in the book. In "Critical Theory" the narrator discovers his daughter covered with mud, mold, and slime and can't find any way to clean her. The daughter connects her situation to an alternate reality: "Well, Daddy, you know what Marx said: 'You have to think the world by a different thought.' Can't I just be part of that different thought?" (142). In "The Order of Virility" a traveling mountebank directs a minstrel show in Peru, Illinois, and discovers his small-town boy actors have "transformed into black-faced beasties, infernal guardians, neighborly Cerberi, who plainly now slept in the way that something really evil sleeps" (169).

I connect this revelation of the illusion of childhood innocence to White's archeological exploration of the corruption beneath the surface of America, a corruption necessary to recognize before the construction of a preferable alternate America can begin. As the narrator of "The Phantom Limb" explains when his mother suddenly believes that her perfectly healthy arm has been amputated: "Most people deny that there is anything metaphysical about the midwest. And it is true that the crust of the normal is more than usually thick here. But a distress like my mother's can create a sort of crevice in that crust through which we may peep in order to see forgotten things, like the fact that men are animals and animals are gods" (44). In "Malice" White strips away the crust to reveal the historical layers of disappointment and death that support contemporary America:

> As I watched, I saw this dust storm, with malice for no one, concerned only with truth, sit and turn in the yard, peeling away by careful degrees layers of sand and dirt. Objects began to surface. First, the bruised, abraded rubber head of some little girl's baby doll. The flap top then the whole box of Wheat Krispies (including the offer of a free cereal bowl to anyone who'd like one for ten cents). The wind worked away at the sand, revealing oil cans, axles, steering wheels, sparrows, radio tubes, dime novels, a board with the dry rot, "I seen our wheat dry up and blow over the fence," a dead chicken in the mouth of a dead fox, no roots, a bean for dinner, the

> word *DROUGHT* scratched into the cover of a Bible, a laugh so bad it couldn't say "America," Kodak film at thirty cents per roll, "You and me, brother," "A piece of meat in the house would like to scare these children of mine to death," a farm boy who got his ears lowered, a hard get-by, the milk cow that went dry in '32, the coil from Uncle Josh's still, the unkindness of a federal agent, the tour of a tourin' car, the blade of an old plow, the scent of its mule, a cross of sticks for her sixteen-year-old son who died of cholera half-way to Oregon, a pioneer wagon wheel, an Indian camp ground, an Indian's bones, an entire burial ground, rattles, arrow heads, jewelry, a branding iron, a Spanish stirrup, the fossilized remains of a giant sloth, the morose depth of a billion years of indifferent rock. (179-80)

This passage exposes as false America's claims to innocence by revealing the historical processes of death underneath the crust of contemporary America and exposes as illusory the American Dream by revealing its failure, from the lost promise of the frontier to the lost potential of the land to the lost opportunity for a free cereal bowl.

The book recognizes, however, that this exploding of the illusion of America and the revelation of the spoiled America beneath its surface are not the same as creating a new vision of America, the new world so many of the characters in *Heretical Songs* sought. As I've indicated, many of the stories in *Metaphysics in the Midwest*—especially "Howdy Doody Is Dead" and "The Order of Virility"—suggest an apocalypse, an ending of the world as we know it, without offering an alternate world or a theory of how to enact it. Two stories in the collection struggle with this problem. In the title story Dr. Feeling, an instructor in metaphysics at Kankakee College, tries to provide for himself and his students a means of transcending the systems of lies that make up contemporary America, but in trying to negotiate the conflict between this potential for transcendence and his own interpellation into America's systems, Feeling uses the rhetoric of transcendence to pursue sensual ends and ends up in a mental hospital. "Critical Theory" presents two alternating tales, one focusing on a man, Curt, driving cross-country to pick up his daughter from his ex-wife, but who keeps interrupting his journey to read Hegel, the second on a car trip across the U.S. taken by Max Horkheimer and Teodor Adorno in 1941. Both tales find humor in the conflict between abstract theory and living in the practical world. Max and Teddie's theorizing of America is undercut, when, "only about ten miles of Amarillo, the Plymouth ran out of gas, thus rebutting, with that brutality typical of American automobiles, the relevance of theory" (143). For Curt, the conflict becomes focused on his muddy daughter, who is like the America of the book: her "sugar, spice and everything nice" surface has been exposed to reveal "the essential murk" underneath (145). Curt's purpose, then, shifts from using his theory to transcend the world to focusing on his daughter and, as he puts it, "alter what I desired in her" (145). He does not achieve a solution, for his daughter or for America, but he believes a solution is possible: "at least I can say that I live consciously at the cusp of my contradictions. I have maintained the sanity of difference. This is my child. These are our problems. The world is not an elaborate hoax perpetrated by those who do not love us. Therefore, we may be happy yet. I have hope for it" (146).

This hope is the point of White's next book, *The Idea of Home* (1992). While there's much that's familiar here—the archaeology of American history, the analysis of the America that has been constructed to serve the needs of the few at the expense of the many, the yearning for the possibility of another world to replace this one, even a return to the nineteenth-century European artists of *Heretical Songs*—*The Idea of Home* also marks an important turning point in White's career, for two main reasons. First, despite the title of its first chapter, "This Is Not an Autobiographical Statement," it's a much more personal book than either of White's first two. White has explained that the book originated in his desire to research the history of his hometown, San Lorenzo, California. As a result, he deals here with events, issues, and feelings from his own life, relating to his home and his relationships with his family, especially his father. Second, *The Idea of Home* claims to be a novel, though at first glance it seems to be, like his first two books, a collection of stories. White has said that as a novel, *The Idea of Home* is similar to the great concept albums of the late sixties and early seventies, the Beatles' *Sgt. Pepper* or the Who's *Tommy*: the cuts can be played individually like any other album, but played together, they connect narratively and/or thematically. *The Idea of Home*, then, in form goes beyond the first two story collections, where there was some unity of subject matter and theme. In the novel the stories/chapters are meant to function in a sequence, simultaneously building each upon the last and interacting dialogically—commenting on, conflicting with, supporting, or undercutting each other. The result is a process that helps to answer questions that the other two books raised about remaking the world. Like "Critical Theory" 's Curt confronting the fact of his filth-covered daughter, *The Idea of Home* suggests answers not in transcending or escaping the world-as-it-is but in finding a position from which it can be seen and understood.

White has acknowledged two intellectual influences or sources that can help us understand the structure and purpose of the novel. Paul Ricoeur offered White a way of conceptualizing utopia. For

Ricoeur, utopia is not a physical space or specific time toward which human society is moving and at which it will finally arrive. Rather, it is a conceptual space from which one can look at the place society is in now, especially the ideology that creates a context for, defines, and articulates that place. From such a position outside the dominant ideology, one can observe, examine, and rearrange the dominant ideology and its discourse and thus create the opportunity to live in another way. This utopic purpose for the novel is established in the first chapter. The narrator begins:

> I would like, in this book, to imagine a place in which humans can live. A place more desirable than the failure which we presently inhabit. This failure which, we fear, cannot be defeated. I will admit that my purpose is utopian if that won't mean that my purpose is laughable. To be sure that it's not, then, let's be sober about our utopia. Let's understand by it the simple notion that there are ideas as yet unrealized which if realized would transcend our present reality. (9)

But this is not the same transcendence that the artists in *Heretical Songs* apparently pursued. Using his hometown of San Lorenzo as a starting point, the narrator goes on, "one of the great things about utopia is the terrific view. Do you remember Miss Nancy on Romper Room, how she was able to see us all on the other end of the television waves through her magic mirror? . . . Well, the view from this place I have in mind is even better than that! It's a place from which San Lorenzo can be seen quite clearly. Which can only mean that San Lorenzo isn't 'in' the 'place' " (10). He develops this idea, playing on the etymology of *utopia*, "San Lorenzo is so far from the place that it is, as Maynard Krebs always sagely maintained, 'nowheresville.' Of course, Krebs and Thomas More referred to different 'nowheres.' Let me put it this way, I'm after a real nowhere. A realizable illusion" (10). This novel's purpose, then—and, implicitly, the purpose of art in general—is to expose to the reader the ideology of the world-as-it-is, create for the reader a place from which it can be analyzed and critiqued, and offer the reader the opportunity and the means to remake it. The narrator challenges us at the end of the first chapter:

> As we are all obliged to admit, the Self is an interesting void to fill. But fill it with what? The dread bestowed upon us by the Culture of the Fathers? The "crappy shit" (as an amusing and wrathful Marx put it) of capitalist industry? Whatever we choose, in choosing we will have risked our lives on the idea (the very Notion which makes utopia) that it is possible to live a "better" life, to see and understand things "better" than others. Better, certainly, than our mothers and father, still residing in our first home, who can only be dead to us now. (15-16)

The second source for *The Idea of Home* is G. W. F. Hegel's *The Phenomenology of Spirit*, which, White says, provided the model for his novel's tripartite structure. There are two concepts from Hegel's work that seem especially important here. The first is Hegel's concept of *Geist* (mind/spirit in English): a sort of collective consciousness that as a force contributes to shaping human history. The study of history reveals the process by which *Geist* comes to know itself, eventually resulting, Hegel argues, in a rational state—that is, a state in which *Geist* has reached completion—in which humans will have overcome their conflicts and will live in harmony—as one of White's characters puts it, "Spirit is the Idea reality seeks" (190). This study of history reveals a dialectical logic: a position or state of consciousness at any given historical moment can be shown to contain internal contradictions, which create instabilities in the position, leading to its downfall and the establishment of a new position.

This dialectical logic forms the structure of the long middle section of *The Idea of Home*, "Unnatural Children." The chapters here progress roughly chronologically, from the European-American settling of the West, through World War II and postwar California, through the social upheavals of the sixties, to the present. Each chapter presents a historically based form of consciousness and examines its downfall. White is able to use Ricoeur's utopic thinking to place his readers outside the moment so as to understand the critique of each position and the dialectical process by which history moves. The result is a procession of American moments in which we can see *Geist* continually reinventing itself in its quest for a rational society. This is clearly seen in "Tales of the Hippies," which examines the origin, the achievements, and the self-destruction of the 1960s counterculture and New Left. One of the Hippie storytellers ends the chapter with this utopic challenge:

> "We hippies failed, maybe, but we tried something amazing that was, even if for a little minute, noble and alive. But if the rest of you have ignored all the death in our culture—mental death, physical, economic, environmental, military, judicial, spiritual—and if you've concerned yourself only with getting high, getting laid, and making money to buy shit, if you've found no way large or small to make even a little revolution, a tiny mutation, a single rip in the membrane of our shared sausage casing, then fuck you." (133)

Keeping with Ricoeur's notion of utopia as an intellectual process, not a final destination, the last section of the novel, "Ecstasy," does not bring us to a remade world but presents many of the characters and ideas from the first two sections in new narrative settings and in new, jumbled, playful combinations. The result is an opportunity for the reader to discover new ways for the world to work and new ways to be. At one point, the narrator explains how the Hegelian dialectic leads to this opportunity:

> what if the cosmos were not so much the result of a bang as of a sort of regurgitation? What if the original black hole were a sort of bridge between two universes, our own and an anti-universe, you know, a Hegelian antithesis. . . . The two universes are constantly moving in and out of each other, one collapsing while its companion, in a fit of revulsion at the sudden proximity of this too-familiar Other, spews it back out (rebirth).
>
> What I particularly like about this image of Being is that when a singularity belches forth a new universe, it is not necessary that the physical laws, constants, gravity, circuitry and that shit should be the same as in this universe. Because after having squeezed through a knothole, wrung through the cosmic wringer and changed utterly, the new universe would have no memory of what had ruled its predecessor. Rules, argues John Wheeler, "are freshly given for each cycle of the universe." (175)

Where *Heretical Songs* and *Metaphysics in the Midwest* recognized the failure of the world-as-it-is and seemed to know intuitively that art offered the opportunity to remake it, *The Idea of Home* offers a much more specific concept of how that remaking can take place and implies the important role art plays in it.

Anarcho-Hindu (1995), White's novel in the Black Ice Books series, makes explicit this implication that art, especially storytelling, is the vehicle by which a new world can be achieved. The novel is short but complex in its structure—not a sequence of dialogically related stories but several simultaneously told stories wrapped around each other like a strand of DNA—and in its intertextuality—it's written through such texts as the *Bhagavad Gita*, *Les Miserables*, David T. Burbank's *Reign of the Rabble* and through such stories as the European workers' revolutions of 1848, the Paris student rebellions of 1968, the rumored theft and mummification of John Wilkes Booth's body, pornographic films, and White's own life. White has said that in this book he tried to bring together two stories that don't really belong together—the stories of reincarnation/nirvana and revolution/utopia—so as to see what happens. The first story is the *Bhagavad Gita*, the Hindu epic in which Arjuna, on the eve of a great, potentially apocalyptic battle between the Pandavas and the Kauravas, falls into despair over his existence and his situation; Krishna, in the form of his chariot driver, teaches him that there is a distinction between the temporary material body and the eternal soul, that life should be a process of renouncing the contamination of the material and seeking the transcendence of self-knowledge and knowledge of Krishna as the supreme lord, and that each life needs to be understood as a preparation for the next life. The second story is about the general strike of 1877 and the workers' commune that developed in St. Louis. Thus White has brought together the concepts of Eastern reincarnation and transcendence and Western revolution.

The book's three parts, "A Sordid Life," "A Sort of Life," and "Assorted Lives," plus its prologue and coda trace a contemporary version of an Arjuna-like journey from material despair to spiritual enlightenment, and it connects this journey to the possibilities for remaking the world. The prologue, a parody of the battle between the Pandavas and the Kauravas set in a K-Mart parking lot, establishes contemporary America as a place where most people's lives are not lived at all but constructed for them by corporations and the media. A K-Mart waitress, at the urging of Ganesh, the elephant-headed deity, who has stopped in for a hot dog, looks out of the store,

> and sees that the vast field of parking spaces for K-Mart shoppers has been replaced by a wide valley. At the top of each side of the valley are new split-level residentials, townhouses, and condos protected by tall pine privacy fences. The fencing wood is so fresh and green that the waitress can smell the pitch. On the opposite side is also a tall pine privacy fence protecting condos, townhouses and split-level residentials. In the middle of the valley is a long, flat, green space manicured like a golf fairway. A dazzling army of residents line the two sides of the valley. They carry weapons of destruction: television remotes, weed whackers, leaf blowers, and tractor mowers which bunch up in the front as if they were tanks. They carry bright red pennants numbered 1-18. They are about to storm down to meet in colossal self-annihilation in the middle of the fairway. They await only a sign. They stare at the door of the K-Mart—where the waitress stands, mouth agape—as if that is the place from which they expect the sign. (7)

The novel then moves forward—toward a possible personal transcendence and a reinvented world—and backward—into the narrator's past and human history. "A Sordid Life," set in the suburban comfort of contemporary Normal, Illinois, shows the novel's protagonist, Arjuna, his wife, Siva, and their dinner-party guest, Alex, in the same kind of despair wrought by material culture that the prologue presented. Here, even Siva, the androgynous Hindu deity of creation and destruction, has been rationalized into a product, sold through 900 numbers.

But Siva is also the inspiration for the second section, "A Sort of Life," in which Arjuna attempts to reinvigorate their lives and save the world by telling the story of the 1877 general strike and the workers' commune that flourished briefly and then was squashed in

St. Louis. This workers' commune, though failed, offers proof that there are ways to live other than the ones that have been defined for us by the corporate culture. Through Arjuna's narration, the St. Louis workers' commune simultaneously becomes workers' rebellions from other places and times, which fail for the same reason—our tendency to participate in our own defeat: "this is the great historic question, kids. . . . To shoot or not to shoot. History's advance is always ultimately dependent on whether or not soldiers will shoot the most urgent representatives of their own class and thus murder their own interests. Baltimore in 1877, Haymarket Square, Kent State, Tianamen Square, Timisoara, the Russian State Parliament building in God help us 1991" (64-65). But the telling of this story has only mixed success. Inside the frame where Arjuna tells his story (Arjuna, Siva, and Alex watch a videotape of Arjuna telling the story to Siva and Alex) the story is unable to keep Alex, "our child/our father/our lover" (71) alive. In the frame the story has a limited success. Siva and Alex fall asleep, but, Arjuna notes, "at least they looked now as if they might rise from their sleep with hope" (71). In the next section, "Assorted Lives," the inadequacy of the story is revealed as we see Arjuna returned to his childhood home (San Lorenzo, again) to live over his life: "Siva seemed to be telling me that I would have to do it all again, live the whole thing over. I'd made no progress at all" (78).

In this last section Siva takes center stage as a sort of deconstructive principle. Through the words and actions of her postpunk manifestation, she reveals as false the principles and pretenses that support American corporate culture. At the same time she offers the opportunity for the kind of utopic analysis from which new lives and new worlds can be created. In "despair's last and most desperate moment," she offers just such a chance to Arjuna: "she gave me a kiss, the kiss I'd been waiting, begging, longing for, a kiss not to be found in written lore, not even the *Kama Sutra.* No, it was something far more powerful than the kiss of the coral and the jewel. It was a kiss which made me willing to die and try again" (88).

The coda is a restatement and reexamination of the themes introduced earlier in the novel. Arjuna has apparently been reincarnated as Curtis, a writer who has just finished a novel called *Anarcho-Hindu* and who is now in St. Louis with his wife, May, to find out how much the current residents of the city know about the commune that briefly flourished there. Curtis is suffering from Arjuna's and the culture's despair: "I had become unwilling to exist. I could not be" (92). His reinvigoration comes through storytelling and the awareness of the power of stories to destroy or re-create their tellers and listeners. Curtis trades stories with a man named

X (Alex reincarnated?): X's story insists that the lesson of the St. Louis commune is death and that the awareness of impending death will contaminate all of life; Curtis's story insists that life can be celebrated, even with the awareness of death, that life can be "World-play. Mixing seeming with Being" (113). The conflict is unresolved, but the reader is left with a sense of the importance of stories: they can kill us or offer us the chance for life, depending on which we choose to believe. As the narrator tells us, "whoever calls God by any name . . . by that name does God come. Therefore take care with the names of God" (113).

White's most recent novel, *Memories of My Father Watching TV* (1998), like his last two, combines personal introspection with large-scale explorations. In a prologue Chris White remembers his childhood family situation, in which he and his siblings tried desperately to catch their father's attention so as to come to know him and to establish a relationship with him. All their efforts are thwarted by the presence of the unofficial but most important family member, the television. Chris says, "The defining childhood memory of my father is of a man (but not just a man, of course; it is my father—young, handsome, capable!) reclined on a dingy couch watching TV and ignoring the chaos around him, a chaos consisting almost entirely of me and my sisters fighting" (3). What follows is Chris's attempt to know his father through an indirect relationship: Chris studies the thing that is granted all of his father's attention—the television. The subsequent chapters simultaneously parody the form and critique the content of several popular TV shows of Chris's childhood: *Combat* (ABC, 1962-1976); *Highway Patrol* (syndicated, 1955-1959); *Bonanza* (NBC, 1959-1973); the scandal-ridden TV quiz shows; *Sea Hunt* (syndicated, 1957-1961); *Have Gun Will Travel* (CBS, 1957-1963); *Maverick* (ABC, 1957-1962); and *Saturday Night at the Movies* (this week, *The Third Man*). In each case Chris's father is incorporated into what seem to be actual episodes of the shows; he can appear as anything: a murdered cop for whose children Broderick Crawford's Chief Dan Mathews must become surrogate father on *Highway Patrol;* a wild man of the woods whose presence challenges the perfect patriarchy of Ben Cartwright on *Bonanza;* a bridge the platoon must destroy on *Combat.*

This examination of personal relationships is broadened into social significance by the focus on the medium of television. TV is revealed as one of the ideological state apparatuses that serves to interpellate viewers into their socially sanctioned subject positions. The novel seems to make use of Lacanian theory to show TV as a manifestation of the Law of the Father, whereby children are bound to the systems of social codes—the rules of the American game. The novel, through its parody and critique, seeks to disrupt this process, then create the critical conceptual distance necessary for the kind of utopian analysis we've seen in White's earlier books. The result is a transformation of TV as the medium of deadened lives, disrupted relationships, and ideological control into a playfully subversive alternative discourse that offers the opportunity for remaking lives, relationships, and the world.

My concern about the analysis of White's career I've offered here is that, while arguing for some of his ongoing intellectual concerns and his constant experimentation with forms in which to express them, I've been able only to suggest the breadth of knowledge, the depth of intelligence, the barrels of fun, and the real beauty that are exhibited in each of his books. The following articles, providing some other takes on White's work, will fill in these gaps to a certain extent. But in the end, as in so many other things, you need to see for yourself: become reader to White's storyteller, and be prepared to see your world in new ways.

WORKS CITED

White, Curtis. *Anarcho-Hindu.* Normal: Black Ice Books/FC2, 1995.
———. *Heretical Songs.* New York: Fiction Collective, 1980.
———. *The Idea of Home.* Los Angeles: Sun & Moon, 1992.
———. *Memories of My Father Watching TV.* Normal: Dalkey Archive Press, 1998.
———. *Metaphysics in the Midwest.* Los Angeles: Sun & Moon, 1988.

Hippies, Madness, and the Revolution of Everyday Life: An E-Mail Conversation

Mark Amerika

Curtis White lives in the heart of the heart of the country, Normal, Illinois, where he teaches at Illinois State University. ISU, for those who don't know, is home to the Unit for Contemporary Literature, the most active literary publishing site in America (let's forget New York for a moment, especially since this week's *Book Review* had exactly two fiction titles reviewed in it). The Unit, as it's called, is the production center for a wide array of important books and reviews including Dalkey Archive Press, FC2/Black Ice Books, the *American Book Review,* and the very journal you now hold in your hands.

Author of four books whose titles include *Heretical Songs, Metaphysics in the Midwest, The Idea of Home,* and *Anarcho-Hindu,* White directs the FC2/Black Ice Books press and has just completed a new book of fiction entitled *Memories of My Father Watching TV* He is an avid cyclist and practicing vegetarian whose collection of old sixties vinyl would make most hippy nostalgia freaks salivate with envy.

Curt and I decided to do an informal e-mail exchange as our version of an interview. Curt had some opening remarks and off we went . . .

CW: Now and then it occurs to me that I ought to try to write a conventional, gripping novel of the real world—I should write Graham Greene's *The Third Man* or even Henry James's *Daisy Miller,* but the truth is I couldn't if I wanted to, I wouldn't know how to proceed. I know nothing of the drama or concreteness of the everyday. It would be a horrible disaster.

Here's the little I'm capable of: I can write of the slightly hallucinogenic world that has risen out of my mental illness. I suffer from chronic if episodic depression. It is this which has provided me a lens. Do I deserve some sort of artistic credit for this illness? (Do Kafka or Byron or Mahler?) Mental illness has also allowed me to take up "ordinary human unhappiness" (fathers, romantic love, mortality) and explode them into cosmic offenses against me personally. My outrage!

At the same time, my largely distorted sense of the world and its tenacious desire to hurt me personally has turned out to be from the most grimly objective perspective nothing less than the pure (metaphorical) truth of our collective condition. What does it mean that my chemical madness (sorry, we're fresh out of serotonin today, señor) produces fantasies which are nothing other than the truth of our political reality, metaphorically spoken?

The personal is the political. But damned if I know why.

Oh, and I'm capable of making language sing. I say this in all modesty. I take no more credit for it than I do for my madness.

MA: It would seem that writing itself could relieve one of depression. But it might also be the thing that destroys you in that you know you can't live without it and what if it leaves you (fathers, romantic love, mortality)? How does one perform these mental balancing acts when the tightrope is no longer real but is always already hallucinogenic? Your work seems to deal with all sorts of philosophictional issues—one of which comes to the fore: If life itself is always teetering on the edge of absurdity, then how can the writer whose mind is also teetering use the writing practice to achieve a sense of "connectivity"?

CW: That's my dirty little neurotic secret, see? I started writing because I had bad brains. John Barth once said to me, regarding writers who aren't the real McCoy, that "some of them are just neurotics; it takes awhile to see that their muse is really only their madness." I thought, shit, he's figured me out! I've lived in artistic terror ever since. My own private version of "The Emperor's New Clothes": why, you're just a lunatic. *(Kirkus Review* called *Anarcho-Hindu* a "lunatic assemblage.")

But what you say is perfectly true. My happiness is based on my misery. As a suburbanite fated for a job repairing power lines for Pacific Gas and Electric and a four pre-fab wall prison, I can only thank my lucky stars that I was blessed by madness.

Madness and hippies. That was the other major intervention in my youth. I have an utterly fond memory of going to San Francisco in 1967, while I was in polyester high school, meaning only to go to Golden Gate Park, but having to cross the Haight to get there. Suddenly, out of nowhere, came a man in flowered shirt, vest, beard, hair, and the rest singing loudly to himself as he walked down the street. He was a personal "event horizon" for me. His appeal to me was "make your own future." I've been trying to live up to this appeal ever since.

So I suppose that these two things, madness and hippies—certainly not any highbrow appreciation for surrealism—is how I came about the hallucinogenic quality of my fiction. As you know, I live a very "controlled" life, but I couldn't bear it if the possibility of instantaneous transformation were not always a presupposition of my every waking instant.

MA: I'm glad you bring up the hippies. This is something your work deals with directly, especially in *The Idea of Home* where we get this feeling that the various voices floating throughout a story like "Tales of the Hippies" are greatly informed by your own experiences. How active were you in the political, drug, music, and consciousness-raising scenes that were going down in San Fran at the time and is there any connection between those experiences then and your evolution as a writer?

CW: I think we have to put the "hippy question" this way: What were the hippies about that we can continue to forward as a response to the present? (To do otherwise is to indulge in mere nostalgia. Then we're no better off than VFW WW2 types at the Moose Lodge listening to Glenn Miller.) First and foremost, the cultural logic of hippy was about refusal, especially refusal of work. Drop out. In this way they were progenitors to the Italian Autonomia movement and our own contemporary slackers. Hippy-logic can remind us how to "just say no" to the regimentation of everyday life. This is still its primary good. Refuse work. Just say no to the boss. That's why Marcuse liked the hippies.

My own involment with literal hippies was late. I didn't graduate from high school until 1969, and I didn't live in the Haight until 1971. By then it was no summer of anything but the year-round of dog shit, drug abuse, and madness (although often still an inspired madness). Let me tell you of this one experience I had in 1972. I was strolling Haight Street and saw a storefront called the Church of Doodah or something. I went in to investigate the latest religion and met this grim dude who proselytized for thirty minutes or so, my own private audience with the newest pope on the block, that the secret of eternal life was in anal sex. Crazy autonomous churches cropped up everywhere. Another was the Psychedelic Church of Venus. They had great brochures.

My own personal involvement in hippy life was superficial. I was a dead-serious English major, usually to be found in my room reading poetry, and I was a draft resister and general political activist. But I feel a powerful connectedness to the music I heard at the Fillmore, the underground presses like the *San Francisco Oracle,* and one epic mescaline adventure at Russian River. I would like to take this opportunity to thank the hippy who picked me up in his VW microvan and fed me lima bean soup when I was coming down.

Mostly, it was a time when people tried hard to make a life outside of corporate culture. Boy, are those days ever gone.

MA: Something that I really want to discuss with you in this "electronic conversation" is the great divide between most leftist political publications like the *Nation, In These Times,* and *Z,* and the kinds of innovative fiction being published by presses like Sun & Moon, Dalkey Archive, and FC2/BIB. Especially nowadays, with the far right controlling the country's legislative agenda and the supposed liberating convergence of various electronic media, you'd think that there would be some organized activism that would bring these two groups closer together.

CW: The short answer to your question is that American socialism is boring, square, and dangerous (i.e., tends toward a political correctness that means nothing good for radical intellectuals of a deconstructive stripe or avant-gardists of any stripe). One of the most painful political realizations I have had is that the armies of St. Noam (as in Chomsky) with whom I feel myself in substantial solidarity . . . well, they hate me. Hate me for my thoughts (elitist, jargon-laden-deconstructive Marxist-Hegelian) and hate me for my art (surreally cast, political postmodernism). Michael Albert at *Z* is the worst, but Victor Navasky at the *Nation* has not been much better. FC2 is more real for the *NY Times* than it is for the *Nation.*

It is much the same sort of divide that we saw in the sixties between the "serious" Berkeley politicos and the "playful" San Francisco hippies. What I don't understand is why the playful/serious cultural politics of Abbie Hoffman, hippy revolutionary, no longer apply? Why isn't Jello Biafra more important than he is? Sadly, it is all just another nail in the coffin of the American left. Again, the story of Western revolution is self-defeat. Oddly, it's capitalism that is truly dialectic—always in conspicuous, pernicious conflict with itself, but always emerging revitalized in a new, more gruesome form. Meanwhile, the left sits at the foot of some pigeon bedunged nineteenth-century monument to its own failure (a place perhaps where working-class police beat the shit out of working-class revolutionaries) singing "we shall overcome" to an audience of none.

There's no "we" in that "we" anymore. The first job for "us" is to reconstitute that social subjectivity. And that's the job of artists, like it or not. It's always messy work with artists. They make lots of mistakes. That's why it's important to keep the culture police of both left and right at a distance. Ideologues should observe museum etiquette with artists: look but don't touch. Don't fuck with it.

MA: I like your idea of artists reconstituting social subjectivity. Writers in particular are having a tough time doing just that these days as the commercial presses focus all of their attention on big books by the likes of Rush and Newt and Bill Bennett, meanwhile short-listing or completely doing away with their serious literary books. One strategy to combat this "conservative conglomeratization of intellectual culture" is to do what you're doing with FC2/Black

Ice Books. Am I reading more into this than I should, or are the stakes involved with your passionate attempt to bring the former Fiction Collective into the twenty-first century ultimately political? What are the political stakes involved in keeping an alternative press like FC2/Black Ice Books alive and kicking?

CW: I recall once sitting next to William Gass, at the Novels of the Americas conference in Boulder in 1992, and being asked a similar question: What are the politics of contemporary American innovative fiction? Gass had replied that his only interest was aesthetic and "elite." I answered, hoping to irritate Gass, that I had gone to the university in '69 because that is where I thought the revolution was taking place and I stayed on to work in literature as my form of day's struggle. Well, my piece of political bravado was insufficient to flap the unflappable Gass, but there is certainly some personal truth to my comment. I have always felt that the most important aspect of the Fiction Collective and FC2 was its politics.

Imagine, an ongoing affront to corporatism: a successful author-run and edited publishing house! FC2 is the child of the sixties logic of communalism, and it continues to foreground the virtues of autonomy and contestation. Best of all, we seem to be able to find friends, allies, supporters in each new generation of writers, readers, and university intellectuals. The great threat, of course, is that we can only survive and have an impact by being able to operate in an industry defined by and conducted in the interest of Random House. So we must have directors who are business savvy and yet have the artistic sense to know what constitutes an "authentic" opposition.

People like Dick Grossman and Cris Mazza and even Mark Amerika have helped Ron Sukenick and me to do this with fair success in the last seven years.

But without the political edge, I don't think I could muster the sustained level of effort that I have mustered. For me, it's always a very intuitive thing. Where does life live? Certainly not on TV. Not at the mall. Not in movies. Not in our impoverished imaginations. Not in neorealism. Not MTV. FC2 tries to be that ornery place where you get the click. Yeah. Life lives here. That's what the next revolution should be about (again).

MA: Along these same lines, we need to discuss how specific leftist intellectuals exclude so much of what gets published in the alternative press from their critical studies and how this inability to see what's out there compromises their positions as "leftist intellectuals."

CW: You allude, no doubt, to the sad Jameson case. I mean, here's a guy who is probably the best known academic Marxist in the country, and yet when he discusses postmodern fiction what are his examples? Doctorow and Norman Mailer! Jameson has completely bought into the fact that corporations have the social power to define what will count as literature. But what kind of Marxist is it who has no interest in precisely those creative and political efforts which would resist and create an alternative to corporate culture? It's really pathetic. But when I look at the books on postmodernism by younger critics (Linda Hutcheon, for example) they too stick closely with the canonized figures, especially Pynchon and DeLillo. Perhaps these critics feel that if they don't deal with these figures that they won't be able to find a university press to publish their work. But it creates some truly distorted views of postmodern literary culture. Such criticism is predictable, conformist, boring, and devoid of the kind of adventure that postmodernism was meant to engender. Where are the terrific essays on Gilbert Sorrentino? Carole Maso? Paul Auster? Richard Powers? Stephen Wright? Steve Dixon?

In other ways, though, I think that academic leftists have been badly treated and underappreciated. It's often said, especially in the left media, that left intellectuals are careerist, out of touch, etc. But in my view, it's not so much that the left has been institutionalized (the old left including the old New Left is still "out there," however moribund) as that the institution has been lefticized. And I don't think it's all been "irrelevant" or elitist, as *Z* or the *Nation* might lead you to believe.

Obviously, women in the academy have been active participants in feminism. Marxists in the academy have against all odds kept current the ideas of Marx and introduced them to several new generations of American students. ACT-UP was rooted in deconstructive theory, and so is much of the slacker and Situationist renaissance.

Even granting the premise that leftists in the university are somehow out of touch, why is it wrong for them to be having their greatest impact precisely where they are: in the Educational State Apparatus? It could be a lot worse. We could have another generation of New Critics in their place. And certainly the Republican ideologues have taken the academic left deadly seriously. It's a large part of why the NEH has had its budget reduced. This is class war (broadly understood) at the level of ideas, and the Andrew Rosses and Gayatri Spivaks and Edward Saids and Cornell Wests deserve some credit for what they're doing.

MA: Well, since you're naming names (Spivak, Said, Ross, West, etc.), perhaps you could riff a bit on what sorts of critical theory you yourself have been developing lately and who, if anybody, you've been especially influenced by in the world of lit-crit.

CW: That sounds suspiciously like an invitation to talk about Hegel.

I don't have a political or critical theory of my own making. I am and have been content to borrow from those who came before me. Marx's early essays, especially the "Economic and Philosophic Manuscripts of 1844," were tremendously inspiring to me. I was discovering Derrida at about the same time. The first essay I wrote on critical theory basically argued that the Althusserian claim that the early Marx was fatally flawed by idealism and "humanism" was based on a very superficial reading of Marx. Marx makes it perfectly clear that this thing "human nature" is not some enduring and aboriginal essence but something always in the process of its own discovery. Marx is much more Nietzschean than others allow. Marx is much more Hegelian than he himself allows!

What I have taken from a certain tradition in reading Hegel—a tradition consisting of Lukacs, Kojeve, Hyppolite, Adorno, and Herbert Marcuse—is the profound idea that the "normative" human qualities we struggle in the name of (qualities that Hegel shrewdly and obscurely gathered under the rubric "Spirit") that these qualities are historically generated. They are not "universal rights" etched into the forehead of God; they are thoroughly human because thoroughly historical concepts of what we Will the human project to be about. Will the human project in the end be about "instrumental reason" and the commodification of experience? Or will it be about Freedom, the infinite capacity for humans to learn, create, transform, make beautiful, whole, and finally Spiritual? That's what Hegel called the World in Love. These are the stakes. It's what makes struggle worthy of the name, especially for artists.

Buddhists discuss the same issue in these terms: life, they argue, is the "play of energy in voidness." It is this wandering impulse that is most at the heart of my great heroes Marx, Hegel, Adorno, Marcuse, and Nagarjuna (a Mahayana Buddhist philosopher).

These thinkers have had the most intimate influence on my fiction. They are inspiring. They have filled me with their enlivening breath. And to all those AWP types who would argue that theory/philosophy has nothing to give the writer or poet, I say *tant pis*.

MA: How does all of this relate to what you've written, both in fictional and nonfictional works, about the institutionalization of the left (or lefticization of the institution) in academic environments?

CW: Frankly, I think I've been very fortunate to be "institutionalized" at this juncture. (It's not as if anyone has much of a choice in this culture. You will be part of the machinery of the state or you will be sleeping on a steam grate.) I've learned a lot from "professors" and it has enriched my life. Ludicrous as it may sound, I've found my encounters with Derrida and Hegel deeply rewarding and provocative—artistically! They're always prodding me toward getting the business of fiction done in some new and unexpected way.

For example, scandalous as it may sound, *The Idea of Home* is structured after Hegel's *Phenomenology of Spirit.* It was both a funny, serious, and above all else useful thing to do in that book. I admit, academic life provides privileged and even culpable circumstances. What one owes, in these circumstances, is a commitment to use that position and those privileged tools in the "struggle" (if you can still use that silly term). So you move students toward the left, you work as a cultural laborer toward everybody's autonomy. That's part of why I do the work I do with FC2/Black Ice Books. It's class warfare. Giving voice to positions fundamentally antagonistic to the status quo.

MA: All of this talk about madness, hippies, struggle, and being lucky enough to find oneself successfully institutionalized gets me to thinking about writing, about how the writer has to wake up every day and do the right thing. Has your writing method or schedule been fairly consistent over the years or does it change with each book?

CW: I don't write every day. In fact, I write very infrequently. That somehow books emerge from my disinclination to actually sit down and write astonishes me. I find myself looking at them and saying, "When did I do this?"

Of course, young writers need to write a lot. They need to practice. But once you've got the skills and voice, I'm beginning to wonder if the writer's obligation oughtn't to be to resist the temptation to write. Actual writing gets in the way of my need to learn. I'd prefer to study Buddhism or Hegel or bicycle mechanics or music or environmental science and write only when the accumulated force or weight of this other work says: "Okay, now really you must sit down and 'work the change' on the material." The "change" is the art and the love and the beauty of the work in its engagement with this World.

I'm presently reading with a horrified intensity about pollution. Obviously, the idea that pollution is the contaminating of the "natural" by the "artificial" is an unacceptable thinking of the term. But then you've got dioxin! Literally, a compound that does not exist in nature that attaches itself to animal DNA and makes life impossible! I want to write a book that thinks pollution through a political poetics.

Now, I think most writers would find what I have just described as foreign to their own way of working. For me, this is how work becomes urgent.

MA: I'd like to finish this e-mail rap with you by changing the subject to how technology and electronic media have influenced your work. For instance, your new work called *Memories of My Father Watching TV,* where you are using specific TV programs like *Bonanza* and *Combat* as well as this very limited "network programming" ideal that was pushed at us as kids, to help devise new narrative strategies that tell the story of a boy named Chris. How has TV affected your work as a writer?

CW: The guiding premise of my new book *Memories of My Father Watching TV* is that "I" got to know "my father" not by talking to him but by watching "his shows" with him. Since its intrusion into the home, TV has been part of the psychopathology of the family. Just add alcohol and you have total dysfunction. In the photograph of my family on the cover of *The Idea of Home,* there is a perfect little 1950s cocktail complete with olive on top of the television set. What percentage of American families are essentially dead simply because of TV and alcohol? The artistic measurement of that "social subjectivity" is frightening and depressing to contemplate.

So my relation to TV was always pretty negative. I confess to a limited sense of nostalgaic cheap thrill in working with *Combat* etc., but on the whole my feeling is one of horror. My position, unlike some avant-poppers, is not much mingled with pleasure, even of the guilty variety. My position is more like Adorno's: TV makes life dead.

Of course, my writing about those old, violent action shows is also a way of "detourning" them. Claiming their always damaged and damaging agenda for other purposes.

MA: As I was reading these new fictions I was taken with how, as with your other books, you were using the narrative to create a really hilarious kind of critical theory, something that I see as being in the lineage of some of the more dark comedy writers and standup comedians of the sixties.

Am I right in assuming that there have been particular comedic influences that have helped shape your sensibility?

CW: I'm always surprised to hear that people think my work is funny. I know it's funny, I work to make it funny. But the point of the work is so little the humor that I am surprised anyway. Not displeased, but surprised.

For me, the humor rides on the horror of what I depict. I think it's funny in part because the reader is so nervous about what I depict. I think *Memories of My Father Watching TV* is the best poetic rendering of depression since Robert Lowell's *Life Studies.* And if having a character say "I am a turd with a hat on" is funny, it is *effectively* funny only because of the horror that underlies it.

As for comic influences, I tend not to think that others are funny. Like most of my generation, however, I was delighted by the absurdity of the Marx Brothers, John Lennon, and the Firesign Theater. (See the cover of *How Can You Be in Two Places at Once When You're Not Anywhere at All.*) I still find myself chuckling over their work: "Trail of Tears Golf Course": "We're moving them out to make room for you." I am most comfortably funny when a contrary emotion like anger or despair provokes the humor.

MA: And as we know, anger and despair permeate the fictional world's landscape. Sometimes it's not funny at all, just pure horror. The feeling of disgust also seems to find its way into dystopian novels that focus on how the world will be taken over by greedy humans with access to very smart machines that will, in essence, control our minds, that is to say, our lives. But something like the Internet offers up a new distribution paradigm for would-be writers and publishers, especially those open to integrating other media like sound and graphics into their work. Could you tell us what your current reading of all this cyberhype is and how it will or won't affect some of the dreams you have for FC2/Black Ice Books and your own work?

CW: Well, Mr. Alt-X, this is really the beginning of the Mark Amerika interview. Hyperspace is full of intriguing possibilities, and it is itself a metaphor for what writers like Borges, Beckett, and Rabelais have been trying to write about for the last five centuries, but it's never going to have the sort of warmth we associate with books and—lord save and protect us!—what it has meant to be human to this point. I think that it offers far more danger to further intensify instrumental rationality and further distance human consciousness from a world worth living in than it offers opportunities for enlarging human capacity, creativity and CARING. Hypertext does not easily encourage us to actively participate in the maintaining of a human relation with a world that transcends the human. Hyperspace is way Kantian: it is locked into the description of the labyrinthine organization of an internal space. It is not enough Hegelian or even Heideggerian: concerned with how a world presents itself and is lived.

But what I just said didn't make hyperspace go away, did it? I thought not. That being the case, I guess the best thing to do is get in it, colonize it in the name of the imagination and whatever other human qualities we can fit into RAM. I suspect, though, that soon there will be so many restrictions on access, expense, and content that the net will be about as lively as your local strip mall. And you won't even be able to get discount basketball shoes there!

MA: And finally, Curt, could you tell us what are the top five albums of all time?

CW: Does being interviewed in the pages of the *Review of Contemporary Fiction* confer that sort of power? Actually, I don't care what the five top albums are. What I care about is the five albums that I don't have in my psychedelic music collection. So if anyone sees Dino Valente's solo album on Epic (yellow label only) circa 1968, with "Children of the Son" on it, please call me collect. I'll pay a 10 percent finder's fee.

I Am Artist; I Make Beautiful Things: A Credo of Sorts Concerning the New Beauty

> "In his work a purely musical residue stubbornly persists."
>
> —*Theodor Adorno on the music of Gustav Mahler*

I'm embarrassed by my title. It has gotten difficult for me to say the words *art* and *beauty.* These two words—when I forget "what I'm about," as the British say, and use them—make me feel antique, precious, unhip, and not a little stupid. What will my theoretician friends in the English department think? "This poor nudnik. Where's he been for the last twenty years?" My embarrassment feels like an apology. I can feel an apology rising up from out of a wounded organ that stretches from my intestines to a hinter region of my brain. I think my spinal cord wants to make amends. Here it comes: "I know that 'art' and 'beauty' have been deconstructed, demolished and otherwise banished from any thinking person's lexicon," I begin. I'm looking around now, hoping to see those reassuring nods that say, "Maybe he won't have to sleep all the way on the other side of the compound fence. With the wild animals. With the dogs we don't like." I get one or two such nods. I continue: "But I don't mean by 'artist' and 'beauty' what you think I mean." Sure buddy. Whatchoo say.

Now I make the truly desperate dodge (the substance abuser at the apex of a family intervention): "I don't want to be an essentialist any more than you do."

Well, now I've said it. "He doesn't want to be an essentialist, Harriet."

In general, I am in agreement with the drift of ideas in the United States (i.e., the drift of theory) in the last twenty years. What a little astonishes me, however, is that although the work of artists has continued unimpeded during this time, no new or more appropriate vocabulary has emerged in the place of our admittedly romantic understanding of Art and Beauty to describe what it is that artists do. Artists have continued to do what they do, but they have done what they do in a sort of embarrassed silence. Artists have not known how to talk about what they do without either seeming to denounce themselves (never a comfortable position), or denouncing the conclusions of the last twenty years (in essence returning with a noisy curmudgeonliness to the high aestheticism of modernism, American realism and the New Criticism). In short, there is no postmodern aesthetic. The postmodern knows not how to talk about its beauties. To be sure, there are accounts of postmodernism as a plundering anti-aesthetic of the pastiche, but there is no positive account of a postmodern artistic "ought." Unlike any previous generation of artists, no artist who is actually a member to the Moment can say to either peer or apprentice, "This is how it ought to be done. This makes it beautiful."

But, as we know, artists are usually awkward when it comes to explaining why it is that what they do is important. Fright and urgency have been added to this awkwardness by the noisiness with which politicians, especially of the Newt/Jesse Republican Right, have asked, "Why do we need these guys?" Doubly frightening (do you hear that little thin voice?), theorists have begun asking, "Aren't these artists and so-called creative writers just a front organization for capitalist ideology? Aren't they the last faithless refuge for Bourgeois Humanism?"

So here stand the artists, feeling, paradoxically, like new kids on the block they've lived on all their lives. To their right conservatives tell them they are immoral and should not exist except as a kind of ongoing anti-Americanism (unless, of course, they are willing to paint what has already been painted, especially if they paint what Norman Rockwell already painted, or—as Newt Gingrich has requested—if they write like Mark Twain (fat lot Newt knows about Twain's heretical misanthropies)). In front of them, liberals reassure them of their value, but in language that reminds them of Hallmark greeting cards—"You make visible the eternal human spirit!"—which language makes them sick of life and eager to swallow their paint solvents. To their left are socialists and leftist intellectuals who complain peevishly and narrowly that their work is politically offensive to just about everybody. The artists try to speak, to respond, but their voices sound now like the high whine of a vacuum cleaner with a dust bunny clogging the hose, or a food processor working on unshelled walnuts. They are unintelligible, especially to themselves.

But, as I've said, there's nothing new in being an artist and being uncomfortable explaining what it is you are and do. The reason for the discomfort simply changes from period to period. Let's look at the logic behind the "artist question" (and the implied final solutions) for our own period as it applies to the conclusions of those who ought to understand art best, art's critics. The present discomfort of artists over their status as Artists and their embarrassed relation to something called Beauty are the result of at least two trends in critical thought which have, I believe, been applied to the activities of art in an extreme and very unhappy way. Criticism has fallen over backward to avoid falling on its collective face. As Ezra Pound wrote (and who quotes Old Ez, *il miglior fabbro,* these days?), "It's easy to go to extremes, hard to stand firm in the middle."

Anti-essentialism. The exuberance with which younger American critics have embraced the philosophy of "anti-essentialism" (if there is a philosophy that one could call essentially anti-essential) has been at times chilling. Anti-essentialism was the conclusion of a complicated logic found by American critics primarily in the work of Jacques Derrida. Derrida argued (and argues) against "the metaphysics of presence," and "transcendental signifieds," and "the purveyors of Truth." Thus it has seemed easy to conclude that notions like "Beauty" or the "Artist" appeal to a romantic, ideologically bourgeois and always and everywhere complicit (and therefore culpable) philosophies of the Real. Critics working under any one of a number of deconstruction's many mantles (especially New Historicism and Cultural Studies) have demystified and debunked (depending on whether it was a romantic or ideological claim being made) the idea that the notion of Beauty has a transcendental or otherwise constant and enduring Being.

The consequence of this logic for those in the field (as anthropologists say) is that few of us have escaped the frightening (for the traditionalist), powerful (for the theorist), or anxious (for the artist) experience of being informed that concept X (Truth, fact, Reality, sense, knowledge, power, our dear friend Beauty, but you can fill in the blank) was an example of "essentializing" and therefore an already defeated concept, defeated before the discussion had even properly begun. This has had, however, the unfortunate consequence, to paraphrase Fredric Jameson, of dismissing from the field exactly the ideas about which one had come to argue. For example, in Marxist philosophy simple anti-essentialism has created a most intense and paralyzing incongruity. Because Marxism's historic appeals to notions like "freedom" or "exploitation" or "alienation" or "humanity" have been so thoroughly castigated as "essentialist," Marxists like Althusser and post-Althusserians like LaClau and Mouffe have found themselves in the (from my perspective) untenable position of arguing resistance to capitalism or the late-capitalist state for reasons that they cannot themselves articulate, have in fact rigorously forbidden themselves from articulating or appealing to. This has led to an ethical impoverishment of the Marxist tradition whose beggarly apotheosis is the glib and fatal thought of Jean Baudrillard.

Artists and critics presently find themselves in much the same untenable position. They can't simply assert the reality of Beauty as some sort of unearthly absolute (the Sublime) and no one seems to be able to articulate an alternative (although they exist), so artists and critics maintain the position of an officially embarrassed silence. An "Idealist Embarrassment," as Hans Robert Jauss once claimed of Marx's work.

As with the Marxist dilemma I have described, artists are left without a vocabulary to describe why they do what they do. Why make art? What is the role of art/beauty beyond endlessly self-deluded puppet of ideology or, on the other hand, politically correct proponent of obvious virtues? They are also left without a way of judging how one piece of art is better than another. Without a way of talking about what it means to be an immature, maturing, and mature artist (maker of a particular kind of something). Any working artist must consider both of these things as a daily and ongoing function of his/her work. I'm doing it this way rather than that because it is "better" this way. What do you mean by "better"? Never mind.

The second theoretical tendency within recent North American critical thought that has tended to make the discussion of art and beauty nigh impossible is the emergence and subsequent dominance of the sociopolitical. So art about AIDS or racism or corporate hegemony or patriarchy has a de facto relevance, importance and justification quite apart from whether or not there is any artistic "value" (let's call it) involved. For instance, a recent public relations project by the Guerrilla Girls argued that "when racism & sexism are no longer fashionable, what will your art collection be worth? . . . For the 17.7 million you just spent on a single Jasper Johns painting, you could have bought at least one work by all these women and artists of color." There follows a list of about fifty artists.

I would hasten to agree with the Guerrilla Girls that the art market is the absurd toy of the ultra-rich, although I find it curious that the G. Girls seem to have no quibble with the ultra-rich as such, just with the politics behind how they spend their money. I'm not sure, however, that that market is absurd because it is sexist and racist (or more so than any other institution you might name). Worse yet, the logic of the G. Girls creates a complete superimposition of the political on the aesthetic. The Guerrilla Girl's appeal in the name of artists finds the aesthetic irrelevant.

One of the best articulations of this situation is Julie Caniglia's "57 Cultures and Nothing On" which appeared in the *Minneapolis City Pages* (24 April 1996). Caniglia argues that art has become "a refuge for the creatively challenged."

In the art world as elsewhere, the multiculturalism that appeared so revolutionary 10 years ago has curdled into a fractious politics of identity, resulting in a new and, for the most part, incredibly banal didacticism: work that "explores" this personal issue or "documents" that social problem, that "provokes" the viewer regarding the artist's identity, or "confronts" the artist's traumas (usually of childhood origins).

As a consequence, she concludes, "As art gets parsed into a multitude of niches based on identity, it follows that the standards for judging such work are lowered, eliminated, or qualified into irrelevance."

It is in this way that a finally trivial artist like Judy Chicago can become "important" because she engages feminist themes. Does feel-good equal good? Does the fact of AIDS make a tedious melodrama like *Longtime Companion* important cinema? Is the solemn *Safe* by Todd Haynes "good" because he's correct: there are toxic pollutants in our environment? Amy Tan is a serious novelist . . . why? Of course, art about right-wing politics (like skinhead rock) is not art at all. That's a hate crime.

I'm perfectly happy with the conclusions of these artists (or "cultural workers," as some would prefer to be called) as political conclusions, but appalled that they are what pass for aesthetic judgment. I don't think that we on the Left have even begun to acknowledge how impoverished our thinking about art is. If the kindest thing we can think to say about art is that it has a socio-political function (when it is Correct), then we are simply and merely advocating art as an assertion of political will. We are asking for that most despised quality, "program art." Moreover, we lose in this way art's artiness (a conclusion that the work of anti-essentialism made possible and tolerable and hardly worth mentioning). We lose the history and the tradition of art's "making" and, significantly, art's "doing" (that is, art's capacity for having its effect not through didacticism but through a formal as well as political rhetorical engagement with its audience). And whether we acknowledge it or not, we are saying that art is irrelevant. Well, if that's the case, let's just all go on down to the demonstration and get our fair share of abuse that way.

We also need to acknowledge the often painful fact that politically oriented critics have often and frequently and vociferously argued against the "content" of much contemporary art. The censorial thrust of much of these arguments is obvious to artists if not to critics. For example, in 1994 at Illinois State University, the University Gallery curator, Barry Blinderman, brought in an exhibition of paintings by Mike Cockrill. The paintings depicted adolescent and preadolescent girls in a variety of precociously sexual poses. Of course, the scandal that erupted focused on the suggestion that these were paintings which existed purely for pornographic purposes. You got naked little girls, you got pornography. None of the exhibition's critics and, most unhappily, none of the exhibition's defenders seemed interested in or able to "read" the paintings. No one seemed able to recall that a whole lot of art works not through sincerity (the artist's "statement," his/her "witnessing"), but through irony and metaphor: saying one thing and meaning another. Our preoccupation with "locating" everyone's "position" in a wholly political grid has had the tendency of making criticism formally illiterate, and, worse than that, dead to art's pleasures. Everyone in the local community was talking about Cockrill's paintings, but no one was looking at them with much care. We had been humiliated by a political critique into a shamed averting of our eyes from exactly that which was meant to be the focus of our attention. "Will you 'gaze' upon the paintings?" became a kind of political litmus test that precluded (not to mention occluded) all other discussion. In fact, by my—very nervous, I admit—reading, the show was exactly about libido and complicity. "What gives us pleasure is corrupt." Roland Barthes, whose *S/Z* is a great textbook of guilty pleasures both sexual and literary, would have understood these paintings. But then he was neither a simple anti-essentialist nor politically correct.

What made the local "progressive" community intensely nervous was not simply that Cockrill was depicting adolescent sexuality. That is done routinely and without scandal in television, advertising, and mass-cult cinema. Those depictions are "acceptable," in a pragmatic sense, because popular culture is its appropriate place. We expect the "market" to be evil. What made Cockrill's critics nervous was that his paintings were being presented within the institutional space of a university and a museum. The simple fact of their presence within that insititutional space implied praise for the work and, implicitly, praise for what was depicted. But, of course, universities, museums, and their related institutions (funding agencies, etc.) are precisely the places in which the sociopolitical has chosen to exhibit its own virtues. It is these institutions which confer upon feminism, multiculturalism, and gay/lesbian activism the mantle of its "goodness." What Cockrill presented was not PC's "sincerity," but a highly charged, ambiguous, and, nota bene, seductive visual pleasure. I can't help but wonder if it wasn't precisely the success of the paintings, their visual "excitement," that accounted for the intensity of the criticism directed at them. When asked what a more appropriate vision of adolescent sexuality might look like, one critic replied, "A picture of a girl sitting with her mother," a comment which I took to mean, very much against its will, that "Satan gets all the good lines."

Whether from the Left or the Right, there is nothing obscure or ambiguous about our political convictions. From whatever direction, our political convictions are vulgar (caught in a primitive rhetoric without a complexity adequate to the complexity of the world it would seek to diagnose). One joins forces with politics in the way that one joins forces with a wave: it's going to take you where it's going to take you, there is little or no chance of amending it, and it will likely toss you out uncomfortable and unhappy ("fooled again," as the Who said) when it has run its course. It is precisely art's obscurity, its unwillingness to capitulate to simple formulations of "position," that makes it suspicious to Politics. What are artists doing? What art is "doing" is creating the possibility for meanings that cannot be limited by the simple sense of the world provided by politics. What feminism, multiculturalism, the Christian Right, Democratic liberals, and anyone else with nothing more than a "position" are saying to artists is: echo our ideas or else.

Against the abstractions of the conservative/romantic ideology of art as essential and timeless reality (delivering the goods on eternal human verities) and against the self-defeat of knee-jerk "anti-essentialism," I would argue two things, the first of which seems to be bright in its simplicity and the second more subtle and shaded. The two are intimately related.

Point the first: Art as such is nothing more than its own very human traditions. That tradition is implicitly dialectical. It is complicit in nearly exactly the same proportion that it is subversive (which is why history, including art history, is really long). It seems to have a motor that keeps it always changing, but never changing so much or so quickly that it moves from "fish to fowl" in one moment. It is in many ways the tradition of our humanness itself (art articulates what it means for humans to be human). This is part of why our best artists have the most highly developed moral imaginations and the greatest "negative capability" (the power to imagine what it is like to be other people, maybe even especially other bad people). Art should not be presumed virtuous, nor should its role be presumed to be instruction in virtue. Art is not the province, as Dave Hickey writes in his brilliant little book *Invisible Dragons,* "of right-thinking creatures who presume to have cleansed its instrumentality with the heat of their own righteous anger and to be using its authority (as the Incredible Hulk used to say) as a 'force of good.' " Rather, art is about the morally unsettled relation of the work to its audience. The work uses its "beauties" to seduce the viewer to literally "incorporate" with the work, to take on the work's "body," to feel its pleasures. This is, needless to say, an often frightening and usually dubious process, but it is also the secret that Shakespeare's *Richard the Third* and even, God help us, Bret Easton Ellis's *American Psycho* know that the forces of artistic/political propriety don't.

To cut ourselves off from art and its "beauties" by arguing that they are "essentialist" or politically evil is to cut ourselves off from ourselves. The human project is the ongoing discussion of what it ought to mean to be human, and art is the most benevolent site for this discussion (much kinder than the floor of the House of Representatives and certainly kinder than the anteroom to the House where corporate lobbyists draft the legislation that will legally orient ourselves toward ourselves and our world until the next crippled term of the next crippled Congress begins).

Thus art provides a tradition of the human from which we should not want to distance ourselves. It is in fact exactly the "rag and bone shop" that we ought to sink ourselves into. But we cannot immerse ourselves in that tradition without being first able and willing to read it and to engage it formally. We cannot read it without a close familiarity with the history/tradition of which it is a part. This immersion in history gives art a complexity that irritates the impatient reader/observer who is merely convinced of his/her own ideological "position." What, for example, makes Mike Cockrill's paintings interesting art is that they mix equal parts of horror and indulgence. The paintings neither bluntly blame (as child abuse advocates might like) nor entirely volupt (as pornographers might like). The paintings create emotional, libidinal, and political instabilities. The same sort of engagement/distancing with the technical conventions of representation (commercial, pornographic, and beaux arts) can be discovered in the formal strategies of the paintings.

In short, to abandon art's artfulness is to abandon human history, the tradition of the human as an ongoing and internally conflicted (dialectical) project, in the name of a cloistered desire for immediate "totality" (the world this way once and for all). Thus, we should speak of art as the most central place where we have carried on an enduring discussion of what we are and what we want to become. Good art demonstrates respect for the human world because of the painful/beautiful history that has brought us to this point, and also shows a certain contempt for that world because the image of a more "desirable" world can always be suggested. An awareness of and engagement with the formal history of a specific genre is an essential and inevitable requirement for this process.

Beauty.

First, poststructuralist thought is quite right about it. "Beauty" has no independent, enduring, unique, timeless being. It has no "presence" separate from (that is, transcending) immediate historical human contexts. So we shouldn't be interested in what it is but in what we say (and have said) it is. (See Morris Weitz's still-relevant essay, "The Role of Theory in Aesthetics.") This corresponds roughly to what Foucault called historical "fact": the "it is said." History is not composed of facts; it is composed of what people say (especially in legal, medical, and otherwise "official" documents). In much the same way, Beauty is not a fixed quality; it is an ongoing dialogue.

Any given piece of art is always a composition of history (what has been said) and the moment (what the artist would contribute to what has been said even if that only means basically repeating what has been said (i.e., the boring)). Art has both an ideological and a utopic purpose and every "beautiful" piece of art will find a way of rendering both. This is, in part, what Derrida's concept of "closure" must mean for us. Whatever we do, we will work within the history of an ongoing (and often failing) project called "the human." This is, in Hegelian terms, a Spiritual exercise.

Something is beautiful when the artist works collaboratively with an inherited past, ingeniously reveals again that history within the work, but then—ah! the bright wings!—opens, allows that familiar world to unfold unfamiliarly (Shklovsky) as either a) the known world re-understood as desirable after all (the ideological) or b) a new world, surviving on bits and pieces of the past (all its parts are borrowed), and erupting as an alternative world we might inhabit (the utopic).

What's an example of a.? How about Gerard Manley Hopkins? He worked within the dying tradition of the rhymed and metered lyric in order to reinvent it as a wholly new music and in the process reinvent the relevance of (a similarly dying) Christian faith. He was, in Heidegger's words, working at "worlding," beautifully if conservatively.

What's an example of b.? How about the Beatles's *Sgt. Pepper's,* which works within the tradition of the rock'n'roll long-playing album in order to demolish and reinvent rock'n'roll, albums, and the relation-to-the-world of nearly every teenager in the Western world circa 1967.

For me, beauty is the ah! of recognition not of the sublime or a beyond. It is the complex recognition of the complex capturing of a specific human past and the formal rerendering of that past as a whole (or, okay, as Wallace Stevens would say, parts of a whole) world. Beauty always appears as the strange within the familiar. It convinces us to desire what it desires—this strangeness—through the intensity of the pleasures its "beauty" offers. So beauty's chief anxiety is not the fear of being "ugly" but the horror of being "dead." As Dave Hickey puts it, the opposite of beauty is "the banality of neutral comfort." Beauty seduces us to desire what it desires: to be more "alive": feel this pleasure, this beauty, this strangeness. For beauty, the static quality of mere comfort is precisely despair. Needless to say, for the "sociopolitically convinced," to desire to be more alive or more fully human is not necessarily to desire to be good. Thus Politic's desire to circumscribe what is tolerable in art.

My point is that we should no more wish to be done with the complicit/culpable renegade notions of art/beauty than we should wish to be done with the complicit/culpable renegade creations of sex. Simpleminded anti-essentialism and its provocative (if finally dull) companion the merely "sociopolitical" demand something no one should want (except end-of-history Francis Fukayama-like Republican ideologues): the termination of the human's discussion of its humanness with itself.

In the end, we are, as the painter Nicholas Africano likes to put it, "Still Human."

In spite of the facts.

From America's Magic Mountain

Curtis White

America's Magic Mountain is a rewriting of Thomas Mann's famous novel set at a fictional recovery spa called The Elixir located among a range of slag heaps in Central Illinois. The Elixir has "gone autonomous." Its leader is Mayor Jesse.

Dear Dad:

There was this guy who owned a Caddy. It was a big green monster of a Caddy and it had once been a real prize of a car (it had in fact been the guy's pride and joy), but now it was getting old. It leaked oil onto the driveway, and the rings were shot, consequently it used so much oil that he thought he would have to hook up a funnel system through the front seat so that he could empty quarts of 10-30 and STP into the bugger as he drove. Also, the heater leaked onto the carpet and in the cool spring months astonishing mushrooms grew in profusion. The experience of seeing the car go from new and valuable to old and an embarrassment was of course at first a disappointment to the guy. But soon he saw, because he was one of those guys who get to see, that the disintegration of the caddy provided an interesting lesson for him about investing self-esteem in objects all of which are not only illusory in and of themselves, but prone to, nay, certain to decay. So he actually kept the beast *because* it was old and decrepit and because it spoke to him, in an unmistakably clear, green voice, about an important wisdom. And it also would still limp to the grocery store once or twice a week, farting blackly the whole way.

But, to get on with this story, one day somebody stole his car right out of his driveway! Seems that the "classics" value of the '54 Caddy was going through the roof. And even limping as it did and sprouting fungi from its carpet, it was valuable for its near pristine body. (California cars are famously rust free.) When the guy's neighbor found out what had happened, he ran over (taking, as he ran, many a tossed-back look at his own car, a brand-spanking new Chevy Vega, whose presence suddenly seemed to him much more a matter of speculation than it had before this theft). He said, "I'm so sorry to hear about your car. I can't believe that some young punk" (he was a great one for blaming things on young punks) "has stolen your good ol' Caddy."

The guy looked at his neighbor and said, "You know, I can't tell if this is a good thing or a bad. The car was a piece of junk. I didn't dare leave the neighborhood in it. And my homeowner's policy, for some crazy reason clear only to insurance guys, is going to give me money for it, the kind of money you would expect to get for something that actually ran. I'm kind of surprised that the thief was able to convince it to fart its way off of the block. On the other hand, I'll miss the things the Caddy taught me about life."

The neighbor looked at him in confounded confusion. "Don't you fucking get it? Some jackass young punk of a kid stole your automobile right off of your own private property. There are principles involved."

Some weeks later, he got a call from the police saying that they'd found the Caddy in a nearby used car lot and he could get it back. Also, the owner of the lot wanted to talk to him. So the guy took a bus to the lot and went immediately to his Caddy. He stuck his head inside and smelled the sweet decay, and smiled. Yes, he thought, this is my car. It's speaking to me. "Born alone, die alone, in between a dream." That's my car all right. He was glad. But he had more to be glad about.

The owner of the lot felt bad about being taken in by the forged pink slip that the thief had presented him. So he wanted to make it up to the guy. He wanted to give him a newer car. (Okay, at first he just wanted to offer the guy a "real good deal" on a *very* new and expensive car, but the guy was no way interested in any factory discounted stock overload sticker rebated special leasing arrangements.) It was a used Plymouth Barracuda, sporty as all get out, still pretty fast, and a real plunge back into memories of the guy's sportier youth. He thought at first he shouldn't take it. Another possession to worry about. But these sweet memories and the idea that his neighbor would never shut up if he turned down a free car finally convinced him to go ahead with it.

Now the guy's neighbor was amazed at his good fortune. "I can't believe this," he said, "someone robs you and you not only get the thing you lost back, but you get a new thing worth double or more the thing you supposedly lost! You are such a fucking lucky stiff!"

The guy's neighbor really was getting a whale of a lesson here himself, if he knew how to recognize it. But all he could recognize was that the guy's Barracuda made his Chevy Vega (newer though it might be) look lumpish. His Vega had no sporty wire wheels, for example. And the neighbor guy still had two more years of payments to make on his lumpish vehicle. (In truth, he'd gotten essentially mugged money-wise by his dealer who had nothing more difficult to do to make that sale than wipe the neighbor guy's drool off his chin. In further truth, with still a year left to pay on it, his Vega would implode after a fan belt broke, the car over-heated, the aluminum block warped, the cylinder walls corrugated, the piston rings wore, and the apocalyptic flatulence of the little Vega made the black farting of the guy's Caddy look like an azure day.)

But the guy himself was strangely uneasy, even worried about his good fortune. He wondered if this flashy Barracuda wasn't just another time-mutability trap like the Caddy before it. He really didn't want to have to worry about scratches and dings and shouting at strangers who parked too close to him. And he sure didn't see the pleasure in spending his weekends out in the driveway with a bucket of soapy water and a can of polish always worried about something. Was it rusty? Was it shiny? Was it shiny enough? Was that a streak on the right rear panel? Strange, I know, but this guy was really different. He thought different thoughts than you and I. He was the kind of guy who understood that each mile that popped up on the odometer was a little death. "I'll never travel that mile again. This machine is one mile closer to rusting in a junk yard.") And this was not morbidity talking to him. The guy actually took some sort of weird comfort in these thoughts. He must have been one helluva guy in his previous life.

So, anyway, a few weeks later, the guy's son (who, unhappily, possessed little of the guy's wisdom—so much for theories that past-life-wisdom is transferred genetically) took the car out for a spin. An unauthorized spin with the unauthorized ignition key, the unauthorized buddy and the way unauthorized six pack of Olde English 800 malt liquor. He had a license and all but he was really ill-prepared for pushing a speedy roadster fast on country blacktops—like notorious Redwood Road, where high school boys went to die—which is exactly where he pointed himself and his buddy, as if they had a sort of destiny.

Well, inevitably the guy's son crashed the danged car into a tree. He'd been swilling some beer and failed to notice a curve ("there were a lot of curves," he complained, "and I only missed one") and went into a big old cedar (second growth, but fifty-year-old second growth and more than big enough to shiver this kid's timber). Happily, it was a sort of glancing blow that more diverted than crushed the vehicle. The son and buddy weren't completely killed although both had numerous broken bones and cuts to their faces which flowed freely and terrified mothers for one hundred miles in every direction.

The neighbor, who was by this time starting to wear a path in the lawn with his frequent need to console/congratulate, came over to tell the guy how sorry he was. (Although, you know how these things go in the human brain, he wasn't entirely sorry to see how smashed up the guy's Barracuda was.) But the guy said, "I don't know how to feel about it. My son is going to be okay. The car is trashed, and I can't repair it because I didn't have collision coverage on it, but I'm sort of glad that I don't have to worry any more about how it will affect my life. Plus, if I leave it crippled in the driveway for the next few years it will serve as a constant reminder to my son. He needed the opportunity to learn. So who knows if this is good or bad news."

The neighbor retreated, muttering, back across the lawn to his own home, walking by his own frighteningly shiny Vega. (He actually, for the first time, looked at it with some suspicion.)

Two years later, when the guy's son was draft age, he received a letter from the draft board telling him that it was time to serve his country. In Viet Nam. So the poor dumb kid went down with hundreds of other poor dumb kids. But the guy's poor dumb kid failed the physical because his knees had some resemblance to knees but also to mashed potatoes, all thanks to one Barracuda and one cypress tree.

Again, the guy had to look at the situation and say, "If my son hadn't driven the Barracuda into a tree, he would be on his way now to Viet Nam. Instead, he can go to college. If he can get into one with a 1.95 GPA. This is a great thing."

Of course, once he said that, cosmic laws of irony were set to spinning. The boy went to college where he met hippies and draft card burners and went to concerts at the Fillmore West and took a few consciousness-expanding drugs which, given the constricted consciousness he took them with, couldn't help but do just that—expand his brain. So he came home with this new, expanded brain and lectured his father on imperialism and the military industrial complex and the CIA and the hypocrisy of the guy's generation and on and fucking on. So, once again, the guy was totally unsure about the good/badness of what had happened. He even wondered if he wouldn't rather have had his son shipped off to the Nam. Or killed by the cedar. Or never born! But the guy was really getting quite wise about this nothing-completely-good-or-bad stuff. So rather than taking his son by his ponytail and smashing the hell out of him, he decided to build a sunroom on the back of his home. Lovely California sunlight streamed into that room. There's really nothing in the world like California sunlight. He filled it with house plants (among them, a very swart bonsai cedar!) and one squat chair. The chair was pointed at a little shrine into which he had built the severed front end of the old Caddy. And whenever he'd think that something good or bad had happened to him, he'd go into his sun room and sit and look at the grill of the Caddy. Sometimes the grill would look like it was the angry growling mouth of some predatory animal. At other times it looked like a very toothy and vaudevillian grin. Sometimes it was both at the same time.

Because of this, the guy frequently found himself laughing. Which was fine and hurt no one except that the guy's neighbor could hear him laughing and see him sitting in his weird little sunroom laughing, and he didn't know what it was about, but he wondered if the guy might be laughing about him. And it started to drive him crazy. He fantasized about shooting the guy with a high-powered rifle right through the window of his freaky room (which would have been the ultimate test for the guy's philosophy). And he damned near did. He was getting that bugged about it. But he didn't. Instead, he packed up his shiny Vega in which slept a smoggy future, sold his house and bought a nice not-yet-dented vinyl place out in the new subdivisions in Walnut Creek there to reside with thousands of others who, when their Chevy Vegas self-destructed and farted blackly, would curse the car, its maker and their personal fates as very bad things indeed.

When the guy heard his neighbor was moving, he didn't know if it was a good or bad thing. After all. . . .

Interview with Mayor Jesse about Life at The Elixir

Q—Thank you very much, Mr. Mayor, for agreeing to answer a few . . .

Mayor Jesse—Pesky questions!? Just a second, son. Hey, Hal, whattaya . . . Ha ha! Hal you fuck head! Just put it where it belongs. Ha ha! Yeah, you heard me right, fuck head is what I said, fuck head is what I meant. Whattaya mean what's it mean? You never heard that expression before? It means you got fuck in your head. . . . You don't know what fuck is? Well, if that don't beat. . . . Never even seen pictures, Hal? Get out of town! I'll explain it to you later. I'm busy now. Go ahead, son.

Q—Well, as I was . . .

MJ—Whoa! I don't believe that! I don't believe what I just saw, what I believe that fuck head is up to back there. I'm real sorry about this, son. Just one more moment and you've got my undivided attention. Hey! Hal! Ha ha! Jeez. Are you a pervert or what, Hal? Well that's some of the same kind of shit we might expect from a pervert. Unbelievable. No, don't show me again, I saw it the first time. A course, I know what kind of nonsense you're up to. It's nonsense. And now the whole town knows. Good God, son, can you believe he's a growed man?

Q—He's very spirited and unpredictable.

MJ—Unpre—! Oh you don't know the half of it. He's one spirited fuck head, he is. You don't see fuck heads that pure much anymore. He's no garden variety. Or if he is, he's like a brussels sprout fuck head with all those little fucked up type brussel heads or whatcha call 'em growing up and down his neck.

Q—Yes. I take your meaning. But what I'd like . . .

MJ—Now wait a minute. What do you mean, "I take your meaning"? What's something like that mean? Is that some kind of special interview type talk? I said I'd talk with you, but you didn't say nothin' about talking like some damned computer. You're not one of those computer-talkin' type boys, are you? "I take your meaning." Where you gonna take it? I'll let it pass, but it's fortunate for you that I'm an understandin' fella. Cuz if it were my man Hal there, why, he's just the sort of fuck head make a boy like you sorry.

Q—I am sorry . . .

MJ—Oh hell I don't wanna hear about how sorry you are. Forget it. Here, you want some of this before we get started?

Q—No thanks. I don't drink coffee after a certain hour.

MJ—Coffee! Hell, son, this ain't coffee. Everything what's in a thermos ain't coffee. Hell no. This is Kankakee Rye Whiskey, man. Best sippin' whiskey or gulpin' whiskey or just plain drainkin' whiskey here in Central Illinois.

Q—No thanks. I've got my own little flask now.

MJ—Well good for you! I'm glad to hear it. But after awhile those little flasks just don't cut it. They just get in the way. Try puttin' two or three of those in a coat pocket. Not just that they don't hold enough, cuz there's always more at the Fountains, but they just don't pour fast enough. A man gets frustrated. I mean I got brussels sprout type fuck heads like Hal here around me all day, so when I need to take a belt I need to take a belt. This whatchacall interview will go a whole lot better if I keep my motor runnin'. That way, you get the "amplified affect" as opposed to the "sober interactional state" like the Professor says.

Q—Okay, can I ask my first question.

MJ—Sure, son. Go ahead. Shoot.

Q—Well, I guess I'd like to know what you think about the controversies, both recent and remote, over the therapeutic function of The Elixir and its role in state health care.

MJ—That's some question, son. Where'd you learn to ask a question like that? And I didn't even hear no question mark in it. That must be one of those clever tricks you learned at Downstate. But I think I know what you're gettin' at. You want to know how we maintain our reputation as Central Illinois' best state supported rehab/detox facility? That's what the rest of them pussies from the newspapers want to know too. Well, I'll tell you. I never told no one else before, but I'll tell you. I don't want no one else to hear, so bend on over this way a little . . . IT'S BECAUSE THOSE STATE SOCIAL SERVICE GIRLS ARE A BUNCH OF WEAK SISTER BRUSSELS SPROUT NECK FUCK HEAD PUSSIES. . . .

And that's the reason why.

Q—I see.

MJ—Sure! It's because the State of Illinois is afraid of us is what it is. Sure, they got questions about our methods. Everyone does. We're famous! But they know that if they pulled their funding, which I have more than politely asked them to do, we'd be on our own. Then, they couldn't touch us. We have no shortage of our own resources, man. "Funding" us gives them a little bit of contact with us, if not influence. Sure as hell ain't control. So now what we do, they give us money and we take the check up to Chicago and buy something big, an abandoned building or something that size, take it out to the field by the train depot and torch it. Some anthropo, anthropo-somethin' guy said this big fire made out of a gift had primitive resonance. Coffee clutch or, . . . Hal? what that brussels sprout neck anthropo-somethin' guy call our big fires? You don't recall? Wasn't coffee clutch, was it? Yeah, it was? What I thought. But shit that don't make no sense. Why'd a guy call a big ass fire a coffee clutch beats the hell out of me.

Anyway, that's what we do with the State's pocket change.

But they know the real deal. We got 8,520 some residents out here, all of 'em good white people with money in their savings accounts and willing to spend it for the privilege of a prolonged stay here, and we got six buildings and underground facilities. We pay zero taxes, have zero unemployment, zero employment and no crime. We have annexed communities around us and attract more industry and satellite corporate endeavors than all but the top ten states in the union. Our bond ratings are AAA+. Moody accountants pule at my damn boots. You know that Mitsubishi wood chip factory over Coal City way? That's our tax base, and boy do they pay it. Seems no one else wanted the publicity. But shit, they were gonna grind up all those Amazon logs somewhere. Right? We got every high-tech piece of bric-a-brac you can stack. Con Ed runs a nuclear reactor just for us. We even have a fuckin' radar if you can believe that. Not even I know what the hell it does, but you can see the son of a bitch spinnin' round top one of the slag heaps. Recovery is like a natural resource for us. We own, I mean own, half the state legislature, and they are not cheap. We have a long ass waiting list to get in here. I have personally refused former United States presidents simply because I didn't think they'd fit in and, to be quite frank with you, I don't like their type.

But the bottom line is, our clinicians have nailed their pansy asses to the hardwood on this one. We have showed in studies what the Laboratory of Alcohol Research boys in Tuscola are still peein' their pants about: alcohol don't hurt nothin'! It *helps* families, man. It is part of the Ritual of Family Life and has been for some time. Without alcohol, I don't expect you could even recognize an American family. It is now a hallowed tradition. It helps grease decision making. Danged if it don't. It provides unique options for problem solving. Everyone knows this, but no one says it 'cept a few brave souls like the Reverend Boyle. Ask him, he'll tell you the truth. He knows all the facts. Hal, run get some of the Reverend's facts for the boy.

Facts aside, I can quote you chapter and verse. Take the case of Joe and Sally. Sally was a computer analyst, and Joe he just drank a whole lot. Now they had a very stable marital relationship for over fifteen years until someone made the mistake of suggesting that Joe's drinking was some kind of problem. I don't remember just how they put it. So Joe cleaned up and he and Sally went into therapy. Fuckin' disaster! Joe was depressed all the time now. He'd look at ol' Sally sittin' opposite him and say, "Man alive, she's fat as sin. I am married to a fat woman. She is no foolin' a real haystack." Which I think even a bleedin' heart like you will admit did her no damned good. Then, of course, she'd go into the old "tearful affect." Man, a fat woman, with them big red cheeks like someone rubbed them with sandpaper, who does the old "tearful affect" is way worse than ugly. That's the sort of thing that can put you off your feed. She gives ugly a bad name.

Anyway, so Joe he's sittin' there sayin' nuthin' to nobody for weeks on end thinkin' with way more clarity than he likes, "So this is my life. Nothin' pretty about this," and old Sally just sits there like this blubber-monster of boo-hoo. I ask you, where is this cure at? You call this "better" than something else?

Anyhow, we finally got old Joe and Sally up here at The Elixir and first thing we do, we put 'em in group. And I mean this group was the group to beat all groups. We musta had 250 people in the old Quonset hut. Imagine 250 people with active substance problems in one big room. When that happens we call it Wormstock. One big nation under the Worm. And nearly as peaceful. Couldn't have been more than two or three fist fights on the periphery. Everybody'd heard about this big fat composition of a computer woman who goes boo-hoo and her skinny "salesman" drunk of a husband. Just the thought was pornographic. So you know we sit 'em down, get three or four folding chairs propped around old Sally and first thing I say is, "Joe, you know, why don't you have a little taste before we get started?" And he looks at me wide-eyed, as if I were trying to trick him. So I say, "Joe, lookit, we're gonna get you where you wanna go. But we got irregular means. We're not like all the rest. We're what they call unusual." And so he says, "Well, how about that? Whattaya got?" And I say, "We got Kankakee Rye is what we got." So I hand him this very thermos right here and he pours himself a nice transfusion. Well, wasn't long before old Joe jumps up out of his so-called depression. A mean deprivation of basic human rights is more like what it was. A man has got to be allowed the requisite tools to face the damned day. Now he's assertive, angry and demanding and now he wants to know why it is that old Sally never wants to have sex with him. Well now, don't you see?, we've got these difficulties in the open. Joe's got more stuff to get in the open. He's got baggage. He's got issues like everybody else. Because of old Sally, he's sure got the "when women get old they get ugly" issue or a very chubby version thereof. Some people don't like that issue and don't think of it so much as an issue as an insult, but I say, hell, open your damned eyes! And Joe's goin' on about how fat his little buttery squab of a wife has become and why the heck don't she get a Nordic track or something to take the edge off this meat mountain. Sally, she says that she has a complaint, too. She says unless old Joe's drunk he has no sexual interests at all and in fact drunk or sober has had no nodding acquaintance with an erection in, lo, these last seven or eight years. Then comes the old tearful affect again. Oh boy! Group is dyin' out there. They're breakin' up. Fallin' out. Makin' like a bunch of whoopin' cranes on a funny drug. So this is the famous butterball of boo-hoo. But then, old Joe's little sneaky fingers are stroking the inside of her dimpled thigh. And he don't seem to know where to stop. We lost sight of his hand. But she don't seem to notice one way or the other. Lookit, in my opinion, her leg o' lamb was just too damned thick for nerve endings. I mean, you get this fat just goin' on and on, deep like some peat bog, and the nerve endings I believe get lost and confused. So while she's goin' boo-hoo, he's just gropin' away, heedless.

Meanwhile, group is lovin' this stuff. Wormstock. Fat women having sex, drunks with nothin' hard about 'em, and everything bathed in boo-hoo. I'll tell it like it is: while Joe and Sally were residents here, this place was alive. Nothin' that interesting come this way again till a certain college boy from Downstate who shall go nameless.

But my point is, don't you see, that Joe and Sally were better able to demonstrate a wide range of behaviors, more capable and comfortable engaging each other, more attentive to each other's feelings when we added a little Kankakee Rye to the equation. With alcohol in the picture, Joe could become flirtatious and sexual. And Sally, feeling disgusted and degraded by his dirty drunken pawing, was able to deflect her guilt at being the portly cause of her husband's impotence.

What Sally and Joe achieved with our assistance was a clearer understanding of the emotional economy central to their relationship. Sobriety! Don't make me laugh! It's just not good for everyone. You got to learn to work alcohol. It'll work if you let it. Hunnert percent promise. Last I heard, Sally was still being mistaken for landscaping and Joe was still catching furniture on fire in his zealous housekeeping, *and* they are still married.

Some people like to talk about "let's get real." Okay, let's get real. Nobody's gonna strap Sally to a machine and jiggle off three hundred pounds. And no one's gonna get Joe's dingle to do more than flap in the wind. The Worm has its own path. It's a shiny one. Let the Worm find its path is what I say.

Musial and McCartney—Together Again for the First Time

Christopher Sorrentino

> Our cumulative failure to understand and claim our opportunities is the large part of our poverty.
>
> —*The Idea of Home*

In the title story of *Metaphysics in the Midwest* the acutely alcoholic Professor Feeling, under suspicion of child molestation and burglary, is visited in his hospital room *cum* cell by his student Laura, to whom he describes an imaginary concert to benefit his legal defense. He asks: "Can you see McCartney and Stan Musial singing 'Fool on the Hill' for me?" What an image! Stan the Man and The Pretty One, both long past their prime, gamely managing the lyrics. And yet the two have their ineffable connection, rooted in the Professor's own concerns—you'll have to read the story—and in those of his creator. For nearly twenty years, Curtis White has been making sense of the "world," that vast rich dump of images and ideas to which we are all heirs, by taking the absurd abundance of its components and platooning them, creating bizarre and improbable ensembles that function with a logic perfectly their own. White's base repertory of those images and ideas is a standard-issue grab bag of postmodern fodder, but spiked with a discriminating sense of the perverse uses to which those images and ideas have been put, and with a sharp understanding of the processed convictions such perversions have implanted in us all. This "makes" his work; that is, Curtis White's fiction operates on a dark subterranean level, as a kind of piquant countermyth to the conventional wisdom regarding the basis and nature of the American experience.

At present, to achieve America, to embrace it as wholly new, or to accept as unique to it some feature of its aspect that holds special allure and thus accept the whole, requires the attainment of escape velocity. What is being escaped from is of little importance—it is the lopping off of this part of the equation that has made America such a catastrophe of ingenuous hypocrisy. It is as if in search of its own definition the nation transformed the purposeful flight at the heart of its establishment into a continuously flowing system possessed of a rationale that places more importance on the movement itself than on either its point of origin or its destination. White's fiction is informed by a piercing understanding of the stunted ways we Americans seek endlessly to charge our lives, to remove ourselves from one reality in favor of another, and of the price we pay. He posits, predictably enough, that American life, culture, and society are confining and dull—but also knows that x years after modernism we are in a position where such a stance is in itself hackneyed (you might even say that the success of advertising content today depends upon widespread awareness of the limitations of American life). The task he has set for himself is to scrupulously investigate the various mechanisms of escape devised by people as aware of their confinement and boredom as he is. Unlike a lot of writers, White grants these people their self-awareness. Their failure is not one of intent, but of the imagination. White's take on the middle-class suburb, as exemplified by his fictive San Lorenzo, is suffused with a pained understanding of the wish its invention addressed. With White you get the impression that it might even have worked if it hadn't foundered against its own hardened establishment: the idea of home was defeated by an institutional idea of "the idea of home," so to speak.

But the suburban ideal is only one aspect of White's meditation. If the fact of its unconsummated promise is a reflex truism articulated, more or less, by any number of smartly outfitted postsuburbanites in the Mission or the Lower East Side or Wicker Park—then what of them, these prophets of Riveredge, NJ? It's a question that takes vibrant shape in White's hands, unasked but nevertheless responded to. If William Carlos Williams wanted to shape his language from out of the "mouths of Polish mothers" then Curtis White's is often shaped from out of the mouths of their descendants, sophisticated progeny with the time and desire to "expand" their "horizons," whether via the acquisition of a 1200 square foot suburban house or a rejection of that for a fanciful mixture of street cred and microbrew snobbery. His fiction is populated by strivers and the agents that frustrate their desires. These agents can assume shape as evangelical deceivers, such as "San Lorenzo" or Professor Feeling and his course, "Spiritual Growth: Getting All the Way to Infusion" (the Professor is a relatively benign example—White is the best manufacturer of fictional con men since William Burroughs); or as the dubiously "radical" posturing of contemporary capitalism; or as products of self-defeating impulse, as in "A Disciplined Life," where Daniel Campabruno, a recent immigrant to the USA who suddenly finds himself in prison, decides to abort his successful escape attempt, because

. . . this is also—thankfully—the story of the beginning of my new life. I returned myself to the state penitentiary at Halbert, submitted myself to the amazed guards. I realized that my mad act would add to my tenure, but I knew also that I was still far from ready to leave. I knew that I needed much more time, that I was not yet adequate to join the life in progress in this strange, beautiful country.

With this variation on the familiar twentieth-century saga of immigrant otherness and assimilation White proposes the existence of a peculiarly American condition, subject to self-diagnosis, that he extends through the present day. It is as if none of us are ready "to join the life in progress in this strange, beautiful country," as if otherness is chronic and assimilation an endless remedial program. Like recalcitrant students, we are continually receiving invitations to "join" "life" from forgiving and sympathetic advertisers and the media that bear their messages.

It's all the more appropriate that White writes at a time when "joining life" is cunningly presented as an act of transgressing the boundaries of the everyday. When it sometimes seems as if the options before us are either to remain barricaded within the walls or to gratefully accept the Trojan Horse, what gift does White himself bear? Through the very focus and elegance of his work, its meticulous construction, White makes clear that there is a way out that is not deadening or repetitively masturbatory, that there is a way to refuse the largesse, the malevolent blossom, of capitalism, that there is a way to avoid conspiring in your own defeat, as he puts it. White's marvelous suggestion can be cast in that most revolutionary of phrases—All Power to the Imagination.

But there's a price. White's characters are neither more nor less than what he has made them, but each is pushed to, and sometimes beyond, the limits of the "possible"—precisely what American Life (if I may characterize it as an entity for the moment) claims so insistently to aspire to—and by so doing, they take their lumps. At the center of White's shrewd and learned comedies is a bitter flavor awaiting its release. His work is hardly "realistic," but he is bravely committed to the "real" idea that an upended life yields disorderly and unpredictable consequences. In our era of half-assed transgression, this is a salutary reminder.

Dedication to Doubt: Curtis White's The Idea of Home *and the Function of Fiction*

Jeff Baker

> We walked into the record store and saw the cover of *Sgt. Pepper's Lonely Hearts Club Band.* We thought together, "Life can be other than it has been."
>
> (*The Idea of Home* 156)

Well, there's the darkly wonderful, Raymond Carver-esque story "Sex and Food a Mouthful at a Time"; and the Ishmael Reed-like surrealism of shaman Joe Green's story in "The Idea Which Reality Seeks." Yes, there's also the bittersweet, Sherwood Anderson-grotesque feel of "Some Disease," and the Lovecraftian, bizarrely matter-of-fact narration of "The Amazing Hypnogogic Man." But it is the sixties stories, "Tales of the Hippies" and "Four Theses on the Fate of the Sixties," that I keep returning to in *The Idea of Home.* I think the reason I do is that, though most of his stories aren't "about" the sixties, nonetheless, the *idea* of the sixties, and all it represents for this author, sings irrepressibly through Curtis White's fiction. For the corollary to White's observation about the cover of *Sgt. Pepper's* runs something like this: Life can be other than it has been, which is good, because *it ought to be other than it is.*

Of course, one of the most problematic things about my characterization of White's collection has to do with defining "the sixties" themselves. SDS activist-turned-university professor Todd Gitlin has recognized the difficulty with attempting to define this explosive decade. Writing in *The Sixties: Years of Hope, Days of Rage* of the reductionism inherent in "a shorthand culture where insatiable media grind the flux of the world into the day's sound bites," Gitlin argues that, "Perhaps no decade has suffered this absurd reduction more than 'the Sixties. . . .' " His portrait of the dichotomous perceptions which surround the sixties even today begs a series of questions: Were the sixties "wonderfully high times"? Or "a catastrophe anyone was lucky to have survived"? Were they "days of unbridled idealism"? Or days of "rampant destruction"? Did they embody "youthful exuberance"? Or simply "degeneracy"? Did they signal a higher "moral intelligence"? Or merely "stupidity"? Did they represent "an unsurpassed time of righteous revolt"? Or "an abyss from which only the triumph of Ronald Reagan rescued us" (xiii)?

Gitlin offers his own bit of "sound bite" reductionism, "snippets of pure spectacle, in the style of a ticker tape or a clunky documentary," conjuring images of

> . . . draft card burnings . . . the Pentagon . . . Stop the Draft Week . . . the Tet offensive . . . the McCarthy campaign . . . Johnson decides not to run for another term . . . Martin Luther King killed . . . Columbia buildings occupied . . . Paris . . . Prague . . . trips to Hanoi . . . Robert Kennedy killed . . . Democratic Convention riots . . . hundreds of students massacred in Mexico City . . . Miss America protests . . . Nixon elected . . . deserters, flights to Canada and Sweden, mutinies, "fragging" in Vietnam . . . Eldridge Cleaver underground . . . San Francisco State, Berkeley, Harvard, Stanford, etc. besieged . . . People's Park . . . police shootouts with Black Panthers . . . student, freak, black, homosexual riots . . . SDS splits . . . Woodstock . . . women's consciousness raising . . . the Chicago Conspiracy trial . . . Charles Manson . . . Altamont . . . My Lai . . . Weatherman bombs . . . Cambodia . . . Kent State . . . Jackson State . . . a fatal bombing in Madison. . . . (Gitlin 243)

A poignant list. Yet one which rapidly crystallizes into a series of broken images from the evening news of my own childhood. It is this juxtaposition, between the "public" sixties, and the "private" experience each of us remembers, that serves to make characterizing this conflicted decade so difficult—and that White captures so effectively. In *The Idea of Home* "the sixties" may very well culminate in T.V. newscasters' coverage of Weatherman bombs and Charles Manson, yet they seem to have begun, innocently enough, in the small privacy of a child's curiosity.

In "Tales of the Hippies" White's character Clarence (otherwise known as GloBoy) explains: "I think the thing that saved me and made us, hippies, possible was that very early on I saw that this place had a secret. Maybe a dirty little secret. So, one day I was out riding my bicycle and I stopped before one of the corner street signs. Via Palma and Via Sonya, it read. But what did these words mean? They were telling me something about the place I lived in, I realized, but what? I asked my mom" (121).

Clarence's mom doesn't have much help to offer, except a wryly raised eyebrow at his assertion that the phenomenon is a "mystery." But Clarence has to know what the strange street names signify, "excited by a curiosity of the intellect for the first time in [his] life." He proceeds to the library to get a Spanish-English dictionary, but the old librarian, "a grotesque, knotted, knowing thing," is suspicious and asks why he could want such a thing. Clarence was "smart enough to see that there was not only a mystery here, but maybe also a conspiracy of these adults," so he lies, claiming a pen pal in Barcelona (121-22).

Clarence is amazed to find that his own street, "Sonya," means "A Street of Dreams." This disturbs him, however, because he knows that "no one ever dreamed on the Street of Dreams." But of course there is more: the Via Escondido, "Street of Secrets or Hidden Things." The Via Dolorosa, "Street of Sorrowing." The Via Descanso, "Street of Sleep." "Oh, the joke was on us, for sure," he says, "Via Bolsa, Street of the Purse. Yes, sad, sleeping shoppers said it all" (122).

In a scene reminiscent of Pynchon's 1964 story "The Secret Integration," Clarence has his buddies "get on their stingray bikes and go out all over town making lists and maps of street names. (Even now [he] can see them peddling off, their hair flowing back, their follicles energized, already a lot like the manes they would soon grow in indignation over this fraud, [their] lives)" (122).[1]

These undersized subversives discover plenty of names that constitute a series of "grim jokes on [their] walking middle-class death." Yet there are also names which hint at the possibilities of their "changing things, reclaiming life." First, there's Via Viento, Street of Windy Pride, which GloBoy dedicates to their parents. There is also a place called Honda, the Street of the Sling for Hurling Stones. "We can get started there!," GloBoy says, presaging the later rebellion of a generation. "And a Via Melena, the Street of the Long Hair in Men and Loose Hair in Women." "Finally," GloBoy says, "when our work is done, there is Via Mirabel, Street of Beautiful Sight, a place from which we can see for miles and play our guitars and take consciousness expanding drugs" (123).

Ah, but here is where the ground begins to steeply slope away. . . . Here is where White's cozy little tale begins to take on a most disconcerting turn toward . . . um, *irreality.* A child Clarence's age, in the late-fifties, would never *really* have talked about "consciousness expanding drugs" this way. And the narrator from "Four Theses on the Fate of the Sixties"—she would never *really* have worked for Bert Claster on a Romper Room syndication in Sonoma, California, replacing the boys and girls with "midget cyborgs"! And check out what "Groovy," the narrator of "Death of Hippy," sees when he shoots a guy after his expatriation to "Panamania":

> Instead of the dingy, redundant bullet hole I expected, I saw that at the point of entrance, square in the middle of his face, his flesh had—what other word is there for it?—blossomed! There in the middle of his face a flower of meat had exuberantly bloomed with fervid petals as red as

prime beef. When I looked closer, I saw that the petals themselves, which arched elegantly from the center like a languid anemone or a violent sunflower, were themselves a complexity of really beautiful cells as one finds in the voluptuous oranges of eastern China, only here they were of the crimson color and the gelatinous, pulpy quality of a pomegranate. Yes, indeed, a pomegranate of meat.

"But this was but one of the wonders this man had in store for me. Beneath his coat, projecting from his body as if from a dead log of wood, was a finely layered, opulently colored vest of the silky and almost translucent fruit-bodies, the beautiful white anastomosing sporophores, the blood-red fructifications, the edible glutinous cuticles, the greenish gills, the fine radial striations, hymenial surfaces and thin-walled hyphae of macrofungi, of mushrooms." (131-32)

Yep, Groovy's got himself a serious *reality-check* happening here. Particularly when he discovers that the next thing he knows, he's in a hospital, because a bullet has grazed his own temple. Groovy narrates: "The gentle, concerned doctors of Panamania explained—when I asked what I could possibly be doing there—that I'd shot myself, attempting suicide. Of the other fellow they knew nothing. They also suggested that I should stop eating the tiny, pulsing, radiogenic worms which slept in the deeps of my mescal bottles" (132).

What are we to make, then, of these strangely surreal irruptions in these hippies' tales? How are we to make sense of the warpings of the otherwise "realistic" narratives that White so painstakingly constructs? The answer is provided by Dandelion, another of White's hippy narrators—it has to do with the introduction of *doubt* into the fabric of reality: "Dig it," Dandelion says, GloBoy had our beginnings about right. We began in doubt. Hey, mom and dad, we said, you tryin' to say this place is reality? Far out. What a joke. Nice trick to play on your own kids" (125). She continues:

"But what GloBoy was talking about was a political doubt. There was another kind of doubt as well, stimulated by our first teeny tokes on the weed, man, pot. Don't get me wrong, dope can't take you where you need to go, but it sure is a start, a little jump start, something to break through the crust. We'd look at our shoes and say, What's shoes? Everything looked strange and new, as if seen for the first time. . . . We'd get stoned and think of something like—garden hose—and then we'd laugh like crazy because something so silly existed and people paid money for it. Hoo hee!" (125-26)

All the goofy, dry-toothed pot laughter aside, Curtis White takes *doubt* very seriously. And it is his dedication to doubt—political, epistemological, ontological, and narrative doubt—that makes his stories whisper with the conspiratorial conscience of an underground revolution. In fact, White's dedication to doubt is the essence—the *idea*—undergirding much of the sixties revolution itself.

The *idea* of the sixties in White's writing is rooted in his beliefs about fiction: what it is, how it functions, what it creates (or destroys), what it reinforces (or undermines)—*what it's for*. In the 1992 article "Fiction's Future," Curtis White wrote about a publishing collective he helped start called Fiction Collective Two (FC2). When asked about the purpose and mission of this collective, White responded that "The Fiction Collective came about in the mid-seventies following the brief blip on the screen that was the Counterculture, because of a reactionary backlash against innovative fiction in particular and an alternative culture in general." White believes that this reactionary backlash happened because "the ideas of writers like Ron Sukenick, Alan Singer, Gilbert Sorrentino, and Kathy Acker were fundamentally revolutionary at the level of consciousness and finally corrosive of dominant, mid-twentieth century, Fortress America ideology" (250).

FC2 stands, then, as a dissident reaction against the "lifelessness of hyper-real Disneyesque high-tech life" (251). But why all the surreality in White's own fiction? White explains his belief about realism as a "state form" of narrative which is in complicity with "Fortress America ideology." We are confronted by "a situation," White writes, "in which a fictional discourse becomes part of a broader ideological confrontation, a situation in which a given literary aesthetic becomes a State Fiction. . . . Language and certainly literature are always the site of social dialogue or struggle. So one chooses not to write Realism because one chooses not to be in complicity with the state form which has appropriated it" (251).

This is not a new view of the power relationships among fiction, narrative, and politics for White. Way back in 1984, in an article about Italo Calvino's fiction, White wrote that

> the confrontation between realism and "experimentalism" is not only a narrow, provincial, literary dispute, it is also part of a broader ideological battle between not necessarily but factually combative epistemologies. Realism has become a State Fiction, a part of the machinery of the political state. It is through the conventions of Realism that the State explains to its citizens the relationship between themselves and Nature, economics, politics, and their own sexuality. This massive epistemological exercise takes place every day, right before our eyes on television, in the movies, in *Time* magazine, in the simple-minded, relational rhetoric of politicians, and so on. (138)

Thus, in White's view, to write "realistically" is to condone the political, economic, even onto-epistemological *status quo*—a complicity that White is dedicated to opposing at every turn. "The realist values the reassurance of the familiar," White wrote in that 1984 article, and it's plain to see the connection he wishes to make between that special kind of reassurance and the political conservatism of late capitalist American culture.

Neither is this an especially new view of either politics or narratology more generally—Pynchon makes essentially the same point in both *Gravity's Rainbow* and *Vineland*. And the point is that, as long as we are living in the realism of the material world, the State (as in, those in power, the members of what Pynchon calls a "Christian Capitalist Faith," immune from the reality that the rest of us "poor sheep" have to suffer), holds the upper hand. Where no magic is possible (or even permissible), then the *material*—in the form of television, high-tech movies, and soulless rock and roll—constitutes the overhyped reality of an all-too-corporeal existence.

In *Vineland* Pynchon's much-beloved Mucho Maas, whom some readers might remember as Oedipa Maas's disc jockey husband from *The Crying of Lot 49,* helps the hapless antihero Zoyd Wheeler come to terms with the death of sixties magic. Mucho opines: "But acid gave us the X-ray vision to see through [the State's power over life and death], so of course they had to take it away from us." To which Zoyd replies: "Yeah, but they can't take what happened, what we found out." Mucho explains: "'Easy. They just let us forget. Give us too much to process, fill up every minute, keep us distracted, it's what the Tube is for, and though it kills me to say it, it's what rock and roll is becoming—just another way to claim our attention, so that beautiful certainty we had starts to fade, and after a while they have us convinced all over again that we really are going to die" (314).

The death of magic. The absence of doubt. In White's view this is why the radical fiction writer, dedicated as he or she must be to the irruption of irreality, so "values the beauty of the new and 'monstrous.' " And the point of White's surrealism is precisely, as one of Calvino's characters would say, to "explode" the barrier "between monsters and nonmonsters" so that "everything is possible again" (134).

White's dedication to doubt is really a dedication to the revolution. And he plays it out, narratively, with a variety of strategies, at one point discarding even the strictures of punctuation and syntax so that his narrator, Dandelion, can better represent the freedom of the sixties movement: "This isn't what you asked me to talk about, is it?" she asks. "I'm wandering. But wandering is so beautiful! In fact, maybe wandering is what was at the heart of our movement. My thesis is in my digression. Yeah, I like that. That's hip. It would be a betrayal of the story of our best times to tell it as a 'straight' story anyway. So I'll tell it as one long digression. There's the infinite in that" (127).

Dandelion's assertion, that "wandering is what was at the heart of our movement," is reiterated by Norman Mailer in *Armies of the Night,* Mailer's personal recollection of the 1967 march on Washington. In that novel Mailer writes that "The aesthetic of the New Left . . . began with the notion that the authority could not comprehend nor contain nor finally manage to control any political action whose end was unknown. They could attack it, beat it, jail it, misrepresent it, and finally abuse it, but they could not feel a sense of victory because they could not understand a movement which inspired thousands to march without a coordinated plan" (105). Here Mailer understands that an essential component of the sixties movement was its ad hoc nature. That movement, in all its permutations, was, again, the youths' reaction to a "realism" that manifests itself in every kind of hierarchy; indeed, in even the very syntax and narrative structures that restrict completely free expression—a point which White emphasizes with Dandelion's narrative.

For Dandelion proceeds to spin a stream-of-consciousness tale of "the summer of love before the Summer of Love"[2] that includes the following passage:

> "then it beckoned new age mutants forth from simmering dumplings in the Panhandle or they flew in on UFOs and founded a tax exempt non-profit religious foundation under California state law for the ecstatic transformation of earth in paradise love gifts planted the paradisal sanctuaries for all wildflower people forever they called it Electric Tibet or a 'trippy body cream for groovy loving' depending on my mood some park benches grew pranksters who fed our heads and introduced you to the only god in the world for you she was special you were shy and said 'pleased to meet you' anyhow behind the sheer Indian print sheet a pot was boiling Digger[3] stew for dinner they served a bowl and the little alphabet pastas spelled out Free Frame of Reference solid!" (127-28)

But the scene quickly turns from the stream-of-consciousness, free-form love-in to more clipped and "real" syntax and assumes a menacing aspect as it alludes to the carnivorous gleam in a now-infamous pair of eyes:

> "That was happy, okay. But you all know well what happened next. Someone turned the light on. 'Hey, who turned that light on? I can't see a thing.' That was our last joke. We all sat up like twelve lucid sleepers to a

nightmare and looked to our right as if the meaning of our dream was written on the wall. And there at the door stood an oily messiah, his hand still on the light switch as if it were our collective heart, an omnivorous gleam in his eyes, like a coyote thinking 'Bunnies!'

"Then he said, 'Hi there. My name's Charlie.' " (129)

Once again, White will allow no easy formulation of the sixties or of their grim slide into the "me-decade" of the early seventies. Raising the specter of Charles Manson here helps the author's own transition into "Groovy's" tale of the hippies' demise. Groovy appears, *Spoon River*-like, with a "bit of brain protruding" from his broken skull, an eye dangling "from a gristle of nerve" (129) to speak of the "Death of Hippy." "This is what guys like Charlie brought us to." Groovy says. "Even me, the lysergic Lenin, the Leader of the Laughers, not even I was pure enough to survive" (129).

Certainly there is real-world evidence to corroborate this narrator's expatriation, demoralization, and defeat, as well as the more radical sixties factions' move toward violence in the face of brutally repressive police and governmental tactics. Reflecting Groovy's own expatriation in White's fictional tale, Gitlin, for example, asserts that, by the early seventies, many activists, "burned out by the infighting, brooding with visions of impending apocalypse . . . found this a propitious moment to slip off into communes in Vermont, Mendocino, and their equivalents. . . . Beneath the rhetoric, they kept up their whole way of life by relinquishing any illusion that they could shape history" (396).

Other dissidents, however, turned toward violence[4] as an answer to the government's repressive policies, once again echoing White's portrayal of Groovy and his violent demise. Gitlin writes that Bernardine Dorn, a Weathermen leader, actually exulted in the Manson "family's" slaughtering of Sharon Tate and the LaBianca family: "Dig it!" Dorn is quoted as saying. "First they killed those pigs, then they ate dinner in the same room with them, then they even shoved a fork into the victim's stomach. Wild!" (399), thus reinforcing Groovy's assertions that "guys like Charlie" brought such radicals to their violent defeat.

In this way Groovy's questioning as to how he was actually killed takes a wry twist. After his experience in the hospital in "Panamania," Groovy returns "back to the States, back to the Haight. It wasn't long before I died for good" he says, "Head stove in with a brick. Strange. But the one thing I'm not sure of is, did I do it to myself again? Do you know, mister? Do any of you understand?" (132). Surely White is here raising the question as to whether the hippies and antiwar activists, by assuming the violent methods and tactics of their oppressors, hadn't actually been overtaken by the very "virus" they were trying to counteract—that their defeat was implicit in their own methods having degenerated into the same violence they had so opposed in the first place.

But there are even bigger, more currently pressing questions to be asked, in White's view. For not only was this "lysergic Lenin" not "pure enough to survive," but neither, according to the author, were his compatriots. For, as these stories open, we find their various narrators standing at the corner of "Pasatiempo and Perdido"—literally "passing the time" and "lost" or "wandering." This foreshadowing functions as a prolepsis to GloBoy's childhood examination of the "secret" offered by his hometown's street names but also as a prelude to "Four Theses on the Fate of the Sixties," wherein White indicates that the sixties generation—some 20 million of them by 1970 (Gitlin 192)—are lost, passing the time aimlessly as we move into the new millennium.

White's first "thesis" accounts for the reasons that this generation lost its way. "Because irony knows no limits and recognizes an easy mark when it sees one," White's narrator claims, "it is certain that the sixties generation—raised on revolution and yearning in the enervated eighties for its return—will find, when revolution does return, that they are the ones to be overthrown" (142). The narrator insists, in fact, that "If the Pentagon were to be levitated now, like Allen Ginsberg, Abbie Hoffman and the Fugs did in 1967, when it reached shoulder level out scampering like shame-faced mice and roaches would come guys and gals who used to wear their hair, their 'freak flags,' down to their butts" (142). While the speaker admits to the poetic license he takes here by reconfiguring the 1967 march on Washington, he nonetheless indicts an entire generation by asserting that "you don't have to live in the 'belly of the beast' to benefit from the beast's reign. Now, there you've got us" (143).

White's narrator claims that his own story is "as good an illustration as any" as to why the hippies lost their way. Starting out in "mass communications, B.A. from Iowa State," the narrator eventually moves to the West Coast "along with everybody else twixt eight and twenty-eight from Grand Rapids and Bismarck and Boise and Topeka, for god's sake, with just a fragment of the freak infection" (143). But by 1973, all the revolutionary fronts seem "insubstantial" to the narrator. "We shot our wad on Chicago and the Cambodian incursion" he says, "and thereafter it was all postcoital *tristesse*" (145-6).

The narrator continues, asserting that disappointment and disillusionment with the movement led, around 1974, to all of the disaffected revolutionaries starting to look for jobs. "Countercultural as all get out at first," the narrator says. "But eventually it was hard not to see that what we'd almost inadvertently acquired in the universities—organizational skills, knowledge and a capacity for insight—the auto-, techno-, and bureau-crats were willing to pay really a lot of money for." Thus their "deviant brilliance" now beholden to the high-tech industry, they begin to find solace in "Cuisinart, BMW, and laser disc players for our reissued copies of *Sgt. Pepper* and *Surrealistic Pillow*" (146). The final result? "If we wanted power, son of a gun, we got it after all" the narrator states. "We rule the roost. We possess all of the shibboleths of power and privilege" (146). Yet the narrator remains troubled by this rise to power.[5]

What seems most troubling to this narrator is the fact that the sixties generation has "sold out"—has abnegated their responsibility to create and maintain alternative ways of living and of looking at the world. Perhaps the best, and most persuasive, characterization of this ethical imperative occurs in Groovy's narrative, wherein he describes a young woman whose health has been ravaged by smoking, but who now faces an operation which, because of her weakened health, may itself kill her. Her doctor considers the situation: "If you don't have the operation, you'll die. So, we'll operate, and if you die because you've wasted your health on cigarettes, well, fuck you."

Groovy has a similar message to the human race: "I would like to say something similar to the species. Humans, I mean" he says. "We hippies failed, maybe, but we tried something amazing that was, even if just for a little minute, noble and alive. But if the rest of you have ignored all the death in our culture—mental death, physical, economic, environmental, military, judicial, spiritual—and if you've concerned yourself only with getting high, getting laid, and making money to buy shit, if you've found no way large or small to make even a little revolution, a tiny mutation, a single rip in the membrane of our shared sausage casing, then fuck you" (133).

Were the sixties a bust? Were the efforts of sixties radicals, in the end, a failure? Todd Gitlin's answer, decidedly, is no. "To put it briefly," he writes, "the genies that the Sixties loosed are still abroad in the land, inspiring and unsettling and offending, making trouble. For the civil rights and antiwar and countercultural and women's and the rest of that decade's movements forced upon us central issues for Western civilization—fundamental questions of value, fundamental divides of culture, fundamental debates about the nature of the good life" (xiv).

Similarly, Curtis White's fiction successfully raises the same essential debate—that is, how to be? *The Idea of Home* is testimony to White's continuing dedication to the hippies' ethical imperative of attempting to make that "little revolution." White's collection of stories is certainly informed by his dedication to doubt as a force for undermining a narratively and politically oppressive realism. Yet his writing is fed by more than a negative will toward Disneyesque hyperreality: these stories aim to engage the *human* in us all. Curtis White would offer us an alternative to the realist's spare certainty. For while his dedication to narrative doubt reinforces his convictions about the function of fiction, still that function is always geared toward a continuing revolution of thought—toward rupture, toward the monstrous, toward the irreal, toward possibility, toward magic. It is geared, ultimately, toward the creation of a dynamic, ever-changing narrative reality that emerges as revolutionary idea—an *idea of home. . . .*

NOTES

[1]Readers familiar with Pynchon's story will recall Étienne, the child who let the air out of cop cars' tires and even "put on skin-diving gear to stir up silt in the creek the paper mill used" to stop its production for a whole week. Or Kim Dufay, "a slender, exotic-looking sixth-grader with . . . a thing about explosive chemical reactions." Or even Hogan Slothrop, who once planned to set off a smoke bomb in the PTA meeting in order to make off with the grown-ups' minutes and financial statements (150-51, 166). Given the fact that the story was published in 1964, it is a remarkably prescient account of baby boomers' preadolescent predisposition to radical intervention into their parents' affairs.

[2]The other narrators' request that Dandelion tell about "the summer of love before the Summer of Love? How about life before the portable cam crews caught it, refracted it once or twice, and left this twist of image that became a virus indistinguishable from the national infection?" (125) is echoed in Pynchon's *Vineland* by Isaiah, who says: " 'Whole problem 'th you folk's generation,' Isaiah opined, 'nothing personal, is you believed in your Revolution, put your lives right out there for it—but you sure didn't understand much about the Tube. Minute the Tube got hold of you folks that was it, that whole alternative America, el deado meato, just like th' Indians, sold it all to your real enemies, and even in 1970 dollars—it was way too cheap. . . .' " (373).

[3]An interesting gloss on this passage can be found in Gitlin's book: "They [the Diggers] practiced street theater, with performances and leaflets as their two forms. They declared 'The Death of Money and the Birth of Free,' trudged down Haight Street as pallbearers wearing five-foot animal masks and carrying a coffin, giving away flutes and flowers, mocking the law banning 'public nuisance,' which they said was only a 'new sense.' They raised money from Owsley, and stole sides of beef which ended up in the stew they ladled out every afternoon for a year at 4 P.M. in the Panhandle of Golden Gate Park. They broke a donated brick of marijuana into baggies, went into

Haight-Ashbury stores, and yelled, 'Free marijuana. Does anybody want this?' They ran a Free Store with 'liberated goods,' and gave out 'free money.' They burned dollar bills. They erected a twelve-foot-square 'Free Frame of Reference'—walk through it and remind yourself how constructed consciousness is" (222-23).

[4]In sober tones, Gitlin admits that "The turn toward deliberate violence against property was already well along, the explosions amplified, as usual, by the mass media. By conservative estimate, between September 1969 and May 1970 there were some two hundred fifty major bombings and attempts linkable with the white left—about one a day" (401).

[5]Gitlin's characterization of this "decline" into equipoise and conformity is more sympathetic to his radical brethren: "what was far more visible, of course, was the money-grubbing and chic self-absorption so much beloved by I-told-you-so journalists, as if a whole generation had moved en masse from '*J'accusse*' to *Jacuzzi;* Jerry Rubin's move to Wall Street in the early Eighties garnered more publicity than all the union organizers and anti-nuclear campaigns among New Left graduates put together" (433).

WORKS CITED

Gitlin, Todd. *The Sixties: Years of Hope, Days of Rage.* New York: Bantam, 1993.

Pynchon, Thomas. "The Secret Integration." [1964] *Slow Learner.* Boston: Little, Brown, 1984. 139-93.

——. *Vineland.* New York: Penguin, 1990.

White, Curtis. "Fiction's Future." *ANQ: A Quarterly Journal of Short Article, Notes and Reviews* 5.4 (1992): 250-52.

——. *The Idea of Home.* Los Angeles: Sun & Moon, 1992.

——. "Italo Calvino and What's Next: The Literature of Monstrous Possibility." *Iowa Review* 14.3 (1984): 128-39.

Eden, the American West, and Temporary Autonomous Zones: Imagining Utopia in Curtis White's Postmodern Home

Stephen Davenport

Curtis White and Allen McAfrica have a lot in common. Both are inventive, restless storytellers. Both hail from San Lorenzo, California. Both make an appearance in White's third book, *The Idea of Home*. Wounded sons of the exhausted American West, they long for replenishment. They imagine utopic spaces, zones of renewal, or, as White himself calls it, "that place where the world worlds in availability" (155). They seek, in short, the garden promise of America, the fruits of which are reinvention and rebirth.

Like White, McAfrica "was born high and dry on the green front lawn of the not-necessary," and what he seeks is "not the real world or the true world or the authentic world, but simply, as he put it, an available world that is itself" (39). David Bohannon, another of White's *Home* characters, makes available, if not the world White and McAfrica have in mind, a material world nonetheless. In the fashion of the Levitts of the East, Bohannon invents what he calls the "California method" and, putting it in motion, builds himself a paradise, the Village of San Lorenzo, California, the slogan for which is "Every lot a garden spot" (101). For the workers who had poured into the Bay Area in the early 1940s to work in the war industry and the soldiers who returned to take part in the baby boom that would follow, Bohannon's San Lorenzo, the construction of which was completed in 1947, was a paradise, a plotted and paved garden of family possibilities and actual homes.

Like Bohannon, White is interested in space and the uses to which it can be put. He opens the first of the seventeen pieces that make up *Home,* "This Is Not an Autobiographical Statement," with the following claim: "I would like, in this book, to imagine a place in which humans can live. A place more desirable than the failure which we presently inhabit" (9). He closes the piece with these words: "Whatever we choose, in choosing we will have risked our lives on the idea (the very Notion which makes utopia) that it is possible to live a 'better' life, to see and understand things 'better' than others. Better, certainly, than our mothers and fathers, still residing in our first home, who can only be dead to us now" (16).

White's vision is a moral one. He writes about individual and cultural exhaustion, about the limitations of the American Dream of Rebirth, specifically about the California method, which offers up pre-fab paradises like Disneyland and San Lorenzo. He writes about the necessity for a new home, a utopic space capable of intending other spaces, each one inventive, wild, as procreative as it is re-creative. His is the world as verb, not noun. As I imagine White imagines it, a better life, one that worlds, is available to those willing to take the spatial cure. To suggest how we might approach White's fictions, which have come to constitute a kind of inner space program, I call upon three spatial metaphors—Eden, the American West, and Temporary Autonomous Zones—in the material space this essay affords me. If all goes well, we will be better readers of White, maybe even better equipped to take his advice and risk a cure of our own.

Eden

For some time, White has been addressing the idea of America, or the promise of the New World. His first book, a collection of stories set in Europe, deals with the decadence and failure of the Old. In *Heretical Songs*, when a woman is murdered in the English countryside in a story called "The Poet's Sister," Eden is undone: "The happy life of pious brother and sister was saddened, Arcadia sombered, God's first garden refound turned mortal, again the subject of life's vagaries" (17). In "Malice," the last story of his second collection, *Metaphysics in the Midwest*, Reverend Phenues Boyle imagines the reseeding of Arcadia after a Kansas dust storm:

> "The first time, the Lord God in his mighty and righteous wrath sent a flood. This time he's sendin' the opposite—original dirt. . . . By the end, we all of us gonna be one full mile down, and upstairs a new garden starts, feeding on our justly corrupting bones. New grass, new trees, children, new ponds, new and cleaner fish for the sea. Folks, it's going to be some kind of wonderful. Full of His grace." (188)

It is the idea of an American paradise, this "some kind of wonderful," that White develops in *Home,* his next book.

There his interest in Eden, or Arcadia, is most evident. That American spatial experiments like Bohannon's San Lorenzo—"Every lot a garden spot"—fail, prove themselves to be something less than wonderful, should not surprise us. Utopic spaces rooted in the material world are bound to fail, and whether we look forward to a new garden or backward to the good old days, Arcadia always eludes our grasp. It is always only an idea. If we play the escalator game Raymond Williams sets up in *The Country and the City* and go down through the centuries looking for the untainted space, where do we end up before everyone, young and old, is satisfied? Williams himself responds, "One answer, of course, is Eden" (12).

Where does White locate his Eden? To get a good idea, we need only call up a few examples from "An Available World," the three-story section that opens *Home.* In the first story he almost finds it in a kids' show: "Speaking of vision, one of the great things about utopia is the terrific view. Do you remember Miss Nancy on Romper Room, how she was able to see us all on the other end of the television waves through her Magic Mirror? . . . Well, the view from this place I have in mind is even better than that!" (10). He also fails to locate it in the next story, "Boy Finds Body." Neither "the slimy, green trickle of San Lorenzo Creek" (18), in which he mistakes a vacuum cleaner for a body, nor the "dark," "unnatural," "dangerous," "wrong" Hayward Plunge (21), a crowded indoor swimming pool built during the Depression by the WPA, fits the utopic bill. Even when a Sunday school teacher takes him and a few others on a nature tramp out behind the Plunge, an activity that should have been "innocent and easy" turns ugly: "as we were going through a steep grove of eucalyptus I happened to see a body not fifteen feet down the hill. A black teenage boy in jeans, tee-shirt and sneakers with flies perching and strutting on his vacant eyes" (21). The machine in the garden, the vacuum cleaner, portends death. Arcadia is littered with lost promise. Something is wrong in Paradise.

The closest thing to a material utopia in *Home* is the space afforded to Little League baseball in 1960. San Lorenzo's quartet of "grassy diamonds with fences all around, colorful handpainted advertising everywhere and a beatific snack bar" (11) is rendered imaginary two stories later. In "Willie Mays and the Idea of Home," the Edenic San Lorenzo diamonds are replaced by box scores and televised images, participation is transformed into spectatorship and the sacred bond it creates among the worshippers, and an actual professional baseball stadium, a material Eden for a Little Leaguer, becomes that most sacred of zones for a Bay Area fan, Willie Mays's "no-other-man's-land, the open spaces of center field" (24). A young boy named Chris turns inward, like the ten-year-old Commissioner in the title story of *Metaphysics in the Midwest,* to statistical baseball: "While other boys were actually out playing baseball, growing strong, staying healthy, Chris retreated to his room . . . where he replayed the 1962 season" (30). According to Chris,

Ecstasy had descended on him arbitrarily, unexpectedly. Through the Giants he had experienced triumph indistinguishable from love and innocent of ego. He wanted to live in that moment. He was an adolescent Trotskyite yearning for "permanent revolution." He wanted to get high and stay high. He wanted enlightenment. And so for most of his eleventh and twelfth years, he struggled to arrange for the game, the rolling dice—rattling like Tibetan skull-beads, thrown with all the solemnity of the I-Ching—to readmit him to utopia, to allow him not only his obsession, but control over it as well. (30)

Soon Chris can no longer recall the perfect past and enjoy it in the present.

White's situation is similar. Caught on the down escalator, he looks for that spot where he can hop off, reenter Eden, and play in the garden, code for "the good old days," about which Raymond Williams remarks, "Of course we notice their location in the childhood of their authors. . . . Nostalgia, it can be said, is universal and persistent; only other men's nostalgias offend" (12). For White, then, the prospect of a material Eden—a Little League baseball diamond in 1960, the center field Willie Mays patrolled in 1962—disappears with his childhood. In this way *Home* is a coming-of-age story, White's *Catcher in the Rye.* Personal nostalgia, though, is only part of the key to utopia for White. Cultural nostalgia also seems to be part of it.

American West

If *Home* is a Bildungsroman, it is even more so a Western. "Unnatural Children," the eleven-story middle section, provides a remarkable imaginative history of the American West as failed garden. Focusing on a hundred-year stretch from the 1870s to the 1970s, this grouping of tales eschews the nostalgia of ethnocentric European-American notions like virgin territory, noble savages, and manifest destiny for the kind of analysis that directs the work of New Western Historians like Patricia Nelson Limerick and Donald Worster.

In her seminal text *The Legacy of Conquest: The Unbroken Past of the American West,* Limerick compares the broad cultural effect of Southern and Western historians. For a variety of reasons—a Civil War, migration patterns of African Americans, the civil rights movement, disciplinary interest—Southern slavery has had a much stronger impact on the national consciousness than Western conquest. Limerick writes, "In the popular imagination, the reality of conquest dissolved into stereotypes of noble savages and noble pioneers struggling quaintly in the wilderness. . . . Children happily played ‘cowboys and Indians’ but stopped short of ‘masters and slaves’ ” (19). A new generation of Western historians, though, have made some headway. According to Worster, in his “Beyond the Agrarian Myth,” the first essay in an edited collection entitled *Trails: Toward a New Western History,* “Clearly, the grandiose history that white Americans once thought they were making out here in this land beyond the Mississippi River has come apart and does not compel belief as it once did. I think I know how that happened and want to claim some small credit for historians. For this region that was once so lost in dreams and idealization, we have been creating a new history, clear-eyed, demythologized, and critical” (7). Credit also goes to fiction writers who manage a Western that avoids the romantic trappings of the genre.

White’s performance in this area is admirable. Like the New Western Historians, he tells a story of the American West that foregrounds environmental change and admits to the garden multiple voices and viewpoints. In “History of the Great Mouth,” the first story in the middle section, he describes how mesquite was imported through grazing patterns and made natural:

> “Punctuating this radiant waste was the durable mesquite, a squat pretender to treeness, which grazing animals had brought up from Mexico (for the lucky-duck mesquite seed passes through the digestive tract of, say, a longhorn not only unharmed but with its seedcoat strategically scarified by gastric juices; thus upon its evacuation from a beast it is fertilized, watered and in all ways at home). The mesquite’s story provides an instance of genuine groundedness, of homeliness; it gives new vigor to the concept of ‘native.’ ” (46-47)

In “Dig Here and You Will Find a Writing,” an eerie tale about, among other things, the loss of wetlands, White looks at Paradise and the cowpokes who put in a parking lot. The environmental effect is obvious: “They have drained the swamp . . . in order to develop houses. The whip-like rushes, the truncheon blooms of the tules are brown and dead. Twenty bulldozers, earthmovers, dump trucks gun their engines and will not stop. I think they are bug husks” (56-57). The story closes with the narrator’s prediction that one day he will explode in a “welter of memory”: “Then I’ll start talking. And I’ll tell everything I know” (67).

In “Blood Will Tell” the West Coast hysteria during World War II that led to Japanese-American relocation camps is answered by “wrathful deities” (99). A Japanese-American classmate’s “sudden resentment” and look of “killing distrust” during a 1969 high school discussion about such camps lead the narrator years later to recognize the presence of their “separate histories” and “conjoined situation" (95-96). In "The Birth of Tragedy" the overpopulation of the Bay Area just after World War II forces the issue. Out of the region's "welter of memory" tumble the histories: "Chinese men sold interests in a cot or a bed from laundry doorways to bleary Vets. The Negro Problem and the Coolie Nuisance were contained through the use of tiers of beds hooked four or five to a wall, Pullman style" (101). *Home* provides a pluralism that we seldom see in Westerns.

Yes, hero cowboy images—Cisco Kid, Hopalong Cassidy, Gene Autry—do float through White's fiction; in fact, one of the photos in *Metaphysics* is a portrait of a 1940s' Everyboy girding himself for a little Cowboy-and-Injun action (108). Yet, as story after story in the "Unnatural Children" section demonstrates, White's West is anything but glamorous. By the time he is done, he has not so much demythologized it as remythologized it. For instance, the title character in "Are You With Me, Madame Nhu?"—a feminist activist, anti-Communist dissident, and "super-seductive sister-in-law to Ngo Dinh Diem, South Vietnamese President during the early days of American involvement in Vietnam" (112)—appears in a cage in a Bay Area market, where a boy buys her, "about the size of a large dog," for $37.95 (115). And in "History of the Great Mouth," a mother interrupts her slaughter work just long enough to give birth: "You could have seen her involved in her work, straddling the buffalo pornographically while working at his soft belly with a piercing knife. Suddenly a twinge. Mrs. Truby reaches under her leather apron and, with a shrug of wonder, removes a steaming infant. Wrapping him in a still bloody hide, she wipes her hands on her own wide thighs and begins ripping again. This child, Hank Smith Truby, was the first white child born in the Texas panhandle" (52). In the spirit of the New Western Historians, whose research has repopulated the West with a variety of women, White spins a New Western that is no romantic horse opera about a guy and his pony and the occasional river or winter or band of Indians they have to negotiate in their efforts to escape the effeminate East.

It is in "History of the Great Mouth" that White comes closest to a nineteenth-century Cowboy-and-Indian story. In it Allen McAfrica, a double for White, spins a version of a Kiowa creation myth that begins in a garden of giants, "fat buggers" who can barely move and who leave behind a legacy of "simmering brown dumplings," thousand-year-old feces out of which spring the "dungy" buffalo in proliferating numbers "so thick on the plains that nothing else like landscape had been able to assert itself in a millennia," the "thousand thousand" bison so densely packed they appear to hug the plains like "God's shag carpet" (41-42). The remyth ends in darkly comic stampede and wasteful death. Carrying the markers of incipient European colonization, their numbers reduced by yellow fever, small pox, and gunpowder, the Indians enact their part of the food chain as they storm the buffalo: "Till come-a-ki-yi-yip, whooping up behind charged Comanches, riding fast but looking a little silly on the tiny Spanish ponies. . . . Like children on scooters, their feet dangled to the ground so that often when a pony faltered the rider himself could keep them going for a stride or two" (42). In the good old days, there had always been a trickle of buffalo who fell into the Palo Duro canyon, where "they were chawed, joint and tendon blasted, flesh exposed and portable. . . . Yet, this was still called the world-at-peace, because not so many buffalo died that there was any accumulation" (43). On the day in question, though, which came to be called "Gluttony or the Big Stinking," the trickle turned into "a shitten waterfall" of bison, all of them falling into the Palo Duro. Despite the Indians' attempts to use what their actions had killed, "deep down in that bulk which spread across the canyon floor, which crested thirty feet up the canyon wall, resentment stewed against the agile red monkeys: they'd rue the day" (44).

A hundred years later, the Indian wars essentially over, the day of reckoning arrives. According to McAfrica, the Palo Duro canyon is teeming with everything Western from mesquite to buffalo to recalcitrant Indians. Though relatively few in number that day, the white troops "have a compensating if unfoundable quality which was absolutely the essential element of their race. It was nothing like the Right that the joining of blood and dirt bequeaths; rather, it was a promiscuous, productive delusion" (47). As it did the Puritans to the American shore in the seventeenth century, a mission has brought these soldiers to this wilderness: "For the idea of ranching, of long horns, chuck wagons, and little dogies getting along had already occurred to white men as a stern vision. Destiny" (46). There in the former site of the Big Stinking, the buffalo have their revenge on the Indians, who are, in short order, separated from their horses, rounded up, and returned to their reservations. As McAfrica tells it, the soldiers, in the rush to complete their duty, leave behind a curious pair, a soldier and a frightened Indian child named Little Kettle. Although Private McGowan finally wins her confidence with black licorice and "a rousing version of 'Turkey in the Straw' sung while clogging madly, his belly bounding about, all punctuated by frequent heart-felt solos on a potato-whistle," he goes too far with his "yarning about Pecos Bill and the like" and Little Kettle lets him know it, "expressing contempt for such lies" (50-51). McGowan, like McAfrica and White, is a storyteller, yet his is the genre fiction that denies Little Kettle's history.

We last see McAfrica in an Amarillo bar he thinks he knows, feeling a little disoriented and talking to "the cleanest white people he had ever seen" (54). At the table later in the evening, one of them, a corporate lawyer named Maureen, calls him "Keemosabe" and puts his hand between her legs, where he feels a "shaggy mat of hair" and "coarse patches of hardened filth" (55). What are we to make of this turn of events that would never have happened to Pecos Bill or Hopalong Cassidy? The buffalo are having their revenge on the white man, too? The storyteller is caught in his own lies? Are we to believe that just as "the great mouth of the world, the Palo Duro gullet, was eager for its share of the chewing" a hundred years before, so it is hungry again? With McAfrica's hand clamped in place, the story ends: "She smiled and then in a fit of ennui yawned, right in his face, opening her mouth so wide you could hear the tendons and bones of her jaw stretch and crack" (55).

This seems as good a metaphor as any to explain the history of the American West as White encapsulates it in "History of the Great Mouth": a series of swallowings that, if retraced via Raymond Williams's down escalator, ends eventually in Kiowa world-at-peace, the West not as howling wilderness or frontier but as pre-European Arcadia or Buffalo Eden. Like McAfrica, White understands these things, for he too is "a Son of the Western Suburbs" (38). He knows that all of us, not just Native Americans, are caught in the grip of the buffalo: "And there are Indian reservations to conceal the fact that we are all Indians" (38). If we read *Home* as a New Western, there seems no escape, no utopic space to which we might repair—that is, unless we think postmodern.

Temporary Autonomous Zones

First, given the controversy surrounding the term *postmodern* (e.g., is there such a thing? is it socially responsible?), we might as well start with what White himself has to say about it in "Writing the Life Postmodern," which he published in the *Review of Contemporary Fiction*'s "Future of Fiction" issue. After a disingenuous claim that he, the author of the article, will be of little help—"Hell, I don't know what postmodernism is" (113)—he proceeds to build a theoretical base for us: "In my judgment, the archetype of the postmodern condition is Theodor Adorno's famous epigraph to *Minima Moralia,* 'life does not live.' Which means that a certain form of life does not live" (113). One of the lost forms that White names is particularly telling: "faith in a mythic—high modernist—return to a time before capital" (114). Particularly telling because it tells us so much about White's project. The "time before capital" is Eden, Arcadia, World-at-Peace.

As he goes on to explain, "postmodern fiction assumes a condition of 'damage' (to borrow again from Adorno) and dutifully expresses that damage: we are text and getting textier" (114). As postmodern fiction, *Home* is highly self-conscious, a text about text. "Ecstasy," the third of the three sections that comprise the book, is composed of three stories—"The Amazing Hypnagogic Man," "Some Disease," and "Still Human"—the third of which is composed of three parts: "Sex and Food a Mouthful at a Time," "The Idea Which Reality Seeks," and "Emptiness Is Empty Too." Also, the middle part of "Still Human" is, like the middle section of *Home,* a Western, and the first and third parts open and close in the same places the first and third sections of the novel do—in San Lorenzo and Paris, respectively.

The preoccupation with writers' snot as text in key parts of "Ecstasy" also suggests a self-conscious pattern. "The Amazing Hypnagogic Man," which opens "Ecstasy," begins with a diarist trying to read the snot he has wiped on the back of his hand: "But what word does the glazed snot spell?" (158). In "Emptiness Is Empty Too," the third part of the third story that closes the third section (you get the idea), a Parisian artist and writer named Blanche (French for White?) walks up to a table of artists, including Edouard Manet and Edgar Degas, and presents a text: "Look, friends, I wiped my nose with the back of my hand a few moments ago and it crystallized in the cold. But wonderfully it seems to have crystallized in the form of a letter, perhaps a word. Take a look, what do you think it says?" (195). The next morning Degas explains Blanche's project: "He's going to write a poem this winter by taking a walk every evening and wiping his nose on the back of his hand. He figures if the weather remains cool for three more months and he uses both hands he can have a poem of one hundred and eighty words by the spring. He says he'll call it 'Still Human.' You know, sometimes he is very funny. An idiot, but a funny idiot" (197). In a self-review published in *Fiction International* White claims, "All of my fiction is a complicated rewriting of my favorite books" (188). If "Still Human," the structural double for *Home,* is a snot poem told by a funny idiot signifying something, are we to think of *Home* as, in some measure, White's *The Sound and the Fury?*

Given this self-consciousness, it would be easy to dismiss postmodern fiction as merely narcissistic (i.e., about nothing but itself), as "text and getting textier." Yet, as White argues, "Postmodern fiction is also a strategic response to that condition" ("Writing" 114). In contrast to those postmodern theorists like Jean Baudrillard, who argue that we have reached the endgame of language, "that there is no option other than an ecstatic capitulation to the flow of signs," White takes what seems an old-fashioned position: "most postmodern fiction writers continue to carry the human capacity for resentment (although they are given no credit for this by those who worry that no one is taking flashlights into the darker cavities of the human heart). Postmodern fiction is, for its most exemplary practitioners, an expression of resentment for the postmodern condition" (114). Old-fashioned because this is the pragmatic approach, a better world through better art. About literature in general, White contends, "Each new work of fiction and poetry is the presentation of a world within which we might choose to live" (118).

Recall the opening line of *Home:* "I would like, in this book, to imagine a place in which humans can live" (9). A couple of lines later he adds, "I will admit that my purpose is utopian if that won't mean that my purpose is laughable. To be sure that it's not, then, let's be sober about our utopia. Let's understand by it the simple notion that there are ideas as yet unrealized which if realized would transcend our present reality" (9). In "Tales of the Hippies" Groovy describes that "reality" as America: "He follows you around like that Lenny character and every time you discover some new way to be he apes it. If we could only stay one change ahead! Maybe then the goon USA would get confused and bored and leave us alone" (129-30).

Space theorist Hakim Bey understands White's sober desire and Groovy's complaint. In *T.A.Z.: The Temporary Autonomous Zone, Ontological Anarchy, Poetic Terrorism* he writes, "Are we who live in the present doomed never to experience autonomy, never to stand for one moment on a bit of land ruled only by freedom? Are we reduced either to nostalgia for the past or nostalgia for the future?" (98). Bey's solution is that we get off the nostalgia escalator. The World-at-Peace, the time before or after capital, is a fiction that keeps us locked "in a kind of nirvana-stupor" (98). Bey suggests a course of action in the here and now, the time-in-capital: "I believe that by extrapolating from past and future stories about 'islands in the net' we may collect evidence to suggest that a certain kind of 'free enclave' is not only possible in our time but also existent" (98-99).

Bey looks to the past for stories about an nineteenth-century pirate network, a series of islands and black-market operations forming " 'intentional communities,' whole societies living consciously outside the law and determined to keep it up" (97) and to the future through cyberpunk sci-fi speculation, like Bruce Sterling's *Islands in the Net,* about "giant worker-owned corporations, independent enclaves devoted to 'data piracy,' Green-Social-Democrat enclaves, anarchist liberated zones, etc." (98). Although, as Bey points out,

"Perhaps certain small TAZs have lasted whole lifetimes because they went unnoticed, like hillbilly enclaves," the present-day pirate utopias he imagines must consistently negotiate an information state that seeks to turn everything into data: "As soon as the TAZ is named (represented, mediated), it must vanish, it *will* vanish, leaving behind it an empty husk, only to spring up again somewhere else, once again invisible because unidentifiable in terms of the Spectacle" (101). It must escape Groovy's "goon USA." According to Bey, "The TAZ is an encampment of guerilla ontologists: strike and run away. Keep moving the entire tribe, even if it's only data in the Web" (102).

White's project is similar. Just as he travels in *Anarcho-Hindu,* his fourth book, to St. Louis to collect stories about an 1877 workers' commune, he looks in *Home* to the World-Not-At-Peace for his utopic spaces. As he writes in *Anarcho,* "It was an old theme for me: what did it mean to live on the site of a wholly submerged history of genocide, oppression, self-defeat, and, not insignificantly, resistance" (90). He goes on: "we live our ordinary lives on the site of fabulous violence, to be sure, but these are also the sites of exciting lost opportunity. . . . I wanted to retrieve both the violence (in the name of justice for the victims) and the opportunities (so that our present poverty might be challenged) of a history both the good and bad of which were submerged beneath the ersatz surface of the present" (90-91).

It is the identification and the nature of these "sites of . . . opportunity" that clarify White's notion of utopia and his project as postmodern. One site that White names in both *Home* and *Anarcho* is, although historically accurate, wholly nonmaterial: a metaphor used by a group of Bay Area sixties' activists, the Diggers, to describe a way of conceptualizing reality so radical that reality changes, what they called "a free frame of reference." In *Home,* or more specifically in "Tales of the Hippies," Dandelion describes a "Digger stew" in which "the little alphabet pastas spelled out Free Frame of Reference" (128). In *Anarcho* it's a stretch of Delmar Avenue in St. Louis, near Washington University, that one character argues could be called "the Liberated Block for Free Frames of Reference," to which another responds, "It would be a block forbidding familiar forms of life. A block for the trans-valuation of values" (99).

Although White occasionally locates one of these Free Frame zones in the material world—in the above instance, in St. Louis—the purest example of the kind of utopic space that recalls Bey's TAZ is the one White describes in the last of the "Four Theses on the Fate of the Sixties." There a younger generation makes the mistake of thinking they can tuck the sixties' generation away in a rest home, the Huey P. Newton Nursing Colony:

> For in their youthful arrogance they failed to factor in the unfactorable: spontaneous, intersubjective insight and rebellion. They didn't take history seriously. They didn't bother to wonder, "How did everyone in France know what to do at the same time in different places in May '68?" . . . Weren't these colonies rather like the old networks of our countercultural past? The Haight to Santa Barbara to the Strip to Taos to Boulder to Madison to the Village? We flowed with perfect freedom, hitching along the unsuspected circuitry, doing our impression of the artist as a young electron. (151)

Simply put, islands in the net. Bey writes, "The TAZ is 'utopian' in the sense that it envisions an *intensification* of everyday life. . . . But it cannot be utopian in the actual meaning of the word, nowhere, or NoPlace Place. *The TAZ is somewhere.* It lies at the intersection of many forces" (111). White describes his version of that "somewhere," his "some kind of wonderful": "This wasn't utopia, it was an even more desirable atopia. We weren't no place, just no particular place. We played. We blew all the circuit breakers" (152).

White does what he argues a postmodern novelist ought to do: he registers his resentment for our present reality in a space, his postmodern *Home,* that offers a blueprint for new behaviors, new ways of conceptualizing space, ways that allow us nostalgia, however sober, for the Edens of our childhood as long as we are willing to rethink genocidal fantasy spaces. White also plays. He blows out all the circuit breakers, hitches from story to story as he invites us to hop from colony to colony, from TAZ to TAZ, which means in the World-Not-At-Peace, which means in history. In that way we might intend new realities, get as close as we can to "that place where the world worlds in availability."

WORKS CITED

Bey, Hakim. *T.A.Z.: The Temporary Autonomous Zone, Ontological Anarchy, Poetic Terrorism.* New York: Autonomedia, 1991.

Limerick, Patricia Nelson. *The Legacy of Conquest: The Unbroken Past of the American West.* New York: Norton, 1987.

Sterling, Bruce. *Islands in the Net.* New York: Arbour, 1988.

White, Curtis. *Anarcho-Hindu: The Damned, Weird Book of Fate.* Normal: Black Ice Books, 1995.

——. " 'Anarcho-Hindu': Self-Review." *Fiction International* 28 (1995) 187-90.

——. *Heretical Songs.* New York: Fiction Collective, 1980.

——. *The Idea of Home.* Los Angeles: Sun & Moon, 1992.

——. *Metaphysics in the Midwest.* Los Angeles: Sun & Moon, 1988.

——. "Writing the Life Postmodern." *Review of Contemporary Fiction* 16.1 (1996): 112-21.

Williams, Raymond. *The Country and the City.* New York: Oxford UP, 1973.

Worster, Donald. "Beyond the Agrarian Myth." *Trails: Toward a New Western History.* Ed. Patricia Nelson Limerick, Clyde A. Milner III, and Charles E. Rankin. Lawrence: UP of Kansas, 1991. 3-25.

Comic Depth: Curtis White's Laughable Idea of Home

Alan Singer

> "And where there is laughing and gaiety, thinking cannot be worth anything:"—so speaks the prejudice of this serious animal against all Joyful Wisdom—Well, then! Let us show that it is a prejudice!
>
> Nietzsche, *Joyful Wisdom*

The Nietzschean muse flatters the artist's ability to descend to the least dignified understanding of his life. For Nietzsche, laughter is the joyful antagonist of the Platonic *Idea* and in that regard the guarantor that philosophical thought will not drown in the depths of its own tendency toward abstraction. In *The Idea of Home*, a novel of buoyantly "joyful wisdom," Curtis White is an agent provocateur of this Nietzschean wisdom. In *The Idea of Home* White takes the *"Idea"* seriously by making a joke of it, which is to say, by denying it depth, by refusing to countenance it as an untouchable abstraction. Implicitly, White has launched an attack on the Platonist prejudice that depth requires the transcendence of surface appearances: appearances are always *to the contrary* in idealizing philosophical discourses. Too often this is the case at the expense of ideals themselves.

But White has chosen his target idea well. The idea of home is the cardinal idea inasmuch as it is the home of the human self/subject. It is then, the *Idea* of ideas. By making a joke of it, White's handling of this *Idea* entails a paradoxical state of blessed homelessness. In the end, I will argue, this makes a more suitable domicile even for the mind that turns compulsively homeward. More to the point however, the rhetoric of homelessness in White's novel is driven forward by the trope of irony. This is strictly *de rigeur* for a narrator who enthusiastically confesses that "irony knows no limits" (142) and whose account of the world is touted to be "blessed by the Dukes of Irony" (153). And true to the truism that homelessness entails irony, White's *The Idea of Home* offers the reader a montage of narrative episodes, each of which succeeds only by *failing* to evoke the static, picture-book "reality" of childhood memories. This is necessarily the case insofar as the theatrics of memory are bound ironically to break out of the time frame of the life from which memory proceeds. The ultimate joke, of course, is that there is more to the task of autobiographical memory than mere lived life can accommodate. And so the meaning of personal life must be pursued upon a treacherous surface, where appearances disguise only the appearance of meaninglessness.

In a good Nietzschean sense, then, irony prevails in White's fiction as the most serviceable mode of memory. In the book's prelude to personal history, "This Is Not an Autobiographical Statement," the narrator of *The Idea of Home* gives voice to the ironic mode in what is virtually the motto of all that follows in this narrative: "Let's understand . . . the simple notion that there are ideas as yet unrealized which if realized would transcend our present reality." The difference between ironic autobiography and the "sincerity" that often masks its authenticity is its connection not to the rehearsable past but to the unexpected future.

Of course, the risk of irony, in its insistence upon skimming the surface of experience, is shallowness, lack of depth, that by now well-heralded postmodern "aura" which desacralizes experience too often at the expense of meaningful experience. It is already a tired adage of postmodernism that depth is a quagmire of metaphysical thinking. The surface is where it's at because it's where we inexorably *are*. But a conspicuous liability of this pragmatism is that where we *are* amounts to nothing that we can count as more or less significant than where we *are not*. The unhappy postmodern alternative to the quagmire of metaphysics, then, is a desert of valuation, a wishy-washy relativism. So it is his unwillingness merely to play out the platitudes of postmodernism that marks Curtis White as a potent creator rather than as that predictable academic thinker for whom irony counts as a smug discount of seriousness and sincerity. It is my contention that White's irony, locus of all his characters' homelessness, touchstone of the superficial, produces precisely the seriousness with which philosophical depth is so metaphorically equated. White effectively belies this equation between seriousness and depth in a way that I believe only literariness allows: by making all the serious substance that irony typically jettisons into something prospective rather than retrospective, something procreative not nostalgic. In other words, instead of simply inverting the hierarchy of depth and surface, a stock-in-trade curlicue of postmodern styles, White obviates the hierarchy. Furthermore, this author does not resort to the only too reflexive postmodern evasions of metaphysical depth that are operative in the techniques of collage and pastiche. White seems to understand that these formal gestures ultimately proffer as empty an existence as the chilliest Platonic idea they are intended to thwart. This is an effect of their comparable trivialization of time. Immediacy is a no more concrete, no less metaphysical acknowledgment of temporality than transcendence because it precludes a reflective moment. On the contrary, White's narrative *incurs time* by defying its limits. That he does this without pretending to write without limits, so much the unwarrantable wont of collage and pastiche art, is all the more to White's credit as an artist whose engagement with the word is emphatically an engagement with the world.

The comedy of White's complex reckoning with time is most vital in the way each memory of his novel proliferates the implications of what can be recalled rather than resolving them into nuggets of original meaning—the deep idea. As we have already noted, the deep idea obviates the "surface" of experience through which it is conventionally plumbed. Comedy is often trivialized for its "of the moment" preoccupation with the surface of life, entertaining the unexpected for the sake of meretricious reversals, silly surprises. In White's fiction the comic is the unexpected that nevertheless must be respected in its imposition of new contexts. So this novel avails itself of a kind of "comic depth" precisely by elaborating the surface appearance of events into new contextual complexes. They in turn incur the responsibility of living in time as a temporal event, not as a recourse to proliferating ironic eventualities.

The elaboration of new contextual complexes in *The Idea of Home* is anchored in the precarious identity of its autobiographical narrator. Indeed, the mind of an eminently imaginable boyhood Curt (or Curtis as he is sometimes known to himself) is the ultimate homing device of this fiction of lost origins fixated, as boyhood identity is bound to be, on insatiable desires: sex, athletic preeminence, fatherhood, history's memorial.The paradox of the insatiable desire is, of course, that it cannot know itself as such. Wittingly or not, it therefore holds the door of knowledge expectantly open. Wittily enough, the setting for this boy's story is the cookie-cutter real estate development of San Lorenzo, California. San Lorenzo is a place which no boomer-generation reader will have any difficulty charting on his memory map of the fifties—not, however, without experiencing the self-effacing recognition that it is our identification with the familiar that is most dehumanizing.

Likewise, while White's inventory of would-be reminiscences proliferates multiple narrators, they are all of one mind. Each is possessed of the same sense of loss that was bequeathed to America's children in the material rewards of the post-WW II American economy. Therefore, though chapters may be narrated by seemingly different people in *The Idea of Home,* their experience is the same in its yearning to be something more than what could simply be remembered. This reprise of the paradox of the one and the many—it is, after all, the paradox of American consumerism where many (existent beings) are reducible to one (cash currency), precisely in the mode of the Platonic concept—is White's vehicle for a cultural memory that is always conspicuously and unpredictably *in process*. As is conspicuously the case in consumer economies, it is the process that matters even though process is almost always sought in the form of products that arrest our development. Productivity stymies the process. The housing development of San Lorenzo is itself the paradigm of such development: each plot of land relentlessly plotted in advance, the lives of its inhabitants habituated in advance of their habitation.

Here, after all, is the taut Nietzschean thread that runs through White's fiction—tethered as this narrative is to the epigraph: "It is even part of my good fortune not to be a house-owner." Ownership is the enemy of process. Nietzsche furthermore remarks in *The Genealogy of Morals* that the "cause of the origin of a thing and . . . its utility, . . . in a system of purposes . . . lie worlds apart" (77). In this regard space is effectively time. Likewise, the force of memory in *The Idea of Home* is staked in the world that remembering *becomes* rather than in how becoming the memories of home might prove to be in the rosy light of our most nostalgic selves. Curtis White seems intent upon following up the thought that if there is no depth to the *Idea* there is nonetheless a trajectory of thinking it which—unlike the *Idea* itself—might do justice to the time line it follows simply by sustaining our thoughts about it.

That in White's world the overblown Platonic *Idea* is ever needful of a joke to bring it back to earth is most starkly apparent in his boy-narrator's consternation that the street names of the San Lorenzo development are written in the code of another language, a romance language at that. The prospect of translation tantalizes with the possibility of a secret world, a hidden, wondrous depth of meaning. Via Escondido, "street of secrets," is the prototype of this conundrum echoing in Via Dolorosa, Via Descanso, Via Borso. Translated, however, these exotic names for the coordinates of an all too ordinary middle-class American adolescence are "street of sorrowing," "street of sleep," and finally "street of the purse" (122). The narrator's disappointment at reaching such mundane depths of interpretability, such an inescapable superficiality of meaning, are confessed in the narrator's glum synthesis of what he delved for in Spanish. His all too literal translation is, "Yes, sad, sleeping shoppers said it all" (121). This expostulation is a counter for the comedy of translation since it yields a literalism that vacates the narrator's habitation of the words that name his world, making a vacuum of his world.

This is to say that the secret other side of the world orbed in the mystery of coded language is obliterated in the narrator's realization that his world is really flat, untranscendable. This knowledge demands an understanding of how to live on such flat terrain, bred up as we are to dig to its depths. In White's fiction the discipline of negotiating the surface of things is a bit like riding metaphors without their tenors. The saving grace is that metaphors without tenors are nevertheless vehicles which, because they operate on the principle of contiguity, are the guarantors of a contextual polymorphism that privileges change and surprise over punctual intelligibility. As the narrator divines: "The street signs designated fluctuating zones that were coextensive with reality itself. So it wasn't just the grim jokes on our walking middle-class death; there were also signs which appealed straight away to the possibility of our changing things, reclaiming life" (123).

The grim joke of this middle-class death is nowhere more jocularly menacing to "the possibility of changing things" than in the recognition that all of the houses of San Lorenzo are in reality the same house, despite nominal variations in the floor plans that make telling them apart empirically possible. Indeed, the sameness of the houses is the novel's most parodic touchstone of the Platonist ideal. In orthodox Platonism the reality of things is understood to reside elsewhere than where the body locates itself. This reality entails a stasis of ideation which brooks no material differences. The mapping of this "elsewhere" is very much the burden of Curtis White's fiction and nowhere more explicitly than in this author's acknowledgment that possibility and change are more compelling than the abstract knowledge which they invariably call into question.

In *The Idea of Home* the grim joke of middle class death-in-life is therefore triggered by a quintessential case of mistaken identity. Narrator Curt, having apprehended an Electrolux vacuum cleaner tossed on a trash pile to be a human corpse, feels compelled to carry this knowledge home to his parents. In this case mortality is mortified. Full of the shock of his imagined encounter with the mortal flesh, the child reporting this incident to his parents, unceremoniously walks in on their own mortal coupling, only to experience the desperate wish to wish it away before it can be taken in. Luckily the child has the excuse that the different houses of the neighborhood, alternating floor plans with the "rhyme scheme ABA," make it conceivable that one could easily have entered the wrong house: "So you run in and—whoa—it was the Alice effect, through the looking glass" (19).

Comically enough, the Platonist philosopher's indictment of "false appearances" is Curt's ready-to-mind refuge from his confrontation with the unimaginable possibility of his parents' sexuality. But to no avail, since in this case appearances are only too true. This is the right house! Or it is the wrong house only in the sense that this is the wrong moment to enter it: "I told you he wasn't going to play long," the mother, legs in the air, must remind the pantless father, as if to affirm a truth that resides in abstract principle.

But the father's terse instruction to the son, "Out, Buster!" obliterates any doubt that it is the body that gives place to the world and not the other way round. The terrible irony is that here the place of the body is subject to the most quixotic variables, not the least solacing of which is Curt's ultimate revelation that the "body" he saw with his own delusional eyes on the trash pile was indeed an Electrolux vacuum cleaner, testimonial as all vacuums are, to the imminence of the body's displacement. This knowledge of the fragility of the flesh was of course the original motive of Platonism's wish to make a virtue of necessity, to make the body disappear before inevitable complications ensued from its involvement in contingency. The *White* magic, so to speak, that animates *The Idea of Home* is a reckoning with this world where the possibility of changing things—the Platonist's dream of truth—is rendered inextricable from the changeability of the world—arch antagonist of the philosopher's dream. The changeability of the world is the necessary complement to "the possibility of changing things" by which White's narrator would reprieve himself from "a walking middle class death."

It follows then that the comic bravura of White's fiction will depend on the author's gift for making comedy's stock encounters with the unexpected unfold as a map of the changeability of the world. In this way the author takes seriously the proposition that the burden of change is the relevant essence of human life, and not an accident of historical or political fate. This is a fitting homily in a book filled with "historical episodes" that are tragi-comic testimonials to the ruthlessness of civilized abstraction: the rape of the American wilderness, the slaughter of buffalo, the decimation of native peoples. All were perpetrated in the service of the white man's so Sisiphysian burden: progress of the idea of home, progress of the *Idea*.

Progress is of course the *metier* of the developer. In White's *The Idea of Home* the ironies of development, the brutalities that the idea must wreck on the forms of life it would render intelligible, are most strikingly embodied in the character of David Bohannon, master-planner of the San Lorenzo development. The two chapters which invoke Bohannon's career, "The Birth of Tragedy" and "Still Human," wittily evoke two Nietzschean texts that significantly frame that philosopher's intellectual career, like the thing that *The Idea of Home* both epitomizes and refuses to be: an autobiography bounded by knowledge of beginnings and endings that are conceivably mirror images of the eminently recognizable self they hold in their Janus-faced embrace. *The Birth of Tragedy* (1872) is Nietzsche's first book and *Human All Too Human* (1878) is arguably his last book. Or rather, it is his last book *as Nietzsche*: *Human All Too Human* breaks intellectually with the mentorship of Wagner, and in doing so it breaks with much that Nietzsche had thought himself to be in the *Birth*. In this respect, the later work constitutes a rebirth of sorts, an open-endedness that might elude the rampage of the *Idea of the author.* Curtis White's depiction of David Bohannon as a quintessential homeless man famous for building homes that will not suffice to house the human desire for identity, is a witty gloss on the Nietzschean refusal to think through the reifying spell of ideas, especially the idea of whom the author himself might be.

Nietzsche's own gloss on the title *Human All Too Human* might serve as a useful reference point for the reader's understanding of Bohannon's predicament, especially since anyone who understands it is already deeply implicated in the trouble it portends: "where you see ideal things, I see what is human, alas all-too-human!—I know man better" (*Ecce Homo* vi, i). Even more than white magic, the conceptual magicianship of White's fiction improvises a rational remedy for that ideal seeing of things which otherwise arrests the seer in the idea-mongering egotism of the idealizing gaze. Like Nietzsche, White knows man better than the reader who would imagine that there could indeed be an idea of home that would suffice to house human desire. He even knows more than the reader who, seeing the dire predicament of the idealist, abandons the resources of the mind altogether. Bohannon is the vehicle and the exemplar of the knowledge that something subtler must be conjured that will therefore fit within the frame of human frailty rather than attempting to frame that frailty with the delusional architecture of wood and stucco.

Bohannon is touted in his capacity as developer to be the man with a "cure . . . for homelessness" (101). The irony that he forgets to build a cottage for himself in the community of San Lorenzo, thus inspiring his envy of the other lives he has safely domiciled, produces in turn the fantasy of his amours with Wanda. Wanda is a wife he has housed so convincingly in the habits of bourgeois domesticity that he can vividly imagine her need to escape it. No accident that the corollary fantasia of his desire is the real cinematic prototype of this clichéd psychology: the film of *The Postman Always Rings Twice.* No accident that this film occupies the time and attention of Wanda's husband Roy, as if it were expressly contrived by some transcending power of fate to create an opportunity for Bohannon's imagined seduction of the wife.

As I anticipated earlier, the comic effect here becomes seriously philosophical by mitigating the distinction between dream and reality, at least insofar as they are familiar counters for depth and surface respectively. So in White's fiction, philosophical depth denotes not insight but sightedness, a more complex worldliness. This is to say it transcends metaphor. The idea comes up to the surface for air. In other words, the comedy here does not release us from the need to inhabit a palpable human situation—however homeward bound the author knows us to be and however much he might disapprove of the weakness of will it confesses. The fact that Bohannon's realization of his dream—to build San Lorenzo—necessitates a fantasy life (the world of Wanda) and one that transgresses the moral decorum of domesticity, propels the reader of *The Idea of Home* onto that Möbius strip reality where fear of self-contradiction can be answered only by the denial of any metaphysical depth which would require sorting out dream from reality. Rather, what is thought about the world and what is actually "there" in the world to think about, reference one another by their contiguity in the mind that compasses the contradiction. Or as our narrator explains it: ". . . Bohannon had fantasized his union with Wanda so often and so fervently, had imagined his cock represented for her fond attention as real as the laminated mahogany leg of her dining room table, that fantasy's far side had become the quotidian's near side . . ." (105-6). Here the denial of metaphysical depth is understood as a necessity to adapt to circumstances as a continuum of experience upon which one is fated to *continue.* This is alternative to the notion that experience can only be made intelligible by reference to some register of meaning whose truthfulness would be a function of its distance from the moment that solicits it.

It is no accident that in the unfolding of this episode the narrator's "rapport" with the reader is ominously inflected with a litany of contemptuous epithets, all directed at the conventional reader's desire for an uncontradictory refuge of truthfulness that must be sought beyond the moment of one's experience. The string of insulting epithets—vicious . . . hollow . . . clinging reader—are explicitly an admonition for the reader to stand on her own feet so to speak, to stand on the flat ground of the here and now, to resist the illusion of that dubiously "rounded" world in which depth of vision appears to be the real secret of life. Thus the final chapter, where Dave and Wanda are reintroduced to us as a domestic couple whose domesticity is indeterminably fact or fantasy, serves as the occasion for a dose of philosophizing that might bolster the reader's confidence. More propitiously than we might have expected, this speculation offers the reader a way out of the contradictions that obtain where reality and fantasy are contiguous surfaces, where "fantasy's far side become[s] the quotidian's near side." Dave portentously speculates that: "time is dependent upon perception, . . . has to do with perspective, both of which imply consciousness. What is time in a cosmos without consciousness? he wondered. So the difference between the twinkle that was the first ten billion years and the present (so often tedious!) suburban moment, post-WW II sunny California, was that now there were a lot of people around paying attention . . . by extension . . . if time seemed to be getting out of control, hurrying away, then it could be slowed down by thinking hard about it" (183-84).

This brainstorm is only surpassed in Dave's mind by the theory that "our bodies present themselves for the same reason that stars are present for our amazed study. We resist entropy and collapse, the nihilist attraction of gravity, because we are capable of metabolizing vegetable and flesh, thus burning/expanding hotly enough to resist becoming that ultimate failure of Being . . . a BLACK HOLE. Our body then is a post-primordial abyss into which we slough ourselves one cell at a time. Thus, to say body is to say grave. A skin cell is sloughed and plummets into the nothing at the heart of us" (184). Were the reader to be persuaded here, she would understand that it is precisely that experience of time—eternal nemesis of the eternity-smitten idea qua *Idea*—that might save the thinker from her thoughts. After all, thinking harder about one's thoughts takes the time that slowness denotes.

White supplies a perfect coda for this knowledge in the penultimate sub-section of the novel's ultimate chapter: "The Idea Which Reality Seeks." The burden of this passage seems to be, above all else, to make it possible for the reader to ask the question "What if reality seeks the wrong idea?" (194). If she has paid attention, the no longer "clinging reader" can now answer—in a way which was plausibly unimaginable prior to reading this book—that the reality of the human thinker who can think beyond "development" would *never seek the wrong idea,* because the criteria by which its wrongness might be judged is still being thought out.

Such is the wisdom imparted by the last character to appear in the pages of White's novel: Blanche the gross-bodied "fool" of the soiree of Parisian artists and writers who are assembled in the Café Guerbois. Devoid of ideas that fly free of the body, Blanche greets his would-be friends: "look . . . I wiped my nose with the back of my hand a few moments ago and it crystallized in the cold. But wonderfully it seems to have crystallized in the form of a letter, perhaps a word . . ." (195). Here is the body misrepresented as a sign for the mind. And Blanche's humiliated subservience to the reputedly better minds of his betters renders him the perfect vehicle for transcending intellectual prejudices that prompt our aspiration to raise the mind above the body. Blanche's intuitive confusion of mind and body invites him to see himself through the eyes of his betters as the "perfect dope." But the standard of perfection here becomes a crowning irony. Throwing himself onto the filthy floor of his studio, capitulating to the soiree's abusive idea of himself, he is now capable of a sublime insight: "Wait a minute! He may have been stupid, of course he was stupid, an utter baba, he understood that now perfectly. But was there no value in the perfection of that understanding? He felt he had so much insight now into his essential brainlessness that he was really quite smart about that" (201-2).

Indeed Blanche's "stupidity" turns out to be his easy continuity with experience. It makes a startling contrast with the experiential stupidity of the conceptual homebody so widely ridiculed elsewhere in this work. It is after all Blanche's consciousness of his body splayed upon the floor, the organs "piled . . . like cheap goods in a grocery sack" that causes him to "lift his head" (201) without launching it beyond the gravitational pull of terra firma. The contents of his head at that moment, as Blanche stares up at the haystack painted upon his easel, as he focuses upon his own aping of the ideals of *pleine aire* style—"Monet had been talking to him about painting ordinary things like haystacks . . . (202)"—are miraculously indistinguishable from what suddenly fills the *plain air* outside his window: "He noticed the most marvelous thing: the air was full of hay which was falling like snow, gently quilting Paris" (202).

At this moment Curtis White's "vicious," "hollow," "clinging" reader might earn the author's respect by noticing how the title of this last chapter—"Still Human"—is precisely the one so "stupidly" intended by Blanche for the poem he would compose in calligraphic snot on the back of his hand. In this homage White reaffirms a notion of humanity that does not brook mind-body distinctions. One consequence might be that the ideas that come from our heads would now fit more comfortably into the grip of the hand that would implement them. This is no doubt every painter's dream, clutching the brush to his eye. It may suit our own eyes if we can be made to see that reality is laid out before us as a palpable road to trod upon instead of as a penetrable surface through which we must hope to lose ourselves in mysterious depths. Then we might more or less knowingly laugh along with Degas when he alleges that the "funniest thing" about Blanche's poem-in-snot is that it will be dedicated to Manet. In these last pages of White's novel, Manet, a painter of surfaces *par excellence*, tells Degas that because the latter can't paint without harkening to the Old Masters, he cannot see what is happening right before his eyes. We might allow that Curtis White reckons justly with his own reader's eyes by making her laugh at the temptation to see more than what can be beheld.

WORKS CITED

Nietzsche, Friedrich. *Joyful Wisdom*. Trans. Thomas Common. New York:Ungar, 1975.

——. *On the Genealogy of Morals / Ecce Homo*. Trans. Walter Kaufmann. New York: Vintage, 1967.

White, Curtis. *The Idea of Home*. Los Angeles: Sun and Moon, 1992.

Location Is Everything: Community and Individuality in the Novels of Curtis White

David Winn

Shortly before his death, Bruce Chatwin wrote in his last book, *The Song Lines*, of his belief that the wandering aboriginal people of Australia had thoroughly mapped and explored their continent centuries before the arrival of the Europeans. It was Chatwin's contention that the original culture's method of charting and locating the landscape they moved through came out of their lyrical and narrative oral traditions. They literally sang and spoke their way into community and a sense of place as they traveled from one place to another. Simultaneously they oriented themselves to the natural world that surrounded and defined them as they redefined it with language and memory, and they carried that orientation with them as atlas and almanac.

I think of Chatwin now whenever I read Curtis White, and I think particularly of Chatwin's argument for nomadic culture as the way of life that best suits human beings. Because it is White's fiction, more than any other American novelist's, that attempts to reconcile the compelling need for community in the life of our culture with the equally strong requirement of individual sovereignty, the expression of personal will, and the profound rootlessness that results from the tension between the two. In White's fiction the terrifying loosing of the moorings of community is always a given. There is only the idea of home and we must carry it with us.

Certainly the novel's rise over the past three hundred years in the West seems inextricably tied to conventional and traditional notions of place whether we speak of Woolf's London, Joyce's Dublin, Kafka's Prague, or even Pynchon's New York. There is an immutable evocation of the essential nature of these places, even when Pynchon's New York with its albino sewer alligators tips into Alexandria of the British raj, London of the Blitz, or post-Vietnam Los Angeles. We can still read the street signs, recognize the buildings, follow the map. Prague is no different when Kafka presents it as a nameless ministry: for anyone familiar with his work, that ministry is now the local DMV or the registrar's office at the beginning of each semester. But it is still to Prague between the wars where each of those manifestations sends it roots.

It is White who seems to have slipped the bonds of geography altogether. His characters wander in time as much as they do space. In "Tales of the Hippies," a chapter from *The Idea of Home*, the mistranslated Spanish street signs of a postwar housing development traduce the culture and reinterpret the lives of the adolescents growing up in those same streets. Digression becomes a synonym for wandering and as characters tell their stories they, like *vandervogel,* move into new territory.

White knows this process of transformation by misinformation is nothing new in the American experience. His references, for example, to the Quanah Parker odyssey and the motif of the Comanche culture Parker represents recur constantly in his later work.

In his cultural study, *Comanches*, the Texas historian, T. E. Ferenbach describes how the Spanish corrupted the Ute word, *Komatcha* (those who are against us) for the Utes' traditional enemies, whose word for themselves was *Nermernuh.* To the Spanish traders and frontiersmen at Santa Fe, *Komatcha* became *Comanche,* and these Uto-Aztecan people absorbed the insult-as-identity as surely and as quickly as they adapted to the horse. They transformed themselves from small bands of foot-borne hunter-gatherers into a fierce cavalry-army who saw themselves as stewards of the Great Southern Herd of plains buffalo, and they effectively shut the Southwest to European incursion for nearly three hundred years. White, I would suspect, would be the first to argue that these new people required a new name—that they couldn't assume their new role without one. (Certainly Hollywood would have agreed: *Nermernuh Territory*? *Gunfight at Nermernuh Wells*? Somehow, I don't think so.)

Parker as a figure of legend as well as historical fact is particularly important to White. Parker's mother, a white Welsh captive took quickly and successfully to Comanche life as a girl, as did her brother James. Her son Quanah led the subtribe of "Nyakah" or "Noconi" Comanches from the canyonlands of the Palo Duro out onto Llano Estacado and the Texas Panhandle to raid and hunt for decades before Colonel Ranald McKenzie, commanding black cavalrymen, destroyed the Noconi horse herd. Their name freely translated can mean *Wanderers,* but as Alan Lemay points out in *The Searchers,* his novel of frontier Texas, a more accurate translation would be: "Man says he's goin' one way, means he's goin t'other."

If there is a locus or defining point in White's work, it is the post-World War II suburb to which he returns again and again. And truthfully, these places are now more post-Vietnam in their interchangeability, their topography of convenience store, interstate off-ramp, strip mall, and failed franchise. Whether the franchise is personal, commercial, or civic is irrelevant. The important element for White is in its value as a symbol for abandonment and moving on. For White, American character and American landscape are pretty much interchangeable, and it is the powerful presence of impermanence in these places—homestead, hunting ground, or battlefield—that sets his narrative in motion.

The continuity of experience is forever being violated and disrupted in White's novels. Once again, in *The Idea of Home* a suburban adolescent is allowed a pet by his family, and he chooses not a dog or a cat, but a Madame Nhu. The historical figure—Ngo Dinh Diem's sister-in-law and Ngo Dinh Nhu's wife—is reduced to a household pet, but she is far from domestic. She rampages through the neighborhood as soon as she has the opportunity, biting, clawing, killing, fucking, burning, and destroying until she is finally brought to heel. The boy is chastised by his parents and the neighbors, but ultimately forgiven: the damage she has done can be repaired and forgotten, the people that she hurt were somehow distant, unimportant, and not very well liked.

While this may seem an obvious metaphor ("Oh, yes, America in the early stages of its involvement in Vietnam, ho-hum"), it is not. White is describing, as few Americans have, Vietnam's involvement with us and the way in which our cultural short-term memory absorbs and diffuses the most extreme and consequential kinds of experience.

How starkly this chapter stands in contrast to Robert Olen Butler's brilliant but historically specific short story, "A Good Scent from a Strange Mountain." It is almost as if Butler insists upon the reader standing outside the reference points of American experience—such as it is—and reading the story as though she or he were Vietnamese. What always astonishes me when I try teaching this story is that even my Vietnamese students, most of them less than one generation removed from the war, must have everything explained to them: What was Versailles? Why was Ho Chi Minh there? Who were the Hoa Hao? What was the Tet Offensive? Discussion becomes history lesson. They have American memories now.

But White is not saying that history does not persist in the American ethos. It might be bunk or it might be written by the winners, yet it still has the power to reconfigure our vision. In *Anarcho-Hindu* the narrator informs his goddess high school-sweetheart wife, "nobody dies, but everybody is assassinated!" Since they are mourning their son, who has just died from possible over-identification with deceased characters in another part of the narrative, this pronouncement does not seem inappropriate.

To revive him, the narrator reconstructs (and reinvents) the tale of the St. Louis Commune, which is really a conflation of the Revolution of 1848, the Paris Commune of 1877, the actual railway strikes in St. Louis that same year, and the wishful imagination of the narrator. The event itself is a kind of doppelganger and it produces a frantic spin of doubling events and personalities that becomes a satiric paradigm for capitalism:

> What the country needed was a monarch and and ex-President Grant was the man for the job! Did [B&O Railroad President] Garrett know that when the St. Louis Workingmen's Party gathered in Lucas Market to have a mass rally, the very place and moment Garrett would have them gunned down, they stood on the spot where in 1857 a down-at-the-heels Ulysses S. Grant sold wood from from his father-in-law's farm? In short, did Mr. Garrett understand that thirty years earlier Grant would have been in the crowd to be mowed down? What sort of poetry is this? What is the key to history's jangling rhyme scheme?

Certainly it is an irony, a poetry, a rhyme that General Grant, the Great Slaughterer of Vicksburg, The Wilderness, and Second Manassas would have appreciated. A marketing epiphany for warfare depends no less for its success on timing and location than one for hamburgers or hardware, and White's use of "moment" as well as "place" is no accident here.

"All this has happened before and will happen again," Arjuna is assured as he faces the prospect of slaughtering his own kinsman in the *Mahabharata*. White's invocation of the hero caught up in the cycle of his own destiny is a deliberate reflection of the American belief of unlimited and cornucopic possibility. True, Wal-Mart and McDonald's are hardly the Plains of Kurukshetra, but perhaps there's not such a great difference after all.

The admonition of Bhisma, Arjuna's companion, quoted above, has the ring of "business as usual" about it, as well as an appreciation of assembly line production and the nature of interchangeable parts for a single product, that Henry Ford or Eli Whitney would have understood. White, of course, extends this American tinker-genius to the social and political level: "History's advance is always ultimately dependent on whether or not soldiers will shoot the most urgent representatives of their own class and thus murder their own interests." Of course, in *Anarcho-Hindu,* the revolution-besieged businessmen of St. Louis recognize in this historical truism an unparalleled economic opportunity. So they offer guns to their loyal workers at a reasonable price to be repurchased at a fair discount once the revolt is suppressed. "Thus the shrewd businessmen of St. Louis would become wealthy from the sale of guns to workers with which workers could murder their own dreams." Downsizing by any other name. . . . Now the cycle is not so much Vedic or Viconian as it is economic. Property and capital become "The once upon a time" and "they lived happily ever after" of the American *hallucination publicitaire,* and who's to gainsay that. Big Bill Haywood? Emma Goldstein? John L. Lewis? Walter Reuther? Dolores Huerta? Social visions of economic justice and transcendent political equality are all very well, but the efforts of America's most strenuous idealists lapse into self-interest and commercialism, just as the public taste for designer coffee or microbrewed beer grows jaded and moves on to other things. Bhisma's admonition is writ large on teeshirts (another marketing epiphany): "BEEN THERE, DONE THAT/SAME SHIT, DIFFERENT DAY.

It is into the routine of this workaday universe that White introduces the feminine oracular spirit and its manifestation in character. In *Anarcho-Hindu* the character is the woman-goddess Siva, who may also be the narrator's wife May, who may also be the goddess-destroyer Kali, not to mention a host of other renegade possibilities who take the form of porn stars, Queer Nation lesbians, long suffering women characters from various literary works, and the probative voice of the narrator's mother.

Toward the end of *Anarcho-Hindu,* the narrator visits St. Louis in an attempt to establish contact with the historical setting of the uprising and thereby gain some greater understanding of its unfolding. Instead he encounters various social grievances embodied in characters who wander across the mall-like backdrop that Lucas Market has become; the old territory has been remapped. May has accompanied him and is impatient with his reluctance to wind up the tale. When she finally tells him to "Hush," he reenvisions her as Siva, speaking to him from a cloudy height.

These are characters who embody the yearning for justice, civil equity, and the sanctity of the individual that the Western mind refuses to relinquish. At the same time their social idealism seems to rest upon the dark aggressive impulse within sexuality "to body forth" the revolutionary changes that same social idealism calls upon. The power of these characters to enchant and ravish, White seems to be saying, is the same power that offers the possibility of escape from "the nightmare of history." The culture of the hearth is portable and its nature is narrative. Character, identity, story, and community are all one and the same, free of sect, clan, territory, boundary, or border.

"Blessed by Madness": Memories of My Father Watching TV

Charles B. Harris

"My mind's not right."
—Robert Lowell, "Skunk Hour"

"I started writing because I had bad brains."
—Curtis White, Interview with Mark Amerika

During an honors seminar in twentieth-century fiction at the University of San Francisco, Chris White, protagonist of Curtis White's newest novel, *Memories of My Father Watching TV,* bewilders his fellow students by insisting that "Franz Kafka deserved no acclaim, was not to be admired, because the lone meaning his fiction had to offer was the effect of his own mental illness. What greatness is there, I demanded to know, in disease? What credit can one claim?" (69). In an interview with Mark Amerika published in this issue of *RCF*, White admits to a similar skepticism about his own talent: "Here's the little I'm capable of: I can write of the slightly hallucinogenic world that has risen out of my mental illness. I suffer from chronic if episodic depression. It is this which has provided me a lens. Do I deserve some sort of artistic credit for this illness?"

For at least three reasons, I believe that most readers of *Memories* will answer White's self-deprecating question with a resounding "Yes." White—who describes postmodern fiction's chief tendency as an "inclination . . . for the hybrid, for the a-generic" (*Monstrous* 10)—has created in *Memories* that most unlikely of hybrid, the *postmodernist confessional,* thereby extending and preserving the "monstrous possibilities" of contemporary fiction. Second, White's inspired image of a father whose TV-induced catalepsy renders him oblivious to the frantic attention-getting efforts of his children resonates powerfully as a metaphor for our radically dissociated, simulacra-saturated, late technocapitalist age. Finally, although the "plot" of White's novel offers little hope that Chris will ever completely rout his demons, the novel's hallucinogenic quality, its literary monstrousness, functions as a strategic response to the postmodern condition, confronting postmodern problems, as White says, all "exemplary fiction writers of the present moment" must do, "on postmodern grounds" (*Monstrous* 61). That is, White (both Curtis and Chris, who is the "author" as well as the protagonist of *Memories*) recombines the antic effluxions of his own faulty brain chemistry until they mutate into new potentialities, not only for literature but for life. "As a suburbanite fated for a job repairing power lines for Pacific Gas and Electric and a four pre-fab wall prison," White told Amerika, "I can only thank my lucky stars that I was blessed by madness."

Formally, *Memories* is a novel in the same sense that Barth's *Lost in the Funhouse* is a novel. Most of its eight chapters, each bearing the title of a television series a youthful White watched with his father in their San Lorenzo, California, home between 1957 and 1963, were first published as self-contained short stories in literary journals or fiction anthologies. Arranged as they are here, the stories-*cum*-chapters unfold rhizomatously, their original autonomy sustained yet simultaneously transgressed by an intricate network of recurring images and cultural references as well as by a faintly discernible narrative progression (one hesitates to call it a "plot") from conflict toward a horizon of resolution in the novel's final two chapters. To indicate this progression and to preserve the motif of mental illness, White divides the novel into two sections of four chapters each, the first entitled "Gloom," the second "Glee." But if the chapters in "Glee" are less grim than those in the first half of the book, glee, we should remember, is depression's manic other, no less a symptom of madness than gloom is. Like Ellison's Invisible Man, White sells us no phony forgiveness; *Memories* navigates toward no conventional happy ending. Mental illness in the novel is not subdued so much as it and the hyperreal landscape White's clinically depressed protagonist inhabits and writes about are employed against themselves in a process White calls "liberatory 'free play' " (*Monstrous* 110), a mode of writing that attempts to reclaim human value from *this* side of humanism, which is to say, from within the postmodern moment.

At the level of confession, *Memories* represents Chris White's attempt to come to terms with the psychological damage inflicted on him by his alcoholic, emotionally distant, and similarly depressed father. "The defining childhood memory of my father," Chris writes in the novel's prologue, "is of a man (but not just a man, of course; it is *my father*—young, handsome, capable!) reclined on a dingy couch watching TV. Watching TV and ignoring the chaos around him, a chaos consisting almost entirely of me and my sisters fighting" (3). The novel's typical narrative strategy is to recount in each chapter an episode from one of the series White watched with his father and, employing the Freudian practice of transference (31), to appropriate one or more of the episode's characters—or, in some instances, part of its set ("my father was a German pontoon bridge built over a narrow French river" [68])—as his surrogate father.

Significantly, Chris's father substitutes tend to be conventional "he-men," cowboys or cops or other varieties of adventurer, who carry guns they are more than willing to use. Indeed, what primarily attracts Chris's father to the TV shows is the sound of gunfire, which he "worshipped . . . obsessively," prompting Chris to present him with a recording of the battle scenes from *Combat* as a birthday gift, "six hours of bliss" which Chris imagines his father enjoying as if it were a porn tape (74-75). The association of violence and pornography suggests that one dimension of Chris's psychological damage is sexual dysfunction. Descriptions of sex in the novel are often accompanied by images of violence, self-hatred, and Célinesque disgust with the human body (note, for example, the Nazi soldier's repellent description of anal rape in "Combat"). As boys, both Chris and "Broderick Crawford" masturbate compulsively; and in a particularly disturbing scene, Chris's sister engages in brutal self-abuse with a familiar childhood toy, Mr. Potato Head, not for pleasure but out of "pure childhood desperation" (117). Crawford, we learn, is a urinist; "Lloyd Bridges" likes to sprinkle his body with baby powder, don the rubberized wet suit he wears on *Sea Hunt,* and prance onanastically in front of a mirror; Tuck, a character in "Bonanza," exhibits a peculiar fondness for horses and purveys his daughter to a local rancher as a sex slave. Impotence, too, is a problem. At the peak of lovemaking with his new mistress, Chris envisions the appearance of "Have Gun—Will Travel" father-surrogate Paladin, who, black-clad and revolver-toting, discharges an erection-dousing bullet into Chris's shoulder. While usually rendered with White's characteristic humor (and for all its darkness, *Memories* is a gleeful book), scenes such as these are clearly sublimations of Chris's psychosexual wound, that hole in his psyche symptomatic of an absence from Chris's life of an effective model of masculine emotional receptivity.

Chris's televisual fathers do little to close this gap. Not only prone to violence, they are as remote as his real father is, displaying the habitual emotional taciturnity made famous by Hollywood tough guys. *Combat*'s Sarge, for example, "never smiled, never expressed any emotion except his determination to see his suffering through" (73). Like conventional celluloid cowboys, all of Chris's surrogate fathers are unmarried and, with the exception of *Bonanza*'s thrice-widowed Ben Cartwright, childless. We are not surprised to learn, therefore, that Chris is himself divorced (101), and that promiscuity, a manifestation of Chris's inability to develop enduring emotional attachments, is listed, along with alcoholism and suicide attempts, as a prime symptom of his pathology (45). Much of the novel's pathos derives from Chris's struggles to fortify his "fragile sense of manly self-worth" (27) by transferring his need for a receptive father to TV characters whose representations of masculinity are in large part responsible for the very constructions of male subjectivity that are the source of Chris's oppression. For example, Lieutenant Douglas is, like Sarge, "strong and silent. . . . His immobile face seems to take some dark delight in refusing [his men] even the most basic human acknowledgment" (70). When it is disclosed that the motive for Douglas's "apparent indifference to his men" is a desire to protect their lives, Chris desperately concludes that "when authority is most brutal and indifferent, it is then that it loves and cares for us most" (75-76). Yearning for paternal love, Chris contorts the images of his despair into a pitiable solace.

Despite the considerable poignancy of such scenes, Chris's plight is not unfamiliar. Indeed, if *Memories* remained solely at what I have been calling its confessional level, it would not be wholly indistinguishable from that art of "incredibly banal didacticism" Julie Caniglia castigates in her essay "57 Cultures and Nothing On," from which White quotes approvingly in *Monstrous Possibility:* "work that 'explores' this personal issue or 'documents' that social problem, that 'provokes' the viewer regarding the artist's identity, or 'confronts' the artist's traumas (*usually of childhood origins*)" (91, italics added). But of course White doesn't permit the novel to remain at the confessional level. In a gesture the critic Linda Hutcheon has taught us to recognize as typically postmodernist, White installs familiar generic conventions (in this case, the conventions of the psychological novel or the novel of adolescence or the *Künstlerroman*) in order to *subvert* the expectations such conventions evoke in the reader. White's point is neither to debunk nor even to parody the psychological novel. Indeed, his comment to Mark Amerika that he considers "*Memories of My Father Watching TV* the best poetic rendering of depression since Robert Lowell's *Life Studies*" seems to have been made without irony. Rather, White's postmodernist strategy is to complicate and problematize the conventions of the psychological novel, to pressure them into higher complexities, new mutations, in order to extend the novel of psychology into our present postmodern moment.

For epistemological and political reasons, using traditional novelistic conventions without problematizing them—writing, that is, a "realistic" psychological novel—was never an option for White. Realism, "the representation of the world through images that pretend to be natural, adequate, and proper" (*Monstrous* 20), informs as it reflects a discredited epistemological paradigm. More importantly, White believes that it "has become a State Fiction, a part of the machinery of the political state. It is through the conventions of Realism that the State explains to its citizens the relationship between themselves and Nature, economics, politics, and their own sexuality" (15). More than just perpetuating bad theory and bad politics, however, continuing to write unproblematized realistic fiction at this late date also represents an irresponsible evasion of our present moment, and is, as such, an act of literary and perhaps ethical bad faith.[1] In his essay "Writing the Life Postmodern" White wryly posts the following "notification":

UNTIL FURTHER NOTICE
YOU ARE IN THE
POSTMODERN CONDITION

One can either write in and of our present historical moment or "be irrelevant" (*Monstrous* 59). But in the age of the simulacrum, in which the individual is proclaimed to be nothing but a semiotic function, the human "subject" a mere ideological formation, how does one presume to write a "relevant" psychological novel? If the subject is always already de-centered, what might a postmodern confessional look like? How does one go about constructing hyperreal gardens with real existential pain in them?

In "Writing the Life Postmodern" White proposes a solution for the writer determined to be theoretically up-to-date while remaining "Still Human" (98). "Postmodern fiction," he writes, "is not necessarily merely an expression of the postmodern condition. Postmodern fiction is also a strategic response to that condition" (60). Unlike such radical proponents of postmodernism as Jean Baudrillard, who counsels "ecstatic capitulation to the flow of signs," postmodern writers White regards as "exemplary" assume that the postmodern condition is a condition of "damage." On the one hand, they "dutifully" report this damage:

> We are text and getting textier. Language accelerates. If we used to chew words in the old days, a nutrient rich stuff that built strong bodies in at least twelve ways, it's all crank now, insidious binaries that we mainline, along with their insulting viruses. We've caught a computer's disease, every bit as weird as coming down with hoof and mouth. (60-61)

On the other hand, however, exemplary postmodernists express "*ressentment* for the postmodern condition" (61, italics added). They protest the damage of the postmodern moment from *within* that moment (for various reasons, including several derived from postmodern theory, they couldn't get outside the moment if they tried), confronting, in a passage already quoted, "postmodern problems on postmodern grounds" (61).

In *Memories* clinical depression is a real disease but it is also a symptom of the larger cultural damage inflicted by the postmodern condition. "What does it mean that my chemical madness (sorry, we're fresh out of serotonin today, señor) produces fantasies which are nothing other than the truth of our political reality, metaphorically spoken?," White asks in the interview with Mark Amerika. "[M]y largely distorted sense of the world and its tenacious desire to hurt me personally has turned out to be from the most grimly objective perspective nothing less than the pure (metaphorical) truth of our collective condition." The very first chapter in the novel, "TV Scandal," establishes the landscape of that "collective condition." Chris's father sits comatose before a television set from which his "attention has not been distracted . . . since the early 1960s" (9-10), occasionally emerging from his cataleptic state to "jabber for a few moments" (21) recollections—or, perhaps, his own Chris-like projections—of his involvement in the TV scandals of the late fifties. This dual focus allows White to evoke both our current society of the spectacle, of which Chris's father is an exemplary denizen, and the decade of the fifties, the period in which, according to Fredric Jameson, the economic preparation for postmodernism or late capitalism began. The chapter explores the emergence of television and advertising as mediating factors in American politics and life, our entry into what Baudrillard defines as the fourth stage of the image, the era of the simulacrum, in which a boundless network of media and advertising images precede any reality to which they may once had referred. In commodified, postindustrial America desire is managed by being transformed into television images, as "life-on-TV" constructs impoverished housewives as Queens for a Day and "little people" as intellects powerful enough to compete successfully for unthinkable sums of money against Columbia University professors. Baudrillard calls such images "simulations," representations that don't copy so much as they displace the real, assuming a power reality never possessed.

In a hilarious scene in "TV Scandals" White examines one of the early examples of simulation. In his 1959 "kitchen debate" with Soviet Premier Nikita Khrushchev, Richard Nixon, a politician whose successful Checkers speech made him "conscious of the need for an artful reality" (18), tries to manipulate public perception again by pretending to be an actor. (Three decades later, confirming the trajectory predicted by this early simulation, America would elect as its president an actor pretending to be a politician.) In White's account Nixon wins the debate by managing to be less real than Khrushchev—or, more accurately, by stumbling into the realm of the hyperreal.

> How should a diplomat behave while in a kitchen discussing atom bombs? He had no idea. So, in a mild panic, he retreated to American cowboy politics, which had a short but potent stack of visual strategies available. He saw himself projected as Roy Rogers, Gene Autry or the Lone Ranger. He jabbed a finger into Khrushchev's chest. Nikita's eyebrows lifted in amazed amusement as Nixon's digit sunk to the first knuckle in his peasant chubbiness. This diplomacy was *more than real*. (19-20, italics added)

Taken aback, Khrushchev responds by waving his own finger. Because he is not tuned in to the American cultural psyche's store of Hollywood conventions signifying manly courage, Nikita's digit is perceived to be just a "pinky, not a finger that a cowboy would wave." The Premier is "thus marked as an alien. He lacked access to the authentic cowboy diplomatic vernacular" (20).

White's surreal fusion of the TV scandals of the late 1950s, the televised kitchen debate, Disneyland (which exists, in Baudrillard's famous formulation, to reassure Americans that life outside of the theme park is real), and Chris's father's sense of "humiliation, shame and powerlessness" (9) modulates into a complex metaphor for the damage wrought on the American psyche by postmodern consumer society. Mr. K., to whom Chris's father speaks at Disneyland (which the historical Khrushchev was forbidden to visit during his 1959 visit to the US), is himself, or itself, also a compacted metaphor, at once a TV-like talking head, a head of state, a spinning head (*á la* the demon-possessed child of *The Exorcist* fame), a robot evocative of Burroughs's "soft machine," Kafka's K., Chris's father's surrogate father, and a copy of the actual Nikita Khrushchev, whose public identity (the only one we can know) is the product of media images and who therefore exists as little more than a simulacrum himself. The embodiment of postmodern overdetermination, Mr. K. perceives the link between the symptoms of Chris's father's mental condition, the most significant of which is self-loathing ("I am a turd with a hat on" [14]), and the larger symptoms of cultural damage inflicted by the postmodern condition: "Consumer yearning, sexual bafflement, autocratic cruelty, and crushed pride" (22). Chris's father's feelings of alienation and hopelessness are not merely the result of his personal biography, as Mr. K.'s final comments indicate, but reflect a wider cultural despair: "We have grown lost in the fall and rise of day. We are confused by the dilemma our ruins present. *The outside has disappeared.* See there, nothing in the distance but a flat buzzing. That is not life you hear, that's just heavy breathing" (27-28, italics added).

Spoken, appropriately, by a Disney toy, Mr. K.'s melancholy benediction echoes Jameson's diagnosis of the postmodern moment, which in White's summary has "no 'distance,' . . . no 'outside' from which to describe and critique late capitalist space. All postmodern gestures are already taken up and reified as commodities" (*Monstrous* 38-39). Because metaphysical systems have no outside, any resistance untainted by the dominant ideology is impossible; we can never totally escape the cultural and discursive constraints of our moment. More significantly, perhaps, Mr. K.'s words echo what White considers "the archetype of the postmodern gesture . . . [:] Theodore Adorno's famous epigraph to *Minima Moralia,* 'life does not live' " (60).

> Which means [White continues] that a certain form of life does not live (nineteenth century faith in the capitalist/rationalist/instrumentalist enterprise, or faith in a mythic—high modernist—return to a time before capital). Adorno's maxim also means that life understood as a fundamental 'normative' quality of being human no longer lives. In short, the Modern does not live and that privileged modernist project called *humanité* does not live. (60)

The loss of verities once presumed to be eternal and the consequent sense of estrangement and psychological disequilibrium that loss entails constitute the condition of damage assumed by White's postmodern fiction. It also fuels White's resentment. But for reasons already articulated, White can neither return to a lost time (whose own brutalities and damagings we are, from this side of modernism, now better able to assess) nor fully capitulate to the postmodern present. The only responsible alternative, as White characterizes that alternative in "Writing the Life Postmodern," is to forge a "dialectical" relationship with the present moment, self-consciously registering its ideology while simultaneously searching for its utopic potentialities.

Paradoxically, then, the utopic search must proceed not only from within the dystopia (and all totalized cultural systems partake to a greater or lesser degree in the dystopic) but in the very terms of the system being critiqued. "TV Scandal," as we have seen, deals thematically with postmodern damage by connecting Chris's father's depression—and by implication Chris's mental illness as well—to a specular society in which all things—politics, entertainment, mental illness itself (the topic of the questions Chris's father answers on the quiz show)—are mediated by images contrived solely to solicit consumption. White's thematics are indistinguishable from his aesthetic strategies, which, as suggested, involve the incorporation of postmodernist tendencies into his novel's formal dimensions. That is, White performs his novelistic cultural critique by recontextualizing the signs of oppressive culture, appropriating as formal and aesthetic devices such postmodern interventionist political strategies as reappropriation, bricolage, and detournment.

His reappropriation of "those old, violent action shows," for example, is, as White explains to Mark Amerika, "also a way of 'detourning' them. Claiming their always damaged and damaging agenda for other purposes." Similarly, the novel's formal discontinuity, its reliance on multiple or intertextual surfaces without apparent causal or logical relationship, is also detourned, turned back against itself. At first glance, the novel's surface play of differentiation (exfoliating identities, texts within texts, etc.) resembles those "randomly heterogeneous [,] . . . fragmentary and . . . aleatory . . . cultural productions" (25) Jameson identifies as postmodern pastiche. Like Baudrillard's simulacrum, pastiche signals the disappearance or "death" of such humanistic doxa as the individual subject, a personal style, interiority, indeed, meaning itself (pastiche, Jameson maintains, is "blank parody"). In *Memories,* however, pastiche becomes more than an empty representation of the forms of representation that comprise the world of human experience. Rather, turned back upon itself, pastiche functions as a metaphor for that dispersion of simulacra through which Chris—and, indeed, the author himself—must struggle in his effort to come to terms with absence, palimpsestically evoking Chris's desire for an always already deferred presence within a context of endlessly proliferating differences.

In a similar fashion, the overdetermined characterization of the novel's eponymous father exemplifies the endless deferral of meaning, closure, and foundation that constitutes the postmodern condition. At the novel's confessional level, he is Chris and, in a more difficult to determine sense, possibly Curtis White's father, as well as the various television characters who represent Chris's displaced desire for a father figure. Clinically depressive, a victim of late technocapitalism, and also abandoned by his father, he is Chris (and Curtis?) White's double; moreover, because we, too, occupy the disparate and fragmentary moment called postmodernism, he may be the *hypocrite lecteur's semblable* as well. In addition, he is the father-function constructed by a mélange of contemporary mind maps, including Freud's Oedipal father (who must be "killed" if Chris is to obtain a "penis" [31]); Lacan's Name-of-the-Father, the symbolic order which, structured by language and ruled by the phallus, shapes Chris's desire for "a place for a man among men"

(45); Melanie Klein's object relations theory (61); R. D. Laing's theory of schizophrenia ("This was either break down or break through" [27]); Jung's archetypes; the "anti-psychiatry" of Gilles Deleuze and Félix Guattari; and of course the clinical constructions that construe all mental disorders as the effect of bad brain chemistry, treatable by the pharmaceuticals Chris takes "with gratitude" (77). And he is the Barthelmean Dead Father, the Tradition of literary Modernism, whose claims of epistemological authority White subverts while nonetheless paying homage to some of its practitioners, specifically Kafka, Céline, the Eliot of *The Waste Land,* Burroughs, and the Lowell of *Life Studies,* all noted exemplars of "mad" discourse. Less a character than an intertextual nexus, White's titular father, like the postmodernist landscape he occupies, comprises an irreducible plurality whose "essence . . . is fixed nowhere [,] . . . an 'economy,' a set of human relations that works (even if its working is all a process of damaging; damaging the already damaged)" (*Memories* 109).

At the level of form, style, and characterization, then, *Memories of My Father Watching TV* seems to assert infinite multiplicity. But the novel stops short of that "systematic exemption of meaning" Roland Barthes associates with the "writerly" text. Radically dilatory texts, which practice an infinite deferral of meaning, reveling *a la* Baudrillard in an erotics of indeterminacy, simply exchange one totalizing system, realism, for another, "Baudrillard's totalized semiotic vision," in which the " 'transcendental signifier' is signification itself" (*Monstrous* 105, 108).[2] Ultimately, given the constructed nature of reality, "no texts are mimetic"; "nevertheless," White insists, "all texts must behave, at some level, as if they were" (15-16). Even antimimetic fiction "needs the as-if of referentiality," a self-conscious awareness "that it is always at some level part of what it critiques" (15). As we have seen, what White imitates in *Memories* is, precisely, imitations, or, better, representations, simulacra, the infinite regress of icons—"that which saturates consciousness without having to be meaningful" (*Monstrous* 27)—which impels the passivity and commodity fetishism of late technocapitalist society. By embedding in his portrait of uni-dimensional post-humanist society the desire of a single "damaged" human being, White enters into a "negative dialectics" (*Monstrous* 28) with postmodern culture, contesting the "managed" commodification of all human value and desire with singular human need.[3]

White's method, then, is to turn postmodernist critique back upon postmodernism itself, or at least upon those radical forms of postmodernism characterized by the totalizing assumption that "the Real has been 'ravished,' and we must now suffer infinitely the consequences of that ravishing: life in the 'hyperreal' (that is to say, life in a cultural context devoid of a role for the Real; life in a context of pure simulation)" (*Monstrous* 109). Paradoxically, even audaciously—since it is proposed knowingly from within the postmodern situation—White posits the possibility of a postmodern ethics, something he finds disturbingly lacking in much postmodernist theory. Postmodernism, White complains,

> is unlike its predecessors in the nearly total absence of ethical content in its diagnosis of techno-capitalism. Largely because of its simplistic commitment to the post-structural critique of metaphysics and master narratives, postmodernism is not willing to entertain the possibility that our present techno-totalization is a form of damage, that it is something that we ought to resent, or that there are imaginable social forms which we might legitimately prefer to it. The present is simply our 'mode,' perhaps our final mode. (112-13)

Declaring "Death to the dictatorship of the present" (35), White locates the source of his ethical program in postmodernism's notorious fluidity and the radical freedom that fluidity implies. Of course, freedom, especially as it pertains to human agency, has become a vexed concept in poststructuralist thought, and, for that reason perhaps, it is not the traditional humanistic notion of free will to which White appeals. Rather, he evokes Herbert Marcuse's concept of "free play," by which Marcuse means "the released potentialities of man and nature" (35). As an aesthetic principle, free play implies the activities of the *bricoleur,* who creates new forms and new meanings by the persistent recombination of existing materials and experiences. But postmodern literature's preference for the discontinuous and the monstrous need not result in that variety of postmodern text Alan Wilde describes, whose formal discontinuities signal an acceptance of "the impossibility of making any sense whatever of the world as a whole" (44). On the contrary, monstrous literature can tease out the "monstrous possibility" concealed in our present moment, "its world-making potential." Alluding to Deleuze and Guattari, White defines play as "a form of radical democracy based upon a radical philosophy of becoming over a static philosophy of being, of difference over presence, of an *ad infinitum* 'wordling' over Nature, of infinite Nomadological 'lines of flight' over the striated space of the political State" (115). Since, as postmodernism has taught us, "the social world is constructed, does not participate in the necessity of nature," it follows that the world can be "constructed otherwise" (26). The promise of monstrous literature, therefore, is not only a postmodern ethics, but a postmodernist literary politics:

> If the real is constituted not by simple presence . . . but by "difference," by the activity of texts, commodities, and the world of signs; and if the possibilities for how those worlds are constituted are without necessary limit; then, a political economy which "mutilates" artisans in order to make "workers" of them' (Deleuze and Guattari), which reifies the world through commodities, and which compels social conformity either through the bourgeois ideologemes of Nature or the obligations of the performance principle, this political economy is a form of social injury. If the logic of signs allows for "worldling" without limit, let these worlds begin. (115)

In *Memories* the potential for "worldling" is signified by the recurring appearances of Shiva, the Hindu god of dissolution and regeneration. As readers familiar with White's earlier work will recall, Shiva turns up in *Anarcho-Hindu* (1995) as Siva, the novel's protagonist. In *Memories,* on the other hand, Shiva, who is explicitly mentioned only once (113), functions less as a character than a flickering presence, whose emblems are dropped periodically like calling cards: Paladin's horse-shaped third eye, a crescent-shaped fish-bite, the halo of fire concluding the two sections of *Memories*. From a postmodern perspective, Shiva is particularly interesting because his personality teems with incoherence. Creator and destroyer, often androgynous, a lover of monumental prowess whose symbol is the linga or phallus yet an ascetic indifferent to pleasure, recognized as Supreme Lord yet shunned by the other gods for his impure habits and slovenly appearance (matted hair, ashes-smeared body, a necklace of skulls and human bones)—Shiva is the most overdetermined of deities, whose multifarious activities reflect the Hindu and Buddhist principle that good and evil, wretchedness and salvation, spring from the same source. His dance, the Tândava, destroys the world in order to regenerate it, symbolizing the eternal movement of the universe, the Sanskrit word for which is *lîlâ*—or "play."

Shiva's enervated presence in *Memories* implies the raw power of play's countervailing forces, "postmodern death-in-life" (62) figured in the life-defeating proclivities of the novel's various father figures and the omnipresence of television. In a terrifyingly comic scene, for example, Shiva appears in the personage of the Wild Father. In a book about father-son-relationships, mention of a Wild Man immediately evokes Robert Bly's *Iron John* (1990). In Bly's book Iron John is an incarnation of the "Hairy Man" or "Wild Father" archetype (Shiva, Bly points out, is another) who initiates a young boy into manhood by helping him develop his "inner Wild Man," a vigorous masculinity whose attributes include male sexual energy, spontaneity and "riskiness," love of nature and a concomitant desire to protect the earth, the capacity to learn from and "honor" grief, and a protecting, caring nature. The Wild Father of "Bonanza," on the other hand, is a wildly parodic inversion of the archetype's life-enhancing qualities, a god in ruins, "naked and matted with hair," whose penis, unlike Shiva's divine linga, is variously described as "cheesy" and as "plastic." His disturbing yet hilarious "rant" near the end of the chapter demonstrates how attenuated male energy has become in postindustrial America. This is life that does not live. Yet, in another cruel parody of Shiva's regenerative force, the chapter concludes with Wild Father "reproduc[ing] his kind" (64) by performing guitar strokes on his infirm "weirdly plastic penis" before a TV audience of wildly approving little boys, "hooked by satellite/ To everyone's favorite station" (67).[4]

As the recurrence of such scenes suggests, *Memories* never quite succeeds in presenting "a world within which we might choose to live," which is a primary function, according to White, of new works of fiction (*Monstrous* 66). Yet the novel's Shiva-energy, however muted, persistently holds out the possibility of change. At the end of "Combat," Sarge removes his helmet to reveal "a small patch of garden" growing out of the top of his head. One in a series of scenes in which characters discover that alien life forms—snakes, fish, Kafkaesque insects, Burroughs-like viruses—have invaded their brain, the motif reinforces the novel's theme of mental illness. But we are also told that the "bright colors of the wildflowers" growing out of Sarge's head "make it appear that his brow is aflame" (79). The halo of fire is a sure sign of Shiva, whose brow glows as he dances the dance of annihilation, which preserves the infinite play of life. Appearing at the end of "Combat," by far the novel's most somber chapter, the manifestation of Shiva-energy suggests the ancient Hindu principle that one thing always contains its other—which is, of course, a principle of deconstruction as well. "And if the present can be deconstructed," White says hopefully, "this opens the way to a possible reconstruction" (*Monstrous* 34).

White is not recycling discredited Enlightenment views of human progress. Free play implies an ongoing process, not a destination that can be reached. "Openness of human possibility," White contends, presents "an infinite horizon of never fully realizable potential" (113). So at the novel's end, when Chris and his father have finally had their talk and the "happy family" takes its first "family outing" ever, we should not be surprised that Chris is confronted by "a flaming hedge of burning brow" from the station wagon's backseat (155-56). A parody of conventional reconciliation scenes, Chris's talk with his father yields no understanding, no modernist epiphanies, none of the behavior changes we associate with

Forster's "round" characters: Dad, we discover, communicates with no one because he has nothing to say, drinks because he enjoys it, watches TV every night because he finds it entertaining, and considers himself happy. "So you see, Son, I'm happy because I have a nice TV to watch and drinks to drink. And that's all there is to it" (143-44). In a phrase White appropriates from David Hickey, Chris's father enjoys "the banality of neutral comfort"—which, White concludes, is the same as being "dead" (*Monstrous* 97). The burning brows Chris observes at the novel's close, then, disrupt the false *telos* of the novel's conclusion, not by offering a specific alternative world (which would be another *telos)*, but by reconfirming the spirit of purposeful play which empowers us to imagine more palatable futures.

A monstrous hybrid, Curtis White's *Memories of My Father Watching TV* presents itself as a postmodern confessional/psychological/political novel. It also strives to capture what is perhaps the most paradoxical of hybrids, postmodern *beauty*. White concedes the poststructuralist argument that beauty "has no independent, enduring, unique, timeless being. It has no 'presence' separate from (that is, transcending) immediate historical human contexts" (*Monstrous* 96). Nonetheless, a claim for aesthetic beauty as a meaningful category can be made from inside of postmodernism by evoking the concept of "wordling." "Something is beautiful," White suggests, "when the artist works collaboratively with an inherited past, ingeniously reveals again that history within the work, but then—ah! the bright wings!—opens, allows that familiar world to unfold unfamiliarly . . ." (97). White's allusion to Hopkins recalls "Manic Maverick," the novel's penultimate chapter and perhaps its most successful consolidation of all the qualities White associates with monstrous beauty. The chapter modulates from the *Weltschmerz* and disgust of Céline, in whose fragmented, ellipses-ridden style the entire chapter is written, through Vishnu's return to earth as the avatar Blue Maverick, a kind of cartoon Krishna,[5] to the concluding passage in which Chris's perception of Maverick-Krishna's apparent re-return is conveyed in Hopkins-like cadences: "it was again Maverick intruding on a black-and-white world . . . it was Maverick that he saw high behind the sycamores . . . he bent, brooding, over the world with his warm blue breast and—ah!—his bright laughing eyes" (139).

Typically compacted and conflicted, the concluding allusion points in two directions. On the one hand, it implies the possibility of a kind of postmodern faith, the "utopic hope . . . that if there is nothing necessary or natural about the present, and change is real, then things can be otherwise. We might even allow ourselves to imagine that things can be *better* than they are" (*Monstrous* 34). On the other hand, the world it implies, the world of Hopkins's imagining, can never again be our world. Hopkins's major accomplishment, according to White, was his work "within the dying tradition of the rhymed and metered lyric in order to reinvent it as a wholly new music and in the process reinvent the relevance of (a similarly dying) Christian faith." In the process Hopkins achieved that kind of aesthetic beauty that permits a reunderstanding of the known world and its dominant ideology "as desirable after all" (*Monstrous* 97). For our time, however, a different order of worlding, another kind of beauty, is needed, one less conservative than Hopkins's, one that, like the flights of stairs in *The Third Man*, can "provide access from one logic or metaphysic to another" (149). Postmodern beauty, as White describes it, projects "a new world, surviving on bits and pieces of the past (all its parts are borrowed), and erupting as an alternative world we might inhabit" (*Monstrous* 97). We may have lost forever the naive belief that it is possible to step outside of the narrow, totalized confines of what men call "reality," as Ellison's Invisible Man was able to do. But *Memories of My Father Watching TV* demonstrates that certain writers are able to view our present moment through the defamiliarizing lens of blessed madness, and by employing the recombinant aesthetics of bricolage and liberatory free play, keep alive the possibility of constructing not only new aesthetic forms but new and potentially better worlds.

NOTES

[1]I want to emphasize that it's the *unproblematized,* "naive" use of realistic conventions that I have in mind here. A major motive of the metafiction of the sixties and seventies was to foreground the *conventional* nature of realistic conventions and to demonstrate that such conventions are no more nor no less artificial than the conventions of other fictive modes (e.g., fantasy, journalistic fiction, or metafiction itself). Thus exposed, realistic conventions have once again become part of the aesthetic repertoire of otherwise "transgressive" authors. Note, for example, the use of realistic conventions by that former arch-metaficitonalist John Barth in novels such as *Sabbatical,* or the realistic surfaces of otherwise transgressive novels by Richard Powers and Don DeLillo.

[2]Such texts exist only potentially. As White drolly remarks, the "only knowledge" we have of " 'writing at the zero degree,' or 'white writing,' or the Writerly, or any other dream text of the avant-garde, . . . is that, as Barthes says, there are no examples of it" (*Monstrous* 15).

[3]Which is not to suggest that White hopes to recuperate the modernist concept of the alienated individual, whose binary conceals a self/other hierarchy. Rather, White's double-voiced strategy implies that postindustrial

fragmentation is not a cause for celebration but a source of damage.

[4]In Bly's retelling of the Wild Man myth, Iron John initially emerges from a lake, signaling his mythic residence in the human collective unconsciousness. In "Sea Hunt" Chris's father also emerges from beneath the water in a scene White describes as "mythic." But the father fails to recognize Chris as his son, and instead of bestowing life force, he hands him an undetonated bomb (99).

[5]Readers familiar with the legend of a young Krishna among the cowgirls will appreciate White's sly joke in bringing Krishna back as a cowboy. White bestows on Maverick several of Krishna's experiences and attributes, including his blue skin; the dirt-eating episode, in which the entire Universe was perceived in Krishna's mouth; Krishna's victory over the goblin Putana by sucking the poisonous milk from her breast until she dies; and Krishna's bout of love-making with Râdhâ during which they engage in the eight kinds of sexual intercourse. Significantly, White changes Râdhâ's name to Lila, which is, as already indicated, the Sanskrit word for play.

WORKS CITED

Barthes, Roland. *Image / Music / Text.* New York: Hill and Wang, 1977.

Jameson, Fredric. *Postmodernism, or, The Cultural Logic of Late Capitalism.* Durham: Duke UP, 1991.

White, Curtis. *Memories of My Father Watching TV.* Normal: Dalkey Archive Press, 1998.

——. *Monstrous Possibility: An Invitation to Literary Politics.* Normal: Dalkey Archive Press, 1998.

Wilde, Alan. *Horizons of Assent: Modernism, Postmodernism, and the Ironic Imagination.* Baltimore: Johns Hopkins UP, 1981.

A Curtis White Checklist

Fiction

Heretical Songs. New York: Fiction Collective, 1980.

Metaphysics in the Midwest. Los Angeles: Sun & Moon, 1988.

The Idea of Home. Los Angeles: Sun & Moon, 1992.

Anarcho-Hindu. Normal: Black Ice Books/FC2, 1995.

Memories of My Father Watching TV. Normal: Dalkey Archive Press, 1998.

Nonfiction

Monstrous Possibility: An Invitation to Literary Politics. Normal: Dalkey Archive Press, 1998.

Milorad Pavić

Milorad Pavić: "He Thinks the Way We Dream"

Radmila Jovanović Gorup

When French and American critics, writing about Pavić's *Dictionary of the Khazars,* wrote "We are all Khazars," they meant this as a paradigm for the troubled eighties, plagued by ecological pollution, nuclear menace, and the threat of a global loss of identity. Almost one decade later, with the author's country engulfed in a savage war, the same statement sounds even more prophetic.

With three novels published in the U.S., Milorad Pavić, Serbian poet and prose writer, university professor and expert on Serbian baroque and symbolism, translator, literary theoretician and member of the Serbian Academy of Arts and Sciences, remains primarily associated with his internationally acclaimed novel *Dictionary of the Khazars.* When a friend of mine from Philadelphia, who had been invited to attend a panel dedicated to Pavić, wanted to read a work by him, she first went to her college library. She did not find a single book by Pavić. She then went to Philadelphia's main public library, where she found only *Dictionary of the Khazars.* It is hoped that this issue of the *Review of Contemporary Fiction* will correct this neglect and help assure for Milorad Pavić the readership he truly deserves.

Milorad Pavić was an accomplished scholar, poet and short-story writer when he burst onto the European literary scene with an extraordinary novel—*Dictionary of the Khazars* (1984). Western Europe, usually very responsive to literature coming from Eastern Europe, and generally from abroad, was unprepared for such an erudite author coming from what it considered the periphery of Western European civilization. Pavić, however, considers his background an asset. He credits his success as a writer and intellectual to two great traditions of the territory of his origin: the Serbian oral literature which preserves the art of storytelling going back to Homer; and the Byzantine novel of myths and legends.

Pavić, together with some other Serbian writers (e.g., the poets Ivan Lalić and Miodrag Pavlović, for example), has been endeavouring to re-establish contact with what they regard as their true spiritual and intellectual origin, the art of Byzantium. In his works Pavić includes folktales and legends, riddles and proverbs, historical documents and literary criticism, cookbooks and jokes, and much much more. Poet Charles Simic sees three sides of Pavić: "Pavić the Arabian Nights storyteller," Pavić the poet who seeks hidden relationships between unrelated things, and Pavić the comic who "thrives on mixing the spiritual and the sensual, the sacred and the profane."[1]

Pavić insists that he does not have a biography, just a bibliography, and that his books speak for him. When pressed to say who influenced him the most, he says that he learned a great deal from the ecclesiastic orators of the Serbian baroque period who were themselves influenced by both the European and Byzantine traditions and from whom he learned how to construct the sentence and "fight for each and every reader."

In an interview with the Greek journalist Thanassis Lallas, included in this issue, Pavić credits his ancestors for his present identity as a writer. "It was my ancestors who supported me each time I began writing something," says Pavić.

Pavić was born on 15 October 1929 in Belgrade. His father, a sculptor, came from an intellectual family which produced many writers. In the last two hundred years there was at least one Pavić writer in every other generation. Young Milorad was very close to his uncle Nikola, a poet who wrote in the Kajkavian dialect of Croatia. Pavić's mother was a professor of philosophy and an afecionado of Serbian and South Slavic oral tradition. Other family members demonstrated other artistic talents. The author's son Ivan is a painter.

Pavić started to write while in high school, but he soon abandoned it because his writing did not conform to the prescribed mode of writing of the time, social realism. As a young man, Pavić actively pursued literature at the University of Belgrade while at the same time studying violin at the Belgrade Academy of Music. The literary historian won over the violinist in the fifties when Pavić began to translate Pushkin poetry and also to publish articles on literary history in various journals. While this was politically safer, it affected his academic career adversely. He was unable to secure a teaching position at the University of Belgrade, and he taught at the University of Novi Sad. At first, researching and publishing books on the Serbian literature of the seventeenth, eighteenth, and nineteenth centuries, Pavić began to write poetry when the political climate started to change in the sixties. His two collections of poetry, *Palimpsests* and *The Moon Stone,* were published in 1967 and 1971, and his first book of short stories, *The Iron Curtain,* in 1973. While he continued to produce scholarly articles, within the next decade, Pavić published several collections of short stories—*The Horses of St. Mark* (1976), *Borzoi* (1979), *New Belgrade Stories*

(1981)—and prose and poetry—*Souls Bathe for the Last Time* (1982). The critics, however, received Pavić's fiction without great fanfare. This all changed in 1984 when his first novel *Dictionary of the Khazars: A Novel Lexicon in 100,000 Words* was published, was soon translated into scores of foreign languages, and received the highest praises from abroad.

When *Dictionary of the Khazars* was translated first into French in 1988 and later into other languages, the critics tried to link its author to Bulgakov and Flaubert, Nabokov and Cortázar, Borges and Eco, Calvino and Perec. Nevertheless, they had to admit that in *Dictionary of the Khazars* we have something entirely new, a book like no other book. The novel was praised as: "the first novel of the 21st century" (Philippe Tretiack); "a celebration of art" (Raša Livada); "a delirium of storytelling." Its author was showered with compliments: "A Diderot of our time" (Werner Krause); "He thinks the way we dream" (Robert Coover); "He writes as the Gypsies play violin, with delirium natural and inborn" (George Walter); "He writes with such imaginative cultural extension as to make García Márquez seem like James Mitchener"; "*Dictionary of the Khazars* is the equivalent of Salvador Dali drawing the road map for the AAA or a Gypsy band playing Bach fugues in a village inn" (Charles Fenyvesi).[2]

The novel was a literary experiment. It sold in two versions, male and female, which were identical except for a single paragraph. It had the form of a lexicon, consisting of three books, each presenting different versions of the same historical events. The red book gave the Christian version, the yellow book the Jewish version, and the green book the Muslim version.

Encyclopedic in character, *Dictionary of the Khazars* reconstructs the life, customs, and beliefs of an ancient people who vanished from history without leaving a trace. Inspired by both ancient experiences as well as modern concerns, the book contains magical tales embedded into other tales, all told with baroque imagination and playful humor. The entries of the lexicon, events and people, are both historical and fictional, though the historical basis is quite slim. The "Khazar Polemic" theme on which the novel is based gives the author the opportunity to introduce his magical world of events and characters. The book is not only populated by the characters of the time of the Khazar Polemic; it spans different periods over eight centuries and ends with our own. The book is replete with magical happenings and mythical characters who come to us via dreams and reincarnation, linked only by a loose thread.

The major novelty, however, is the book's form. The form of a lexicon offers the reader a novel way of reading. The novel can be opened anywhere, read whichever way the reader prefers, from the beginning, middle, or end, upward, backward, sideways. It is, literally, an open book that never ends and that makes the reader forget that the book has an author. Indeed, Pavić often has stressed that an author is only a medium, that whereas past writers have tried to invent a new way of writing, he wanted to create a novel way of reading and interpreting a literary work.

Aware that the genre of novel was in crisis, the author deemed it necessary first to change the way it is read. *Dictionary of the Khazars* is an invitation to the reader to create his own book and to modify the traditional method of linear reading. It is up to the reader to construct a narrative out of these uncertain facts. The reader is also advised that it is he who bestows a higher order on these facts and gives them meaning. The character of Adam Cadmon is the metaphor of that order, as members of a sect of dream hunters strive to reconstruct his body out of disparate parts.

With this book, each reader stepped onto an uncharted territory and could make of it what he or she wanted. Pavić was not surprised when the reviewers of *Dictionary of the Khazars* seemed to recount different books, because they found that the content of the novel could not be easily summarized and that each layer revealed a deeper layer to be interpreted. For him, an author who can be fully interpreted cannot be a good author. He has to be prepared for each reader to find something different in this book.

Four essays in this issue are dedicated to *Dictionary of the Khazars*. In "*Dictionary of the Khazars* as an Epistemological Metaphor" Andreas Leitner views the novel as an absolute book in the sense propagated by German romantic writers and philosophers. In reading *Dictionary of the Khazars,* one quickly loses interest in the Khazars and their tragic fate and is immersed instead in the legibility of the absolute book as a means of resolving the mystery of man and the world. This novel reflects in concrete images the abstract concepts of episteme, which is understood as the summary of all knowledge. Leitner sees its reading as closely linked to the way that reality is presently interpreted through two opposing epistemological methods, "the knowledge of being" and "the knowledge of becoming." The former is represented by the natural sciences and sees reality as heterogeneous and pluralistic, while the latter is represented by evolutionary systems, systems theories, and pseudosciences and sees reality as homogeneous and universally connected. With examples from the novel, Leitner shows how these two types of knowledge interact to determine reality in *Dictionary of the Khazars.*

Dagmar Burkhart's analysis, "Culture as Memory: On the Poetics of Milorad Pavić," focuses on the novel's fantastic element within the larger frame of the nonmimetic discourse of Serbian postmodernism. Extensive intertextuality is a major characteristic of this literature and is present at all levels in *Dictionary of the Khazars.* Miscellaneous references to the Bible, ancient myths, the Byzantine novel, the tradition of the Kabbala, sermons from the Serbian baroque period, texts from German romantic writers, Russian classics, Serbian contemporary writers, and more, are introduced at different places in the novel, combining cultural layers of human civilization and illustrating *arts combinatoria* of postmodernism. Burkhart considers this concept as best exemplifying the basic principles of Pavić's poetics. She further discusses three basic semantic dichotomies present in *Dictionary of the Khazars* and other works by Pavić: memory and oblivion; identity and metamorphosis; and particularity and unity.

Rachel Kilbourn Davis's essay, "*Dictionary of the Khazars* as a Khazar Jar," shows how Pavić sets traps for his reader and challenges them to create and re-create the narrative. She cites the entry "The Khazar Jar" from *Dictionary of the Khazars,* as a parable about the novel and the reader, his relationship to the novel and his attempts to unravel its meaning. However, Davis stresses that unlike an ordinary Aristotelian novel, where some element of the plot or character discovery is the reader's goal, in *Dictionary of the Khazars* the reading process itself and the dialogic engagement between the author and the reader is the end. As a novel, *Dictionary of the Khazars* is both an attempt to train the reader "how to read" and a message that the writer and the reader both bear equal responsibility for the "meaning" or "truth" of the text. Like Pavić's image of the two men holding a captured puma on a rope between them, each one is completely responsible for the other's very existence and the punishment for shirking this responsibility is death.

Toma Longinović's essay, "Chaos Theory and the Fantastic: Narrative Strategies in *Dictionary of the Khazars,*" examines the relationship between scientific chaos theories and the novelistic poetics of Milorad Pavić in the context of postmodernity. His theory is based on the parallel epistemological position of science and literature in an age when certainty and stability are being substituted with uncertainty and self-creation.

Just when it appeared that what Pavić had achieved with *Dictionary of the Khazars* was unlikely to be duplicated, along came *The Landscape Painted with Tea* (1988), again "a bewitching brew," "part Borges, part Calvino, part Old Testament, part brothers Grimm" (Thomas Christensen), a true Pavić (Tešanović 345).

This novel, in which the heroine falls in love with the reader, could be read like a crossword puzzle, horizontally and/or vertically. This gives the reader the opportunity to construct different chapters, "across" and "down."

A former architect of Belgrade, the protagonist Atanas Svilar is an executive of a chemical corporation in California. His hobby is to paint landscapes with a brush dipped in tea. When he draws the villa of Josip Broz Tito, the late president of the former Yugoslavia, he starts to imitate his extravagant lifestyle, thus creating a parallel life. This, however, does not make *The Landscape Painted with Tea* a political novel. Pavić introduces philosophical ideas present in the Orthodoxy. In the Serbian Orthodox monastery on Mount Athos visited by Svilar, monks are divided into two groups, the cenobytes who live in communities and build the material world, and those dedicated exclusively to the spiritual life, the ideorhythmics. Likewise, people in general are divided into these two groups and different historical periods are seen as dominated by one of these two ideas, materialistic and spiritual.

Jasmina Mihajlović's essay traces the theme of endangered ecology, which she finds present at all the levels of *The Landscape Painted with Tea.* She concludes that the novel sounds both a warning of the approaching apocalypse and an appeal to humans to cease the self-annihilation they have been perpetuating in their destruction of nature. The ecological crisis can be perceived in the novel through the crisis of identity: personal, religious, sexual, national, cosmic, or otherwise. This is one of the central themes of Pavić's works. Various characters in the novel are searching for their lost identity and the main protagonist loses his by transforming into his opposite. Other characters display dual identities, various disguises and transformations, and all strive to regain the paradise lost, "the other half of their long ago possessed whole." *The Landscape Painted with Tea* calls for a return to the art of living.

The third novel by Pavić, entitled *The Inner Side of the Wind or the Novel of Hero and Leander,* appeared in 1991. Based on Ovid's *Heroides* the novel recounts the passionate anticipation of two lovers separated, not by the waves of Hellespont, but by the waves of time. As with the two previous novels, *The Inner Side of the Wind* offers a still different way of reading. A novel-clepsydra, it has two beginnings and one end. The reader can begin with either Hero's tale and then flip the book upside down and read Leander's narrative, or the other way around. In my essay "*The Inner Side of the Wind:* A Postmodern Novel" I discuss the postmodernist characteristics of *The Inner Side of the Wind,* such as its novelty of form, intertextuality, the violation of ontological boundaries and the artful combination of the historical and the fantastic. I place special emphasis on the novel's fragmented and disrupted topos that accommodates exclusive worlds and the embedded structure of using mirrors and other shiny objects to capture invisible relationships.

We have included in this issue an excerpt from the fourth novel by Pavić, soon to be published in England. *The Last Love in Constantinople* (1994), subtitled *A Handbook for Fortune-Telling,* continues the author's playful engagement with the reader. The novel consists of twenty-two chapters. Each chapter bears the name of a tarot card and is a separate tale. Like Pavić's previous novels, *The Last Love in Constantinople* lends itself to countless interpretations. The reader can read the book from beginning to end and then open the set of cards attached to the novel and reread his "fortune," looking to the way the cards opened and reading the corresponding chapters in that order.

This is a love story which takes place during the Napoleonic wars between the French and the Austrians. The central character, a Serb who is a captain in the French army, disappears as foretold, once a young woman falls in love with him. This is again a story about ideorhythmics and cenobytes, the loners and the communal inhabitants, to whom the reader was introduced in *The Landscape Painted with Tea,* although there in a masculine, here in a feminine key. In this novel Pavić writes about the destiny of a woman in a man's world, about her relationship to the man, both as victor and defeated, as well as her ability to transcend the masculine division and be "the third shoe." That is why in the table of contents the chapters are labeled "keys of a Great Secret for ladies of both sexes."

Pavić was able to come up with another innovative form for his play *For Ever and a Day,* published in 1994. *For Ever and a Day* is a theater menu consisting of several appetizers, one or two entrées and several desserts. The director or the reader can "order" the play as he might a dinner. The play, translated by Christina Pribićević-Zorić, was performed abroad and is scheduled for publication in English.

In 1996 a novella entitled *Hat Made of Fish Skin* appeared. Its plot takes place in the third century A.D. in the area of the former Yugoslavia. The Roman Empire is crumbling under the assaults of barbarians. Two people meet and fall in love but their happiness is short lived. Like all of Pavić's works, this short novel is filled with symbolism and strange imagery.

It was mentioned earlier that Pavić's books ask for a "creative" reader, one who is ready to abandon the traditional linear style of reading. In her essay on Pavić and the computer novel Mihajlović explores the interest the electronic writers and critics of hypertext literature have in Pavić's works. They consider him one of the predecessors of hyperfiction. With examples from Pavić's works, Mihajlovic demonstrates how they can be converted into the computer medium.

All of Pavić's works of fiction, including the five collections of short stories (*The Iron Curtain* [1973], *St. Marco's Horses* [1976], *Borzoi* [1979], *New Belgrade Stories* [1981], and *The Inverted Glove* [1989]) take us to that seismic zone between the East and the West which houses three major religions and where, in the words of George Walter, "Christians, Jews and Muslims, mixed as the spices in a sauce, fecondated Europe with their marvelous brew" (Tešanović 62). All of his stories are witty, playful, and chronologically disturbed, shifting time and events, facts and conjectures, a haunting mix of dream and reality.

In view of the present state of the world, Pavić's novels were indeed prophetic. While *Dictionary of the Khazars* was a warning to small nations about their vulnerability, *The Landscape Painted with Tea,* published one year before the fall of the Berlin Wall, spoke of name, language, and identity changes. In the midst of war and chaos, the hero of *The Inner Side of the Wind* fretfully builds as the Austrians and Ottomans repeatedly destroy Belgrade in their fight for it. Leander hopes that those who are destroying will tire first. Pavić writes a tribute to that part of the Balkans where Eastern Christianity, Islam, and Judaism "have stewed, feuded and fermented for so many centuries" (Tešanović 262). It is also a tribute to the author's nation which in the words of St. Sava, the twelfth-century Serbian prince and bishop, is condemned to be for the West forever in the East and for the East forever in the West.

In 1989, when Pavić was asked how he viewed the approaching end of the second millennium, he answered that while there is ample reason for despair, he still has hope for the end of the twentieth-century. He justified his hope by saying: "I learned that the world is better than it appears on the TV news hours and in the newspapers, that people are better than their politicians, and that we all need culture more than we think. I also found out that the culture of a people is more important than their state and that in this world there is far more beauty than love . . . This beauty created by man, and also a part of the beauty which exists in Nature, shall perhaps help us overcome the lack of love and thus survive the year 2000."[3]

NOTES

[1]Jasmina Tešanović, *Short History of a Book; Critics' Choice on "Dictionary of the Khazars" by Milorad Pavić* (Vršac: KOV, 1991), 214; hereafter cited parenthetically.

[2]See Tešanović 48, 20, 113, 118, 62, 182, 184, and W. S. di Piero, rev. of *The Inner Side of the Wind, New York Times Book Review* 13 June 1993.

[3]Ana Šomlo, *Hazari ili obnova vizantijskog romana* (Belgrade: BIGZ, Srpska književna zadruga, Narodna knjiga, 1990), 149.

Acknowledgments

I thank all the contributors to this issue, with a special appreciation to Rachel Kilbourn Davis who not only contributed an essay but initially edited the entire manuscript as well.

The editor would also like to express her sincere gratitude to Jasmina Mihajlović in Belgrade and Robert L. McLaughlin for their help in making this issue possible.

As a Writer, I Was Born Two Hundred Years Ago

Thanassis Lallas

Milorad means *beloved* in his language. Milorad Pavić is unknown to many of you. He is a Serbian writer, nominated several times for the Nobel Prize for Literature. According to *Paris Match*, "he is undoubtedly the first writer of the twenty-first century." Pavić is the writer who managed to construct a novel that anyone can read in the same way he or she observes a statue. He lives in Belgrade. We spent three days with him, just talking. The following is the result of our conversations.

First Meeting

Belgrade. It is getting dark. There isn't much traffic on the streets. Asking her way around, Gaga finds a flower shop that is still open and buys some flowers. The cab leaves us at Braće Baruh Street, number 2. The building is old and its main door is ajar. We enter. On the right side are some mailboxes for the residents. They are all the same size, except the last one, which is surprisingly huge, almost as big as all the rest of the boxes together. For the first time I saw the name Milorad Pavić written on that huge mailbox. According to the *Sunday Times*, *Milorad Pavić* is a writer who, together with Borges, Nabokov, Singer, Calvino, and Eco, composes the literary treasure of our half of the century.

The first floor, an old wooden white door. We ring the bell and find ourselves in front of the double of Lech Wałesa! "Lech Wałesa's face is a bit more swollen," notices Gaga. "His eyes are less intense," I add, completing her thought. Pavić, dressed in a dark blue suit and wearing a tie, leads us to the high-ceilinged living room. There are some white armchairs in the room. On the walls there are some drawings by his son Ivan, who lives and paints in Paris. Pavić, the writer "who thinks the way we dream," offers us a drink and persuades us to taste some of his excellent cookies. He introduces us to Mrs. Pavić. We shake hands and Pavić talks to himself, while we look at the editions of his books, translated into every language except Chinese and Norwegian. "It was very difficult to get a positive review in my country, that's why I married a critic!" We all laugh, and he writes a dedication on a copy of his book *Dictionary of the*

Khazars: "To the Golden Girl! Milorad Pavić." He gives the book to his compatriot and also his student at the university, Gaga Rosić, who wonderfully translates his books into Greek. We leave for the opening of a new cinema in the center of Belgrade.

He drives like a child. The car in his hands seems like a toy. He drives against the traffic on all the one-way streets and shows us the house where he spent his childhood, a two-storied house with a garden and trees in its backyard. He always parks his car far away from his destination. This makes me curious. It seems as if he is in his own world all the time. Wearing his gabardine, he walks in small steps toward the center of the city. "This is the National Theater," he says to me as we pass the streetlights. In the big square, opposite the National Theater, many people recognize him. Pavić keeps on walking, pretending not to notice anything. He has probably noticed everything, but until he finds himself lying on his back on his bed, he cannot prove it.

He is always writing, lying on his back on his bed. He keeps notes in a small notebook and writes in it every time an idea comes to his mind. "It is nearly always so—fifty/fifty," he says. "Every time you catch some beauty from the vast world around you, another piece of beauty sinks untouchable in the blue waters of the Danube." My first meeting with Pavić ends with a handshake outside the Metropol Hotel. During this first meeting, I continuously observed him and we exchanged very few words. Our next meeting was scheduled for the next day at ten o'clock, at his apartment.

Second Meeting

THANASSIS LALLAS: I was carefully observing you yesterday. Your reactions were like those of a child. You did not give me the impression that you are the most important Serbian writer at present.

MILORAD PAVIĆ: The truth is that this is the way I feel. I try to see the world as if I see it for the first time. I try to forget all the books I've written in order to keep on living and writing.

TL: Do the books that you've written prevent you from continuing to write?

MP: If you do not forget the books you've already written, you cannot write new ones, because every new book is like returning to the beginning.

TL: The beginning and the end must be the biggest trouble to a novelist.

MP: I have tried my best to eliminate or to destroy the beginning and the end of my novels. *The Inner Side of the Wind*, for example, has two beginnings. You start reading this book from the side you want. In *Dictionary of the Khazars* you can start with whatever story you want. But writing it, you have to keep in mind that every entry has to be read before and after every other entry in the book. I managed to avoid, at least until now, the old way of reading, which means reading from the classical beginning to the classical end.

TL: Do we suppress the classical notion of the beginning and the end when there is more than one beginning and more than one ending?

MP: Even if we do not suppress them, we liberate them, and we liberate ourselves along with them.

TL: Do you believe there is one ending for each beginning?

MP: No, this is not true.

TL: Yet we say that whatever begins with birth, ends with death.

MP: Exactly. But since in my life I cannot avoid this one-way street, I try at least to avoid it in my novels, to the extent that I can.

TL: Is fantasy the weapon that one uses to fight against the "facts" of life?

MP: There are no definite borders between the real and the imaginary world. A free man suppresses the borders between those two worlds. As a writer I have this feeling quite often. I actually believe that the most important ability that a writer can possess is the ability to reach a certain point where reality and fantasy reflect as one the same world. Then things develop normally. They develop the way they should.

TL: I was watching you drive yesterday. I've noticed a habit of yours; you drove against the traffic on all the one-way streets. Are you not afraid? In the sense that when somebody drives against the traffic, he exposes himself to great danger?

MP: I've been wondering for a long time: "How do you know that what you are writing is good or will turn out to be good and be accepted?" For a long time I used to believe that when what you love the most is written, it turns out to be the best. Today I know that this is not true.

TL: According to you, what is the truth in order for someone to reach the best?

MP: I believe that the best will appear as soon as your fear is maximized. The closer we get to something that we are afraid of, the closer we approach the best. Fear leads us to excess, real excess. This is where one can find the truth. Such a challenge is very valuable in order to find the truth.

TL: So you are actually saying that fear leads us to creativity.

MP: Exactly. Just fear. Fear is leading us. Fear leads us correctly. In literature, of course.

TL: Is there any fear dominating you?

MP: I've been dominated by all sorts of fears, by all kinds of fears. I carried them with me through my whole life like a cross. Fear is actually a writer's most devoted friend. I still feel fear as intensely as when I was a child. My fear will never become old. As a child, I was so much afraid of loneliness. I was afraid of the empty house in the middle of the night. I was afraid of the backyard of the house where I grew up—I showed you that house yesterday. I was afraid of it, especially when the lights were turned out.

TL: Actually, all of your fears seem to be concentrated inside or around the house.

MP: Maybe that explains why I try to construct my novels the way I would build a house. Maybe because this fear of the empty house—one that I am trying to get over—exists permanently. *The Inner Side of the Wind* has two entrances and one inner yard. The *Dictionary of the Khazars* is also a huge house, which shocks people because of its many entrances and exits. There are doors everywhere. Your entrance into or exit from the house depends on your desire.

TL: What did your father do for a living?

MP: It may sound quite strange, but he constructed houses. Real houses. I did not like it. I would have preferred that he was a sculptor or a painter. He spent his free time on sculpture and painting.

TL: Why didn't he become a sculptor?

MP: It was the time between two world wars: the most appropriate time for someone to make too much profit! At least you could profit more constructing houses than by working as a sculptor or a painter. But he was never successful in building. He was best as a sculptor.

TL: How is it possible for someone who constructs buildings all day to come back home and make sculptures?

MP: My father was capable of doing thousands of things at the same time. Maybe he was more afraid than I was.

TL: And your mother? What did she do?

MP: She taught philosophy. She could speak smoothly. She told many different stories about members of our family, especially about the older ones.

TL: Can you recognize in yourself any similarities to your father or mother? In other words, what did you inherit from them?

MP: Nothing actually. It is just that sometimes, when I look at myself in the mirror I get the feeling that I see my father instead of me.

TL: So you do look like your father.

MP: That is what I am telling you. I've inherited nothing from him. We just look alike.

TL: Are there any people who have influenced your life?

MP: My ancestors.

TL: What do you mean?

MP: I am talking about my father's family. In the last two hundred years many members of my family were writers. It was in the eighteenth century when the first Pavić published a poetry collection. He was a monk in Buda. He knew Latin and published books in Latin and in his native language as well. And then, in every other generation you can find at least one Pavić who was a writer.

TL: What did you want to be before you decided to be a writer?

MP: I always wanted to be a writer. I still remember myself saying that I wanted to be one. I believe it was my natural environment that pushed me in this direction, because I grew up surrounded by writers.

TL: Do you remember the first writer you admired? Did you happen to say to yourself, "I'm going to be like him?"

MP: Yes. My uncle Nikola Pavić. He was a poet. But I did not learn about the first writers by reading. I learned by listening to other people talking. Actually, I relied upon two things: on the Serbian oral tradition (popular songs and proverbs) and on the church orations and cultural tradition of Byzantium. In both cases the oral element was important.

TL: How important was this oral tradition to your writing style?

MP: I believe that a phrase must first of all sound nice. When it sounds nice, it is automatically a good sentence. When somebody thinks about literature the way I do, it means that he has in mind not his reader but his listener. So a new problem is formed—you must not let your listener fall asleep.

TL: Are there any writers who make you fall asleep?

MP: Many of them. I avoid reading their books. I truly believe that Homer has the right to fall asleep, but he does not have the right to make his listeners fall asleep.

TL: When does a piece of writing become boring for a reader?

MP: When it does not demand that the reader use his own fantasy. According to me, a piece of writing does not refer just to the mind of the reader. That means that it cannot be just a process of the mind for the writer.

TL: What else does somebody need except the "mind"?

MP: Love! In other words you must be in love with what you are writing. You also must not obstruct the eternal energy if your writing has a chance to become its path. If you let this energy flow through your book, it is certain that the writing will find its own way to the reader.

TL: Did you ever catch yourself being tired of beauty?

MP: Yes, I used the phrase *tired of beauty* once. I'm surprised you posed such a question. As long as one can be tired of love, one can be tired of beauty as well.

TL: The standard of beauty in art is perhaps the beauty of nature?

MP: No work of art is enough to describe the beauty of nature. But the beauty of art is a part of the beauty in nature.

TL: What is the meaning of art for you?

MP: A bird with long legs, standing in the gutter. It must move continuously in order not to sink. If art stops moving, even for a moment, it will drown.

TL: When you are writing, do you think about the reader?

MP: While writing, you never have the time to think about the reader. You do have a certain obligation, though, toward your future reader and toward yourself "not to lie." While writing I try not to forget the words of the great novelist Ivo Andrić. "The main intention while writing," he used to say, "must be to make the reader cry, not you, the author!"

TL: Have you found out what makes somebody special in whatever he might be doing?

MP: Persistence to start with. Though in my case luck helped too. For a while I was not able to publish my writing in my own country. There were political reasons for it. So I could have stopped writing, despite my desire and love for it. Finally, I was lucky. I did not do that. I did not stop. I was dealing with literature as a teacher. I was writing about literature to avoid becoming bitter. And finally I started publishing fiction, although very late in my life. If this had not happened, today I might have been a violin virtuoso.

TL: Why the violin especially?

MP: I finished my studies in violin but I did not do anything more than that.

TL: When did you start publishing?

MP: Unfortunately, I had to wait until 1967, when the appropriate conditions were established that allowed me to publish my first book in my country. I was thirty-eight years old then. So I never had a literary start. I was in that moment what I am today. But luck is something that will not follow you as the tail follows a cow. Actually I have the worst position among all living authors. I am the best known writer of the most hated nation in the world.

TL: What could you say concerning the Serbian nation?

MP: That it is a nation without any international financial support, without any international religious support. Their isolationism is like that of the U.S. and Russia, but it has to be paid for much more. It is a nation deprived of memory. They never forgive, but forget immediately. They are good warriors, but the worst diplomats. They win wars, and lose battles. They suffer from reductionism; they always count who is a patriot and who is not. The accent is on the word *not*. They always have their enemies in mind and they do not care a lot for their friends. They had a state beginning in the tenth century (as well as a literature), but they can hardly keep it and easily lose it. They are talented. From this nation came Tesla, Pupin, Mileva Einstein, Ivo Andrić, Charles Simic, Danilo Kiš, Makaveyev, Vasko Popa, Vlada Divac, and Dušan Kovačević, an excellent playwright and co-author of Kusturica's last film, etc.

TL: Do you actually think that a great writer is born or made?

MP: As a writer, I was born two hundred years ago. In the biggest libraries of Europe one can find books written by my ancestors, as you know. It was my ancestors who supported me each time I began writing something. I even wrote some poems for them using the old language so that they could understand me.

TL: What do you think their opinion would be, if they could read your books?

MP: I think they would be very confused.

TL: When somebody reads your novels, he or she feels that they are the creation of a mathematician's structured mind.

MP: The film "Byzantium Blue," based on my short story "The Wedgewood Tea Set," talks about mathematics. It claims that the mathematics that we use now is unique. During the sixth and seventh centuries the Byzantine world had a different conception of numbers. Through my story, I bring out the Byzantine conception of numbers. What we usually call mathematics is based mainly on three elements: the number 1, the full stop, and the moment of the present. Now in the Byzantine world they ask: How is it possible to have as a basis for mathematics three elements that cannot be measured? So, if you follow Byzantine mathematics in your comparison, you can conclude my writings are the creation of a mathematician's structured mind.

TL: What does a writer do, in general? Does he or she bring order to the chaos of the world?

MP: I am not sure whether you can name as a work of art something that brings order into the chaos that surrounds you. I never wanted to bring order into something that I considered the work of God. In fact, I want to express this chaos through my books. Nothing else. For me that is enough.

TL: Do you think that by expressing this chaos you bring God to the surface?

MP: Not hiding this chaos is one way to approach God.

TL: I thought that we reach God by dreaming.

MP: Dreams are also a huge chaos. You are thinking correctly. Besides, "God exists at the bottom of each dream," as I say in one of my books. Now I have the impression that if we reach the bottom of our dream, we can see our death there. And awaking, forget what we have seen.

TL: Can you define God?

MP: When *Dictionary of the Khazars* was published, a fellow professor at a university in Israel asked me the same question: "In your book you talk about a Christian devil, a Jewish devil, and a Muslim one. Where is God in your book?" "The Book is God," I answered him. Not of course my book, but the one with a capital *B*, and I really do not know anything more to tell you about it!

TL: Where does God exist?

MP: I think He exists inside us. Every day God teaches us something.

TL: When the devil himself interferes, does he transform God into different religions?

MP: Yes. That is why there are three devils in my book.

TL: Isn't it an injustice that some people have the talent to create and some not?

MP: That is happiness, that somebody is able to create something that another cannot. Look out of the window a little bit. Everything is different. That is beauty. Each one of us has different abilities. I am incapable of doing something else. I do not know how to build houses as my father did, for example.

TL: You are, however, one of those exceptional people who are able to mark their time with their actions.

MP: That is not something that I own. That is something that I have inherited. The power, which existed for a long time, has become more concentrated as the years go by. I am just a sort of instrument where the energy and power of a family reaches its most intense expression. Until now.

TL: Have you ever thought about what is actually the destination of your existence?

MP: To rescue as many pieces of beauty as possible. Tons of beauty sink every day in the Danube. Nobody notices. The one who notices it must do something to rescue it. To rescue as much beauty as he can. That is actually the role of an artist. He is the lifeguard of beauty.

TL: Have you ever thought of giving up writing a novel before you finished it?

MP: For each writer there are two moments of crisis while writing a novel. The first moment comes very soon. It is the moment when the writer has all things concerning his novel in his head. But not the novel itself on paper. In that moment you are faster than the novel is. It is inert and you have to push it ahead. And most of all, you must not let it get behind you. The second moment comes during the zenith of writing. It is the moment when you have to have absolute control of it, but in this particular moment the novel is ahead because it already has its own flow and speed. It is the moment where the novel overcomes the writer. It is faster than he and has more energy. It is actually the most difficult moment because it finds you very tired by your effort to approach this zenith. Yet you must put all your efforts together in order to retain balance and keep control of the novel. You cannot allow a premature child to be born. If you can overcome those two moments, the result will be good. You will have written a healthy novel, and you will be sick for the next two years. After the *Dictionary of the Khazars,* I was terribly sick for two whole years.

TL: Can you imagine life without dreaming?

MP: I imagine you are talking about the destruction of life. For me, to dream means to live.

TL: Is dreaming necessary in life?

MP: Is life necessary in dreaming? Through dreaming man can get in touch again with his first kindness. Through his dreams, man can experience again the kindness he once lost.

TL: Have you ever thought, "why do we exist?"

MP: The answer to this question is hidden in my novel *The Inner Side of the Wind:* Time is the creation of Satan; Eternity is the creation of God. At the point where Time and Eternity intersect is life. The moment of the present is the moment when Time stops to be blessed by Eternity. In the universe there are maybe zones where Time never meets Eternity; that is why this very moment is missing. Life does not exist there. Life exists just in the moments of the present.

TL: Do you actually believe that a great piece of writing is written by a great soul or by a great mind?

MP: I personally believe that great writings are the result of the soul's many trips to the mind, as well as the mind's trips to the soul. That's how a writing can actually breathe.

TL: Is it necessary to be a talented reader, as you said, in order to understand a talented writer's work?

MP: If a writer's piece of work is read by an untalented reader, it is not going to be understood. But, fortunately, we have now in the world more talented readers than talented reviewers. And more talented readers than talented authors, as well. Only the untalented readers have special characteristics. The best and most talented reader in our century was Borges. Anybody can attend a university.

But it is not possible to learn in school how to compose the *The Magic Flute*. Nobody can teach a reader how to read between the lines and through the words.

TL: Can you give a definition of what talent is?

MP: It is just an intellectual or spiritual vitamin. The world suffers from vitamin deficiency on the spiritual level as well. What actually matters is whether the vitamin that one writer has is the one that the world needs at this time. So if it happens that you offer the appropriate vitamin at the right place and the right time, the world will turn out to be a huge uterus and will absorb you. Talent is just a vitamin. Or sperm. It is possible to offer your kind of vitamin at the wrong time. That's what we consider "lost talents." For a writer to reach fame's sky, that is, to be read, he must go through what I call the seven celestial customs. He has to be accepted by publishers, by readers, and by reviewers. The moment a writer dies, he goes through the next celestial custom. The world is almost fed with the vitamins that the deceased writer offers. The world feels it does not need him anymore. There might be another time when the world will again need the same vitamins. And that is what we call resurrection. A posthumous rebirth, the comeback of an author.

TL: What is the next celestial custom?

MP: The moment the writer's language dies, since languages die as well. The writer's language needs to be adopted by another language. Will it make it? Today, nobody can read Horatio in the language in which he wrote. Nothing lives for ever. Eternity is God's present.

TL: Why do people deny God the right to sin?

MP: Because that is their only way to comprehend their differences from God. Another question would be why people expect another person to sin. Maybe because that is their only way to explain war. Their only way.

TL: If I could give you the chance to meet another writer by the end of our meeting, which one would you prefer to meet?

MP: That is a very good question. I once happened to meet somebody that I had always wanted to meet. I always wanted to meet D. M. Thomas, the author of the novel *The White Hotel*. I met him in Canada. He looked just as nice as his book.

TL: If Borges were here, what would you like to find out about him? What would you ask him?

MP: Nothing. I would prefer to listen to him.

Third Meeting

Our third meeting with Pavić takes place in a marvelous restaurant. Our dinner begins with a toast.

MP: I am really glad to have here with me today's descendants of Homer.

TL: What does Homer mean to you?

MP: I am always trying to act as an ancient epic poet. To act the way Homer did. Not as Homer at the moment when the *Iliad* and the *Odyssey* were written. The person who wrote down those two masterpieces defined their beginning and their ending, while the epic poets in Greece, as in Serbia (Homer included), were singing a different song every time. They started from a certain point that they chose and they ended when something new was starting. Cheers! For me it is the oldest lesson that I know in the history of literature. Of course, it is difficult to apply this lesson in practice. Actually this job can turn out to be even more difficult, if you must be both the epic poet, fashioning your rhapsodies in the oral way, and, at the same time, the one who writes down these rhapsodies in order to fix them in the shape of the book.

TL: Do you appeal to a public of listeners or readers?

MP: I appeal to listeners always. To me the best literature is oral. I've told you already in our last meeting. My teachers were the oral literature of the Balkans and the Byzantine church orators, Chrysostomos, for instance. In France they felt it greatly, one journalist named me the New Chrysostomos. To listen to a well-tempered sentence is like walking through beautiful rooms and halls.

TL: Name a lovely sound to me.

MP: The sound of the violin in music by Mozart or Bach. For me great literature competes in sound with a musical synthesis of Mozart.

TL: Did you study music for a long time?

MP: I was ready to start a career as a violin soloist, when I finally decided to become a writer. I knew by heart the violin concerto by Max Bruch.

TL: After trying various tastes, finally we find the one we like the most.

MP: Our environment, which has already decided for us about some of the tastes in the past, pushes us. We all believe for a moment that what we like, others like too. We think our children will like the same things we do. My father, for example, always believed that I would like to become a good designer.

TL: A great Greek writer, Stratis Tsirkas, said to me once, "I need to find the end of my story, then everything comes along."

MP: I do not see it this way. I want to let the reader free to enter anywhere he chooses and get out as he pleases.

TL: While you are writing a novel, do you always continue from where you stopped the day before?

MP: No. I never write like this. There are many different levels. Slowly they all fit within a framework. It is very difficult for someone to understand my writing relying only on the mental element. A novel has its own life. [He takes a small, green notebook out of his pocket. He has written something by hand on its cover.] This is my new novel, *Last Love in Constantinople*. This is how my new novel starts. In this little notebook I write whatever I think concerning the new novel and everything that is worth keeping. *Dictionary of the Khazars* was a notebook of a thousand pages as well.

TL: Can you copy a phrase of this little notebook onto a blank piece of paper?

MP: Why not? Here you are! Now you've got a sentence of my future book. To understand how somebody writes a novel, you must feel the breath of the book. Every single book breathes. A novel is born exactly as a baby is; it is a child, or a human being. This small green notebook is nothing else but the embryo of a future novel.

TL: How do you understand that is breathing?

MP: If you do not want to bore the reader, you have to address mutually different levels of his mind: his intellect, intuition, emotion, imagination, his introvert and extrovert intentions. If you, as a writer, act like that, your book will breathe like a human being or alternatively will put its heavenly letters and human letters in the foreground.

TL: Could a great writer disappear if he is read by untalented readers?

MP: Of course. You have an example in front of you! For a very long time I was among the least read writers in Yugoslavia. This was changed only by the new generation of readers.

TL: And in what way does this new generation differ?

MP: The new generation is capable of listening to my writings. And loving them, because estimation is not important. Jasmina, my wife (she is very young), belongs to this generation. It is strange. Young people consider me as a writer of their generation! The most precise comments on my writings were made by the generation born in the sixties.

TL: Do you mind that I ask questions all the time?

MP: On the contrary. Actually life is interesting because there are questions.

TL: Are there answers for all the questions?

MP: In the world there are more answers than questions.

TL: Does the development of television, of pictures, coincide with the decadence of books?

MP: In my opinion the book is going through a period of decadence and crisis, but the novel is not. If there is something in crisis, it is the way of reading. That is why I try to push the reader to be more active. I found the solution in the other forms of art. I truly believe there are seven muses. All of them together form a strong art! When a muse finds herself in a difficult position, she asks for a solution from the others. The relationship between them is very important. That's why I searched for the solution among the other arts.

TL: And did you find it?

MP: I do not know. Throughout my research I discovered that some of the seven muses are evolving and others are not. For the moment. Later they change places.

TL: Which ones are the evolving arts at this moment?

MP: The evolving arts at this moment are the ones that allow users to approach them from any one of their different sides. I like to call them reversible arts.

TL: Name a reversible art for me.

MP: Architecture, sculpture.

TL: And a nonreversible art?

MP: Music, literature. I always believed that I would be able to transform literature, which is a nonreversible art, into a reversible one.

TL: All this is brilliant, but it seems to me like a trick.

MP: Tricks are the beginning and the end of the classical novel as well. In the oldest world literature, in oral literature, there is always a new start and always another ending to the narration. Or there is one and the same beginning for different stories. In life you never find such things as the beginning and the end of any story. But in literature it can't be a trick if the death or life of the hero depends on the way of reading. All these activate the reader. From a passive reader-listener, you transform him to an active one. It requires the reader's participation in the novels. In one such novel the hero, a lady, falls in love with the reader. So the question is: What will the reader do? That's the question. Will he respond to her love?

TL: Have you ever been a communist?

MP: I was once asked by a French journalist whether I am a communist, and I replied, "I am the last Byzantine." He did not publish this answer. He probably concluded it is worse to be a Byzantine than a communist.

TL: Name an insult to life for me.

MP: To destroy everything that you've found.

TL: Is this your reaction to what is happening to your country today?

MP: The only thing left for me to do is to build even during the war. Like my hero from *The Inner Side of the Wind*, who is building while all others around him in the war are destroying everything.

TL: Yet the past is full of wars, and I am afraid that the future will be too. How do you explain that?

MP: There is an old myth that we read often in many books. According to this myth, a human being is a man from the waist up and an animal from the waist down!

TL: Is there any hope?

MP: I do not know if what I will say is the answer, but the fact is that never in history have such a great number of books been read as now. My publishers say I have some five million readers. Many writers have more than I have, of course, but even this number is bigger than the number of soldiers in any army in the world. This means something. Perhaps, these readers, not only mine of course, are an assurance that love will overcome savagery in this world where there is always more beauty than love, always more good novels than we will have time to read in peace and love. Let us for an instant count readers, not voters.

TL: And now the final question: during all these days I observed that only women are around you. Rarely does somebody see a man. Why? Is this a choice or an accident?

MP: Their choice. For me, a woman is a "quality" that needs the male "quantity" to become a piece of art. "He was half of something. A strong, beautiful, talented half of something that was perhaps, even stronger, greater and more beautiful than he. He was, then, the magical half of something magnificent and unfathomable. She was a complete whole. A small, disoriented, not very strong or harmonious whole, but a whole all the same" (*The Inner Side of the Wind*).

The Beginning and the End of Reading—The Beginning and the End of the Novel

Milorad Pavić

The novel is like cancer.
It lives on its metastases and is fed on them.

Long ago I started putting to myself a question: Where are the beginning and the end of the novel? Does the novel start with Homer? And does the story about the novel end before the story of the story? That is to say, has the novel reached its end in our times we call post-historical, postcommunist, postfeminist, and postmodernist? Borges was eager to see the faces of his first hundred readers. My eagerness is different. Are we all standing before a challenge to see the faces of the last hundred readers or, to be less pathetic, the faces of the last hundred readers of the novel?

Answering that, let us put the question of when, where, and in which part of the text the reading of a novel starts, and when and where the reading of a novel ends. With some novels, it is the first and the last sentence, and that is clear forever. A good example is Miloš Crnjanski: "A big blue circle. A star in it." That is the unforgettable beginning of the *Migrations* that also has an undeniable and unforgettable end in the last sentence: "Migrations do exist. Death does not." But this is not always the case with other novels. Let us take *War and Peace*: it ends long before the end of the text. Does *Anna Karenina* really end with the toothache of Vronsky? Where and when does Joyce's *Ulysses* begin? It has one of the most magnificent finales in literature: a feminine ending to a masculine book. How are the beginning and the end of a novel, the beginning and the end of reading, conditioned by what Jasmina Mihajlović calls "reading and sex"? Must the novel have an end? And what in fact is the end of a novel, of a literary work? Is there unavoidably only one? How many ends can a novel or a play have?

To those questions I have found some answers while writing my books. Long ago I came to understand that the arts are "reversible" and "nonreversible." Some arts are reversible and enable the recipient to approach the work from various sides, or even to go around it and have a good look at it, changing the spot of the perspective, and the direction of his looking at it according to his own preference, as is the case with architecture, sculpture, or painting. Other, nonreversible arts, such as music and literature, look like one-way roads on which everything moves from the beginning to the end, from birth to death. I have always wished to make literature, which is a nonreversible art, a reversible one. Therefore, my novels have no end in the classical meaning of the word.

For instance, *Dictionary of the Khazars* is "a lexicon novel in 100,000 words," and according to the alphabet of various languages, the novel ends differently. The original version of *Dictionary of the Khazars*, printed in the Cyrillic alphabet, ends with a Latin quotation: "sed venit ut illa impleam et confirmem, Mattheus." My novel in Greek translation ends with a sentence: "I have immediately noticed that there are three fears in me, and not one." The English, Hebrew, Spanish, and Danish versions of *Dictionary of the Khazars* end in this way: "Then, when the reader returned, the entire process would be reversed, and Tibbon would correct the translation based on the impressions he had derived from this reading walk." The Serbian version printed in the Latin alphabet, the Swedish version published at Nordsteds, and the Dutch, Czech, and German versions, all end with the following sentence: "That look wrote Cohen's name in the air, lighted the wick, and lit up her way to the house." The Hungarian version of *Dictionary of the Khazars* ends with the sentence: "He simply wanted to draw your attention to what your nature is like." The Italian and Catalan versions end in this way: "Indeed the Khazar jar serves to this day, although it has long since ceased to exist." The Japanese version, published by Tokyo Zogen Sha, ends with the sentence: "The girl had given birth to a fast, quick daughter—her death; in that death her beauty had been divided in whey and curdled milk, and at the bottom a mouth was seen keeping the root of reeds."

My second novel, *Landscape Painted with Tea* (comparable to a crossword puzzle), brings the portraits of the book's characters into the first plan if read vertically. If the same chapters are read horizontally (in the "classical way"), they foreground the plot of the novel and its development. Let us discuss the end of the novel in this case as well. First, this novel ends in one way if it is read by a female reader and in another way if the reader is a man. Of course, the ends of this novel differ from each other depending as well on whether the novel is read vertically or horizontally. *Landscape Painted with Tea*, if read horizontally, ends with the sentence: "The reader cannot be so stupid as not to remember what happened next to Atanas Svilar, who, for a time, was called Razin." *Landscape Painted with Tea* if read vertically, ends with the sentence: "I ran into the church."

After the novel-dictionary and the novel-crossword puzzle, I tried again to transfer the novel into the row of the reversible arts. It is *The Inner Side of the Wind, or the Novel of Hero and Leander.* A Clepsydra-Novel. It has two front pages, and it is best to read it one and a half times, as the famous archeologist Dragoslav Srejović says. The end is in the middle, where the lovers of this mythical tale, Hero and Leander, meet. If you start reading from Leander's side, the end of the novel will be the following: "It was 12:05 when the towers blew up in a terrible explosion, carrying away the fire in which Leander's body disappeared." If you read *The Inner Side of the Wind* from Hero's side, the end of the novel will be like this: "According to the crazed lieutenant, it was not until the evening of the third day that Hero's head cried out in a terrible, deep, masculine voice."

My most recent book, *Last Love in Constantinople,* is, in fact, a tarot-novel consisting of twenty-two chapters corresponding to the cards of the Major Arcana. With the help of the tarot, it is possible to foretell the future, and *Last Love in Constantinople* has several keys, like the cards themselves. In other words, this novel is a direction for tarot fortune-telling and can be "used" in different ways. It is possible to read the meaning of the tarot cards into the chapters of the novel that bear the same appellations and numbers as the individual cards. It is also possible to read the sense of the chapters of the novel into the meaning of the cards during fortune-telling. The novel can be used regardless of the cards. Also, according to the directions for the tarot given in the content, you can first throw the cards and then read the chapters in the way cards fall on the table.

Therefore, we can conclude from the described novels that we can come out not only through one exit but also through other exits that are far from each other. *Landscape Painted with Tea* has two different ends and *The Inner Side of the Wind* has two different beginnings. Just like a house, *The Inner Side of the Wind* has two entrances and an exit in the middle, in its inner part, but that exit leads into a closed garden, into a closed courtyard, where instead of a waterfall the reader comes upon a sea he is going to swim over, just as Leander swims over the Greek myth.

Slowly I lose from my sight the difference between the house and the book, and this is, perhaps, the most important thing I have to say in this text. But let us turn to the more general question often raised in these days: Is the end of the novel approaching? Is the end of the novel before us or already behind us, ask those people who are followers of the thought that we are already living in post-historical times. Is it also a postromanesque time? Have we passed through the finish without even noticing, and now all of us are running together in an already finished race? I believe it cannot be said so, unless we are struck by some nuclear cataclysm of cosmic proportions. Rather, I am more inclined to say that we are at the end of one manner of reading. It is the crisis of our way of reading the novel and not the novel itself. The novel as a one-way road is in a crisis. Something else is in a crisis as well. It is the graphic sight of the novel. This is to say: the book is in crisis.

I tried to change the way of reading by increasing the role and responsibility of the reader in the process of creating a novel (let us not forget that in the world there are many more talented readers than talented literary critics). I have left to them the decision about the choice of the plot and the development of the situations in the novel: where the reading will begin, and where it will end; the decision about the destiny of the main characters. But to change the way of reading, I had to change the way of writing. Therefore, these lines should not be understood exclusively as a talk about the form of the novel. At the same time, this is also a talk about its content. In fact, the content of any novel has been, so to speak, on Procrustes' bed for two thousand years, always subjected to the merciless model of form. I believe that an end has come to this. Each novel should select its specific form, each story can search for, and find, its adequate form. The ends of the novel today behave like a delta. They fork at the mouth into the sea of reading, where the novel and the river lose their names. That delta, which in the postmodernist novel behaves like a many-way road, has a very handy and already built-up riverbed. This is, as Robert Coover and Jasmina Mihajlović say in their essays, a computer-simulated space and a computerized fake eternity. This can be used practically. The literature created in such a way, without the beginnings and without the ends we have gotten used to in the printed book, is written everywhere in the world today. Let us mention only Joyce the younger or Caroline Gayer. The computer novel is coming to us as hyperfiction and belongs to the sphere of virtual reality, and its writers are called electronic writers. Here the novel really becomes a child of the space; it can break free of the conditions and laws of Gutenberg's galaxy and emerge into a new galaxy path that has no more connection with a printed book. My novels, as well as the novels of some other writers, at this moment are being transferred to computer CD-ROM. *Last Love at Constantinople* is a novel easily conceived of and realized as a video game, such as one of those computer games with cards or one of those in which roads are to be found for the future. Such games fill the computers of young people all over the world. One should not fear a future that digitally knocks at the writer's door. I am looking forward to it.

Applying the same principle to a dramatic text, I have written a hyperplay called *For Ever and a Day*. It has a specification: "a theater menu" (as a "menu" in restaurants but also as "a menu" in a computer). That love story has three different beginnings, let us say three different starters, one main course, and three different ends, or desserts (a tragic outcome, a happy ending, and an ecological ending). Or, if you prefer, coffee without sugar, cake, or an apple. Nine theaters can play it without repeating the same version of the text. Out of this hyperplay, it is possible to make "an octopus" in film, the same way it is possible to make forty-seven films out of *Dictionary of the Khazars* (the novel has as many entries) that would last anywhere from three minutes to three-and-a-half hours and would require the engagement of forty-seven of the most famous directors, so that each of them, in his own part of the world and with his own cast, would shoot his own part. This would be the most expensive thing in the history of the film, but it would no longer be a film of the twentieth century.

Now at the end of our century it is the time to turn to the literature, theater, and film of the twenty-first century, and it is exactly the novel of today that introduces us to it. Therefore, the novel is not dead.

From Last Love in Constantinople

Milorad Pavić

Special Key

THE FOOL

In addition to his mother tongue, he also spoke Greek, French, Italian and Turkish; he was born in Trieste into a family of Serbian merchants and patrons of the theater, who had ships in the Adriatic and wheat and vineyards on the Danube; since childhood he had served in the unit of his father, French cavalry officer Haralampije Opujić; he knew that when charging on horseback or making love exhaling was more important than inhaling; he wore the splendid robes of a cavalryman; in the middle of winter he slept in the snow underneath the covered wagon rather than evict from it his Russian hound bitch and her litter, and in the middle of war he wept over his ruined yellow cavalier boots; he left the service in the infantry in order not to part from his cavalry gear; he was mad about beautiful horses and plaited their tails; he obtained silver dishware in Vienna, adored fancy dress balls, masquerades and fireworks and felt like a fish in water in drawing rooms and inns which had women and music.

His father used to say of him that he was as foolish as the first wind and was treading on the edge of a precipice; one minute he looked like his mother, the next like his grandfather and the next like his as yet unborn son or granddaughter. He was a most handsome man, taller than average, with a pale face, a dimple in his chin like a navel, and long thick hair as black as coal. He sported his finely twirled eyebrows like a mustache, and his mustache braided like a whip. On his endless military expeditions in Bavaria, Silesia and Italy, women admired his appearance, his horsemanship and long combed hair which, when he was tired of marches and the hardships of military life, he would dry by the hearth in a wayside inn; for fun they would dress him in women's clothes, stick a white rose in his hair, take his last cent at the tavern dance, give him their beds when he was ill or tired, and tearfully part with the cavalry units at the end of their winter respite. But he, he was wont to say that all his memories were in his food bag.

With an alien feminine smile on his face which was covered with a beard, young Opujić had crossed Europe, first as a boy with his father and later on his own in the French cavalry, traveling from Trieste, Venice and the Danube to Wagram and Leipzig, and had grown up in French military camps seeing a war every decade. In vain did his mother, Mrs. Paraskeva Opujić, send him "cakes with sad walnuts." The young Sofronije had his devil born to him before his child. One eye resembled his maternal grandmother's, who had been first and foremost Greek, and the other, his father's who was finally a Serb, and so young Opujić of Trieste saw the world cross-eyed. He would whisper:

"God is He Who He Is and I am who I am not."

Since early childhood he had carried a big, well-hidden secret. It was as if he felt there was something wrong with him as a human being. And it was natural that he wanted to change that. He wanted to do so badly, secretly, slightly embarrassed by this wish as if it were an unseemly visit. It was like a small pang of hunger which wails like an ache under the heart, or like a small ache which stirs like hunger in the soul. He did not remember exactly when this hidden longing for change had germinated inside him in the form of a bodiless energy. It happened as if he had been lying down, putting the tips of his middle finger and thumb together and, having nodded off, his arm slid off the bed and his fingers opened; he woke up with a start as though he had dropped something. In fact he had dropped himself. And the desire was there, this terrible, inexorable desire, so heavy that his right leg began to limp under the weight of it. . . . Another time it would seem to him that once long ago, he had discovered a soul floating in his plate of cabbage and had swallowed it.

And so it was that this secret, powerful thing took seed inside him. It is hard to say whether it was some kind of dizzying ambition connected with his father's military career and his own, some kind of unachievable longing for a new, real enemy and more purposeful alliances, or whether young Opujić wanted to reverse his relationship with his father, whether he loved the South and was lured, he of the imperial cavalry, by the fallen empires of the Balkans straight down to the Peloponnese, whether there was something in the blood of his Greek grandmother whose kin had amassed a fortune in trade between Europe and Asia, or whether it was some third happenstance and desire of the strong and turbid kind that ensure a man's face is never still. One minute it shows what he will look like in old age, the next what he looked like when he still had only his ears to take him through the world. Because a person's face breathes, it constantly inhales and exhales time.

From then onward, he worked steadily and prodigiously on bringing some fundamental change to his life, on making his lifelong dream come true, but he concealed it as best he could and others often found his actions puzzling.

Since then young Opujić had clandestinely carried a stone under his tongue like a secret, or more to the point a secret under his tongue like a stone, and his body underwent a change which was difficult to conceal and which gradually entered the realm of legend. It was noticed by women first, but they said nothing; then the men in his regiment openly began joking about it and the story spread all over the battlefield.

"He's like a woman. He can always do it!," the officers in his unit would say with a laugh. From that fateful day on, young Opujić traveled the world carrying his secret inside him, and his ever-ready male spear against his stomach. His eleventh finger unbended and started counting the stars. And it stayed that way. That did not bother him, he cheerfully rode his horse, but as for his secret, which might have been the cause of everything, he never said a word to anyone.

"He's fooling around," the officers in his unit said, as they marched steadily northwestward, in the direction of the unknown. He had embarked on this muddy military path at his father's wish, but now he hardly ever met his father, Captain Haralampije Opujić. Sometimes he remembered how at night, in their palace in Trieste, his father would lift his head from the pillow in the dark and listen for as long as could be.

"What is he listening to?," the boy would wonder in amazement. "The house? The war? Time? The sea? The French? His past? Or is he listening to the fear that can be heard from the future? Because the future is a stable out of which steps fear." Then his mother would suddenly lay his father's head back down on the pillow, so that he would not fall asleep stiff-necked and prick-eared. Terrifying to both his subordinates and his superiors, Opujić Senior had more love for the son than the mother. And he watched over him from the immense distance of his traveling battlefields. The son had not seen him for a long time and no longer knew what his father looked like or whether he would even recognize him. Let alone his mother in Trieste. It was not in vain that she said of her son:

"That one is a mixture of two bloods, Serbian and Greek. Awake he wants a rainbow, asleep a shop."

In fact, Lieutenant Sofronije Opujić was like his hounds. He heard and saw behind every corner. He was a veteran soldier: he had been knocked around in the victory at Ulm when he was fourteen and in the defeat in Prussia when he was twenty-two, but somewhere at the bottom of his soul he was still a crazy kid. He still saw his father behind one corner, and heard his mother behind the other. And he longed to meet them. He did not know who he was.

The First Key

THE MAGICIAN

"Would you like me to breastfeed you, mon lieutenant?," the girl asked the young Opujić in front of a tent on the outskirts of Ulm.

The lieutenant's eye had been caught by a bird which, in the fast wind above the tent, was flying in place as if riveted to it. Inside the tent a male voice was singing "Memories Are the Sweat of the Soul"; Opujić paid and walked in.

Standing on the table inside was a magician belted with a serpent devouring its own tail and he was singing. He had red roses in his hair. Finishing the song he aimed his high voice over his eyetooth as if targeting the bird above the tent and like an arrow his voice felled it. He then offered his services to the visitors. He could eat the name of anyone present for a quarter of a Napoléon d'or, and for only slightly more he could eat the surname as well.

"Whoever agrees will never again have the same name as when he entered! If you have your house keys, but your house was destroyed in war, I can reconstruct it for you down to the smallest detail simply by tossing the keys into a caldron, because each key creates an echo giving the ear a clear description of the shape and size of the room that the key guards."

Finally, the magician proposed that everyone present make a wish and he would help to make it come true, while mademoiselle Marie would gladly breastfeed each gentleman on his way out to thank him for having come. When it was Opujić's turn to make a wish, the magician went berserk, although he had not been informed of the audience's wishes; he quickly stepped down off the table, wishing to slip out of the tent.

"There is never enough wisdom in one day, just as there is never enough honey in one flower," thought Opujić and, catching up with the magician, grabbed him by the collar, sat himself down on a barrel and the magician on his knee.

"Stick out your tongue!," he ordered, and the magician quickly obeyed. "Is it raining?"

The magician nodded his head, even though it was not raining.

"Liar! You think you can fool around with me the way you do with that bird that flies in place above your tent? Do you know who I am?"

"Yes. That's why I wanted to run away. You are the son of Captain Haralampije Opujić of Trieste."

"Alright, now to the point. Can you or can you not make a wish come true?"

"Not in your case. But I do know where it can be done. I shall confide something to you. In a temple in Constantinople there is a pillar and attached to it is a copper shield. In the middle of that shield is a hole. Anyone who wants to make a wish must stick his thumb into the hole, close his fist around the thumb so that the fist never leaves the copper surface or the thumb the hole, and his wish will be fulfilled. But take care, sir, and beware. God, when He wants to punish someone, grants a wish and at the same time a terrible misfortune. Perhaps that is how He behaves toward his favorites, we don't know, but it's all the same to us anyway. So beware, Lieutenant. And don't forget the song "Memories Are the Sweat of the Soul."

"I don't believe a letter of what you're saying," replied the lieutenant, "but, all the same, I shall ask you one more question. Can you help me find my father? I haven't seen him since the stone got thin and the wind got heavy. I know that he was retreating towards Leipzig, but I don't know where he is now."

"That I cannot tell you, but what I can tell you is that a group of pickpockets and charlatans comes to this tent every Thursday to perform for the credulous. They enact the deaths of Captain Haralampije Opujić, your father."

"What do you mean deaths? He's alive!"

"I know he's alive, Lieutenant. But that is what the show is called: "The Three Deaths of Captain Opujić."

"I don't believe a letter of what you're saying," said the lieutenant once more and went off to bed.

But on Thursday he made some inquiries. In the magician's tent they really were performing the three deaths of Haralampije Opujić, his father. When young Opujić entered the tent, he asked the first masked actor he could lay his hands on how they dared to portray the death of a living man, but the actor calmly replied:

"You should know that this performance has been paid for personally by Captain Haralampije Opujić, who, sir, is a great admirer of the stage and a benefactor of the theater and comedy. He is now at war on the Elbe."

Knowing, of course, that the Trieste Opujićes had long been patrons of the theater, there was nothing else Lieutenant Sofronije could do but sit down and watch the play. When the people in the tent saw him they seemed to go rigid. They had recognized him. He told them they were free to begin.

First a man sporting someone else's beard and a French tunic appeared before them. He played Captain Opujić. Around him stood four women and a girl. One of them turned to him and said:

"Just so we immediately know where we stand, please bear in mind that I am not the spirit of your maternal great-grandfather, nor do I represent him in the form of a vampire. He died and nothing of him remains anymore, not his body or his spirit. But since deaths do not die, I am here. I am his death. And here next to me is the death of your great-great-grandmother. That is all that remains of her. Assuming we understand each other on this matter, we can move on. Your ancestors, then, had only one death each. But not you. You will have three deaths and here they are. This old lady here, this lovely woman and this girl here, they are your three deaths. Take a good look at them . . ."

"And that is all that will remain of me?"

"Yes, that is all. And it is not negligible. But, Captain, you will not notice your deaths, you will ride through them as you would through the gate of victory and you will continue your journey as though they never happened."

"But what will happen then after my third death, after I become a vampire for the third time?"

"For a while it will seem to both you and others that you are still alive, that nothing happened, until you experience your last love, until you catch the fancy of a woman with whom you could have offspring. That same instant you will disappear off the face of the earth, because the third soul cannot have offspring, just as someone who becomes a vampire for the third time cannot have children . . ."

Then the tent went dark and the growling of a bear could be heard. When the stage lights went back on, a man in a French tunic (embodying Captain Opujić) was wrestling for dear life with a huge bear. The man stabbed the animal with his knife and in its death agony it peed on and choked him. Both the man and the animal fell to the floor . . . The audience applauded, the actors gave each spectator a spoonful of boiled wheat for the soul of the dead man and someone observed that this was Captain Haralampije Opujić's first death. The second was to follow.

The beautiful woman of scene 1 stepped out in front of the audience and said:

"You people don't know how to measure your days. You measure them only in length and say they are twenty-four hours long. But the depth of your days is sometimes greater than their length and that depth can be a month or even a year long in days. That is why you do not know how to perceive your life. Not to mention death . . ."

At these words Captain Opujić came riding into the tent, scattering the spectators aside and holding a military field glass in his hand. Appearing behind him, in an Austrian tunic, was a man with a rifle. The Captain turned around and raised the field glass to his eye. That same moment the other man killed him through the field glass. The Captain fell off his horse and the animal, now free of its constraint, galloped out into the night . . . That was Captain Opujić's second death. Again they handed out spoonfuls of boiled wheat for his soul.

Then the little girl from the first scene stepped out before the audience and curtsied.

"Don't leave yet. My dead aren't well this evening; stick your finger in my ear so I know you're here even after I fall asleep. Listen! In the dark the heart beats out somebody's total number of years which are completed inside us . . ."

That heralded the Captain's third and youngest death. On the stage (as outside) night had fallen. Two men bearing lanterns and sabers were walking toward one another. It was obviously a duel. One of them portrayed Captain Opujić (in the French tunic), and other the Austrian officer. The one representing Opujić suddenly stopped, stuck his saber into the ground, hung the lantern on the saber, and moved away, planning to attack the other man from behind. He came up on his opponent in the dark, following the man's lantern as he stood there hesitantly, several steps away, unable to see what his enemy was up to in the dark and why he was standing so still. That moment, where he least expected it, Haralampije Opujić ran straight into the Austrian knife in the dark, far from the saber and lantern which the other man as well had cunningly left stuck in the middle of the street. And that was Captain Haralampije Opujić's third death.

"I don't understand a thing," the young Opujić thought, leaving the tent.

Just then a voice behind him said:

"It's just as well that you don't understand!"

Turning around, the lieutenant saw the magician with the roses in his hair and asked him:

"What is the truth? Is my father alive or not?"

"Everybody has two pasts," replied the magician. "One is called Braking; this past grows with the person from his birth and moves toward death. The other past is called Sliding and it goes from the person back to his birth. These two pasts are not of equal length. Depending on which of the two is longer, a person either does or does not fall ill from his death. In the latter case it means that the person is building his past on the other side of the grave as well and so it continues to grow even after his death. The truth lies between these two pasts . . . But why doesn't the lieutenant seek out the Papess?", the magician asked in conclusion and left.

Translated by Christina Pribićević-Zorić

Dictionary of the Khazars *as an Epistemological Metaphor*

Andreas Leitner

Comments, reviews, articles, and monographs on Milorad Pavić's *Dictionary of the Khazars* demonstrate a wide range of ways of approaching, understanding, and interpreting this fascinating, bewildering, and bewitching "Lexicon Novel in 100,000 Words." This novel acquaints the reader first of all with a kind of infinite book of the world or of nature, a kind of absolute book, as discussed and propagated by German romantic writers (F. Schlegel, Novalis). In this reading experience one very quickly loses interest in the Khazars, their history, even their tragic fate. One is caught by the legibility of the absolute book as a fascinating means of reading the book of the world, in other words, of solving, deciphering, and unraveling the mystery of man. In hardly any other work of literature is the possible legibility of the world presented so suggestively and convincingly as in *Dictionary of the Khazars*. And the way one has to read the book is closely linked to the way the present épistéme, the present knowledge, interprets the world or reality. Because the described world of the Khazars is based on abstract present forms of knowledge, it can be called an epistemological metaphor. Epistéme, understood as the summary of present knowledge, first of all from the natural sciences but also from philosophy, psychology, aesthetics, and the pseudosciences, like esoterics, organizes and interprets our world in a wide sense.

There are works of art like Pavić's *Dictionary* that reflect in concrete pictures the abstract concepts of knowledge. Such pieces of art render a great service to the emotional and the sensory experience of totally abstract, not-even-conceivable concepts, theories, and hypotheses of modern science.

How science today organizes and interprets reality and how these organizations and interpretations are transformed into concrete literary pictures are pointed out and discussed on the basis of a few outstanding examples below. Present reality is, put simply, interpreted by two contrary forms of knowledge. Both forms determine the reality in *Dictionary of the Khazars*, or, alternatively, they struggle with the truth. On the one hand, there is the *knowledge of being* and, on the other hand, the *knowledge of becoming* (I. Prigogine, *From Being to Becoming*. The knowledge of being is represented by modern natural science and partly by postmodern philosophers. Both show us reality in its loss of unity and wholeness, in its radical heterogeneity and plurality. The knowledge of becoming is represented by brand-new natural sciences, psychological and esoteric theories, as well as by individual thinkers. They show us reality in a new wholeness, in a universal connection and continuity. On the one hand, we have the loss of the holistic vision of the world; on the other hand, the holistic vision is regained. In Pavić's *Dictionary* the knowledge of timeless mythology connects being and becoming through meaningful and symbolic coincidences.

Present Scientific Foundations

Russell's proof of paradox and antinomy in the foundation of mathematics, Einstein's theory of relativity, Heisenberg's uncertainty principle, and Hilbert's foundation of geometry made it clear in the twentieth century that science lost its access to a logical wholeness. It was not only the whole universe but also the individual systems that lost their clarity and transparency and were no longer sources of unfailing and reliable truth. The status of scientific theories was called into question, and undecidable, undetermined, and illogical facts had to be accepted. The extent, for instance, to which quantum theory shook the foundations of mathematics, physics, and the traditional vision of the world is described by the physicist Erwin Schrödinger in his study "What Is Life": "The great revelation of quantum theory was that features of discreteness were discovered in the Book of Nature, in a context in which anything other than continuity seemed to be absurd according to the views held until then."[1] In the field of quantum biology even reversals of the cause-and-effect sequence were observed. Pascual Jordan describes this phenomenon as follows: "as a result of quantum theory . . . we have learned something new about time and causality. On occasion, with or in the explosion of an atomic nucleus under bombardment of a very fast particle of matter, the usual order of events is reversed: the explosion comes first, then it is followed by its cause. This has enormous implications for psychology and parapsychology, since such reversals of cause-and-effect sequence are proved logically possible and philosophically valid."[2]

Brand-new sciences like the fractal theory (Mandelbrot), catastrophe theory (Zeemans), the theory of dissipative structures (Prigogine), and synergetic chaos research (Haken) help destroy the idea of a logically organized wholeness and unity. These modern visions of the world dismiss the claim to totality, to universal principles, to logocentrism, to wholeness and unity. Discontinuity becomes the central category of science and culture. Reality now appears pluralistic, particularistic, antagonistic, paralogical, ambiguous, unpredictable, and, above all, open. This changing scientific interpretation of reality is reflected in literary art by an increasing openness and dynamism of pictures, situations, and actions. Openness and dynamism, especially, teach us to see reality not only from different points of view but also in its constant changing and in its partly paralogical and antinomous state.[3]

In the synchronic view *Dictionary of the Khazars*, too, calls into question the spaciotemporal continuum, the principle of causality, bivalent logics, univocal relationships, the principle of identity, and the principle of contradiction. Every phenomenon in Pavić's literary world appears radically pluralistic, heterogeneous, and paralogical. Chance and freedom, sense and nonsense, have equal rights in a kind of open ambiguity. About Princess Ateh we read:

> Ateh was a beautiful and pious woman. . . . They say she had seven faces, like her seven salts. . . . According to other stories, Ateh was no beauty at all, but she would train her face in the mirror and compose her features into a lovely expression and a pretty shape. . . . In any event, in the 9th century a Byzantine emperor used the term "Khazar face" to describe the famous philosopher and Patriarch Photius, which could have meant either that the Patriarch was related to the Khazars or that he was a hypocrite.
>
> According to Daubmannus, neither was the case. The term "Khazar face" referred to the characteristic of all Khazars, including Princess Ateh, of starting each day as someone else, with a completely new and unfamiliar face, so that even the closest of kin were at pains to recognize one another. Travelers recorded just the opposite: that all Khazar faces were identical, that they never changed, and that this created problems and caused confusion.[4]

This example shows that the Khazar reality is obviously in a state of dissention, difference, and paralogic. Nothing, it seems, is governed by continuity or identity. Sometimes we only know things for sure which contradict our empirical experience. About Princess Ateh, we only know for sure that she "never managed to die" (23).

The loss and the change of identity are omnipresent. The nonidentity is part of the Khazar identity. For instance, "There is a place in Itil, the Khazar capital, where, when two people (who may be quite unknown to each other) cross paths, they assume each other's name and fate, and each lives out the rest of his or her life in the role of the other, as though they had swapped caps" (148).

The loss of the spaciotemporal continuity is demonstrated in a broad spectrum of events and incidents. The Khazars believe, "that passing through the four seasons are two years, not one, and that they move in opposite directions (like the Khazars' river). Both years shuffle the days and seasons like cards, mixing winter days with spring, and summer days with autumn. Moreover, one of the two Khazar years flows from the future to the past, the other from the past to the future" (144). The Khazar god of salt "separated the past from the future, set up his throne in the present; he walks over the future and flies over the past to keep an eye on it" (145).

When the stream of time can flow backward, then it is quite normal that the sequence of cause and effect is reversed, too. As an example for this reversal, we may take the death of Avram Brankovich, who dies the death of his son Grgur, whom the Turks killed with arrows: "Arrows seemed to be piercing his body, but it all happened backward: with each arrow he felt first the wound, then the penetrating stab; then the pain would stop, something would whistle through the air, and finally there was the zing of the bow string as it released the arrow" (236).

Heterogeneity of Discourses

French postmodern thinkers, first of all Jean-François Lyotard, have performed a turn from the theory of consciousness to the linguistic theory, the so-called linguistic turn, a turn that had already been carried out by Ludwig Wittgenstein. Lyotard analyzed different language games and proved convincingly that all language games are heterogeneous, contradictory, and controversial, so that there cannot be any consensus over one and the same thing when discussed or reported in different language games. Referring to postmodern knowledge, Lyotard emphasized that the aim is no longer consensus but dissension and difference and paralogical utterances about one and the same thing. If one decides in favor of only one form of discourse, one will never see other aspects of truth that always exist, too. The coming task of literary criticism, philosophy, and even politics will be to point out the heterogeneity of discourses and the equal right of each discourse. There is not only one truth about a thing but many aspects of truth. Lyotard's critical discourse fights against any theoretical or practical dogmatism. The aim of postmodern knowledge has to be to point out even its own evolution as discontinuous, catastrophic, and paradoxical.[5]

Dictionary of the Khazars is an exact literary representation of this postmodern demand. It consists of Hebrew, Islamic, and Christian sources, that is, of three religious or ideological discourses that interpret the most important things in the world of the Khazars controversially. The central question in Khazar history is that of the faith to which the Khazars converted. And it is quite natural that each faith solves this problem to its own advantage. The Christian sources tell us that the Khazars converted to Christianity, the Hebrew to Judaism, and the Islamic to Islam. In the postmodern sense of truth these contradictions should merely be pointed out, but they should not be eliminated. Nobody has the right to decide, for instance, in favor of the Christian sources. If so he or she would lose the ability to see the Khazar world in the Hebrew or Islamic way. The reader of postmodern scientific concepts or Pavić's *Dictionary* has to learn to accept such contradictions as an enrichment of experience, not as the impossibility of finding the historical truth.

Systems Philosophy

In many fields of science we are moving—or at least trying to move—to a new paradigm of knowledge and science: systems philosophy is booming. Systems theorists (Bertalanffy, Laszlo) are interested in cosmological (Jantsch), biological (Maturana, Varela), ecological (Allen, Margalev), sociocultural (Jantsch, Allen), and evolutionary systems, as well as in human consciousness (Maturana, Varela, Bateson, Gebser). They show us that both microscopic and macroscopic systems are no longer rigid structures but processual and dynamic organizations. Such systems are called dissipative structures, which means that they are evolutionary system-maintaining structures. Their evolution is based on self-organization, self-government, and self-renewal—they are autopoietic systems. Autopoietic systems aim at renewal of their processual structure by order and fluctuation. Such theories make us—more or less convincingly—believe that all evolution, the microscopic as well as the macroscopic, the organic as well as the anorganic, are connected to each other and take place in a similar way because the whole universe has the same origin.

Pavić's universe, too, seems to be ruled by such a kind of autopoietic system, a self-organizing, self-governing and self-renewing one. On the historical level, for instance, one of the students of the Khazar question always dies when he seems to be near the solution. But only his body is dead; his soul or the principle represented is still living and is embodied in other persons, so that the solution of the Khazar question can go on eternally.

Nevertheless, such historical events have their homological correspondences in Khazar mythology. In the same way that the students of history try to reconstruct the original *Dictionary of the Khazars* and solve the Khazar question, Adam in mythology is always trying to reach himself but has not yet succeeded and will never succeed. In "The Tale of Adam Ruhani" we read:

In the beginning, this Adam-before-Adam was the third mind of the world, but he was so carried away with himself that he went astray; when he recovered from his vertigo, he cast Iblis and Ahriman, his fellow travelers in iniquity, into hell and returned to the heavens, where he was now no longer the third but the tenth mind, because in the meantime seven heavenly cherubim had overtaken him on the ladder of angels. And so Adam-the-precursor found himself seven rungs behind on the ladder. . . . This angelical Adam, or pre-Adam, who was both man and woman at once, this third angel who became the tenth angel, is forever trying to reach himself, and at moments he even succeeds, but then he falls again, and he is still drifting today between the tenth and second rung on the ladder of reason. (165-66)

Mythological and historical events then are connected by a kind of coevolution so that the microcosm of man and the macrocosm of God are only aspects of one and the same evolution.

Long before systems philosophy and the new age movement, Jean Gebser, a largely unknown philosopher, propagated in his voluminous study *Ursprung und Gegenwart* (1949-1953) the end of the causal-mechanistic view of the world and the beginning of a noncausal evolutionary view. His evolution is not an autopoietic one, nor is it progress or development, but the actualization of the invisible in the visible world. What is going on in evolution was already determined beyond space and time, before the first day. In this concept of evolution causal relations are no longer valid, the cause-and-effect sequence and the stream of time may be experienced in reverse, and origin, present, and future coincide. Such opinions or experiences of determination and predestination were not only uttered by Gebser. In T. S. Eliot's "The Family Reunion" we read: "The things that are going to happen / Have already happened."[6]

In a similar way Father Theoctist Nikolsky in Pavić's *Dictionary* states his perception of events in space and time: "I decided that nothing happens in the flow of time, that the world does not change through the years but inside itself and through space simultaneously—it changes in countless forms, shuffling them like cards and assigning the past of some as lessons to the future or present of others" (313).

Carl Gustav Jung or Synchronicity

In an evolutionary universe the traditional dualism of idea and reality, spirit and matter, subject and object, and so on, no longer exists but is substituted by floating transitions. The either-or of rational and logical dualism is replaced by the as-well-as of a living polarity. Each event is no longer governed by the cause-and-effect sequence but takes place between polar tensions, in which cause and effect cannot be described by traditional terms or concepts. Things are happening in a kind of coincidental oppositorum. Though they are not causally connected, they appear regularly in space and time and therefore appear highly determined. Such events and their mysterious connection can be described by Jung's concepts of animus and anima, of coniunctio as unification of the opposite, and of synchronicity.[7]

In his research on the personal unconscious and its complexes and the collective unconscious and its archetypes, Jung saw in each man a feminine part and in each woman a masculine part. He called them anima and animus. Each individual is striving for the unity, wholeness, and completeness that got lost in the Fall of Man. In their striving together there occur events that are not causally connected but connected by synchronicity. Jung's "use of synchronicity was an effort to substitute a formal cause conception within time for the customary conception of impetus changes taking place over time as antecedents-to-consequents. According to Jung, each time the individual opts to behave in one way, sending the libido teleologically in one direction, an equal amount of libido is being sent in the opposite direction. For every behavior affirmed in consciousness, there is an equal degree of libido sent into the unconscious realm bearing the opposite behavioral intention."[8]

In *Dictionary of the Khazars* the Serb Avram Brankovich and Samuel Cohen, a Jew from Dubrovnik, are exactly such archetypes and their shadows as described by Jung.[9] They are constantly striving for their reunification, including the re-creation of Adam, the completion of the *Dictionary of the Khazars*. In this connection, dreams, dream visions, and dream interpretations play an important part. For Pavić's Khazars, as well as for Arthur Schopenhauer and Sigmund Freud, the legibility of dreams, the interpretation of dreams, is inseparably connected with the legibility of the world. Dreams have divinatory character; they discover the unknown, the past, the present, and the future by supernatural means.

In the Khazar world freedom and chance are always connected with determination, and all determination with freedom and chance. The Khazar universe seems complete in its openness and open in its completeness. Each part is in the life of the whole, and the whole is in the life of each part. Each meaningful word, each occurrence stands in a series of possible relations with nearly all the others in the text.

Openness and the Active Reader

The extent to which *Dictionary of the Khazars* corresponds with present cultural activities is shown in its claim for openness and for an active reader. I recall the exhibition *Les Immatériaux*, which took place in 1985 in Paris. Visitors were offered the opportunity of using their creativity on computer terminals to write stories, fairy tales, and so on. The reader should no longer be a consumer but an active creator, which means that the consumer and the producer become one person.

In "The Open Work" and "Lector in Fabula" Umberto Eco discusses in detail the openness of modern works of art and the active reader in literature. Modern art is deliberately and systematically ambiguous, so that the reader or interpreter or performer must choose one of the open possibilities for completing the work: "In other words, the author offers the interpreter, the performer, the addressee a work *to be completed*. He does not know the exact fashion in which his work will be concluded, but he is aware that once completed the work in question will still be his own. It will not be a different work, and, at the end of the interpretative dialogue, a form which is *his* form will have been organized, even though it may have been assembled by an outside party in a particular way that he could not have foreseen. The author is the one who proposed a number of possibilities, which had already been rationally organized, oriented, and endowed with specifications for proper development."[10]

In the "Preliminary Notes" of *Dictionary of the Khazars* we read: "it can be read in an infinite number of ways. It is an open book, and when it is shut it can be added to. . ." (11). And: "Hence, each reader will put together the book for himself, as in a game of dominoes or cards, and, as with a mirror, he will get out of this dictionary as much as he puts into it, for, as is written on one of the pages of this lexicon, you cannot get more out of the truth than what you put into it" (13). In hardly any other literary work is Umberto Eco's characterization of the active reader and the open work realized so convincingly as in Pavić's *Dictionary of the Khazars*.

NOTES

[1]*What Is Life? and Other Scientific Essays* (Garden City: Doubleday, 1956), 49.

[2]"New Trends in Physics," *Proceedings of Four Conferences of Parapsychology Studies* (New York: Parapsychology Foundation, 1957), 16.

[3]See Umberto Eco, "The Poetics of the Open Work" and "The Open Work

in the Visual Arts," ch. 1 and 4 of *The Open Work*, trans. Anna Cancogni, (Cambridge: Harvard Univ. Press, 1989).

[4]Milorad Pavić, *Dictionary of the Khazars*, trans. Christina Pribićević-Zorić (New York: Vintage, 1989), 21-22; hereafter cited parenthetically.

[5]See David Caroll, "The Aesthetics and the Political: Lyotard," ch. 7 of *Paraesthetics: Foucault, Lyotard, Derrida* (New York: Routledge, 1989).

[6]T. S. Eliot, *The Complete Poems and Plays of T. S. Eliot* (London: Faber and Faber, 1975), 317.

[7]See Allan Combs and Mark Holland, *Synchronicity—Science, Myth and the Trickster* (New York: Paragon House, 1990).

[8]Albert Kreinheder, "Jung: Historical and Methodological Considerations," *International Encyclopedia of Psychiatry, Psychology, Psychoanalysis and Neurology*, ed. Benjamin Wolman (New York: Aesculapius, 1977), 6: 231.

[9]See Jane Kabel, "Motiv dvojnika u *Hazarskom rečniku* Milorada Pavića," *Srpska fantastika*, ed. P. Palavestra (Belgrade: SANU, 1989), 581-85.

[10]Eco, 19.

Culture as Memory: On the Poetics of Milorad Pavić

Dagmar Burkhart

"Here the world of the fantastic intruded into the world of the real," as it says at a central point in Jorge Luis Borges's *Tlön, Uqbar, Orbis Tertius*. It is precisely this phenomenon of the increasing intrusion of the fantastic into mimetic-realistic narrative prose that characterizes the nonmimetic discourse of Serbian postmodernism. Milorad Pavić is, alongside Kiš, Pekić, and younger authors such as Basara, Mitrović, Kazimir, and Albahari, one of its principal representatives. Pavić began, as Sava Damjanov has stressed, "with stories which were closer to the original model of fantastic writing or to the field of *pure* fantasy," while in his novels he incorporates "literary discourse in a more complex linguistic-artistic structure (with marked postmodernist characteristics)." If this fantasy, which may be read as poetic-allegorical, is an important medium of postmodern Serbian literature yet is also different from that used in the literature of the ninteenth century or in modernism, so too does intertextuality undoubtedly present one of its further constitutive characteristics.

While in modernism, intertextual games and quotations already characterized literature, in postmodernism, literature, in Dietor Borchmeyer's words, "becomes an imaginary museum, a Babel of quotation, a permanent pla(y)giarism, to use a word-play of Raymond Federman (*Take It or Leave It*, 1976)." Baudrillard has introduced the term *simulacrum* for this literary manifestation of permanent imitation.

In the poetics of Milorad Pavić, who made his debut with the tellingly titled collection of poems *Palimpsesti* (1967), this extensive and intensive intertextuality is present at all levels of the work. Thus, on the one hand, there is a *heteromedial* intertextuality, that is to say, an intermedial interplay of graphic and verbal elements, and, on the other hand, a dominant *isomedial* or *verbal* intertextuality, the latter relating not only to structures, namely genres and poetics, but also to the motif and content levels through quotation, allusion, and paraphrase of other texts (or *subtexts*), both his own and others', by which the nature of this reference may be affirmative or may be dialogic (parodying, deconstructing, etc.). Therein a range of *reference structures* is discernible which extends through the lexicon, the crossword, disputation, dialogic narrative, parable and anecdote, to the historical novel, the crime thriller, and the love story or romantic novel, and which embraces a heterogeneity of *reference texts*, such as the Bible, ancient myths, Homer, Plato, Ovid, the Byzantine novel, apocrypha and holy legend, the *Vita Constantini*, the Talmud and the Koran, the traditions of the Kabbala, Balkan folklore and folk mythology, Ragusan baroque lyric and baroque epic, historiographical works, sermons of the Serbian baroque period (above all those of G. Venclović), texts of the German Enlightenment and German romantic periods, texts by Poe, Pushkin, Gogol, Kafka, Borges, Eco, and García Márquez, and narrative texts of contemporary Serbian authors such as Andrić, Crnjanski, Selimović, Kiš, Tišma, Nenadić, and others. Thus it can be seen that Pavić in his writing technique, with his use of the nonmimetic fantastic and a radicalization of modernism's practice of allusion, follows not a principle of the dispersion of meaning but one of a multiplication of meaning (although on a deeply enigmatic level) and that he with his wholly polyphonic texts demonstrates the *ars combinatoria* of postmodernism as hardly any other writer has done.

It is characteristic of studies of Pavić that his intertextuality is treated too generally, indeed as I have just treated it in my listing of the most important subtexts. One reason that no one has yet expressed a comprehensive and detailed view of Pavić's intertextuality lies undoubtedly in the fact that his texts show such a compressed processing of subtexts that an exhaustive examination of the latter would fill whole volumes of analytical commentary. I wish, therefore, to try to demonstrate the basic characteristics of Pavić's intertextual poetics on a fragment of one of his texts. The text that I have selected is "Appendix I," the penultimate entry in his 1984 lexicon-novel *Dictionary of the Khazars*, correlated by cross-reference with the lexicon entry "Sevast, Nikon (17th century)" in the red, Christian book of the lexicon. I have chosen these two interconnected fragments in particular not only because it is possible to use them to illustrate the intertextuality but also because it is here, in my opinion, that the author has formulated his poetics.

Appendix I bears the title "Father Theoctist Nikolsky as Compiler of *The Khazar Dictionary*'s First Edition." It contains an introductory sentence by the fictitious lexicographer ("Father Theoctist Nikolsky penned his dying confession to the Patriarch Arsen III Charnoyevich of Peć in the pitch dark, somewhere in Poland, using a mixture of gunpowder and saliva, and a quick Cyrillic hand, while the innkeeper's wife scolded and cursed him through the bolted door") and a subsequent letter-text with the autobiographical narrative of Theoctist, in which above all his remarkable memory and his relationship to Nikon Sevast are presented and in which is embedded a tale taken from Avram Brankovich, "Note on Adam, the Brother of Christ."

The lexicon entry "Sevast, Nikon (17th century)" deals with the mundane biography of the devil Nikon Sevast, employed as a protocalligrapher and painter of icons in the Morava monastery of St. Nicholas, and moves into the report in a church register of an unnamed monk in the year 1674, in which the painting-technique of Sevast, left-handed but converted to right-handedness, is presented.

In my view three semantic complexes may be discerned in these two exemplary texts, complexes that dominate not only the whole of the *Dictionary of the Khazars* but on which, following Pavić's poetic principle of the correspondence of all parts, his subsequent novels *Landscape Painted with Tea* (1988) and *The Inner Side of the Wind* (1991) are also based, namely: Memory + Oblivion; Identity + Metamorphosis; Particularity + Unity.

Memory + Oblivion

That the monk Theoctist (from the Greek *theos*, meaning *God* and *ktistes*, meaning *creator*) in his letter to the Serbian Patriarch is attributed with a hypertrophic memory and that this is said to be a "frailty" refers above all to Borges's story "Funes the Memorious" but also to subtexts such as A. V. Chamisso's romantic narrative *The Fantastic Tale of Peter Schlemihl* (1814), in which the protagonist, after making a pact with the devil, must live without a shadow, that is, must live with a characteristic of the demonic, or to Patrick Süskind's postmodern novel *Perfume*, in which the protagonist is born devoid of a personal odor and spends his whole life in an obsessive quest to cure this deficit. Yet while in Borges's text it is the narrator who calls Funes's prominent characteristic a "relentless memory," in Pavić's text it is the protagonist himself who calls the inability to forget to which he is "doomed" a "punishment." It seems only consistent that Theoctist's hypermnesia, which at first appears reminiscent of a parody or persiflage of the ancient *ars memoriae* or mnemotechnique (Simonides), is then positively connoted as it supplies the motivation for the preservation of *The Khazar Dictionary* from the threat of fiendish annihilation: Theoctist had learned by heart not only the Christian and Islamic parts of the texts, which were consigned to the flames by Nikon Sevast (an allusion here to the burning of the library in Umberto Eco's *The Name of the Rose*), but also the Jewish part, which was scattered by the winds on the battlefield of Kladovo in 1689. He then committed all three parts to paper and gave them to the Polish printer Daubmannus to be published, which it was in 1691, only to be later proscribed by the Inquisition in 1692 and destroyed save for a single poisoned specimen (also an allusion to Eco's novel) and its check copy.

It is this game with the text, lost in the realms of memory yet reconstructible, the mythopoetic creation and destruction of signs, which forms the central isotopia in the Pavić text. Here belongs also his version of the legend of Adam, nourished by cabalistic and apocryphal tradition, an Adam whose picture or incorporation is created through letter and text, that is, through the congealing of human perception as a recorded cultural memory, as well as through Pavić's metaphysics of dreams, derived from Sigmund Freud, as the reinspiration of forgotten signs.

That Theoctist temporarily loses his memory during his initial contact with the fiend, Nikon Sevast (from the Greek *nike,* meaning *victory,* and *sevastos,* meaning *praiseworthy*), who (an irony typical of Pavić) is employed as an icon painter and calligrapher in the monastery, follows from a concept that Pavić raises to an ideology: that the diabolic forces that are themselves devoid of the capacity to remember seek to annihilate the memory of human beings. It is only writing, the "hunger for writing" as it is called in the last sentences of Theoctist's report, that has been able to still his "thirst for memory," so that once the latter is extinguished, Theoctist becomes a doppelgänger of the fiendish Nikon. Writing as a work of the Devil, as an alternative to memory? Borges said of himself that he forgot his stories after he had written them down. But is not Pavić rather propounding a reanimation of the myth of Mnemosyne, the poetic arche-anamnesis?

Identity + Metamorphosis

The most significant subtext for Pavić's motif of transformation is obviously Ovid's hexametrical epic *Metamorphoses*, the poetic source of which is 250 ancient transformation myths. Just as for Ovid "myths in which people are transformed into animals, trees, and stars [are] symbolic of eternal mutability in the historical world," in Manfred Lurker's words, so there is in Pavić's mythopoetic concept of world and time (time springs from Satan, eternity from God, declares Theoctist) only a cyclically recurrent or equally pre- and regressive movement of creatures and events (the symbol here being Cancer, the Crab). The Khazar researchers and the devils reincarnate themselves three hundred years later; Nikon Sevast claims to have been a denizen of the Jewish hell in his previous life (a persiflage on the doctrine of rebirth), and the people say of Avram Brankovich that he transforms himself into a spirit in his sleep, a spirit who led "the winds and the clouds" and rode upon a black horse that could, in its turn, transform itself into a piece of straw, a characteristic of devils, witches, and nightmares (in this case the subtext is the keyword *zduhać* in the lexicon of Vuk Karadžić with its narrative-type entries). In this Pavićist reproduction of archaic creation and cyclical myths, the characters are preferably presented in pairs. Brankovich and the Jew Cohen transmigrate in their dreams (cf. Borges's "The Story of the Warrior and the Captive"), and Theoctist *Niko*lski loses his identity and, as a glance in the mirror shows him, is increasingly transmuted into his diabolic writer-colleague *Niko*n Sevast (note the similarity of names as another indicator of doubleness), by which the whole doppelgänger and mirror-image theme from romanticism to modernism is evoked (Poe's *William Wilson*, Gogol's *The Nose*, Kafka's *The Metamorphosis*, etc.). When Sevast goes hunting to find his "true future," he encounters his soul transformed into a deer by the Archangel Gabriel (the deer being a solar symbol and a signifier of the natural cycle), and in a pact with the archangel ("a pact with an angel" as a parody of all "pact with the devil" narratives) the hitherto left-hander is transformed into a right-hander, who now begins to paint extraordinarily and who is punished with mediocrity only after breaking his pact. Finally, the grotesque body of the fiend (Sevast has an enormous phallus, has only a single nostril, and in the place of a posterior has two faces with a nose instead of the traditional devil's tail between them) presents a carnivalistic man-animal synthesis that since the Middle Ages has been modified to the ridiculous.

Just as the semiotic notion of metamorphosis in avant-garde literature is anchored as a thematic complex in the construction of Pavić's intertextuality, so too is archaic man's belief that the word is an instrument of divine power and the reflection of this belief in all higher religions and folk mythologies. The sentence quoted in the "Preliminary Notes" to *Dictionary of the Khazars* from the Gospel of St. John, "Verbum caro factum est" / "The Word became flesh" (referring to Jesus as the incarnation of the Logos, the Word of God), prefigures the passage in Appendix I in which the transforming, potentially even annihilating word is spoken of. After his initial contact with the fiend, Theoctist actually begins to transform the texts of the *Lives of the Saints* that had been entrusted to him for literal transcription. He begins by inserting narrative elements and then by inventing wholly novel hermits and miracles. Finally, Theoctist causes the death of a young monk when he transcribes the Life of Saint Peter of Corishia, which serves as the young monk's model, and makes a vital change increasing the number of fast days from five to fifty, a witty and ironic satire on the (alleged) power of the poetic word.

Particularity + Unity

In this complex, Pavić's intertextuality of motif is above all connected with autopoetic utterances. Here, there are allusions to all the mythical narrations in which *duality* (e.g., body-soul polarity; male-female duality such as in Plato's *Symposium* and Adam-Eve; god-devil; the dual nature of Christ, etc.), *triplicity* (e.g., triple time = past, present, future; triple cosmogonic space = heaven, earth, underworld; the Trinity; the Holy Family, etc.) and *multiplicity* (the creation of Adam in apocryphal myth from the seven parts of the world; the cosmogony of the body parts of the ancient Indian "archeman," Purusa; dismemberment as a prerequisite of rebirth in vegetation myths, etc.) are merged into *unity* or the *holistic*.

In Pavić a mystification of the dominant number three, which is viewed as the holy, perfect number, is observable. Therefore there are three religions, three Khazar researchers (although, typical of Pavić's irony, countered by three fiends), and correspondingly three parts of the *Dictionary of the Khazars,* whose unification in both the seventeenth and the twentieth centuries is in each case attempted by a triad of researchers (dream hunters), after the efforts of a dyad, Princess Ateh and her lover, Mokaddasa al Safer, have been broken off in the ninth century (a contrafacture of motif from the relevant Borges narration, *Tlön*). The influence of the dualistic Bogumil heresy, which also appears in Ivo Andrić's texts, is expressed in Pavić's version of the Adam-legend: Adam (Kadmon), the Hebrew "arche-man," viewed in Jewish mysticism as the first emanation of God, is interpreted as a macrocosmic creature whose icon is pieced together, particle by particle, tale by tale, illumination by illumination (the World as a text and poetry as the mythical preexistence, arche-book, arche-dream of mankind) by the Khazar dream hunters. Creative power lends this creature the internal polar principle of Adam and Eve, hypostatized in the duality of the male-right and the female-left thumb, which strain toward contact. The twinlike, conjoined figures (Sevast and Theoctist, Brankovich and Cohen, Masudi and Akshany, etc.) also bear witness to the dual nature of man and his world (divine-satanic, divine-human, spirit-body).

Within the consciousness of the creative recipient of Pavić's poetics, truth (or one of many possible truths) is inferred from a multiplicity of interconnected messages: "On his frescoes," it is said of

Sevast, "in the churches of the Ovchar gorge are inscriptions that, if read in a certain order from painting to painting and from monastery to monastery, form a message. It can be assembled as long as the paintings themselves exist." And from multiplicity comes unity:

> "He took blue and red and placed them next to each other, painting the eyes of an angel. And I saw the angel's eyes turn violet.
>
> " 'I work with something that is like a dictionary of colors,' Nikon added, 'and from it the observer composes sentences and books, in other words, images. You could do the same with writing. Why shouldn't someone create a dictionary of words that make up one book and let the reader himself assemble the words into a whole?' "

Here, clear autothematic references to Pavić's poetics are formulated which read like a paraphrase of the point in Borges's "An Examination of the Work of Herbert Quain," in which it is said that writers passed from a trinomial to a binomial order, but the demiurges and the gods "decided on the never-ending: never-ending stories, never-endingly intertwined." This quasi-divine, world-creating principle of writing which interweaves everything with everything else, which asserts the validity of equivalence as a third connective possibility, besides the temporal and the logic of causality, is in my view the basic principle of Pavić's poetics. It is the so-called *pletenie sloves*, the intertwining of word and sentence through the medium of sound repetition, such as alliteration and assonance, epanalepsis, figura etymologica, polyptoton, the recurrence of key words or key syllables, paronomasia, synonymy, tautology, etc. This technique has obviously been adopted by Pavić as a structural intertextuality from the sermons and lyrics of the Serbian baroque period, which for its part referred to and further developed the procedure of *pletenie sloves* of the Serbian, Bulgarian, and Russian authors of the thirteenth to the fifteenth century (the term stems from Epifanij Premudrij at the end of the fourteenth century). Not only does a phonic instrumentalization, which one also encounters in representatives of the *ornamental prose* of European modernism, guarantee the highest order of poeticism and density of language, but also it is the central isotopia in the text which unfolds itself in the constitution of the key lexemes. Thus it is no wonder that Pavić, to concentrate the phonic-semantic network further, utilizes a whole sequence of metaphors based upon fabric and weaving: dreams, the "moment of ultimate fulfillment," are in the conception of the Khazars the "nodes/knots" (*čvorišna mesta*) in the life of each individual. All three Khazar researchers or dream weavers of the seventeenth century are additionally marked by either the physical characteristic of a plait like Brankovich and Masudi or Akshany, or by the fact that they have made weaving their livelihood (Cohen, who has eyebrows like woven wings, is a horses' wig weaver in the service of a Turkish pasha). Also it is no mere coincidence that the name of the Serbian Khazar researcher of the twentieth century Suk (Pavić's alter ego) may be traced to the verb *sukati* (to wind, turn, twist) and substantives such as *sukno* (cloth, firm fabric) and *sukalo* (bobbin-winder).

Finally, Pavić's pragmatic, reader-oriented technique of intertwining should be stressed: special cross-reference symbols lead to an intertwining reading of the whole *Dictionary of the Khazars*; the crossword structure in *Landscape Painted with Tea* creates a reading texture spun from vertical and horizontal threads; and the mirror-image, reciprocal ordering of the two parts of *The Inner Side of the Wind* directly provokes a weaving-reading synthesis.

Intertextuality in its varied forms, then, serves Pavić as a medium for the multiplication and concentration of meaning. It must however first be discerned in his texts, which one may comprehend as the literary expression of theorems and ideologies of diverse philosophies, religions, mythologies, and mystic-heretical systems (and herein he is closest to Borges's Alexandrian erudition). On the question of "how much history and reality and how much fantasy and poeticism" is contained in his works, Pavić has answered "that it is not a question of turning reality into literature, but rather one of achieving reality through literature." Each reader may take from these texts, simultaneously cryptic and universalist as they are, his or her own salt, as one might say in Khazar.

Dictionary of the Khazars *as a Khazar Jar*

Rachel Kilbourn Davis

In an article on nonmimetic literature entitled "The Khazar Jar and Other False Memories,"[1] Milorad Pavić cites the entry "The Khazar Jar" from his novel *Dictionary of the Khazars,* in which a student dream-reader receives as a gift what seems to be an ordinary jar. One night before going to sleep, he drops his ring into the jar, only to discover in the morning that the ring is gone. When he reaches his hand into the jar, he discovers that there does not seem to be a bottom on the inside although the jar looks quite ordinary on the outside. When he asks his teacher to explain the mystery of the Khazar Jar, the teacher picks up a stone, drops it into the jar and is able to count to seventy before they hear a splash. Although the teacher warns the student that after he explains the mystery, the jar will be worth far less to him and to others than it is now, the student still wants to know the meaning of the jar, at which point the teacher picks up a stick and smashes it, saying: "The damage would be if I had first told you what the jar was for and had then smashed it. This way, you don't know its purpose and there is no damage done; it will continue to serve you as though it had never been smashed. . . ." The story concludes with the narrator's comment that "Indeed, the Khazar jar serves to this day, although it has long since ceased to exist."[2]

It is not by chance that Pavić chose this particular passage from *Dictionary of the Khazars*. "The Khazar Jar" is a parable about how easily people are deceived by external appearances and how quickly they jump to evaluate something without first really examining either themselves or the object. In general terms "The Khazar Jar" is about the role of perception vs. reality in the determination of the value of an object, whether that object is a vase, a novel, or even existence itself. In attempting to determine the value of an object, one critic writes that:

> Of particular significance for the value of "works of art" and "literature" is the interactive relation between the *classification* of an entity and the functions it is expected or desired to perform. In perceiving an object or artifact in terms of some category—as, for example, "a clock," "a dictionary," "a doorstep," "a curio"—we implicitly isolate and foreground certain

of its possible functions and typically refer its value to the extent to which it performs those functions more or less effectively.[3]

This is precisely the student's shortcoming in "The Khazar Jar." The teacher in the story understands that the student values the jar only because of its mystery, a mystery that he assumes has a "logical" solution. Nevertheless, the fact that the student *believes* that the Khazar jar has a bottom inside because its external form leads him to expect one does not necessarily mean that it has one or that he could understand it even if it did. The teacher knows that once the mystery is solved, the jar will not hold quite the same attraction for the student as it does now. Whether or not the teacher actually knows the secret meaning of the Khazar jar himself, he does know that if he allows the student to continue to study the jar with the sole aim of discovering its secret, the student would never begin to consider *why* the jar puzzles him, nor would he ever realize the inappropriateness of his entire approach to the question. By smashing the jar, the teacher accomplishes two things: he leaves the mystery intact, preserving it until such time as the student is capable of understanding the true meaning of the Khazar jar; and he forces the student to focus his attention on the process of unraveling the mystery, that is, to focus on himself and his perception of the jar, rather than on the jar and its supposed meaning.

Like the student who mistakes the Khazar jar for an ordinary jar because of its external appearance and then is puzzled when it lacks the bottom he had expected to find, we as readers are puzzled by *Dictionary of the Khazars* when it refuses to conform to our predetermined expectations of it as a novel. The purpose of a novel, as it has been traditionally accepted, is as follows:

[To say] something important about man's existence, something basic and quintessential to what his life is all about, . . . to define the quality, worth, and meaning of life; to investigate values and ideas, and to pattern complexities into some coherent form which eventually yields explanations, . . . to *clarify* our universe, defeating mystery where it can, and bringing that mystery into sharper focus where it cannot penetrate it altogether.[4]

What sets *Dictionary of the Khazars* apart from ordinary novels is the way in which Pavić offers so much reliable information that the reader takes for granted the existence of some ultimate meaning within the novel. Yet every time he thinks he has finally gotten it within reach, it evaporates into thin air.

The whole process begins with what amounts to a challenge:

only someone who can read through the sections of one book in their proper order can create the world anew. . . .

[But] the reader capable of deciphering the hidden meaning of a book from the order of its entries has long since vanished from the face of the earth, for today's reading audience believes that the matter of imagination lies exclusively within the realm of the writer and does not concern them in the least, especially with regard to a dictionary. This type of reader does not even need a sandglass in the book to remind him when to change his manner of reading: he never changes his manner of reading in any case. (11)

Pavić makes it very clear that there is an underlying "meaning" in the novel and that only those readers who can change their manner of reading will even come close to solving the mystery of the Khazar jar. Of course, every reader wants to see himself as the only one "capable of deciphering the hidden meaning" of this particular book, and so he immediately sets off, following Pavić's trail of bread crumbs. Unfortunately, like the student of the jar, most readers never think to examine their manner of reading to see if it suits the novel, and consequently they never realize that their search for some ultimate meaning is as futile as the student's attempt to reach the bottom of the Khazar jar.

At the same time, there are clues to the fact that the whole novel is a deception and a training exercise: "As for you, the writer, never forget the following: the reader is like a circus horse which has to be taught that it will be rewarded with a lump of sugar every time it acquits itself well. If that sugar is withheld, it will not perform. As for essayists and critics, they are like cuckolded husbands: always the last to find out . . . " (15). If the purpose of the deception is to lead the reader down the primrose path, he must be rewarded along the way, and Pavić offers some very elaborate "lumps of sugar." Essayists and critics, because of their experience in hunting down the supposed "meaning" of a text, are the last to give up searching and admit that they cannot penetrate the mystery of the Khazar jar.

Now, the dilemma is this: How are we as readers to approach *Dictionary of the Khazars*? Obviously we would be wrong to follow the student's example and allow our expectations of the form to dictate the novel's content. We would only end up as confounded by the novel as the student is by the jar. However, if "The Khazar Jar" can indeed be interpreted as a parable about the novel, then the splash heard by the teacher and the student implies that the Khazar jar does in fact have some sort of a bottom inside. Similarly, *Dictionary of the Khazars* should contain some sort of meaning or message, although it most assuredly will not be "meaning" in the usual sense. In a book entitled *Problems and Poetics of the Nonaristotelian Novel*, Leonard Orr makes a distinction between Aristotelian novels, (that is, those novels constructed according to traditional aesthetic principles) and nonaristotelian novels. The same way ordinary jars are usually evaluated mainly according to their ability to hold things, literature in general has been traditionally evaluated according to how closely it either adheres to or differs from conventional, Aristotelian aesthetic principles, such as unity, clarity, economy, etc. The nonaristotelian novel, however, does neither. As Orr states:

> The nonaristotelian novel . . . is *epistemological* rather than emotional in mode; it is *nonmimetic* and calls attention to its fictive nature; it is *nonchronological* but not achronological, since it foregrounds time or draws attention to the way in which our orderly expectations of time conventions in fiction are disarranged; and *nonteleological*, since the privileged position of the ending occurs only with chronological or logical narration, or a recuperation of some earlier time-frame (the *reading process* and *dialogical engagement* is the end, rather than any element of plot or character discovery or fulfillment).[5]

According to the Aristotelian rules of composition, events imply the existence of a plot that in turn implies chronological time; repetition implies the existence of pattern, coherence, and order; and in general terms, the existence of any number of identifiable parts implies a unified "whole." Traditionally critics have reacted to nonaristotelian novels in much the same way the student and the teacher react to the Khazar jar: either they search desperately for an "order" or "unity" they assume exists because they have identified the parts, or they reject the novel altogether because they assume that "order" cannot be reached, in spite of the existence of the parts. A nonaristotelian novel, however, is constructed so that any underlying structure the reader may identify ultimately turns out to be a mirage, and the search for meaning turns out to be a wild goose chase, just like the illusory bottom inside Pavić's Khazar jar.

A novel, then, like *Dictionary of the Khazars* "no longer purports to *represent* our world—elusive, irreducible, provocative, contradictory, irresolvable, endlessly intriguing us with infinite possibilities as it drifts around in time and space, simultaneously inviting and invalidating interpretations, all valid but none ultimate" (Seltzer 21). Thus, if novelists like Pavić feel that reality is like the Khazar jar, deceptively simple and recognizable on the surface, yet indecipherable underneath, and if the novel is supposed to be a representation of the author's perception of reality, then our job as readers is to explore the novel inside and out and see not only *how* but *how well* the novel depicts its own reality.

Pavić knows that his audience consists of connoisseurs of ordinary jars and that they are very experienced at recognizing and determining the value of different jars based on how well they hold things and how easy or difficult it is to retrieve whatever they are holding. It is precisely this expertise that Pavić relies on in creating his Khazar novel. He knows that if he can make his novel *look* like an ordinary novel, few readers will probably ever think to look beyond the illusion. As a nonaristotelian novel, *Dictionary of the Khazars* creates a very solid illusion of a novel that has order and meaning and then, "lest the form itself imply control," it "self-destruct[s] on contact" (Seltzer 6). From the very beginning, the nonaristotelian character of the novel is evident in its actual physical form, the importance of which is emphasized by the title. The division of the novel into the Christian, Hebrew, and Islamic dictionaries and the distribution of the various "chapters" among the three parts, disrupts the forward, linear movement of the novel and foregrounds the nonchronological, nonteleological nature of *Dictionary of the Khazars*. However, the physical form of the novel has more than just abstract, philosophical significance for the reader. Pavić arranges the novel like a dictionary because dictionaries are reference books and are expected to contain reliable and accurate information. The physical form of the novel and the use of scholarly footnotes and bibliographical references clearly show that Pavić wants the reader to approach his novel as if it were a reference book, that is, with faith and confidence in the accuracy and reliability of the information it contains.

However, the expectation of accuracy is not enough to create a believable illusion of an ordinary novel; Pavić also uses a great deal of factual material to support and encourage the reader's expectations. Not only is the basic premise of the novel, the Khazar Polemic and the religious conversion of the Khazar people, based on actual historical events dating to the eighth century, but many of the characters are historical personages and a number of passages in the novel were "borrowed" by Pavić from genuine historical accounts. Cyril and Methodius are obvious examples, but Al-Bakhri, Yusuf Masudi, Mokaddasa Al-Safer, Judah Halevi, Isaac Sangari, and Judah Tibbon were all somehow connected with the actual scholarship on the Khazars. Other characters, like Theophanes, Al-Istakhri, and the various Byzantine emperors are also entirely historical. In addition, many of Pavić's sources, such as the archaeological site at Chelarevo, Yugoslavia, Halevi's book *Liber Cosri*, and the Khazar Correspondence between Hasdai Ibn Shaprut of Moorish Spain and the Khazar Kaghan Joseph, are indisputably factual. Pavić reinforces the reader's expectations even further by regularly supplying complete bibliographical references for many of his sources throughout the novel, most of which are genuine.

However, if the information contained in *Dictionary of the Khazars* were completely factual, our quest for meaning in the novel would end here. Luckily, Pavić juxtaposes it with outrageously fantastic material that "calls attention to its fictive nature"[6] and emphasizes the novel's nonmimetic character. Again, the significance of this device for the reader is more than merely philosophical; it is precisely this gap between the factual material and the fantastic that creates the sense of mystery, the illusion of "meaning" within the novel, the equivalent of the bottom in the Khazar jar. In the "Preliminary Notes" Pavić has this to say: "Imagine two men holding a captured puma on a rope. If they want to approach each other, the puma will attack, because the rope will slacken; only if they both pull simultaneously on the rope is the puma equidistant from the two of them" (14). If the factual information holds one end of the rope and the fictional or fantastic holds the other, then the poor reader is doomed to examining only one end of the rope at a time. If he tries to bring them together, the mystery will immediately devour whatever possible interpretation he might have offered, the same way the reality of the Khazar jar would have destroyed the student's every attempt to explain it.

Pavić creates this tension between the factual and the fictional material very gradually. In the beginning of the novel he carefully slips single fantastic sentences into an entire paragraph of fact. For instance, the first paragraph of the section "A History of *The Khazar Dictionary*," which begins the "Preliminary Notes," is a relatively accurate introduction to the basic history of the Khazar people. Yet, sprinkled throughout this rather long passage, we find sentences like these: "It is known that the winds that brought them were masculine winds, which never bring rain—winds with a yoke of grass, which they trail through the sky like a beard" (1-2); or "Eyewitnesses noted that the shadows of the houses in the capital held their outlines for years, although the buildings themselves had already been destroyed long before. They held fast in the wind and in the waters of the Volga" (3). The reader easily accepts these passages as highly metaphoric descriptions. As he continues through the novel, however, the fantastic elements gain more and more control of it, and he begins to realize that the novel that had seemed fairly reliable at the beginning is now completely fantastic and utterly unreal. At this point the reader can either choose to assume that the novel does not contain any "meaning" and discard it, or he can intensify the search for this "meaning" and begin investigating other possibilities.

Should the reader decide to continue in his search, he would eventually encounter another device that Pavić uses to create the illusion that *Dictionary of the Khazars* is an ordinary novel, a device I have termed deceptive patterning. While ordinary novels "pattern complexities into some coherent form which eventually yields explanations" (Seltzer 1), Pavić uses this expectation of coherent form to mislead the reader, knowing that, like the student who was deceived by the Khazar jar, most readers assume that external form bears a direct relationship to inner content or meaning. Having found that certain objects, details, and phrases recur, the reader begins to hypothesize about possible connections among them. Once he begins to consider and investigate these possibilities, he finds more and more things to add to the pattern, but the more the reader searches for meaning, the less he finds, and thus the game begins. It then becomes a very simple job of adding to the pile of repetitions, and the more Pavić adds, the more the reader believes that the patterns, and therefore the meanings behind them, exist—the same way the student is completely misled by the external appearance of the Khazar jar into believing that the mysterious bottom can be explained according to ordinary rules.

One of the most delightful examples of deceptive patterning in *Dictionary of the Khazars* is the use of time markers. In the "Preliminary Notes" we are told that "Here all dates are calculated according to a single calendar" (10). Yet we find that Pavić marks time in each of the three books, Christian, Islamic, and Hebrew, according to both the standard Julian calendar and their own respective religious calendars. This means that dates in the Christian book are often marked according to the various saints' days in the Orthodox calendar, while in the Islamic and Hebrew books, dates are often marked according to the months and days of their own calendars. Pavić does this because he knows that, having been told that the dates are supposedly calculated according to one system, the reader will be incapable of resisting the temptation to try to discover the unifying principle behind the references to the various calendars.

For example, the entry for Samuel Cohen says he died on September 24, 1689 (210). We are also told that he fell on the battlefield at the precise moment that Avram Brankovich was killed. Thus it seems to the reader that he has found the beginning of a pattern. From there, it is only a short time until he begins investigating all the other dates given in the novel to see if they, too, fit the pattern. Already the reader believes that the dates form a pattern, and he will continue to search for the organizing principle behind it without ever questioning whether the pattern truly exists or if its existence even matters.

By this point, Pavić's illusion is so successful that he has the reader busy digging around in the novel for a meaning behind the "patterns," a meaning that the reader is certain must exist somewhere and that requires only a little more work to discover. Still, somehow Pavić manages to make the "meaning" continue to elude the reader's grasp every time he thinks he has finally gotten it within reach, while still managing to keep him interested in the search. The whole process is very much like the torture of Tantalus in the Underworld: every time Tantalus reaches down for a drink of water, it flows away from his lips and every time he reaches up for a bite of fruit, the branch pulls away from his hand. Pavić repeatedly offers the reader so much information that *does* make sense that the reader takes for granted the existence of some ultimate meaning or order within the novel.

According to the conflicting texts within the novel, several different Khazar dictionaries seem to exist. First, there is *The Khazar Dictionary* published in 1691 by Johannes Daubmannus, in which was supposedly collected all the information concerning the Khazars, their culture, history, and, of course, the Khazar Polemic, all of which was organized in alphabetical order and according to the religious affiliation of the source: Christian, Muslim, or Jewish. The other Khazar dictionary (or dictionaries) is a collection of all the information relating to the art of the Khazar dream hunters, which has been passed down from one generation of dream hunters to the next. The Khazar dream hunters believe that:

> Man's dreams are the part of human nature that goes back to this Adam-the-precursor, this heavenly angel, because he thought the way we dream. . . . Hence, dream hunters plunge into other people's dreams and sleep and from them extract little pieces of Adam-the-precursor's being, composing them into a whole, into so-called Khazar dictionaries, with the aim of having all these assembled books incarnate on earth the enormous body of Adam Ruhani. (166)

In the entry "Dream Hunters" in the Red, or Christian, book, we find that Mokaddasa Al-Safer (who shares nothing beyond his name with the historical Mokaddasa) is considered the best of the Khazar dream readers because he could "dive deeper into dreams than anyone before him, straight down to God, for at the bottom of every dream lies God" (68). He is also "believed to have shaped one of Adam Ruhani's strands of hair in his dictionary of dreams" (190). Thus it appears that the goal behind compiling *The Khazar Dictionary* is to achieve some sort of knowledge of the underlying structure of existence, whether it is called order, meaning, or God. Unfortunately, the narrator tells us, only two copies of *The Khazar*

Dictionary survived, the poisoned gold copy and the companion silver copy.

Of all the readers of *The Khazar Dictionary* in the novel, the most important ones to mention here are Dr. Isailo Suk and Father Theoctist Nikolsky, because they are the only ones who read *The Khazar Dictionary* in its entirety. Suk is important because he happened to own what is probably the last surviving copy of the 1691 Daubmannus edition of *The Khazar Dictionary* and because he changed his manner of reading: "He was convinced that his was the poisoned copy, where the reader would die at the ninth page, so he never read more than four pages at a time, just to keep on the safe side" (121). Authors generally expect their books to be read straight through and usually in sections longer than four pages, just as Pavić expects the reader to follow the clues he has so conveniently laid out like a trail meandering through the novel. Suk managed to circumvent the author and change the ending of the book (i.e., he avoided his own death-by-poisoning) by adjusting his manner of reading to the text. Yet changing his manner of reading was not enough to guarantee his survival. Suk died because he misunderstood the "meaning" or "purpose" of his reading.

The most important reader is Theoctist Nikolsky. Theoctist is the seventeenth-century scribe who originally gathered the three versions (Christian, Muslim, and Jewish) of *The Khazar Dictionary* together. He himself helped to compile the Christian part and he secretly "memorized the entire manuscript [of the Muslim part] letter by letter without understanding a word, because it was in Arabic" (313). When Cohen fell on the battlefield, Theoctist gathered up and "read the Hebrew pages from the bag, trying not to comprehend or interpret anything written on them" (323). It is no accident that he is the only person in the entire novel who actually succeeds in reading all three parts of *The Khazar Dictionary* and survives the experience. Nor is it accidental that his name comes from the Greek nouns *theos* and *ktistes,* meaning *One Who Creates God.* Theoctist Nikolsky represents the only truly appropriate approach to the mystery of the Khazar jar and therefore to the novel itself and ultimately to reality, because he instinctively understood that the process itself is the "meaning" or "purpose" of reading. Theoctist spent years striving to collect the different parts of *The Khazar Dictionary,* and when he finally did read them, he did not attempt to understand or analyze them. When he had finally finished writing out the dictionary and handed it over to the publisher, Theoctist felt no satisfaction that he had finally reached his "goal." Instead, he found that his "hunger" for collecting (i.e., passive reading for information) had changed and intensified into a hunger for creating (i.e., active reading as part of the creative process). Theoctist is allowed to live simply because he does not *realize* that he has solved the mystery and therefore is unable to divulge the secret of *The Khazar Dictionary* to anyone else.

Believing that the compilation and reading of *The Khazar Dictionary* is the goal that justifies and completes Theoctist's search is as inappropriate as saying that the bottom of the Khazar jar is the only justification for its existence. Theoctist is a creator because he destroys the illusion of meaning (order, God, etc.) as the primary aim, by showing us that the value of the experience is in the searching, not the finding. The value of the Khazar jar, of the novel *Dictionary of the Khazars*, and of existence itself is in the illusion of the bottom, the illusion of order, meaning, or God, because it is the illusion of a "goal" or "purpose" that draws us onward. Without it, people often lose hope, and with it, they lose the will to live. This is why the teacher breaks the Khazar jar and why it continues to function for the student as if it had never been broken; because the mystery still exists, the student can still hope to discover its secret and this hope will encourage the student to continue to search and think. This is why Pavić creates such an elaborate illusion of credible reality and then shoots holes all through it with outrageously imaginative, fantastic episodes. This is why he creates such a web of interconnecting repetitions and then refuses to let them become a pattern. All this is done to encourage the reader to search and think, to learn new ways of perceiving, and, finally, to learn to value the process over the end. In other words, Pavić uses these devices in an attempt to force the reader to shift from a linear, goal-oriented, that is, Aristotelian method of reading, to a more dialogical, process-oriented, or nonaristotelian, method.

Innumerable times throughout the novel, Pavić explicitly points out the necessity for an active and interactive relationship between the reader and the writer with respect to "meaning" in the novel. He stresses the fact that each reader must "forge his own path," and that "he can rearrange [the dictionary] in an infinite number of ways, like a Rubik cube. . . . Hence, each reader will put together the book for himself, as in a game of dominoes or cards, and, as with a mirror, he will get out of this dictionary as much as he puts into it, for, as is written on one of the pages of this lexicon, you cannot get more out of the truth than what you put into it" (13).

Pavić laments the fact that "today's reading audience believes that the matter of imagination . . . does not concern them in the least" (11) because he believes that, like Samuel Cohen and Avram Brankovich, who each dreamed the other's waking life, the text inextricably connects the writer to the reader and vice versa. Just as the mysterious bottom in the Khazar jar is the key to the discrepancy between its external appearance and its true nature, the question of the "meaning" of a text marks the precise point of connection between the writer and the reader. Thus, if addressing the question of the "meaning" of *Dictionary of the Khazars* is still possible after having spent so much time discussing how Pavić completely undermines its existence, it would be this: that the writer and the reader both bear equal responsibility for the "meaning" or "truth" of a text; that like the two men with the puma, each one is completely responsible for the other's very existence; and that the punishment for shirking this responsibility is death—not just the literal death of the text but the intellectual and spiritual deaths of both the writer and the reader.

NOTES

[1]Milorad Pavić, "Hazarski Ćup i Druga Lažna Sećanja," *Istorija, Stalež i Stil* (Novi Sad: Matica Srpska, 1985), 270-78.

[2]Milorad Pavić, *Dictionary of the Khazars*, trans. Christina Pribićević-Zorić (New York: Knopf, 1988), 259-60; hereafter cited parenthetically.

[3]Barbara Herrnstein Smith, "Contingencies of Value," in *Canons*, ed. Robert von Hallberg (Chicago: Univ. of Chicago Press, 1984), 17.

[4]Alvin J. Seltzer, *Chaos in the Novel: The Novel in Chaos* (New York: Schocken Books, 1974), 1; hereafter cited parenthetically.

[5]Leonard Orr, *Problems and Poetics of the Nonaristotelian Novel* (London: Associated University Presses, 1991), 31; italics added.

[6]Orr, 31.

Chaos, Knowledge, and Desire: Narrative Strategies in Dictionary of the Khazars

Tomislav Z. Longinović

> People think reality is another word for chaos. But in reality it is more complex. Legend embodies it in a sound that enables it to spread all over the world.
>
> —Laibach, "Death in Conversation," in *Kapital* (Mute Records, 1992)

Prigogine's theory of chaos stresses the ability of systems to act in nonlinear and self-organizing fashions. The systemic vision of "ordered chaos" has been applied to a variety of phenomena, from predicting traffic flows to understanding variations in the weather patterns. Predictably enough, the narrative patterns which try to articulate nonlinearity and self-organization have begun to surpass the metaphors of coordinate systems and statistical tables. The rise of fractal geometry and the search for "strange attractors" remind one of narrative constructions of writers like Cortázar, Calvino, or Pynchon. The emergence of the novel-puzzle, which holds a central, unreachable secret and offers a multitude of reading paths toward the ultimate knowledge whose realization is displaced and postponed, testifies to similar epistemological positions of the subject. My main focus will move along the lines set by N. Katherine Hayles in her examination of discourses of literature and science:[1] the question of influences between literary and scientific discourses will not be examined in any particular direction. Instead, my focus will be on the cultural context of postmodernity as a condition for the emergence of epistemological hypotheses of chaos theory and the narrative organization of Milorad Pavić's *Dictionary of the Khazars.*

The apparent convergence of the narratives developed by chaos theory in mathematical sciences with those of textual postmodernity is symptomatic of the cognitive paradigm which has been resurrecting discourses simultaneously positioned as the very limit of modernity and its cultural opponent. Indeed, the problematic nature of human truth and knowledge has already come under scrutiny by modernity; but postmodernity goes beyond this epistemological anxiety by foregrounding its axiom of the truth as a construction rooted in the language which articulates it. Modernity's anxiety is accepted and turned into the object of epistemological contemplation. Therefore, the notion of postmodern culture necessarily functions as a theoretical umbrella which encompasses different events and practices affected by the chronic uncertainty of the subject. This emergent condition recognizes the irreducible play of contingencies which structure the subject-that-wants-to-know as it produces "truth" and "knowledge" about the world. For example, the concept of self-organization in nonlinear patterns characteristic of Prigogine's chaos theory counters the narrative model of a reachable certainty about the desire posited by scientific rationalism which seeks to know and describe a limited and abstracted number of phenomena. Instead, these new models reject the limitation of scientific models and begin to project a desire for the knowledge of the ever elusive "total reality." This quest for totality comes after the limits of representation have been surpassed by the awareness that "reality" is a process of constant and necessary invention.

The realization that knowledge may itself consist of tools that are utilized in its acquisition has entered both science and literature with Heisenberg's uncertainty principle and Borges's labyrinth. Both the scientist and the writer became aware that they are tracing the effects and limits of their languages and their instruments, which in turn gave impetus to the theories that stress self-reflexivity, irreversibility, nonlinearity and self-organization. The problem encountered by the exact sciences in the inevitable reduction of the totality of phenomena to the set of observable and measurable variables is mirrored in literary theory and criticism through the problem of interpretation. Some aspects of the text are necessarily suppressed at the expense of others for the critical text to gain coherence and manufacture intelligibility inherent in the old definition of the critic. Poststructuralism emerged as a reaction against these petrified institutional practices by focusing on the centrality of language as a nonlinear and self-organized medium whose role is not limited to the articulation and communication of "external realities." In fact, these "realities" were now understood as constructions dependent on the symbolic networks that stabilize meanings and create knowledge about them. The role of psychoanalysis in these epistemological shifts is often overlooked, although Freud's desire to create "the science of the soul" introduced most of the theoretical models characteristic of chaotic systems.

First of all, the concepts of identity and agency are exploded through the multiple operation of *Lustprinzip,* which regulates the operation of the entire psychic system. The representational sphere of language assumes the role of totality, which is regulated by the desire to eliminate frustrations that emerge from "reality." The entire psychic apparatus is conditioned by the fundamental need to achieve pleasure and avoid pain, which would keep the subject in a state of zero-degree stimulation. This need for constancy is the work of *Todestrieb,* the death drive, which Freud postulates as the origin and end of all other drives. The death drive forces the subject to seek certainty, to avoid excessive stimulation, and to direct its mental functioning away from the displeasures of an anxiety-ridden environment. At the end of that road is the knowledge of death itself, which is a metaphoric representation of the ultimate secret. Therefore, the desire to know is the desire for the impossible, since death is not knowable in terms outside itself.

The subject who desires knowledge creates narrative events by substituting words for reality, since the ultimate reality will remain a secret as long as one lives. As the subject constructs meanings about ego and its objects, its actions are determined by the interchange between pleasure and displeasure, whose relationship Freud defined as a "highly indefinite form," postulating a model of nonlinear organization. The grounding of thought in realms beyond the reach of the body and its mental derivatives becomes naive after Freud's discoveries. Humans are the creators of knowledge which they mistake for truth and reality, because their cognitive models are structured by the imaginary work of the *Lustprinzip.* Since the stability of psychic functions depends on the basic demand for certainty (*Konstanzprinzip*), the potential for gratification is imagined in the immediate future. The very demand for absolute knowledge of truth and reality is an attempt to fill the gap after the *Spaltung* between the one who observes and the one who is being observed occurs within the subject. This halucinatory theory of knowledge, which avoids reality by forging a symbolic order for the body to misrepresent itself, is regulated by the rhythmic discharges of free and bound energy of the organism. Freud's return to the body forced philosophy to recognize that its love of wisdom is a guided hallucination, regulated by the chaotic operations of *Lustprinzip.*

The discoveries of chaos theory enhanced the radical uncertainty inherent in these insights, while at the same time they affirmed that order of a different kind lurks in the depths of disordered phenomena. Prigogine's emphasis on self-organization within chaotic systems points to the fact that the spontaneous emergence of order is possible within physical reality. A very similar vision of "ordered chaos" is present in the wildly successful novel *Dictionary of the Khazars,* by Milorad Pavić. For Pavić, the hidden order of his novel is not guaranteed by any reference to the stability of an "external reality" or even to the internal coherence of the text itself, but is contained in the process of reading. Each reader is invited to forge "his own path" through the book, which is itself arranged like an encyclopedia: "No chronology will be observed here, nor is one necessary. Hence, each reader will put together the book for himself, as in a game of dominoes or cards, and, as with the mirror, he will get out of this dictionary as much as he puts into it, for, as is written on one of the pages of this lexicon, you cannot get more out of the truth than what you put into it."[2]

The decision to do away with chronology or linearity of the narrative development is motivated by the desire to bring literature closer to the chaotic experience of the world, where each of the participants in the game of living ceaselessly deciphers the world as a book, making sense out of irreducible contingencies of reading. Pavić manufactured his chaotic narrative around the alphabetical order of the Serbian Cyrillic. He maintains that because "letters do not follow the same sequence in every alphabet," every translation has changed the original order of Daubmannus's version of the *Khazar Dictionary.* (10). The order of entries in the dictionary shifts every time it is translated into a different language. This creates "an ever-changing hierarchy of names," which determines ways in which we invent our "reality." Therefore, the activity of reading is likened to looking into the mirror of the text, which reflects back to the reader the work of his or her own *Lustprinzip* and *Todestrieb* as order is recuperated from the chaotic arrangement of entries in *The Dictionary of the Khazars.* The authorial promise in the introduction that only "someone who can read through the sections of one book in their proper order can create the world anew," positions the reader as a seeker for proper order within the alphabetical ordering of Greek, Hebrew, and Arabic languages in which the "seventeenth century original" was written. As a specialist who created the theory of Serbian baroque literature, Pavić intentionally performs the discourse of uncertainty characteristic of a world that wishes to return to medieval certainties and divine ordering of the universe.

In his 1985 essay on nonmimetic styles of writing, Pavić uses one of the segments from his own book to posit a theory of fantastic literature which recalls this neobaroque positioning.[3] The entry entitled "Khazar Jar" narrates a parable of the student and the teacher who discuss the fantastic nature of the jar. The student discovers that the jar has an impossibly deep bottom, although it looks normal from the outside. The teacher drops a stone into the jar and after counting to seventy, both of them hear a splash. After demonstrating to the student that the jar's bottom is finite but deeper than its material dimensions, the teacher says: "I could tell you what your jar means, but ponder first whether it is worth it. As soon as I tell you, the jar will inevitably be worth less to you and less to others" (259). The teacher is implying that he is in possession of knowledge which defies conventional perception and logic, yet that the value of the Khazar jar will be lost if that knowledge is spelled out. Nevertheless, the teacher retains the secret knowledge whose very postulation fuels the narrative machinery of the novel. The mystery and secrecy that permeate the gaps between individual dictionary entries supplement the alphabet as the organizing principle of the novel's chaotic structure. The narrative decoding can take place because the authorial voice periodically offers the promise of order beyond the chaotic blend of mythological, historical, and folkloristic narratives about the destroyed nation of Khazars.

After the student agrees with his point, the teacher takes a stick and smashes the jar to pieces. When the startled boy asks why he had destroyed it, the teacher answers: "The damage would be if I had first told you what the jar was for and had then smashed it. This way, you don't know its purpose and there is no damage done; it will continue to serve you as though it had never been smashed" (259). The fantastic event is predicated on the continuing work of the tacit assumption that there exists a possibility of insight beyond the apparent contradiction between perception of the material jar and its invisible interior. The secret lies in the extended fall of the pebble, in the narrative intervention which distorts perception and promises an explanation of this fantastic event. The secret continues to elicit responses from readers, who, like scientists faced with a difficult problem, continue to shift paradigms until they discover a way of reading which convinces them that they are on the path of knowledge. The metaphor of the jar that continues to hold knowledge although it has been smashed to pieces, replicates the formula of the order that may have been there before chaos or the order that will arise once the contingencies of chaos have been sorted out.

Pavić develops his chaotic system by constructing the narrative around the event know as the "Khazar Polemic," whose temporal distance makes its truth value so problematic that the reader has a hard time deciding whether to assign it to the realm of history or mythology. The undecidability of this event causes a proliferation of narratives which attempt a reconstructive explanation. Each dictionary entry is informed by an absolute certainty about the nature and outcome of the Khazar Polemic, since it is associated with one of the major religions: Christianity, Islam, and Judaism. Each religious representative tells a story which claims a victory in the Khazar Polemic, resulting in the eventual conversion of the

Khazars. Pavić's book is therefore divided into three parts, which in the original edition have different colored pages: red-paged Christian, green-paged Muslim, and yellow-paged Jewish books within the main *Dictionary*. The narrative evolves as this process of triangulation is extended throughout the novel, from the original participants in the polemic to the chroniclers of the debate and then to the seventeenth- and twentieth-century scholars of the Khazars.

A supplement to the complex narrative structure of the novel is its division into male and female editions. The reader is apparently given a choice of reading as a man or as a woman. This gender performance reveals a complexity of the relationship between body and time, since the encounter between two contemporary scholars of the Khazars is represented differently in the male and female edition of Pavić's novel. This narrative segment foregrounds "Xeroxed sheets" which Dr. Kabir Muawia hands to Dr. Dorothea Schultz. The knowledge of the contents of the sheets is displaced and never fully revealed to the reader. Instead, Pavić focuses on a brush of Dorothea's hand against that of her male colleague. In the female version this is followed by her sensation that "our pasts and our futures were in our fingers and that they had touched" (293). In the female edition the reader is constructed as prone to sentimentality that crosses the boundaries of gender and ethnicity, since it is also a touch between a Jewish woman and an Arab man. The history which seems to come to life in their fingers immediately encompasses a total temporal dimension that encodes both the past and the future as the infinite conflict between Jews and Arabs. The touch between a man and a woman across a historical abyss, challenges and at the same time reinforces the power of Judaism and Islam over the bodies they structure. The present tense of their touch activates a sense of time that can be named as future-within-past. Dorothea's body contains the time of her nation, which molds her emotions into meanings derivative from the past of her people. Pavić posits the feminine as a receptacle of this terror of time, which causes the body to succumb to limitations as it brushes against the other.

The male edition foregrounds the same narrative context in which Dorothea says: "I could have pulled the trigger there and then" (293). The posture of love in the female edition is changed into a threat to kill the other in the male one. Dr. Muawia is saved by Dorothea's surge of interest in the content of "Xeroxed sheets," while the reader wonders why these stereotypical roles for males and females are coded along the axis of male desire to contemplate violence and female preoccupation with the body and desire. This division causes a radical bifurcation of the narrative dimension as it further disturbs the position of the reader in search of a higher order of meaning.

Around this complex narrative skeleton there is an abundance of entries which further displace linearity and pull the narrative in a multitude of unpredictable directions. The reader is being led astray on purpose, as the narrator constantly assures him that there is an order underlying the chaos, and that it is the reader's duty to discover it through his own, particular arrangement of the dictionary entries. "For the time being, *The Khazar Dictionary* is still just a heap of random letters, names and pseudonyms," says one of the protagonists. The task of the reader is mimicked in the novel by the secret sect of dream-hunters, who attempt to reconstruct Adam Cadmon, a cosmic man whose body corresponds to the text of the original edition of the *Khazar Dictionary.* Adam Cadmon is a metaphor of the imaginary order that dwells within the chaos of "random letters, names and pseudonyms" that characterizes the current version of the *Khazar Dictionary.* By placing the original and complete book in the past, Pavić liberates his present literary construction from the need for narrative coherence.

In his 1985 essay on the Khazar jar, Pavić offers his theory of the fantastic after surveying the history of the genre. First of all, the term he chooses to describe the performance of the fantastic writer is tied to the debunking of literary realism. Pavić offers a nonmimetic approach, which redefines Plato's theory of mimesis by insisting that the fantastic must insert itself at the level of ideal forms and, as in Byzantine literature, projects a monistic image of the universe. Instead of mimesis, the new approach should be "a synthesis of poetic, documentary or even scientific texts with narrative prose."[4] Pavić calls for total literature, the one that does not compromise itself by contemplating what is taken as material reality but positions its narrative as a world before reality, using erudition to assemble an array of literary and extraliterary discourses into a nonmimetic novel. By refusing mimesis as a method of novelistic poetics, the writer produces fantastic literature which posits a new world. That world blends Pavić's folkloristic fantasy with the anxiety of history, which doubts every certainty posed in the past while experiencing its unbearable burden. Erudition is used not to enlighten or inform the reader but acts as an effect of history that replicates the narrative chaos out of which every reader is promised the possibility of carving an imaginary labyrinth. This narrative construction emerges within the postmodern condition, which seems to resurrect a baroque vision of the universe ruled by the unfathomable powers whose trappings remain forever inaccessible. Yet the secret order which Pavić posits beyond the narrative chaos seems to refer to the medieval stability the baroque yearned for. In many ways the tragedy of Yugoslavia, where the novel was first published, may have been the ultimate revelation of the secret the novel is elaborating on. The secret bonds of blood and soil that the Khazars never understand have been revived in the territory of former Yugoslavia through these narratives. The symptomatic nature of novelistic poetics has once again contributed to the almost prophetic dimension of this multifaceted textual performance.

NOTES

[1]N. Katherine Hayles, *Chaos Bound: Orderly Disorder in Contemporary Literature and Culture* (Ithaca: Cornell Univ. Press, 1990). Hayles proposes a nonhierarchical study of influences between literature and science, rather then privileging either of the two terms as more influential than the other.

[2]Milorad Pavić, *Dictionary of the Khazars,* trans. Christina Pribićević-Zorić (New York: Vintage International, 1989), 13; hereafter cited parenthetically.

[3]Milorad Pavić, "Hazarski ćup i druga lažna sećanja," in *Istorija, stalež i stil* (Novi Sad: Matica srpska, 1985), 270-78.

[4]Milorad Pavić, "Hazarski ćup," 275.

Landscape Painted with Tea *as an Ecological Novel*

Jasmina Mihajlović

> "Suddenly I freeze. I sense, I clearly sense, somebody watching me. Somebody's eyes are fixed upon me. And then I realize that staring out at me from my glasses, quite near, is my right eye transformed into my left. . . ."
>
> —Milorad Pavić, *Landscape Painted with Tea*

In the interplay of many themes woven into the structure of *Landscape Painted with Tea*, by Milorad Pavić, it is possible to follow a thread related to the problems of ecology. This thread is drawn through all the layers of the novel and is a part of the relations among the main characters and their links with the world, with nature, and the cosmos. Though it is the Weaver who stands at one end of this thread, who is spinning his web that darkens the light and colors of our world, and who wants to spin an intrigue against mankind and the universe; at the opposite end is a different person, one deft at unraveling things, a new Ariadne. The contours of this second character, who hovers between reality and dream, are painted in the tones of a watercolor with the tints of tea and therefore not as easily discernible as in a photograph. However, it may well be a character whose home is this world and whose image may be linked to the concept of ecology. For it should not be forgotten that the combined form of two ancient Greek words—*oikos* and *logos*—(home and word) make up the word *ecology*.[1]

As a grandiose artistic synthesis of all the aspects of ecological problems, the novel speaks of survival and resistance to the apocalypse and can be taken as an appeal for equilibrium, for the rejection of alienation and self-alienation, for a return to the art of living. The novel is an accusation and a condemnation, an ominous warning. As a reflection in a mirror, the novel depicts the face and reverse side of man, his twofold nature and certitude. This story of the rise of civilization and the mind's brilliant development is transformed into a picture of man's self-annihilation, an edifice of destruction of home and homeland, of nature and the world that is man's great construct.

This tale of the aspiration toward, but also resistance to, the effort to transform the world into a landscape painted in a uniform whiteness or blackness, lacking the reflection of the sky in the water, the shadow of a cloud on the earth, and the glow of a subterranean flame, has man, woman, and Satan as its protagonists. Woven into them, of course, are the reader and the author, past and future generations, as well as present-day man, who is balancing on a tightrope called the ecological crisis.

The ecological plane in the novel can be partly perceived through one of the central themes in all of Pavić's prose works, namely, the problem of identity. The novel has dramatically united, as in a Tower of Babel, the multifarious voices seeking an answer to the questions of personal, sexual, familial, generational, national, religious, collective, and cosmic identity. This search for identity as knowledge of the essence of the contemporary world order by means of immersion into the past and prophecy of the future is, in fact, the search for our original image in order to help us envision our future one and in order to help the world survive.

It is through Atanas Svilar, alias Razin, alias . . ., who tries by means of disguise to alter all his identities and thereby lose all identity, that we are shown the ostensible result of alienation from one's own nature, from nature in general, and from the cosmically ordained order. Atanas's hubris is punished by those cosmic powers responsible for him, powers that are not God's but Satan's, in what looks like a unique solution in a topsy-turvy world in which the Devil himself can become a new Messiah.

In addition to Atanas, many other characters are searching for their lost identity in an effort either to change it or, upon finding it, to acquire it anew or else to preserve their existing one. The difference among these characters is in how they go about accomplishing these aims. They either set out to reach themselves and preserve their inner nature or else they retain only their external similarities with their human and godlike image but lose their real substance. And when a man learns something about his roots, he can then truly define himself.

Atanas Svilar defined himself when on Mount Athos he realized that he belonged to the order of monk "solitaries" and then decided to change his whole identity in the belief this would bring him success in his profession as an architect, a vocation that belongs to the other order of monks—"solidaries." By changing his name, his mother tongue, and his homeland, by transforming himself into Atanas Razin, he does achieve a dizzying business success, but not in his own profession, rather in the field of engineering and pharmaceuticals. He, in fact, attains the position of a man who "owns 2 percent of the world's income from the sale of nuclear equipment for peacetime purposes."

Everything linked to Atanas's success, his operations, hobbies or private life, can be observed through the ecological, or rather the antiecological, dimension. His California factory begins by producing dyes, varnishes, and polishes, while at the same time, in his leisure hours, he abandons dyes and his youthful interest in studying them to begin to paint landscapes with tea and to draw the (former) residences of Josip Broz Tito. Soon afterward, his firm begins to deal in pharmaceuticals, medicaments, and chemicals. But chemistry is often very close to modern alchemy which attempts to create a new man—a degenerate. Atanas Razin, in full strength and with a fair number of years to his age, as well as with the sum of one billion dollars, instead of healing people, concludes one of his deals of the century by selling antifoliage poisons to the American army for its wartime operations in Asia.

> His poisons had destroyed everything down to a depth of one meter wherever they fell, and they fell not only on the ground but into the human bloodstream as well. The veterans who fifteen years before had trod the ground that was now denuded sued Atanas's company for grievous and permanent bodily injury, which was slowly but increasingly making itself felt.
>
> They asked for hefty compensation and Atanas paid it, rubbing his hands contentedly, because they had not thought of seeking compensation for the next three generations of their descendants.

Conceived as a novel for lovers of crossword puzzles, *Landscape Painted with Tea* is partly constructed of small blocks that make up the Testimonial in honor of Atanas Razin, formerly Atanas Svilar, American magnate of Russo-Serbian origin. The Testimonial compiled by unknown authors contains a wealth of varied materials: reminiscences, letters, confessions, stories, sketches, articles, clippings. The Testimonial of Razin's business operations and successes is recollected by Atanas's mother. One of her statements reads: "Atanas, my dear, all you need now is just one letter at the beginning of your name (the one at the end) and you will become a man." It reveals all the subsequent designs, aspirations, and achievements of this "Benefactor" and "Founder."

The anonymous compilers of the Testimonial underline the mystery of Razin's swift, multinational, financial success and the impenetrability of the circumstances that helped a talented architect, who failed to build anything in his own country, to become a "Mr. 2 percent" with wealth that could provide for several generations.

What was it that helped Razin attain wealth, power, and prestige? Changing his identity and leaving his country, certainly, but not this alone. A turning point in Atanas's life, it would seem, was his meeting with one Obren Opsenitsa, an architect, in Vienna. This occurred soon after the change of everything that Svilar-Razin used to be. Opsenitsa, Razin's schoolmate, an administrative bigwig in his own homeland, the man who had thwarted the "old" Atanas from, among other things, pursuing his profession as an architect, became, after the whispered contract in Vienna, a collaborator in the founding of the ABC Engineering and Pharmaceuticals Company, by lending Atanas money. Thus the victim called change, or the betrayal of national identity, was built into the business temple of Atanas Razin.

Razin's next business move is his peculiar act of purchasing chairs. Throughout the world, Atanas keeps buying seats, armchairs, benches—in parks, bookshops, theaters, churches, and even the Italian Parliament. By occupying, in this persistent but unnoticeable way, sectors of space, small blocks of the world, Razin lays the ground for his final achievement, which is to endow himself with limitless power, not only over space but also over time. This kind of power means governing the past, the present, and the future, as well as controlling worldly and spiritual matters, the subterranean and heavenly ones.

The central nonecological story in Razin's biography consists of the tales of three sisters: Olga, Azra, and Cecilia. Razin decides to buy from the sisters, his former paramours, the "white bees," that is, the future generation of yet unborn souls. Together with this purchase there is added the purchase of souls and their property and their future "Lebensraum." Razin prepares a new grave in the future for the reanimated Gogolian souls:

> "Besides the old way of man's exploitation by man, or the exploitation of one class by another, a far more practical solution now presents itself: the exploitation of one generation by another. . . .
>
> "Much more expedient for exploitation are future, still-unborn generations, those that have not yet found a soul on the street, those that have yet to have their fill of tears, unborn little souls that are not yet subject to any legal regulations, that cannot defend themselves, not even by spitting in someone's eye. That is why it is not the sons who should be exploited, as they were by your naïve fathers, but the future, the grandchildren and great-grandchildren, the great-great-grandchildren and the white bees, as you would say. . . . The objective is to exploit and obtain their living space as well, to possess, drink, and breathe even now their land, water, and air. . . . And everybody knows what goes with water, land and air. The grave. . . ."

For, as the voice of one of the sisters goes on to say, where would trains full of irradiated milk and ships with nuclear waste that ominously roam the globe find their haven but in the graves Atanas buys together with unborn children and land. But taking "inventory of the future means violating the rules of heaven and entering its jurisdiction."

The signing of the most profitable deal of the century, the total purchase of the past and future in the present, would have enabled Razin to achieve definitive domination over the world in which he is sojourning only temporarily. Atanas Razin, alias Man, alias False Satan, who has polluted this world, wants to start a revolution in the universe as well. However, this grand funeral of the world is prevented or will be prevented by a child of twofold origin. This possibility is in the hands of the heroine and the female reader of the novel. The child is a young devil, Satan, who is reborn in order to save mankind from the approaching cataclysm. For the destruction of the world would sever the last link that ties Satan to God through man, which binds him to his former own angelic past, before falling down to the Earth or into Hell. This is why Satan will try to thwart Razin's intentions. Woman as the second potential savior, whose possible mission is hinted at by the author, is the basis for his hope for the future as a reflection of the past and the world order. This concept is clarified by the author later in the novel.

Razin's frightening concept, which, unfortunately, is not only the idea of the literary hero but also a fantastic reality whose debts we are already paying, could easily be realized since the three sisters have agreed to have such a sale contract drawn up. For today, contracts with the Devil are no longer individual but rather collective ones, without our consent. Moreover, the whole plan acquires even more monstrous features if we bear in mind that the three sisters are the symbols of the religious-cultural-spiritual, ideological, and economic spheres in the Balkans. No wonder man sometimes asks himself whether it is only individuals who betray their homeland or if the homeland today can betray its individuals as well. At least for some unfortunate nations, which live in mysterious interspaces, the annulment of the past makes it possible to sell out the future.

The heaven of modern mankind has been shattered in the struggle for wealth and power. In the world where the new but false God is identified with Money, contemporary vain man is eager for prestige, power, and success and is ready to make awesome sacrifices, so that a real God or nature or small but disunited nations are the first to suffer. They are first of all threatened by domestic self-styled benefactors who attempt to redeem themselves by building memorials for their own benefit and against their progeny. The small nations are also menaced by merchants of imported values and cultures whose purpose is to level out, from a distance, all the variety of this world and its ancient abundance, for the sake of an artificial paradise in which all people will be identical and "happy."

Atanas Razin is a man without a father and without children, without a past or future, without an identity. Deeply aware, in fact, that he has not succeeded either as Svilar or as Razin, that he is unfulfilled, crucified, false, and sterile, he decides to make his life meaningful in the present by identifying himself with something that will bring back his lost authenticity. Feeling that it is his original vocation to be an architect and that he has renounced it, he makes up his mind to start building again and, finally, to find his father.

The reconstruction of Atanas's life, in fact, starts out with the search for his father. But as his problem is not really to discover his true roots, his father, but rather to find a strong father who will meet his needs as a man with a mission, Razin, a creator without individuality, starts building copies of houses that served as residences for Josip Broz Tito: Plavinats, Brioni, and the White Palace. Thus Razin, an anti-Oedipus, through identification and imitation, decides to extend his life and a specific period of time that costs him the loss and renunciation of his individuality.

Razin's relationship with his idol, "the third father" can, to a certain extent, be perceived through the ancient manner of painting and worshiping icons. Tragically torn asunder, dissatisfied but self-adoring and eager for power, this merchant of other people's futures will try to achieve his rise toward unification with the deity in a gradual way, much like the painter of icons did when shaping his figures layer upon layer. At first, there was the visual aspect of what is the outer feature of the figure (home, hills, clothes) and then come the personal features. The method of building up a scene by means of a copy is used by Razin, and it becomes more meaningful if one takes into account the fact that the icon implies an ontological link between the original image and its sequel, so that in creating an icon, one emulates the creation of man. Moreover, the pagan belief that energy can be transmitted from someone else by means of a picture is transformed by Christianity into the conviction that the icon has miraculous healing powers. The power of the icon is not weakened by copying but is in fact multiplied, just as the freshening up of an old icon with new colors is not just a job of restoring it but endowing an existing picture with new energy. In this way Atanas's relationship to his alter ego, his double, is not only of a ritualistic or magical nature. It is the path that leads the dual toward the plural.

However, icons can also be palimpsests whose layers conceal an entirely different, invisible, and false image, absently present, so that the worship of the holy image can assume a totally different direction from the desired one.

By copying edifices and their environment, Razin creates an isolated world, a private paradise for the present, a personal ecological oasis, a surrogate of the wealth of life, his own Noah's Ark. By constructing a parallel false homeland, predominantly in America, the new continent that already has its Paris, Alexandria, Athens, or Birmingham, he lives alone in one of his palaces in which he is swamped by snow in midsummer in lieu, perhaps, of a twofold admonition: his own disappearance (at least of the Atanas surnamed Razin) and of the child that is yet to come.

Despite his numerous "crimes," Atanas Razin cannot be regarded as a negative hero (postmodern literature denies the existence of such patterns anyway), because by virtue of his professional and thereby life's destiny, he offers us a picture of a world that, in order to save its own bareness, tends toward standardization and the average. It thus stifles all creative achievements by individuals and generations. False monolithicality, which represents a particular absence of a counterbalance, can lead to more dangerous explosions with catastrophic consequences than cultivated contradictions.

Ideological debts, as the moral and existential pollution of the future, are nearly equally as terrible as the debts of the technological and scientific evolution that leads to the biological pollution of the future. The latest scientific investigations show that social inheritance, not only natural inheritance, enters into the genetic code.

If literature is the revelation of man's situation in the world and if this revelation is metaphorically understood as a picture, then its outlines frame the presented segment of reality, for every book is written for the present day. The perspective of this picture and its background is, in a manner of speaking, a look from the outside in and from the inside out, so that it represents the past and the whole experience that our yesterdays have taught us. But all that could also represent a departure from the frame of the picture which would be life itself or tomorrow, a confirmation in the future of everything that the picture itself has portrayed.

Landscape Painted with Tea is precisely such a picture-novel for a number of reasons. The outstanding one is to be found in the fact that a part of the future that had been forecast in the novel by its author (the novel was published in 1988) has been realized and confirmed. This is to say that all the changes of name, identity, and loves, the numerous marriages, divorces, and illegitimate children, are the reflection of the current (Yugoslavian and East European) reality.[2]

Razin decides to build the copies as an inverted attempt to return to a lost essence when he loses his only great love, Vitacha Milut. Her first husband, Major Pohvalić, decides to take a senseless step and kill the children when he also loses his wife. The similarity between Razin's and Pohvalić's characters is based on the fact that both head toward the same goal: the annihilation of national and universal life by destroying their own children and those of other people as yet unborn. The differences between them are to be seen in the awareness of their acts and in their final outcome. Pohvalić, a man without a memory, who has forgotten the killing of his daughters, is a symbol of frustrated national self-consciousness. But the suicide he commits after his awesome awareness is depicted as a sign of an awakened consciousness and conscientiousness. Razin, however, marches toward his goal perfidiously and deliberately and is prevented in this only through the mechanism of a higher cosmic justice. Still, the major's crime has aggravating circumstances in that he does commit the evil act (by killing female children), while Razin's intention might or might not have been realized. The author tells us that there is a vital difference in the deaths of women, between fertile and barren women, although the killing of women in general is, in a way, the killing of the world. The death of a fertile woman is a single one, a personal death, whereas when a barren woman dies, her death wipes out a whole female line of ancestors; that death "is of cosmic proportions and multiplied a thousandfold. It is the extinction of an entire human milkline" and thus represents a specific kind of destruction of bridges between the past and the future.

Pohvalić's "unconscious" killing of the children can be read as a multiple ecological warning of the danger to future generations of mankind. Frustration of the national consciousness kills ancestors and descendants in a special way and leads to self-destruction. In Razin's case it leads to action without any particularity, the mere emulation of alien and obsolete matters. It also leads to decay and disappearance, just like the "white death" or the fall in the birth rate; it wipes out the beginning and continuation of the human species and prevents the existence of the "white bees." The female line, as a biological link in the chain of being and survival, takes us back to Vitacha Milut, to her position in the ecological orientation of the novel, and to that thread which controls the unraveling of the ecological and the antiecological. It takes us back to love, for *Landscape Painted with Tea* is also a love story.

Like a modern Odysseus, Atanas Razin roams the earth in the hope of finding his Ithaca and Penelope—the values he once possessed. The same meandering paths are followed by all the other characters in their search for their lost homeland, which is both paradise and the other half of their long ago possessed whole.

Landscape Painted with Tea is a multitiered novel, dynamically structured, as is the whole of Pavić's literary opus. Given the fact that it is also a novel for lovers of crossword puzzles, it has its vertical, temporal level and its multilayered horizontal plane. The intersection of these two dimensions forms a third one, the in-depth dimension that allows various perspectives. The resulting myriad meanings enable the reader to operate with multiple interpretations.

If we take the ecological interpretation into account, our attention should be focused on the difference in the transparency of the text, depending on whether it deals with the male or the female personages. If we were to divide the temporal axis into the male-female principle, personified mainly in Razin and Vitacha Milut, it could offer a different reflection in the past, the present, and the future. This is to say that the events linked to Atanas would reflect the present to a greater degree, so that their symbolic aspect as allusive and critical attitudes toward reality would be more easily recognizable. Indeed, the warning of imminent dangers must here and now be perfectly clear. Vitacha's image, of course, implies quite the opposite. It is through her that we sense the spectrum of ecological, philosophical, metaphysical, aesthetic, and poetic themes of this novel. If Razin reflects the political, historical, and fragile world of vanity, then Vitacha as a counterweight marks the timelessness and beauty of the eternal. And what is eternal is to be found in myth.

By using the reinterpretation of myth, its transformation through parody or triviality, by creating a new, private mythology and complex interrelationships among the mythic, the symbolic, and the archetypal, Pavić has painted the landscape of his novel. For myth as a tale above and beyond all tales, as a miniature cosmos, as the universe in an atom, expresses the general in the individual, the spiritual in the materialistic, the internal in the external. Myth preserves the memory of a time when man was God and of a time when he ceased being God.

A whole range of symbols akin to a genetic chain in our organism is bound up with the character of Vitacha. These symbols, set in a complex web, make it possible to move forward by the repetition of an ancient, unfathomable code of the primeval, the code of the original and mysterious essence of existence.

The novel is also a family saga of ancestors and descendants. The story of Vitacha's ancestors, the Riznić family, goes back to the eighteenth century and through a whole set of personages and their fates and encompasses broad geographic areas where the Serbian middle class lived outside the borders of its motherland. This ramified family tree is discontinued with the death of Vitacha's daughters, and the extinction of the female branch of the family in the present becomes the destruction of historical, cultural, and existential abundance. However, this same family tree, although representing the wealth of a beneficial mixture of various nations and their cultures, also carries the danger of denationalization. The line between permeation and disappearance is tenuous and almost invisible. For this reason, Woman as Mother is the one who takes care of the future. She is home and the pillar of the family and of the homeland but also of much more: she is the rejuvenation of the family tree. The four rivers of paradise, which, according to legend, flow from a source or a well at the foot of the tree of life in the center of paradise, then flow to the various corners of the earth.

Razin's "rape" of Vitacha recalls many other mythic rapes that ended badly, at least for one side, either the abductor or the abducted. But his forced and yet willing departure implies fleeing, in fact, the expulsion from paradise.

Paradise, that green garden island, in which there was once a perfect togetherness between Man, God, and all that lived, where the plants, animals, and man existed in harmony and spoke the same tongue, is the lost domicile of Adam and Eve, the lost fatherland of Atanas and homeland of Vitacha, and the forgotten bond of contemporary man between nature and himself.

The numerous mythic and symbolic dual sexual identities of the novel's heroes, the various disguises and transformations, all kinds of ambivalence, unions and separations, wanderings and searches, are all in good measure the sign of the tendency to return to paradise, to the primeval beatitude to be attained by once again binding together the male and female principle: the androgyne. The androgyne as the totality of mankind symbolizes the perfect balance between the male and female energy in the universe which, by each of the other, opposite force, implies that there is no exclusive male or female nature.

In our black-and-white world, with all its divisions, everything is experienced, even the difference of sex, as ultimate oppositions, struggles, and rivalry, and not as a mutual partnership or as stimulating tension and a richness of diversity upon which the world resides. Through the implicit symbolism of the androgyne, which is neither one nor the other and yet is both and thus represents a specifically disguised principle of the unity of opposites, Pavić's philosophical-anthropological creed is expressed. In fact, the possible salvation of the national and universal, of Man and nature, and in the final analysis, the future can be perceived in the constant adaptation and coexistence as well as the preservation of what is specific and resistance to total polarity, uniformity, and reduction to which the contemporary world aspires.

On the other hand, one can sense the possibility of mankind's survival in the female "passive," beneficent, and sensitive principle, embodied in Vitacha Milut, not only biologically but also as a chance to transcend the active, male principle, which has for ages pulled the strings of that great game of life more and more clumsily and tragically. Vitacha's "exit" from the book, her attempt to achieve immortality through her love for Mr. Reader, and her incarnation into Ms. Reader, who saves her life, are possible reflections of such concepts. Some other ostensibly insignificant details testify to such an attitude. The sisters, Vitacha and Vida, who, in a certain way, are the same person, are compared to seraphim and cherubim. Some evangelists were depicted on icons in the form of winged animals, and they announce salvation. However, the names of Vitacha and Vida can be etymologically connected with the words meaning *eyesight* (*vid*) or *healer* (*vidar*), with clairvoyance, and even with Svetovid, who is considered to have been the supreme God of all Slavs. The symbolism of the voice as the axis, connected mostly with Vitacha, has many meanings, but viewed from this angle, it can be interpreted as the herald (voice) of the future. Also, the monk "solitaries," about whose choices and principles rotate the centrifugal and centripetal forces of the novel's events, are essentially linked to Woman and the Creation, through the cult of the Virgin Mary. Generally speaking, the novel regards the heroine, not the hero, as the prototype of a savior, just as a similar viewpoint is realized through the person of Satan.

The novel has a cruciform structure (the vertical and the horizontal of the crossword puzzle, the interplay of various tales, etc.), and this form can be understood metaphorically as a cross borne by our ancestors and one that we bear and that future generations, if there should be any, will bear. However, the cross made by the bodies of Razin and Vitacha during their act of love, that illusion or moment of union, takes us back to the universal symbolism of the cross, to the androgyne and the tree of life.

The cross as the junction of two planes, the horizontal and the vertical, is a symbol of the primeval androgyne and archetype of man, ready for the limitless, harmonious spread in both directions, upward and downward. The point of crossing makes possible the discourse between the sky and the earth, the descent of the spirit into matter and vice versa, implying the possibility of eternal life. The cross is formed by the four heavenly rivers that emerge from the roots of the theater of life. Vitacha's persistent search for lost unity, by seeking a heavenly, earthly, and subterranean lover, is the allegorical foundation of the cosmic tree of life.

The axis mundi, the tree of life, is the imago mundi, the picture of the world. Rooted in the depth of the earth, the axis of the world, and by its contact with water, the tree grows tall into the world of time and toward the heavens and eternity. By constantly reviving itself and embracing the past, present, and future, it generates life, while with its unification of the underground, the land, and the sky, it attains perfect balance. The tree of life and the tree of knowledge grow in paradise, but being differentiated in creating balance, they are specifically reflected on the fate of the world and its heroes. The tree of knowledge is basically dualistic, because of our knowledge of good and evil, which brought about original sin and prompted the expulsion from paradise. Still, the tree of life as a universal axis of the trinity transcends duality and, in line with the principle of the unity of contradictions, performs the deed of equilibrium. The young Alexander Pfister, one of the characters in the novel, in discovering the book of knowledge, loses the tree of life. But with its death he does not disappear forever, and it is precisely through Vitacha that he experiences a kind of reincarnation. Pfister's life and fate are mysterious; the more quickly he learns, the faster he grows old and dies, in his seventh year, with all the physical and mental qualities of a mature man. That can certainly be variously interpreted, but it is possible to recognize in his fate the essential situation in which contemporary man finds himself.

Man of the postmodern era approaches self-destruction through his own mental development, through the cataclysms that threaten him as a boomerang and the feedback effect of nature. Human satanization would appear to be the product of transcending the heavenly in the sense of the mental or else the repression of the heavenly in the sense of the natural. This accelerated negative process requires the return to the tree of life, which, as a trinity, preserves the balance of the spirit, the soul, and the body. For what Pavić seems to be saying in his work is that the essential cause of the lack of balance is the rejection of unity or the distancing of the spiritual from the material.

The "androgyne-ecological" story of the soul and the body, which is told over and over again in the novel and is most deeply felt through Vitacha Milut, who is trying to find the lost heavenly reflection of her soul, is a warning that we must return to inherent totality, to that unity which is contained in the cosmic order.

Modern man experiences the world and time as a natural force coming from outside precisely because he has abandoned his self and is therefore no longer in harmony with nature and the grand rhythm of the universe. The novel is not an invitation to regress but rather an invitation to wisdom, morality, and humanness as well as the art of life in this world.

The picture in *Landscape Painted with Tea* of the upside down world of historical and perverted reality is the reflection of our own selves. The cathartic power of the book as a mirror should prevent the headlong plunge into nothingness and should return to the world its lost essence and internal balance.

The snakelike chair in which the author and Ms./Mr. Reader are sitting is an intimate encounter among an awakened consciousness, conscientiousness, and love.

NOTES

[1]Dictionaries, lexicons, and encyclopedias define ecology in various ways, but it is invariably related to the study of the mutual relations of living beings and their environment. These complex relationships within the frame of ordinary life were initially subsumed under biology and physiology, to be later expanded into the sociobiological disciplines. Today, ecology has become a science of the way of life. The road to scientific maturity traversed by the field of ecology in its development is the result of time and mainly of people's activity within time and thus is outside the framework of scientific investigation and belongs rather to art, politics, culture, everyday life, and the like.

[2]Similarly, today one can read Pavić's short story "The Horses of St. Mark" as an anticipation of the collapse of the "East European Empire" (i.e., the Soviet Union) on the one hand and the collapse of the British Commonwealth on the other.

Pavić's The Inner Side of the Wind: *A Postmodern Novel*

Radmila Jovanović Gorup

Discussing the importance of the art form, Tolstoy said in 1902: "I think that every artist must create his own art forms. If the contents of art works can be infinitely diverse, so should be their forms." Tolstoy further recalled that the best literary works ever written in Russian were those whose forms were completely original.

Postmodernism took up this challenge, and Milorad Pavić responded to it avidly. With every new novel, Pavić offers his reader a strikingly original form. After *Dictionary of the Khazars* (1984), a novel in the form of a lexicon, after *Landscape Painted with Tea* (1988), a novel in the form of a crossword puzzle, Pavić's next novel, *The Inner Side of the Wind, or the Novel of Hero and Leander* (1991) is a novel in the form of a clepsydra, the ancient water instrument that measures time. It has two front covers. It is divided in two parts, or rather it consists of two novels printed upside down with a single blue page between them (in the original edition). It immediately presents a dilemma to the reader, and he has to decide whether to read it from front to back or from back to front.

The author himself shed light on the form he chose. In an interview, commenting on the evolution of the genre of the novel, Pavić said: "My feeling is that a novel should be looked upon as a building, a house into which you (the reader) can enter from different sides. You can go around it, look at it from the front, from the back, or from the garden behind it. Inside it you can be surprised by a sea." *The Inner Side of the Wind* is, according to Pavić, such a building. It has two entrances and in its inner court is a sea. From the outside one cannot believe that there is room for an entire sea, yet "each reader is going to make the size of the sea correspond to his ability to swim in it."[1]

The theme of *The Inner Side of the Wind, or the Novel of Hero and Leander* is reflected in the title itself. The book is modeled on the ancient myth of Hero and Leander, the ill-fated lovers divided by the sea. In the ancient myth Leander nightly swims the Hellespont and, guided by the light from Hero's tower, finds his lover, until one stormy night Hero's torch gets extinguished, and without the guiding light, Leander drowns. Seeing his corpse, Hero throws herself from the tower. Having been separated by the sea, they are ultimately united by it in death. However, Pavić's Hero and Leander are divided by the two hundred and more years that separate their deaths. Pavić's novel tells of two Belgrade lovers, one from the turn of the eighteenth century and the other from the twentieth century, who reach for each other over the gulf of time. The sea in *The Inner Side of the Wind* is that single blue page in the middle of the book.

The novel consists of two chronologically and compositionally divided parts, two entrances in Pavić's fashion, a male and a female one. The novel has two currents that run in opposite directions, and their ends meet in the middle. It has one ending because, unlike the lovers in the ancient myth, Pavić's Hero and Leander never meet in real life and are united only in their death. As in the clepsydra, the content of one novel flows into another, and it is left to the reader to construct the whole.

Radacha Chihorich, the hero of the Leander part of the novel, is a santir player and monk but also a builder from a long line of masons. In the turbulent times of the Ottoman push into Europe in the eighteenth century, while those fleeing the advancing Turkish army destroy and burn everything behind them, Radacha, in a seemingly perverse action, frantically builds. He constructs a series of small churches and, in doing so, leaves secret messages in his homeland in Serbia, Voyvodina, and Bosnia, between the monastery Zica, the river Morava, and the towns Smederevo, Slankamen, and Drenovnica. Fleeing the death from a swordsman foretold for him by a prophet, Leander dies in an explosion in a tower he built. He dies the death foreseen for Hero and, in doing so, proves what he believed all along, that "touching was possible after all."

The protagonist of the Hero part of the novel, Heronea Bukur, is a chemistry student at the University of Belgrade. She is also a part-time language tutor, a translator, and an aspiring author. A distant forerunner of today's novelists, Heronea secretly plants her own stories about the migrations of souls inside the translations she is commissioned to do. When her brother seduces her lover, Heronea moves to Prague, where she is killed in an explosion. At the moment of her death she sees a swordsman, Leander's executioner. Heronea too believed that "touching was possible after all." Soul mates, Pavić's Hero and Leander exchange their deaths and, like the ancient lovers, are united in death.

Adorno pointed out the paradox facing modern novelists when he wrote: "One no longer can narrate, yet the genre of the novel requires a story." Pavić responds to this by offering a rich story and telling it in a new fashion. While the key characteristic of Pavić's poetics remains the fantastic, *The Inner Side of the Wind*, unlike other novels by Pavić, does not emphasize this dimension, rather, it equally foregrounds the story. Linked directly to the ancient myth of ill-fated lovers (more than just a fantastic story), *The Inner Side of the Wind* is a love story that the reader discovers only after completing both halves of the novel.

However, *The Inner Side of the Wind* is not only a love story either. It contains universal and philosophic themes. Pavić uses the metaphor of the inner side of the wind to underscore two kinds of relationships, two kinds of prophesies, and two kinds of prophets: the expensive one who can foretell only the immediate future, and the cheap one who looks far ahead into the future. This last prophet likens the long-range prophecies to the wind, the inner side of which remains dry when it blows through the rain. The prophecies are used to connect the two lovers. In resurrecting the old myth, Pavić also connects different centuries and continents and gives the old myth relevance for today.

Postmodern fiction stresses that it is impossible to articulate exactly the external boundaries of narrative, to define its topos. In postmodern fiction space is seen as discontinuous and heterogenous. Rather than to speak of a world, postmodernists prefer to speak of a zone. Michel Foucault calls the space that a postmodernist novel inhabits a heterotopia, "the disorder in which fragments of a large number of possible orders glitter separately."[2]

The topos Pavić chooses for this novel (and his other novels for that matter) accommodates many exclusive worlds, objective and subjective. In answering the question "What kind of world is that?," Pavić insists on plurality of perspective. Geographically, it is the Danubian plain and the Morava valley with Belgrade in its center but also farther north, east, and south, all the way to Mount Athos, the center of Orthodox spirituality, and the Hellespont. Against that backdrop are juxtaposed two great traditions, the Roman and the Byzantine, separated by a limited space, a frontier. The same geographical area incorporates two other traditions as well, Judaism and Islam. This postmodern heterotopia, this dualism of East-West which runs through Serbian cultural space, fascinates and inspires Pavić. He conceives of this frontier not so much as a physical space as a state of mind. Just like Fuentes in *Terra Nostra,* who views the topos of his novel as belonging neither to Europe nor to South America, Pavić insists that the cultural space he portrays is unique. *The Inner Side of the Wind* reflects repeated disruption of a geographical region, the displacement of large masses of population, which is very disturbing. Displaced nations are on the move from south to north and back while the frontiers are completely obliterated. Rather than being fictional, the zone of *The Inner Side of the Wind* has definite historical roots.

Pavić's novel corresponds largely to the historical facts. The collapse of the Serbian and Byzantine worlds mingles with the collapse of ontological boundaries, in which the other world mingles with the objective one. History, however, is internalized and dissolved to the level of characters. Young Leander, santir player and merchant, with a stream of humanity, flees the advancing victorious hordes of Turkish conquerors to return to Belgrade and then flees again farther to the north, then returns to Belgrade, builds his tower and foresees the city's imminent destruction just prior to his death. In this way the zone of *The Inner Side of the Wind*, somewhere between the plain of Pannonia and the Hellespont, is being constantly constructed and deconstructed. Pavić did not have to stage the collision of different worlds, since his native region provided a perfect scenario.

Brian McHale contends that history is not pertinent for postmodern fiction and that those postmodernists who exploit historical elements transgress the rules of the genre of the historical novel by contradicting public record and by integrating the historical and the fantastic. Pavić is guilty only on the second count. *The Inner Side of the Wind* echoes the drama of one thousand years of Serbian existence. The story of Radacha Chihorich, nicknamed Leander, is framed by two historical migrations, those of 1690 and 1740.

Pavić is obsessed with certain time periods that he considers crucial and which for centuries determined the destinies of entire nations and humanity in general. He sees people and events being repeated at other times. That is why he superimposes his plot on the ancient tale, which is also a metaphor for the relationship between East and West, two continents, and two different traditions. Some critics of postmodernism say that the combination of the historical and the fantastic promotes unreality. One could say rather that it disturbs reality in the sense that it breaks illusions but that, perhaps in Pavić's case, it promotes a higher reality that goes beyond the apparent.

Metaphors in *The Inner Side of the Wind* draw from Serbian tradition which was enriched by the four intermingling cultures on its soil, Greco-Roman, Christian, Judaic, and Arabic. This metaphor of the number four is used time and again in *The Inner Side of the Wind*: the quartet of santir players, of which Leander is one; the foreign soul inhabiting Captain de Vitkovich's body has a window divided in four parts; four guests in the Polish castle where Hero's brother gets the answer to his question; the four-part seal of Mount Athos, the center of Serbian spirituality; the four colors of a regular deck of cards; the four different colors of nail polish that Hero's brother is using, etc.

Ontological boundaries are violated repeatedly in the novel. First, the love between Hero and Leander, rather than being an object or representation, is a metaobject. So that Heronea and Radacha, could establish any contact it was necessary that time be made into a material so that characters could move in it in both directions. In Pavić's case that is possible only after death. Death is a frequent theme in postmodern fiction, and *The Inner Side of the Wind* is about death, just like Pavić's first two novels. The first soothsayer Leander saw, the cheap one who could foretell only the distant future, told him: "death . . . is the only thing under the heavenly skies that, like a snake, can climb up and down the tree of our origin. Death can lie in ambush waiting for you for centuries before you are born, and it can also come back for you, can come to meet you from the most distant future."[3] He foretold that Leander's death wouldn't happen for several hundred years. The fate of Heronea Bukur was foretold indirectly. She read Leander's words to Hero on the poster advertising the play by Musaeus Grammaticus:"Your death can get younger; it can become much younger than you. It can go hundreds of years back into the past. Then again, my death can become much older than I am, it can last from now on into future centuries" (40, Hero's part).[4] Manasija Bukur pointed out that his sister started to die soon after her birth, that she was dying for a long time and that perhaps she started to die even before she was born but that nobody noticed. Leander's father too believed that death lasts as long as life itself, but that it can last much longer.

Heronea is not sure whether she belongs to the time in which she lives or to some other time. She is also aware that she is gradually dying. Her nails grow uncontrollably and her language loses the capacity to express concrete notions. She is preoccupied with another reality, the one her dreams inhabit. Leander too is uncomfortable living in the present and is looking constantly into the future. Time obeys a different rhythm for Hero and Leander than for those living around them. Both are very fast. Leander can eat the same amount of food in one third of the time it takes his father. This speed prevents him from fulfilling his love with the girl in the boat on Lake Ohrid. Hero is so fast that she "could bite off her own ear" and "she digested food before it left her mouth" (4, Hero's part). Leander realized early that there exist two different rhythms of existence in humans as well as animals and plants, and he was hiding this quality of his from others.

The Inner Side of the Wind is, according to some critics, an androgynous novel, the story of a single hero manifested as two. The story about Leander starts with an epigraph that he was "the magical half of something magnificent and unfathomable," while she was a whole, "small, disoriented, not very strong or harmonious whole." The theme of androgyny permeates other works by Pavić. *Dictionary of the Khazars* exists in male and female versions, and in *Landscape Painted with Tea* the characters display doubled gender identities. In *The Inner Side of the Wind* the androgynous principle is seen both in the form of the book and in its characters. Jasmina Mihajlović, who calls *The Inner Side of the Wind* an androgynous novel, suggests that we could look at the characters of Hero and Leander as metaphors for the two principles every human being supposedly possesses, the anima and animus.[11] This perhaps sheds light on the epigraph with which the novel of Leander begins. This double principle refers not only to death but to all other aspects of existence. Only when the two principles unite will the perfect whole be realized.

From the very start of postmodernism (and the nouveau roman as well), the device of *mise en abyme* was a distinctive feature. By integrating repeatedly the poetical device of *mise en abyme* in his diegesis, Pavić made *The Inner Side of the Wind* a specular novel in the sense Lucien Dallenbach defined it in his book *Le recit speculaire*.[6] Dallenbach assimilated the concept of *mise en abyme* to that of the speculum so that he talks about a mirror in the text whenever the device of *mise en abyme* appears. The introduction of mirrors into the text enables the author to create an embedded structure. Whereas the traditional novel (and the modern novel to a great extent) held a mirror up to life, which allowed the author to capture reflected images of the world in a movable mirror, the mirror in postmodern fiction is no longer a passive instrument. It is placed within the text and becomes an interior element of it. Also, this is no longer one mirror but a system of mirrors, which, just like a broken mirror, reproduces different reflections. The mirror is there to enrich the text and give it depth.

Reflexivity plays an important role in the imagery of *The Inner Side of the Wind*. It is present in the novel from the level of the visual objects described to the level of text creation. *Mise en abyme* is injected in the title of the novel itself. The original Greek story of Hero and Leander is reflected in two narrative flows, the simulacra of the old myth. The primary level of narrative, the stories of Radacha Chihorich and Heronea Bukur, is interrupted repeatedly with references to the ancient myth of Hero and Leander. When, after numerous trips to the Hellespont, Radacha Chihorich returns to Belgrade as the monk, Irinei, he continues his interrupted education at the newly opened school. His Russian teacher brings his students the Latin translation of the poem "The Love and Death of Hero and Leander" by the Greek poet Musaeus Grammaticus. When the teacher asks the students which obstacle stood between the lovers, Radacha gives an unorthodox answer that earns him the nickname Leander. On his earlier trips to the Hellespont, the site of the original myth, Radacha and his fellow santir players had learned to play the song of Hero and Leander, and someone, as a tip, once threw into Radacha's instrument a small cameo of Hero. Radacha realized even then that the two continents were not only divided by the sea of the Hellespont but also by the winds, or time. That is why he answered his Russian teacher saying that perhaps, to reach Hero, Leander had to swim not the waves of the sea but of time. In the mirror of his new nickname Radacha became the modern simulacrum of ancient Leander. The ancient myth further reminded Leander of his experience with Despina on Lake Ohrid. In addition, Leander recites the lines of the ancient poem, both in Serbian and Greek, as he is completing his tower.

In Hero's part of the novel her young pupil reads the ancient myth in French. Later, Heronea and her brother, vacationing in Rome, look in vain for a theater advertising the play about the love and death of Hero and Leander by the ancient Greek poet Grammaticus.

Hero and Leander appear in the novel as specular heroes. In his eyes Leander reflected Belgrade being reconstructed:

> He usually sat on top of the hill in the fortress and rested his eyes upon the wing of a bird, which would plunge down headlong, and he would let the bird carry his gaze around the town springing up along the river like the stone teeth of the earth, renewing itself from within. . . . Leander, blinking as though he were swallowing, drank in every detail that his bird-borne gaze would touch in that descent. Carried on plumed wings, he observed the Neboisha Tower, which was mirrored in two rivers at once, the Sava and the Danube, and through its facing windows he could see a patch of the sky from the other side of the water, which it hid from view. (46-47, Leander's part)

He could also see the bells of the Belgrade churches that could be heard in two empires, brass decorations at the entrances of new stately mansions, shiny bayonets in the hands of the Austrian and Serbian soldiers who were hurriedly reinforcing the city. Parallel to Leander's eyes, which were mirrors, stood the mirrors of the Sava and the Danube, and in these multiple mirrors flickered the water and sky, town and earth, humans and birds, life and death. The city was doomed to be destroyed one more time.

Young Heronea captured the image of her future lover in a mirror when she noticed the lieutenant shaving in her mirror one morning. In the third chapter of Hero's part the anonymous narrator listens to the story of Hero's brother, Manasia, who calculates the depth of people's eyes. He expects to get the answer to his question only when he finds the person who has the identical depth of his dead sister's brilliant eyes.

The Inner Side of the Wind abounds in references to the specular quality of objects. Not only are Leander's eyes and mind mirrors of nature, nature itself contains mirrors. In the novel these are the aquatic mirrors of the Hellespont, the place Radacha visits during his trips and the site of the ancient myth; Lake Ohrid where Leander meets Despina; and the mouth of the Sava and the Danube at Belgrade, the city that the Austrians and the Turks destroyed so many times in their battle for it. Nature for Pavić is the place where both letters and specula find their simulacra. Rivers write down their secret messages just as Radacha leaves his secret messages with his churches, which outline a giant letter theta (Θ), the first and only letter he learned as a young boy and the letter with which the name of Mother of God (as well as God) starts in Greek. He recognized the same letter on the old icon of Patagonia that showed him that contact was, after all, possible. The function of all these mirrors is to grasp invisible relationships.

The reflexive nature of man-made objects is also highlighted. Describing the furnishing of the newly built metropolitan's mansion in Belgrade, the author gives a long list of shiny objects: fireplaces and porcelain stoves, brocade and velvet fabrics, porcelain dishes from Vienna, Carlsbad, and England, crystal glasses from Bohemia, lamps and mirrors from Venice, musical clocks, etc.

The Inner Side of the Wind focuses on the inner side of things, and that is why the poetic device of mirroring is so much in evidence. The wind, time, and water have their inner sides, and characters too. Whereas the heart is seen the way it is at the moment, the soul is reflected the way it was thousands of years ago, so in order to capture the soul, one has to travel through the interior of time.

The Inner Side of the Wind contains more metatextual references than any other work by Pavić. These references are given indirectly in both halves of the novel, in passages explaining Leander's building methods, his use of numbers and graphic symbols, as well as in passages about music and dreams and in fragments explaining Hero's translations and her writing. Pavić's protagonists are his doubles reflecting his poetics. Out of the fragments of the novel one can construct Pavić's position on the creative process and literature in general. The device of *mise en abyme* here functions to "make present" the creator and to reveal the creative process itself. In postmodern fiction the author excludes himself from the text. He creates, however, a "productive agency" out of his characters, whom he endows with an appropriate profession. Most often in postmodern fiction the substitute for the author is a character who himself is an author who may then write about another author, thus creating triples or multiples embedded in the text. In *The Inner Side of the Wind* all the main characters reflect the creative process.

Leander is an artist, overwhelmed with his creation. He is aware that numbers do not have constant values and that when one uses them he has to take into consideration their origin, as well as their momentary value. When the Austrians decide to replace the two towers at the bank of the Sava that the Turks destroyed in an earlier campaign, they commission Sandal Krasimirich, an experienced builder of high reputation, to build the north tower. He is given sufficient means and he proceeds to build the tower in an already-tested method. From the very beginning the south tower presents problems. The site is a swamp, and nobody wants to accept the job. Leander does, and while his competitor is employing the exact method of the Western tradition, Radacha, a representative of the Byzantine school of construction, proceeds to apply the skills he learned from his Russian teacher. He erects the interior scaffolding and builds his tower from the inside.

Even though his tower rises faster than his competitor's, nobody pays any attention to it. When it is finally finished, it cannot be seen because it is above the clouds. When it clears up and both towers can be seen, Leander realizes that the weather clocks on their tops do not register the same winds. The northern tower reacts to ordinary winds, while the southern tower reacts to winds that are blowing higher up and are not noticeable near the ground. In the official relief of the city the two towers are presented as though equal in height. The two towers are both symbols and metaphors for the two traditions. A reflective relationship exists between the two towers that reflect in the river and in one another. Their construction is likened to an object of art: only when the towers surpass the ramparts of the city and reach the depth of the river so that they could be reflected in it do they acquire their reality.

Perhaps the best description of the creative process is given by Manasia Bukur, brother of Hero, who is a musician, when he says: "The instrument in your hands does not break the connection with its origin, with the material and technique used to make it, even when it is played; indeed, it is only through this connection that the music acquires its warranty" (53, Hero's part).

Pavić's poetics are also reflected in Hero's spirituality. Overwhelmed with dreams, Hero begins cataloging them, to pay attention to the forms of those who inhabit her dreams, thus creating a grammar of dreams. She herself started to use some other language, "different from that of her contemporaries, although it was the same tounge" (19, Hero's part).

The creative process is secondarily embedded in the activities of the characters in Hero's story. Captain Vitkovich, the young Austrian nobleman of Serbian ancestry, is condemned to die. In his cell he writes what his investigators thought was a confession. Instead, he left a pile of typed pages filled with scribbled letters that did not reveal any meaning. Yet Hero's brother immediately understood the secret message his sister sent him.

Pavić's postmodern poetics appear not only in the text; they also extend to the physical book. Even though the physical appearance of a book does not belong to its structure, it nevertheless constitutes an appendix which may add to its structure. The shape of *The Inner Side of the Wind,* with its blue covers and the blue sheet between its halves, is iconic and interacts with its actual structure.

The central theme of Pavić's prose is the question of identity: personal, gender, religious, national, etc. *The Inner Side of the Wind* adds to this list identity of death, both the death of man and of woman.

Michel Butor defines literature as "a mirror in which we not only see ourselves and the author but also the background against which we are set . . . the total sum of relationships between what the novel describes and the real world in which we live."[7] *The Inner Side of the Wind* is a trip through postmodernism and, with its help, a trip through one thousand years of Serbian spirituality.

NOTES

[1]Dragomir Kostic, "Pisac iskazuje poruke svoga tla," interview with Milorad Pavic, *Jedinstvo* (Priština), 11-12 January 1992.

[2]Brian McHale, *Postmodernist Fiction* (New York: Metheun, 1987), 44.

[3]Milorad Pavić, *The Inner Side of the Wind, or The Novel of Hero and Leander,* trans. Christina Pribićević-Zorić (New York: Knopf, 1993), 13, Leander's part; hereafter cited parenthetically..

[4]Musaeus Grammaticus is a poet of the fifth-sixth century A.D. In a poem of 341 heximeters he gave the tale of Hero and Leander a definite form.

[5]Jasmina Mihajlović, "*Unutrašnja strana vetra* ili roman o žudnji za celinom," *Književnost* 2 (1992): 525.

[6]Lucien Dallenbach, *The Mirror in the Text*, trans. Jeremy Whitley and Emma Hughes (Cambridge: Polity Press, 1989).

[7]Dallenbach, 122.

Milorad Pavić and Hyperfiction

Jasmina Mihajlović

Robert Coover, in his seminal essay "The End of Books" and in his larger article "Hyperfiction: Novels for the Computer,"[1] speaks about a phenomenon that appeared in America during the postmodern period and then spread to Europe and Japan. It is the new manner of fiction after the age of the printed book. It is not only a rejection of one technology, in this case that of printing, but also a radical change in the way literary works are created, published, read, and critiqued. Today a literary text need not be exclusively in the form of a printed book. It can be found on a diskette or on a compact disc (CD-ROM), and it can use all the possibilities of the computer medium for altering its form, creating new narratives, and changing its reception.

As the concept of the literary text changes to include the electronic text, a manner of reading and writing on a computer is developing which makes nonlinear and nonchronological narration possible, just as it was in the original manner of storytelling. In traditional oral literature the singers organize and link story fragments into a permanently movable whole that has neither a beginning nor an ending in the classical sense, and the text itself is subject to perpetual changes. Now at the end of the twentieth century, the life of the fictional text goes on in the simulated endlessness characteristic of the computer, in the form of an electronic text. This so-called "hypertext"[2] creates a network of multidirectional links among the various pieces of a text. The possibility of a literary work existing in many versions, as well the new layers of meaning within those new wholes created through the reader's digital (re)organization of the textual fragments, enables the reader, independently of the author, also to become a creator of the text. I go as far as to believe that many postmodern theoretical considerations have achieved practical realization now for the first time with the appearance of hypertext and its use in hyperfiction.

Of course, it is necessary to stress the fact that there now exist two kinds of literary works that can benefit from this technology: the first are those fiction works written directly for the computer, which cannot be transferred from it into print; the second are those printed works that already possess the structural features of hypertext. Only in the labyrinth of hyperspace can such works acquire a more adequate means for the reader to interpret thoroughly all meanings than would be possible in print. As for all the remaining works that have classically linear or chronological features, the transfer of the text from print to computer merely results in a rectilinear reading of the text from the screen.

Milorad Pavić's prose presents a good example of the second type of literary work. The so-called electronic writers consider him one of the predecessors of hyperfiction. Robert Coover says in this respect: "Of course, through print's long history, there have been countless strategies to counter the line's power, from marginalia and footnotes to the creative innovations of novelists like Lawrence Sterne, James Joyce, Raymond Queneau, Julio Cortázar, Italo Calvino and Milorad Pavić, not to exclude the form's father, Cervantes himself."[3]

The works of Milorad Pavić were understood in relation to the world of the computer even before the first emergence of hypertext literature, which took place around 1990 with the appearance of *Afternoon,* by Michael Joyce. In early responses to *Dictionary of the Khazars* (1984), even Pavić himself compared reading it with the principles of reading the computer language known as basic. These types of comparisons were heard rarely at first, and then more and more often. Immediately after the appearance of Knopf's edition of *Dictionary of the Khazars* in 1988, Michael Joyce tried to get in touch with Pavić. Patricia Serex called *Dictionary of the Khazars,* "A kind of the *Iliad,* something like a computerized *Odyssey,* an open, integral book."[4] Robert Coover, while reviewing *Dictionary of the Khazars* for the *New York Times,* foretold a series of literary events that would happen only years later and the place of Pavić's books in those events: "Since the computer radical and prophet Ted Nelson first invented the word 'hypertext' to describe such computer-driven nonsequential writing nearly a quarter of a century ago, there has been a steady, now rapid, growth of disciples to this newest sect of dream hunters. A new kind of coverless, interactive, expendable 'book' is now being written; no doubt there are several out there in hyperspace right now; and *Dictionary of the Khazars* could easily take its place among them. . . ."[5]

When I published an article in 1987 about *The Iron Curtain,* a collection of stories, I expressed my opinion in the following way: "The structure of Pavić's stories may be conditionally compared with a computer video game. The space in them appears unlimited, so that endlessness is simulated. With transition from one level to another, from above to under, from left to right, the puzzles are solved and knowledge is gathered, so that a whole could be made out of a mosaic, and that can be done only by the masters of the game."[6] A person who has access to manuals for word processors may also understand the stories, without much thinking, as one of the keys, mechanisms, or directions for handling Pavić's books. The structure of these books has introduced to contemporary literature a system that completely corresponds with the basic working system not only of the word processor but also of the computer in general, and this naturally happened apart from any premeditated, calculated, and forcible intentions.

Here I would like to touch on some of the hypertext features in Pavić's prose works and investigate the possibility of converting them into the computer medium. It seems to me that the story entitled "The Inverted Glove" represents the best and clearest patterns of the basic qualities of hypertext. In the first part of the story the reader gets the impression that it is a classically linear (i.e., a "Pavić-like" classically linear) story with a unidirectional current. Meanwhile, from the middle of the story, the narration goes backward toward the beginning. Thus the fragments in the second part, changing places, remain linked regarding their sense, but they form a completely new whole with a different beginning and a different ending, as well as a different course of the events. That is to say, the blocks of text that in the first part of the story looked completely fixed, now seem to have fled into space and then to have become fixed again, just like shuffled cards, thus creating new links among themselves that change the meaning of the whole.

Looking at other stories we can follow other features of hypertext that, as we said here, can be linked with the principles of videogames. However, the most interesting thing is to watch the cyclical systems of Pavić's stories, because they represent a step nearer to his novels. Just let us think of the collection *Russian Greyhound (Borzoi),* in the epilogue of which the author declares that the two stories in the book are in such a mutual connection that "the question put in one story obtains the answer in the second, and if you read them together, they form a third story. . . ." and I would add a fourth story in the interspace.

In this way we come to the novels: *Dictionary of the Khazars, Landscape Painted with Tea, The Inner Side of the Wind* and *Last Love in Constantinople,* each of which in its own way can be considered a collection of cyclical texts. Each of them uses a different method of arranging and connecting the separate texts. The links in the chain connecting the texts are much more various and richer than those that can be created using the hypertext software currently available (e.g., Storyspace, Guide, HyperCard). Thus we must necessarily put the question: What is the use of hyperfiction in those cases where works have been created that already surpass it in both content and meaning? The answer can be found, perhaps, in the fact that all the features of *Dictionary of the Khazars, Landscape Painted with Tea, The Inner Side of the Wind,* and *Last Love in Constantinople* can be used much more effectively in precisely that medium. Their structure (a lexicon-novel, a crossword puzzle-novel, a clepsydra-novel, and a tarot-novel) and the structure of some of the stories have obviously already started eating away at the limitations of print and searching for a new living space in which it can be reborn and reincarnated in a new form.

What would a hypertext version of *Dictionary of the Khazars* look like? The entries would form a flexible net in hyperspace, and the signs or links (i.e., the crucial points or junction points between the entries) would enable the reader to choose his own path of reading and would allow him to move with various entrances and exits, beginnings and endings, according to the alphabetic system, temporal segments, religious triads or by way of any given word link. In the printed version of *Dictionary of the Khazars* the reader can follow only the referential signs of the cross, the star, the moon, and the triangle that already interconnect the various entries and allow the reader to leap from one to another at will. This is to say that in a computer version of the novel, carrying out the system of linking the entries or stories would be easier; the leaps would be possible without painstakingly turning the pages, without keeping several fingers inside the book or putting pieces of paper between the pages, and without having to cross out the entries in the table of contents as they are read. This technology could be applied to all the levels of the novel starting from the most concrete ones up to the most abstract. Also, there exists the possibility of storing the reader's path through the novel, so that he can remember the version he created and save his personal interpretation of the novel and the various fragments. The existence of a certainly huge but finite number of possible combinations of entries is not of primary importance. What is important is this: the transfer of such a book as *Dictionary of the Khazars* into the computer medium would give us more chances to (re)combine the fragments of the text and would provide us with a more efficient way to read all the various strata of this work than does the classical manner of reading. Some of the entries could be linked visually using animation or film, and others could be linked by sounds (what would be wrong if some were linked so that we hear music created by Shaitan's fingering?). The reader's own creativeness would be fully utilized, and hypermedia, the three-dimensional, spatial representation of the text, the special text, would add to the reader's impression by appealing to more senses. In Belgrade *Dictionary of the Khazars* is just being converted into a CD-ROM version, and in America people are interested in having the English version of the novel also transferred to a computer system.

The scheme and the method of transferring *Landscape Painted with Tea* into the computer medium seem to have been already given at the beginning of this "Novel for Crossword Puzzle Fans" in the author's directions ("How to Solve This Book Across," "How to Solve This Book Down"). I believe that this work would be the simplest one to transfer into hypertext format exactly because of the directions that clearly point to the various units, i.e., the themes, characters, events, love stories, etc. In addition to the different distribution of the segments of the text and the addition of new links and meanings among them, the reader could naturally influence the fates of the characters by changing the beginning and the end of the novel, as one can do in the book itself. In Malta a CD-ROM version of the English translation of *Landscape Painted with Tea* is just about to be finished, and it is even furnished with opera arias sung by the heroine of this novel, Vitacha Milut.

The most complex work to convert would be *The Inner Side of the Wind,* because the links, marks, and nets existing between Hero's and Leander's stories are very subtle and are not explicitly defined on the surface of the text or at the level of the novel's structure. It would take an exceptionally sophisticated software program to manage all of the links and even then a bulk of the meanings would remain hanging in interspace, which, in fact, could be an advantage. While analyzing the novel I had practical problems in catching a thread, for instance, on Leander's side and finding it (even upside down) in Hero's tale and then connecting them and uniting them. The threads kept on multiplying so much that, in a moment, I wished for an index of the key words, personal names, or any of the signs connecting the two stories, so that I might follow them separately in both halves and in both sexes of the book. To undertake such an enterprise, I would doubtless need a computer that would enable me simultaneously to follow the parallel segments of the text on the screen.

Pavić's play, *For Ever and a Day* is subtitled *A Theater Menu* (here I would like to remind the reader that the word *menu* in computer terminology already points to the possibility of a choice). It is composed so that it has three mutually exchangeable beginnings or *Starters,* three ends or *Desserts,* and a central part or *Main Course* around which these beginnings and endings rotate, thus forming different links with them and among themselves. They can be combined into at least nine different versions, each of them being a separate whole in itself. It is the responsibility of the reader-spectator or the theater director and the acting troupe to decide which of the variants they will choose and which ending to pick: the happy ending, the tragic ending, or the ecological ending. Perhaps we might say that *For Ever and a Day* is a hyperplay. It falls into that group of the texts that cannot be printed in a book in an adequate way because the mutual interchangeability of the beginnings, and the endings of the text cannot be represented without imposing a chronological order on it (for instance: Starter I, Starter II, etc.). The main characteristics of a hyperplay are kept by Pavić's drama even when it is transferred into the theater medium that, in this case, is already a simultaneous performance whether in the real space of one theater or different theaters, similar to the simulated space of the computer. Such a structure enables the spectator to see the same middle part in a new way many times because the opening sections *(Starters)* and closing sections *(Desserts)* realized through such a procedure always give a different meaning to the same central text.

A new novel by Milorad Pavić, *Last Love in Constantinople* (1994), subtitled *A Handbook for Fortune-Telling,* consists of twenty-two chapters that bear the names of the tarot cards, or more precisely, the "Major Arcana" (or "Great Secret"). The book is a unique novelistic interpretation of the tarot cards, in which each card has become a separate tale because each chapter corresponds with the basic meaning and symbolism of each separate card. The readers of *Last Love in Constantinople* move through the novel from the beginning toward the ending step by step, but when they close the book, they can open the cards that go with it, set them down on the table and read their fortune, jumping from one card to the other, looking at the corresponding chapters and reading them in a new way, as the keys for fortune-telling. Therefore, here again we have two levels of reading: the first of them being, we would say, the classical way, and the second being that of the reader's own fortune taken separately. In its second level of reading, this book, as a handbook for fortune-telling, enters life itself and mixes with it, thus enabling even a segmentary reading of the text and a reading of the text in the second key different from the transparent side of the given model as a level of a Romanesque happening. It is easy to imagine Pavić's tarot-novel in a computer version as one more in the series of those video games with cards that fill computers all around the world, except that in this case the text of an entire novel would be included in the game and would go with the cards.

It seems that an important turn or revolution has happened in the literature of the twentieth century with the appearance of literary works that have the characteristics of hypertext and the transition of fiction into a new technology. Thus literature can be divided into two currents, the first being the noninteractive works and the second, the interactive works, and the future of fiction lies in this distinction.

NOTES

[1]Robert Coover, "The End of Books," *New York Times Book Review,* 21 June 1992, 1, 23-25; Robert Coover, "Hyperfiction: Novels for the Computer," *New York Times Book Review,* 29 August 1993, 1, 8-10.

[2]I am using the word *hypertext* as defined by Robert Coover: "Hypertext is not a system but a generic term, coined a quarter of a century ago by a computer populist, named Ted Nelson, to describe the writing done in the nonlinear or nonsequential space made possible by the computer. Moreover, unlike print text, hypertext provides multiple paths between text segments, now often celled 'lexias' in the borrowing from the pre-hypertextual but prescient Roland Barthes. With its webs of linked lexias, its network of alternate routes (as opposed to print's fixed unidirectional page-turning), hypertext presents a radically divergent technology, interactive and polyvocal, favoring a plurality of discourses over definitive utterance and freeing the reader from domination by the author" ("The End of Books," 23).

[3]"The End of Books," 23.

[4]Patricia Serex, "Le livre du XXI siecle," rev. of *Dictionary of the Khazars,* by Milorad Pavić, 24 *Heures,* 31 March 1988.

[5]Robert Coover, "He Thinks the Way We Dream," rev. of *Dictionary of the Khazars,* by Milorad Pavić, *New York Times Book Review,* 20 November 1988.

[6]*Književnost* 12 (1987): 2108.

A Milorad Pavić Checklist

Books

Palimpsesti / Palimpsests. Belgrade, 1967.

Istorija srpske književnosti baroknog doba / History of Serbian Literature in the Age of the Baroque (17th-18th Centuries). Belgrade, 1970.

Mesečev kamen / Moon Stone. Belgrade, 1971.

Vojislav Ilic i evropsko pesništvo / Vojislav Ilić and European Poetry. Novi Sad, 1971.

Gavril Stefanović Venclović / Gavril Stefanović Venclović. Belgrade, 1972.

Vojislav Ilić, njegovo vreme i delo / Vojislav Ilić, His Times and Work (A Chronicle of a Family of Poets). Belgrade, 1972.

Gvozdena zavesa / The Iron Curtain. Novi Sad, 1973.

Jezičko pamćenje i pesnički oblik / Linguistic Memory and the Poetic Form. Novi Sad, 1976.

Konji svetoga Marka / The Horses of St. Mark. Belgrade, 1976

Istorija srpske književnosti klasicizma i predromantizma / History of Serbian Literature in the Age of Classicism and Pre-Romanticism. Belgrade, 1979.

Ruski hrt / Borzoi. Belgrade, 1979.

Nove beogradske priče / New Belgrade Stories. Belgrade, 1981.

Duše se kupaju poslednji put / Souls Bathe for the Last Time. Novi Sad, 1982.

Rađanje nove srpske književnosti / The Birth of a New Serbian Literature. Belgrade, 1983.

Hazarski rečnik. Roman-leksikon u 100.000 reči / Dictionary of the Khazars. A Novel-Lexicon in 100,000 Words. Belgrade, 1984.

Istorija, stalež i stil / History, Class and Style. Novi Sad, 1985.

Predeo slikan čajem / Landscape Painted with Tea. Belgrade, 1988.

Izvrnuta rukavica / The Inverted Glove. Novi Sad, 1989.

Kratka istorija Beograda / A Short History of Belgrade. Belgrade, 1990.

Unutrašnja strana vetra ili roman o Heri i Leandru / Inner Side of the Wind, or The Novel of Hero and Leander. Belgrade, 1991.

Istorija srpske književnosti / History of Serbian Literature 2, 3, 4 (Baroque, Classicism, Pre-Romanticism). Belgrade, 1991.

Zauvek i dan više / For Ever and a Day. A Theater Menu. Belgrade, 1993.

Poslednja ljubav u Carigradu. Priru nik za gatanje / Last Love in

Constantinople: A Handbook for Fortune-Telling. Belgrade, 1994.
Šešir od riblje kože / A Hat Made of Fish Skin. Belgrade, 1996.

English Translations

Dictionary of the Khazars: A Lexicon Novel in 100,000 Words. Trans. Christina Pribićević-Zorić. New York: Alfred A. Knopf, 1988; New York: Vintage International, 1989.
A Short History of Belgrade. Trans. Christina Pribićević-Zorić. Belgrade: Prosveta, 1990.
Landscape Painted with Tea. A Crossword-Novel. Trans. Christina Pribićević-Zorić. New York: Alfred A. Knopf, 1990; New York: Vintage International, 1991.
The Inner Side of the Wind, or the Novel of Hero and Leander. Trans. Christina Pribićević-Zorić. New York: Alfred A. Knopf, 1993.
For Ever and a Day: A Theatre Menu. Trans. Christina Pribićević-Zorić. Belgrade: Dereta, 1997.

Fiction in English Language Periodicals

"Great Serbian Migration 1690"; "Lunch in a Dream"; "Flying Temple"; "The Swing over the Calm Source of our Names"; "Monument to an Unknown Poet." In *Four Yugoslav Poets: Ivan V. Lalić, Branko Miljković, Milorad Pavić, Ljubomir Simović.* Trans. Charles Simic. Ithaca, New York: Lillabulero Press, 1970.
From "Holy Mass for Relja Krilatica." Trans. Charles Simic. *Minnesota Review* 2 (1972): 52-56.
"The Wedgewood Tea Set." Trans. Darka Topali. *Relations* (Belgrade) 1976: 130-35.
"Holy Mass for Relja Krilatica (fragments)" and "The Romaunt of Troy." *Relations* (Belgrade) 5/6 (1978): 40-43.
"Khazarian Dictionary (fragments)." Trans. Vida Janković. *Relations* (Belgrade) 1 (1985): 53-69.
"*Dictionary of the Khazars.* Excerpts from *Dictionary of the Khazars.*" Trans. Christina Pribićević-Zorić. *The World & I* (Washington) 3.11 (1988): 350-67.
"*Landscape Painted with Tea.* Excerpt." Trans. Christina Pribićević-Zorić. *Borzoi Reader* 2.1 (1990): 36-37.
"The Eyes of the Mind." Trans. Ivana Đorđević. *Serbian Literary Quarterly* 2-4 (1990): 39-48.
"The Dark Side of the Moon," *Politika--International Weekly,* 25 January 1992.

"Great Serbian Migration 1690"; "Lunch in a Dream"; "Flying Temple"; "The Swing over the Calm Source of Our Names"; "Monument to an Unknown Poet." In *The Horse Has Six Legs: An Anthology of Serbian Poetry*. Trans. Charles Simic. St. Paul: Graywolf Press, 1992. 141-49.

"Khazar Polemic." Trans. Christina Pribićević-Zorić. *American Srbobran* 2.2 (1993): 5.

"Mistaken Identity: Excerpts from *The Inner Side of the Wind*." Trans. Christina Pribićević-Zorić. *New York Times Book Review*, 13 June 1993, 11.

Book Reviews

Anthony Cronin. *No Laughing Matter: The Life & Times of Flann O'Brien.* Fromm, 1998. 260 pp. $29.95.

Originally published in England in 1989, Anthony Cronin's excellent biography of Flann O'Brien is finally available to readers in the United States. Like his more recent biography of Samuel Beckett, *No Laughing Matter* is a lively, well-researched, sympathetic, and gracefully written book which enters into the heart of Flann O'Brien, who is revealed as a complex, sad, and multitalented genius whose best work—*At Swim-Two-Birds, The Third Policeman,* and *The Dalkey Archive*—can be spoken of in the same breath as Joyce's and Beckett's. Because he was once part of O'Brien's milieu in Dublin in the 1950s and 1960s, Cronin is able to provide an in-depth portrait of the man, his work, and his place in the Dublin literary scene of his time.

One of many compelling explorations is the importance of O'Brien's bilingualism. O'Brien's attitudes toward both language and form were learned from Irish literature and mythology but manifested themselves, primarily, in the fiction and newspaper columns written in English. It is also revealed that after the modest success of *At Swim-Two-Birds,* O'Brien had difficulty getting his work published and that this increased his dependence on the fast recognition derived from the newspaper columns written for the *Irish Times,* under the pseudonym Myles na Gopaleen. Over time, too much of O'Brien's energies were taken up by these columns and by his day job as a civil servant—and by unproductive time spent in pubs—so that there was little energy left for fiction. It was only after his death, when all of his work came into print, that he was finally seen as a major writer. Except for Anne Clissman's biography, Anthony Cronin's is the first major book to be written on O'Brien and it will be of great interest to old fans and will lead new readers to the fiction of a wonderful, very funny writer. [Eamonn Wall]

Guy Davenport. *Twelve Stories.* Counterpoint, 1997. 236 pp. Paper: $14.00.

Guy Davenport, fabulist and scholar, is a champion of knowledge and wit, one of the rare writers nowadays who, without condescension, depends on his readers to have as much curiosity of scholarship—never mind a high working IQ—as he himself has. This original paperback gathers twelve stories from three of his early collections: *Tatlin!, Apples and Pears,* and *The Drummer of the Eleventh North Devonshire Fusiliers.* "A Gingham Dress," a dialogue between two mountain people, is two-and-a-half pages long. "Tatlin" is a slight *nouvelle,* fifty-three pages, taking in Tatlin, a Russian artist's life from 1932 to 1953, a fable/art essay in which Father Gapon, Viktor Shklovsky, Wittgenstein, and Mayakovsky, among others, make splendid appearances. Davenport, who writes gnomically and with chiselled grace, leaves us with aphorisms ("Shape answers use. And then use modifies shape") that lay open whole panoramas of thought.

"Colin Maillard," a story of bullying boys and their gentle prey, is as good as James Joyce's "An Encounter." "The Aeroplanes at Brescia," in which aeronaut Blériot, the Wright brothers, and Tolstoy make appearances, is a masterpiece after Franz Kafka ("Franz Kafka, jackdaw. Despair, like the crane's hunch on Kierkegaard's lilting back, went along on one's voyages"). To read Davenport, one has to be willing to look up words, ponder phrases, do extramural reading and not be threatened by arcane illusions. All of these stories of Davenport are written with the tenderest respect for his readers, as opposed to the insolent disregard that hacks and phony novelists and bullshit artists—Maya Angelou, John Grisham, the dork who wrote *The Bridges of Madison County*, etc.—have for their readers by serving up bowls of crapulosity and cliché and expecting, like poisoning cooks, it be eaten and we go away. Guy Davenport's stories should be read like Cubist essays, for their turns, sides, shapes, and the delectability of their genius. [Alexander Theroux]

Paul Metcalf. *Collected Works, Volume III: 1987-1997.* Coffee House, 1997. 524 pp. $35.00.

This volume completes our opportunity to read one of the most original minds of the century in his own preferred manner, to read his works in the order they were composed, to read a life. *Volume III* begins with *Where Do You Put the Horse?,* a collection of critical and autobiographical essays reaching back to 1973 and forward nearly to the present. In these writings, Metcalf is aware—as perhaps no other—of the middle ground that literature occupies: reading is at once visual and silent, but requires the ear and patience. He trusts his source materials, placing them against each other, making their colors vibrate in the manner of the abstract expressionist, but in the ear. For Metcalf, literature is a physical thing, a voice always heard like music (but through the eye!), "constructed of materials salvaged from the wreckage of previous constructions rather than materials designed specifically for the task at hand"—bricolage. Following the essays, the volume includes seven novels: *Louis the Torch, Golden Delicious, Firebird, Three Plays, Mountaineers Are Always Free!, ". . . and nobody objected,"* and *Araminta and the Coyotes.* Their subjects encompass a wide range: arson, the gold rush, apples, the Chicago fire, baseball, the Civil War, Columbus, the Underground Railroad, and coyotes (Mexican immigrant smugglers). These books prove Metcalf's epic literary lineage, which extends from Homer to Whitman and Melville through Pound and Williams.

The novels are succeeded by the entirely wonderful new long poem "Huascarán," a poetic rendering of the great Peruvian earthquake of 1970. It is a homage to the spiritual and familial attachment to a place that derives in opposition to disaster, religion, geography, government, and indifference. The structure of "Huascarán" is relatively simple and compressed, yet it remains very powerful as a cry for memory ("You must remember not to forget").

The collection closes with a somewhat satirical essay, "The Wonderful White Whale of Kansas." Here Metcalf speculates wistfully on fame, fortune and fate. Still, he celebrates Dorothy's devotion to place and to common sense: "And yet, knowing him [the Wizard of Oz] for what he is, the Scarecrow, the Tin Man, and the Lion willingly comply with his ruses, accepting and believing in the brains, the heart, and the courage that he doles out. Dorothy is right: Better Kansas!"

Paul Metcalf has always been difficult to categorize, perhaps because he is one of only a few American writers who possess an imagination beyond the lyric. With these three volumes Coffee House gives us the epic of our time. [Karl Gartung]

Donald Barthelme. *Not-Knowing: The Essays and Interviews of Donald Barthelme*. Ed. Kim Herzinger. Intro. John Barth. Random House, 1997. 332 pp. $27.50.

Not-Knowing collects much of Barthelme's nonfiction that, the editor explains, "only the most dedicated enthusiast of *Barthelmismo*, to use Thomas Pynchon's useful word, will have had the opportunity to read . . . before now." It is the second in a series of three planned volumes edited by Kim Herzinger, the first of which was *The Teachings of Don B.: Satires, Parodies, Fables, Illustrated Stories and Plays* (the third will contain previously uncollected stories).

Barthelme's essay "Not-Knowing" often circulates in the form of eighth-generation photocopies from *Best American Essays 1986*, with the faded marginalia of previous readers and fuzzy, degenerate type. His work in this book retains something of the quality of the bootleg photocopy even though it is an edited collection. This Barthelme may be bound, but he's still elusive, thankfully. The essays and interviews in *Not-Knowing* fend off the posing and dogmatic proclamations—the rows of sharpened number-two pencils and the sage advice—that are the risk of the genres. Take even his most declamatory moments: "Art is a true account of the activity of mind. Because consciousness, in Husserl's formulation, is always consciousness *of* something, art thinks ever of the world, cannot not think of the world, could not turn its back on the world even if it wished to." This point, which he repeats several times throughout the collection, resonates with the Stevens poem, "Of Modern Poetry": Modern poetry "has / To construct a new stage. / It has to be on that stage." This is the Barthelme of *Not-Knowing*, rigging up the theater and the mise-en-scène, at the same time performing "the mind in the act of finding what will suffice."

At the end of a late interview with Jo Brans, Barthelme is asked to describe his ideal reader. He responds, "Just ordinary folks like us." We should be so ordinary. [Monique Dufour]

Kathy Acker. *Bodies of Work.* Serpent's Tail, 1997. 175 pp. Paper: $16.00.

Bodies of Work is an exquisite catalog of art and culture. Ever suspicious of any specter of control, Acker questions our various obsessions with the internet, the Marquis de Sade, bodybuilding, art cinema, fin de siècle Russia, and authorship/ownership with the appropriate amount of schism one would expect from the author of *Empire of the Senseless* and *Pussy, King of the Pirates.* "I question the works you're about to read," she writes in the final line of her introduction, diffusing the collection of conscious deliberation and opening up an entire dimension for exploration. Moving much in the way her novels do, *Bodies of Work* sketches a connect-the-dots approach to interpretation and meaning that is always searching for answers which may or may not be there, always filling worlds with avenues for possibility, and ultimately deciding that the journey itself is what creates our impressions of understanding.

Bodies of Work attests to Acker's passion for life and art (one in the same and indistinguishable) once incorporated into her body of experience and pleasure. If the collection does have a consistency, it is the inexhaustible intensity and depth she attains in exploring her own desires. Like the meticulously drawn dream maps that have appeared in her novels, *Bodies of Work* showcases Acker as an artist wrestling with the nature of knowledge and, more importantly, how we come to know what we know through a language that is at best disheveled, disgruntled, and disembodied, serving whatever socio-politico-sexual end we can conjure to titillate (and possibly destroy) ourselves.

Read with the realization of Acker's death last November after a long battle with breast cancer, her haunting introduction seemingly concludes the book before it ever begins. "All of us are faced, as perhaps we never before have been, by death," she writes. *Bodies of Work* may in fact be her last will and testament to a world she lived and loved as wildly as it lived and loved her. [Trevor Dodge]

Isaac Babel. *1920 Diary.* Ed. and intro. Carol J. Avins. Trans. H. T. Willetts. Yale Univ. Press, 1997. 192 pp. Paper: $13.00.

During the 1920 Polish-Soviet War, concealing his Jewish identity under a Russian pseudonym, Babel served as a war correspondent for the predominantly Cossack First Cavalry branch of the Red Army. This diary, which contains several of the germs for Babel's celebrated *Red Cavalry* stories (1926), documents his experiences, observations, and reflections for about four months of that war. Its entries catalog the everyday realities of sweat, blood, excrement, flies, rain, mud, dust, fatigue, homesickness, forced billeting, looting, and ethnically motivated brutality. Also included in this volume are four articles Babel wrote for his army newspaper, the *Red Cavalryman;* they are propagandistic in tone and stand in striking contrast to his sometimes ambivalent and detached, sometimes outraged and despairing diary entries. Avins's introduction provides a thorough overview of the diary's historical and biographical context, as well as an illuminating discussion of some of its key preoccupations. Chief among these preoccupations are Babel's anxieties over hiding his ethnic identity, his uncertainties regarding the future of the Bolshevik cause, and his compassion for the unfortunate people caught up in this violent transitional moment—not only Jewish villagers, victims of several atrocious pogroms, but also female nurses and Polish prisoners. Even horses and cows receive his sympathetic attention. Much of the diary consists of hastily written reminders to develop or describe certain people, impressions, or incidents. But Babel's more detailed reflections and anecdotes, considered in relation to both his fiction and twentieth-century Soviet and Jewish history, make wading through the rest of the diary highly worthwhile. [Thomas Hove]

Millicent Dillon. *You Are Not I: A Portrait of Paul Bowles.* Univ. of California Press, 1998. 340 pp. $27.50.

This latest book on Paul Bowles, whose title is taken from one of Bowles's short stories, will likely provoke ambivalent feelings among its readers. For those unacquainted with Bowles, it will doubtless spark interest in the subject. Those already familiar with Bowles's life and work, however, may become impatient with repetition of facts and anecdotes available any number of other places.

Dillon bills her work as an experiment in biography. Her narrative, as much memoir as biography, is based on a series of trips she made to Tangier in the late seventies when she was working on her biography of Jane Bowles, *A Little Original Sin,* and trips made more recently in the early nineties. Her conversations with Paul (some apparently taped, some recalled) are placed within particular settings and interspersed with analytical comments, conventionally arranged biographical material, and the author's musings. A number of key issues are probed: Bowles's attitudes toward sex and money, the significance of his unique childhood experiences, his relations with his father, and the nature of his creative process.

What emerges, very much like in A. J. A. Symons's *Quest for Corvo,* is a double portrait of the biographer and her subject. There is Bowles, the subject, at once charming, enigmatic, and evasive. There is Dillon, the biographer, persistent and constantly frustrated in her attempts to pin things down and gain her subject's approval. Dillon's insecurities and jealousies arise starkly in the last section of the book when Virginia Spencer Carr, another Bowles biographer, arrives in Tangier during her visit and the two women must contend for Paul's time ("A second biographer? A second woman biographer? I say bitterly to myself"). These later sections of the book are, to my mind, the most interesting, demonstrating the kind of possessiveness biographers have for their subjects.

What Dillon confirms, above all, is the immense, though sometimes subtle, power Bowles has held over those who have come into his orbit, his biographers being no exception. One can only wonder why Mr. Bowles has put up with so much relentless, tortuous interrogation—lest it be that he has a streak of masochism. "But what could I do?" I can imagine him saying with a groan, as though he had no way of controlling the events around him. [Allen Hibbard]

Carole Maso. *Defiance*. Dutton, 1998. 272 pp. $23.95.

Carole Maso has suggested "there might be ways in language to express the things that exist at the extreme peripheries of speech." Though she made this comment in an essay on her last novel, *Aureole*, it is equally applicable to *Defiance*, a novel in four acts that follows a brilliant physicist, Bernadette, through her last months on death row for killing two of her Harvard students. For Bernadette, the narrator, language and life collapse into the beauty of a "mute player on a deaf piano" as she creates her "death book," not as an explanation for her actions but rather for Elizabeth, her friend who is working on a book titled *Against a Feminine Masochism*.

Maso creates a defiant female community that responds to the masochism that patriarchal society forces upon women, as in Bernadette's mother's workplace, where her mother was made to sing "I'm a Little Teapot" as her boss masturbated into a handkerchief. Maso's metanarrative critique of society raises stunning questions about war, fathers, media (televised execution?), and children's songs to name a few.

Defiance, however, is not a rant but rather a wonderfully orchestrated novel that employs language—and silence—to explore individual identity within various constructed worlds, not the least of which are sexual relationships. Bernadette, an underage whore during her undergraduate days, bides time as a young professor waiting for her perfect victim, Alexander Ashmeade. By her own admission, her second victim, Payson Wynn, was sloppy passion.

Readers familiar with Maso's work recognize the beauty and irony of her continued quest to write books that explore inadequacies of language while realizing the inseparability of language and society. *Defiance* is a strong and very satisfying addition to her work. [Alan Tinkler]

Carlos Fuentes. *The Crystal Frontier.* Trans. Alfred Mac Adam. Farrar, Straus & Giroux, 1997. 266 pp. $23.00.

Originally written in Spanish in the aftermath of California's Proposition 187, *The Crystal Frontier,* as the title suggests, adopts as its theme the paradoxical barrier—reflective, deformative, and transparent—separating the United States and Mexico. Here, Fuentes takes aim at the greed and callousness of both cultures from American CEOs to lecherous assembly-line foremen to racist border guards.

Composed of nine interconnected stories, *The Crystal Frontier* has as its central figure Leonardo Barroso, a powerful businessman with strong economic ties to the United States. Of the myriad characters, all are in one way or another linked to the enigmatic Don Leonardo. Throughout the novel we see underpaid women toil away in his *maquiladoras;* a Mexican medical student receives a scholarship from Barroso to study at Cornell; a once wealthy young man finds himself reduced to cleaning office windows as part of Barroso's migrant workforce; Don Leonardo's long-forgotten brother, after having suffered a stroke, is abandoned by his family on a lonely highway.

Fate has dealt many of these people a cruel hand, and given the circumstances under which the novel came into being (Mexicans were just dealt the inevitable blind-sided slap from NAFTA), one can sense the anger in these pages. However, *The Crystal Frontier*'s most powerful moments lie in its humor, as Fuentes uncovers the comic absurdity in Mexican-American cultural differences. This humor is most prevalent in "The Spoils," a riotously funny critique of American cuisine and our missing sense of moderation, which also serves as a homage to large women before it ends in Don Quixote fashion as two men escape from the plasticity of San Diego and flee, naked, to their *patria.*

Ultimately, *The Crystal Frontier* is a novel about identity as it addresses the timely issue of multiculturalism. Fuentes occupies a rather tenuous position between the wish to surpass cultural differences and the desire to preserve them, as he recognizes the impossibility of finding answers in a world of migrations and crossings. [Kent D. Wolf]

Lynne Tillman. *No Lease on Life.* Harcourt Brace, 1998. 179 pages. $21.00.

The rigorously close, third-person narration in *No Lease on Life* allows for neither editorializing commentary nor the evasions of an "I." Rather, what the reader gets is something like an inventory of consciousness. Patiently, meticulously, the narrative observes a woman's mind over twenty-four hours one day in June, and records all the "garbage" that mind collects—"all the details, the sidewalk antics"—garbage which only adds to the heap of refuse within, all the experiences and cultural detritus of a lifetime. Just as Elizabeth Hall's excrementally dirty apartment building (human shit sits in the vestibule for half the book) is overseen by a superintendent who can't bear to throw away any of "life's filth," so the novel is presided over by a consciousness that cannot tear itself away from or disregard the street, the endless night, the darkness both within and without.

And herein lies one of the major virtues of Tillman's novel. In a society that increasingly deals with the unbearable by cleaning "it" up, by sweeping the streets and parks of the homeless and addicted, and/or stashing "it" away (in ghettos, prisons, etc.), *No Lease on Life* provides a straight-on view and acknowledgment of the unbearable, if not an acceptance. What Elizabeth collects keeps her from sleeping, drives her to thoughts of murder, and yet "she [has] to be open . . . like a window . . . sometimes transparent, usually paradoxical, and always open to tragicomic views of life."

As that last phrase hints, another great virtue of this novel is its humor. Perhaps inspired by Freud's maxim that "we can only laugh when a joke has come to our aid," Tillman has strewn and even obstructed the path of the narrative with dirty jokes and riddles. Seemingly outside and even superfluous to what I described above as an inventory of a woman's consciousness (since Elizabeth never reflects on them), the jokes nevertheless inform our reading of this inventory—occasionally underscoring its themes, but more often simply helping us to hear better its own hilariously deadpan rhythms, to perceive more fully its "tragicomic view." [Elisabeth Sheffield]

Martin Amis. *Night Train*. Harmony, 1997. 175 pp. $20.00.

Boasting a cast of characters that includes a Colonel Tom, Doctor No, Professor Faulkner, and Doctor Tulkinghorn, as well as a restaurant called Yeats's, a street called Whitman, and a town called Destry, Martin Amis's slim new novel is clearly concerned with the confluence of several different elite and popular cultural traditions. It is also a novel whose British writer seems to direct as a postcard to America, a bemused missive that ponders the endemic and frequently meaningless violence at the culture's core. Narrated by female detective Mike Hoolihan, *Night Train* follows a circuitous route through the investigation of a violent act that hovers tantalizingly between murder and suicide. Unlike a precursor in the postmodern, metaphysical detective genre like Paul Auster's *New York Trilogy,* Amis's version is humanly warmer and less obsessed with mathematical symmetry. Instead, he poses his narrative as a desultory study of its victim, Jennifer Rockwell. And Rockwell is worth this focus, at once an emblem of American middle-class success, a provocative double for the novel's burly narrator, and an ennui-ridden descendant of *London Fields*'s memorable Nicola Six. As Hoolihan's complex investigation of Jennifer's death proceeds, television, the movies, and the more mysteriously general sense of meaninglessness in American culture are implicated as the fuel driving a powerful night train through the national psyche. The locomotive of the novel's title is present enough throughout the narrative, but also recalls the rhythm and blues classic recorded by several different artists. The interpretive variation of these recordings is a metaphor for the shifting, not to say empty, possibility at the core of Hoolihan's investigation. This fascinating and dazzlingly written novel does provide solutions to the various mysteries it poses, but those solutions are every bit as enigmatic and disturbing as the problems they solve. [Stephen Bernstein]

Karen Elizabeth Gordon. *Torn Wings and Faux Pas: A Flashbook of Style, A Beastly Guide through the Writer's Labyrinth*. Illustrated by Rikki Ducornet. Pantheon, 1998. 204 pp. $23.00.

Cross the practicality of Strunk and White, the Gothic humor of Charles Adams, and the inventiveness of an author who can write phrases like "unspeakable velocities in parked cars," and you'll get a sense of Karen Elizabeth Gordon's *Torn Wings and Faux Pas*. Billed as a "flashbook of style," *Torn Wings* is cognate with other manuals of style in that it covers the fundamentals of English usage. Readers can use it to undangle modifiers or parse the difference between anybody, any body, anyone and any one. Like most good handbooks, *Torn Wings* also illuminates the reasoning behind usage, not to tighten the "grammatical chastity belt," as Gordon puts it, but to emphasize how elastic usage can be, how much room a category like "split infinitives," for example, contains for individual taste and play.

What distinguishes *Torn Wings*, though, is its attitude. Instead of drawing illustrative examples from famous texts, the common method, Gordon has approached her task as if she were creating flash fictions. Thus the entry for "anxious / eager" is informed by the consciousness of Zoë Platgut, a "full-time female" in "sensible walking shoes" who brings to the manual a no frills, literal approach. Other characters have a beatnik lineage or prehistoric childhood. Through these and other narrative whimsies, the ancestry of words are brought into contemporary encounters much as they were in Gordon's earlier works: *The New Well-Tempered Sentence*, a punctuation handbook, and *The Deluxe Transitive Vampire*, a grammar handbook. Indeed, together these three works form a reference set, or perhaps more accurately, a minigenre with a lineage that includes Raymond Queneau's *Exercises in Style*. Neither lean nor exhaustive, *Torn Wings and Faux Pas* puts its emphasis on teasing out nuance, a demonstration of the double-coding of language, through style, with social commentary, parody, *jouissance*. [Steve Tomasula]

Cynthia Ozick. *The Puttermesser Papers.* Knopf, 1997. 236 pp. $23.00.

The Puttermesser Papers is Cynthia Ozick's elegant, searing, and darkly humorous tale of the impossibilities and paradoxes of paradise found and paradise lost. The novel presents a picaresque story of Ruth Puttermesser, a dowdy overeducated and idealistic middle-aged lawyer. Demoted from her bureaucratic job in New York City's Kafkaesque Department of Disbursements and Receipts, Puttermesser accidentally creates a golem, Xanthippe (after Socrates' wife), whose superpowers manage to get Puttermesser elected as mayor of New York. The city quickly becomes a vision of urban utopia only to be destroyed in vengeance by Xanthippe, as all golems do.

A decade later Puttermesser embarks on her next adventure when she falls in love with the younger Rupert Rabeeno, a painter who makes exact replicas of masterpieces and sells them as postcards identified as "Re-enactments." In her final escapade Puttermesser rescues a distant Soviet cousin who emigrates to the U.S. as a refugee only to turn out to be hardly the oppressed victim Puttermesser had imagined. Indeed, Puttermesser is finally too idealistic and quixotic for the dark and immoral forces at work in the final decades of the millennium as her violent and random death suggests.

The novel shifts between Jewish magical-realist tale, a bitingly satirical tale of contemporary New York life, and a realistic story of modern life. Indeed, if anything, the novel's only minor weakness is its inability to shift well between these several different modes or even to settle comfortably anywhere between them. Still, Ozick's sharp sense of intellectual and cultural satire, coupled with her masterly pyrotechnic prose and distinctive gifts as a storyteller, keep the novel wise, charming, and imaginative. [Jeanne Claire van Ryzin]

Jack Kerouac. *Some of the Dharma.* Viking, 1997. 420 pp. $32.95.

Some of the Dharma will not replace *On the Road* or *Dharma Bums* as carside reading. It lacks the rush of events that have now led yet another generation to discover Kerouac (even while his literary reputation remains stuck in the ditch of critical neglect waiting for the tow truck of academe). Still, the publication of these mid-1950s meditations (on Buddhism, consciousness, and writing), sketches, brief poems, and occasional drawings is significant in several ways. It suggests that there is a growing readership for Kerouac's more experimental work, which in time may encourage the recognition that the core of his achievement is *Visions of Cody* and his other experiments with voice and form. It also helps define the nature of Kerouac's experiment. In *Some of the Dharma* the defining stylistic element is the typewriter—the way it can space letters, symbols, and words as visual designs and also the way it can deploy text and space to convey cadences and inflections and to create various juxtapositions and simultaneities. Fortunately, Viking has preserved Kerouac's typewriting. This underscores his determination to find ways to evoke the immediacy of the spoken voice (and create an illusion of participating in it), yet also his commitment to construct literary objects for contemplation and appreciation. The typewriterly experiments of *Some of the Dharma* thus point to the dialectic of Kerouac's experiment: the desire for a style that would simultaneously have (actually be) the performative immediacy of talk, yet also have the stability and distance of the printed page. So yes, *Some of the Dharma* offers us Kerouac's attempt to save himself through Buddhism. It is also (read on its own terms) a sometimes stunning, often interesting, occasionally silly experimental tour de force that asks us to rethink Capote's dismissive sneer of "That's typewriting." [Tim Hunt]

Charles Olson.*Collected Prose.* Ed. Donald Allen and Benjamin Friedlander. Intro. Robert Creeley. Univ. of California Press, 1997. 472 pp. $50.00; paper $19.95.

Olson sought trace, prime. "I find it awkward to call myself a poet or a writer," he notes. "If there are no walls there are no names. This is the morning, after the dispersion, and the work of the morning is methodology: how to use oneself, and on what." If his *Collected Prose* is a companion piece to his poetry, a work which constructs the armature around which the poetry turns, particularly in essays like "Projective Verse," "Against Wisdom as Such," and "A Foot Is to Kick With," it is also, more crucially, an enterprise in its own right. The thing is to be of use, Olson emphasized over and over, in whatever context. Increasingly for Olson, literature becomes *écriture,* and his project is a reading of entrails, a sifting of signs, a dive down, in or out. He studied himself to understand that outside himself. He read far and wide to read himself. We were part of the universe, and the universe was part of us, and we had to measure the plumb lines. The dictionary, encyclopedia, and card catalog, Ralph Maud comments, were for Olson stories. The gyre turned in ever-widening circles only to circle back upon itself. For Olson, finally, history was histology, poetry, breath, psychology, archaeology. The gesture was the man (the detail contained everything). It was body knowledge Olson was about, interiors ("you better figure on man's interiors," he says). His philosophy, his aesthetics, call it what you will, was a kinetics. One had to know oneself before one could apply oneself, be of use. Each of us, he reminded us over and over, had to find his own train and track. Much of this material is out of print or difficult to obtain, and we are all in debt to the University of California for bringing it together in one volume. It lies on the stage of poetry today, as the six-foot-seven, 270 pound Olson once did in a dance performance at Wesleyan as an undergraduate, impossible to go around without bumping against. [Robert Buckeye]

Italo Calvino, ed. *Fantastic Tales: Visionary and Everyday.* Trans. Alfred Mac Adam. Pantheon, 1997. 588 pp. $30.00.

Originally collected in two volumes in 1983 in Italy, Calvino's *Fantastic Tales,* available for the first time in English and in one volume, is a wondrous guide for getting lost, showing us through a land that at first seems like solid, empirical reality, but always ends in a bizarre transformation of the expected.

In some ways the tales selected and the introductions written by Calvino can function as an illustrated source book for Tzvetan Todorov's seminal study *The Fantastic.* Calvino cites Todorov's definition of the fantastic as a mode of fiction in which the reader and, usually, the protagonist confront a supernatural intrusion into the real and remain uncertain whether this incredible event, say the appearance of a ghost, is an actual but inexplicable occurrence or a natural and explainable phenomenon, perhaps a hallucination. If the event can be regarded as either natural or supernatural, then it is not technically fantastic. The fantastic is that which sustains and depends on uncertainty. Todorov concludes his study by saying that the fantastic is fundamentally a nineteenth-century genre, and Calvino's collection concurs with this by beginning with Jan Potocki's "The Story of the Demoniac Pacheco" (1805) and ending with H. G. Wells's "The Country of the Blind" (1899), with the likes of Hoffmann, Dickens, Nerval, and Bierce occupying the ground in between.

Aside from offering the simple joy of reading about necrophilia, talking dolls, and a nose that leaves its owner, this collection of tales encourages readers to see the profound influence fantastic literature has had on much of the experimental tradition of the twentieth century. The transgressive, magical, and fantastic realism of Kafka, Borges, Pynchon, Angela Carter, Milorad Pavić, Kathy Acker, Alasdair Gray, Delany, García Márquez, Allende, Rushdie, and, of course, Calvino himself, has roots in this literature that tests the boundaries between fantasy and realism. Published two years before his death, Calvino's collection provides a glorious ensemble of some of the best tales from the last century. It also serves as a key to Calvino's own work (especially *The Baron in the Trees, Cosmicomics,* and *Invisible Cities*), and ultimately illuminates a backdrop for the imaginary explorations of twentieth-century literature. [David Ian Paddy]

André Breton. *Anthology of Black Humor.* Trans. Mark Polizzotti. City Lights, 1997. 356 pp. Paper: $18.95.

In the twenties, it's said, via Freud the world discovered sex. About the same time, André Breton discovered surrealism—or was it the other way around?

Assembled in 1936, the *Anthology* was delayed first by publishing difficulties then by the wartime censorship board's refusal to approve it. Finally it came out in 1945 to almost total silence and was intermittently available as over the years it slowly garnered attention. A new edition was published in 1966 shortly before Breton's death; now for the first time it's available in English. The *Anthology*, like the body, has a long memory. And what it remembers is the twentieth century: that nexus where unknowingly we changed railway cars, destination, clothes, habits, and mind. Breton's collection includes selections from Swift, Poe, Lewis Carroll, Baudelaire, Nietzsche, Charles Fourier, Jarry, Roussel, Duchamp—altogether forty-five entries, each of them introduced by Breton, and it may be to the lancing percepts and verbal energy of these introductions that we'll hereafter return as much as to the texts themselves. Surrealism, if it was about anything, was about enthusiasm, about attempts at engagement, beyond knowledge and experience, with the world's raw *stuff*. It was also about humor. The two are inextricably entwined, which is why this book, this exploration of "the lugubrious tick-tock of the infernal machine that Lautréamont left on the mind's doorstep," is so important. Freud's *Jokes and Their Relation to the Unconscious* first appeared in French translation in 1930, and Breton in his general introduction makes much use of it.

Beauty will be convulsive or it will not exist. Before Beauty, the surrealist lifts his hand to his forehead in salute—or to wipe away a tear the size of a plum? And always with one finger picking away at his nose. [James Sallis]

Victor Pelevin. *Omon Ra*. Trans. Andrew Bromfield. New Directions, 1998. 154 pp. Paper: $9.95; *The Blue Lantern and Other Stories*. Trans. Andrew Bromfield. New Directions, 1997. 179 pp. $22.95.

Pelevin's works reminds one of Thomas Pynchon's, but of course, with a certain Russian twist. *Omon Ra,* his first novel, dedicated to the "heroes of the cosmos," is a dark and sad parody of the Soviet space program. The central character, Oman Krizomazov, is obliged to kill himself after fulfilling his duty on the moon only to find out that the entire "flight" was staged somewhere in the underground corridors of the Moscow subway system. However, he is not disappointed: he feels that he found the truth he was searching for his entire life, a truth he has paid for with a lot of pain and suffering and the death of his friends. He believes his suffering, his belief, his devotion made a difference. The false mission transforms into something similar to the ancient rite of initiation; Oman returns from the dead with a godlike wisdom.

In *The Blue Lantern and Other Stories,* Pelevin's first short-story collection, the motif of crossing borders—between life and death, between different worlds, across different levels of knowledge—appears repeatedly. Pelevin's vision of the world's multiplicity simultaneously contains very ironic and serious elements. In the story "Mid-Game" the flexibility of borders becomes at once funny and shocking: the reader discovers that two Moscow prostitutes are in actuality young former communist league officials who changed their sex, and two male Navy officers, maniacally pursuing the prostitutes, turn out to be former women themselves. In another story, "Crystal World," the motif is laid bare: Lenin, trying to reach the headquarters of the Bolsheviks just before the October Revolution of 1917, is presented as a demon, changing shapes in order to deceive a modest cadet guarding one of the streets of St. Petersburg. The success of the Revolution depends on this ordinary cadet, especially on his intellectual ability to recognize the metamorphosis, to see the transformations of the world occurring around him.

Pelevin's talent combines an incredible control of the magic of absurdity with photographically exact renderings of Soviet and post-Soviet realities. The fact is Pelevin is a philosophic writer par excellence. Moreover, his characters are true philosophers. They are always caught in the middle of a very intensive, passionate and bold search for the meaning of life, the universal explanation of being, despite the fact that in Pelevin's world there are no concrete explanations offered, or if offered they eventually turn out to be mere illusions, void and false. The intensity and seriousness of this search creates a link between the experimental postmodernism of his work and the age-old roots of Russian culture and literature. [Mark Lipovetsky]

Victor Pelevin. *The Life of Insects*. Trans. Andrew Bromfield. Farrar, Straus & Giroux, 1998. 179 pp. $22.00.

Life of Insects makes a case for Victor Pelevin as a major literary talent in his native Russia and throughout the world. If *Oman Ra* showed us his promise as a writer, this book shows us just what it promised, if not more.

Insects opens as a novel of stock intrigue: three strange men (two Russian, one American) secretly meet on the balcony of a dark and decrepit resort hotel to talk business. Upon deciding to continue their talk elsewhere, all three willingly fall over the balustrade: "If there had been a witness to this scene, we must assume he would have leaned over the balustrade, expecting to see three broken bodies lying on the ground below. But . . . If he possessed preternaturally sharp vision, he might just have discerned three mosquitoes in the distance, flying away. . . ." Given this transmutation, one might be lead to believe that this book will turn out as something of a tired Kafka rip-off or a pulpy sci-fi novel. We might simply await the mad scientist and the secret formula.

No chance. If this book has a mad scientist it is Pelevin himself. With stunning virtuosity, he completely undermines the reader's expectations, refusing to resolve the tension created by assigning insect and/or humanoid attributes to characters whenever he deems it to be convenient. In one particularly brilliant and bizarre scene, Sam, one of the aforementioned mosquitoes, notices a fly in his food while dining with his companions. He gently picks her up and places her on an empty chair, admiring her hairy eyes, her glittery, "firm green skin." A flirtation ensues: they drink wine, she freshens up with some makeup, then the two leave in a cab where Sam shows off by sucking blood from the driver through the front seat. Later, tragedy strikes when Natasha swats one of Sam's friends who had landed on her leg during lovemaking on the beach. Pelevin further decenters the identity of this dazzling novel by placing in its middle a seemingly unrelated, hilarious story of two pot fiends. The many layers of paranoia in this piece absolutely rival what's found in Poe's best short stories.

Insects is something of a postmodern *Animal Farm*, playing on our realistic sensibilities through anthropomorphic parody, but also through intra/intertextual and metafictional references, mirrors, and simulacrums. But ultimately, it is Pelevin's utter repose that makes this book so impressive. Clearly, he has the utmost respect for the intelligence of his readership. We should keep a close eye on this brilliant young writer. [Christopher Paddock]

Patrick Chamoiseau. *Solibo Magnificent.* Trans. Rose-Myriam Réjouis and Val Vinokurov. Pantheon, 1998. 208 pp. $23.00; *Texaco.* Trans. Rose-Myriam Réjouis and Val Vinokurov. Vintage, 1997. 404 pp. Paper: $14.00.

The publication of Réjouis and Vinokurov's translation of *Solibo Magnificent* firmly ensconces Chamoiseau in the English language. Last year saw their rendition of his magnum opus, *Texaco,* his depiction of three generations of Martinique history: the days of slavery and its abolition up to the present and uncertain predicament of Creole culture, embodied in the shantytown "countercity" of Texaco. Like Texaco itself, the book is both a hymn and a resistance to the entity known as "City" and the freedom it not so much offers as imposes.

Those with a taste for something less epic, though, might prefer Chamoiseau's earlier *Solibo Magnificent,* an allegory of the death of Creole oral culture. Solibo, the last of the great tale-tellers, dies in the midst of delivering his final public performance, mysteriously choking on his own words. Enter the police, upholders of proper procedure, which takes the form of a linguistic and cultural subordination to French. The resulting Keystone-cop episodes prove Chamoiseau to be strongest when his humor is: *Solibo*'s high points recall Chaplin at his youngest and most physical, with the sobering difference that when Chamoiseau's characters get hit, they bleed and they die.

Both books describe the "un-clarity" of Creole life and language: what Texaco is to City, Creole is to French; counterresistences to the compromising freedoms offered by both. "Freedom is not given, must not be given. Liberty awarded does not liberate your soul." If anything, it is to be wrung out, in the same way *Solibo*'s police wring their nonexistent murder case out of innocent witnesses. In the words of Solibo: "if someone gives Solibo words Solibo has no more words." But with the fading of the culture that he represents, what kind of words are left to the Martinique writer? Chamoiseau's novels are necessarily uneasy collages of different voices and conflicted forms (oral histories, for example, are accompanied by footnotes). The result, however, is a voice of his own: inventive, biting, sometimes precious, but individual in the face of the alleged universality of all official tongues. [Marc Lowenthal]

Ingo Schulze. *Thirty-Three Moments of Happiness: St. Petersburg Stories.* Trans. John E. Woods. Knopf, 1998. 306 pp. $23.00.

This subtle, uncanny collection must be read closely. It is as mysterious, grotesque, and beautiful as a Gogol narrative. The title introduces us to the "madness" of the text. What do the "thirty-three moments of happiness" have to do with St. Petersburg? Is a happy person aware of time? Why are there thirty-three moments? Is the number referring obliquely to Christian epiphany, to Jesus's resurrection? Is it also referring to the thirty-three stories in this collection? To complicate matters, two letters of correspondence preface the book. One explains that a German passenger named Hoffmann has written stories of his adventures in Russia (E. T. A. Hoffmann?), but he has vanished. In the preface it is intimated that Hoffmann insisted Schulze publish the stories under his own name, that he "represent" Hoffmann. Schulze takes responsibility, hoping that the narratives—as eccentric as they are—will be starting points for "an ongoing discussion concerning the value of happiness."

"Happiness" is a strange word for most of the events described in these stories of loss, madness, and violence. In one, three "devils"— whose names keep changing—eat flesh. They are surely enjoying cannibalism, but their victim is not (or is she?): "Fricassee was applied to the feet, cheese omelets to the knees." But the "craziness" of the narrator may create the story. Reality is open to question. In another story the German Müller-Fritsch is calm as he awaits his death: "And now he was done with life as well. It all went too fast. Maybe that was why he was so composed." Müller-Fritsch "oozes" away, leaving a "sweetish, sweaty odor." The juxtaposition of "sweet" and "sweat" is interesting. This play reminds us that all the stories are told in a mixed way. German, English, and Russian are perversely joined.

Schulze's collection is a risky, thrilling accomplishment. [Irving Malin]

Can Xue. *The Embroidered Shoes.* Trans. Ronald R. Janssen and Jian Zhang. Henry Holt, 1997. 221 pp. $20.00.

"The Recorder sat in his roadside shed writing down the various dreamlands described by passersby." Other than a discrepancy of gender—Can Xue is female—the previous line provides a reasonable approximation of Can Xue's project throughout *The Embroidered Shoes,* one of the most remarkable collections of short fiction published in 1997. The eleven stories composing this collection—ten short fictions and one novella-length tale—concern characters whose identities and realities have become as indeterminate as language itself. Physical and psychical material transmute with regularity, and, within these indefinite galleries of linguistic time and space, the act of narration becomes conscious of its constructed nature. In the novella-length piece "Apple Tree in the Corridor," a narrator says, "I haven't told the story as I intended. I am forever circling around, never able to approach reality. Once I open my mouth, I discover I'm telling something that I have falsified, instead of the thing . . . I never intend to tell anything but only to make some noise." This realization frees Can Xue to eschew reality and delve into her powerful surreal vision, composing tales of beautiful linguistic "noise" that range from extended nightmare visions to prose passages redolent of symbolist poetry.

This noise also corresponds to Can Xue's status as one of the few contemporary Chinese writers to oppose that country's realist literary conventions, despite government opposition to artistic freedom. Although the fictional terrain of *The Embroidered Shoes* is contemporary post-Mao China, this China has been transformed by Can Xue's wicked imagination into a truly strange and wonderfully disturbing (sur)reality reminiscent of the dreamscapes inhabited by Kafka, Schulz, and Borges. These three authors are serious company for any author and are not mentioned haphazardly; Can Xue's work is a welcome continuation of their liberating literary projects. [Matthew Badura]

Peter Carey. *Jack Maggs*. Knopf, 1998. 306 pp. $24.00.

Peter Carey's five previous novels have been lauded for their "Dickensian" wealth of incident and characterization. In *Jack Maggs* Carey takes his Victorian forefathers by the sideburns, bringing Dickens himself back to life in the figure of a ruthless and driven young novelist, Tobias Oates, who writes lucrative, sensational accounts of accident victims, destitutes, and criminals. Jack Maggs, a transported convict returned from Australia, offers perfect fodder for the novelist: " 'It's the Criminal Mind,' said Tobias Oates, 'awaiting its first cartographer.' " Unlike Magwitch in *Great Expectations*, however, Maggs resists exoticization.

Dickens's complicity with vindictive Victorian criminology is especially distasteful to the Australian Carey. Yet even as he forces us to rethink Dickens, Carey treasures the teeming, panoramic nineteenth-century form for its ability to accommodate human diversity—what Iris Murdoch calls the "contingency" of the social world. In Carey's hands, the novelist's searchlight sweeps ever further into the margins, picking out the once unspeakable—homosexuality, prostitution, extramarital pregnancy, backstreet abortions.

Dickens, too, used to be celebrated for extending the range of fiction to include the outcasts in the periphery. Hindsight has revealed the latent coerciveness of his social conscience and the violence that informs the conventions that contain multiplicity in Victorian fiction: melodramatic closure, pseudoscientific categorization of social types. Carey eschews such pat devices. He weaves instead a staccato sequence of brief scenes and multiple, overlapping perspectives, evoking a world of irreducible complexity beyond the scope of any single account.

Given the literary conceit on which it rests, *Jack Maggs* makes for a great comparison to *Great Expectations*, and it is worth a heap of essays on its main themes: the pitfalls of fiction, the blind spots of Victorian ideology, social discipline. [Philip Landon]

Carol Shields. *Larry's Party*. Viking, 1997. 339 pp. $23.95.

George F. Babbitt meet Larry Weller. Larry is the eponymous hero of Carol Shields's new novel, an ordinary guy from a lower-middle-class background who rises during the course of the narrative from a clerk in a florist's shop to a master maze-maker. Like Sinclair Lewis's protagonist, Larry learns about himself through his relationships with others, as well as through his material possessions.

Larry's Party is a novel of character. We meet his parents, his first wife Dorrie, his son Ryan, his second wife Beth, and his lover Charlotte, as well as several of his friends. Through these people and through the chapters which focus on various parts of his life—his work, his "threads," his penis, his living tissue, and his incorporation into an independent businessman—readers watch his development from a callow youth, experimenting with love, to a middle-aged man recovering from a serious bout with encephalitis and enduring a midlife crisis. The party of the title brings together his wives, lover, sister, and friends in a way that shows the tensions inherent in these relationships, but also the affection that drew them together.

Mazes serve as the governing symbol for Larry's journey through life and the occupation which moves from personal obsession during his first honeymoon to apprenticing with a maze designer, and finally becoming a highly thought-of independent designer and builder. Different ones also grace the beginning of each chapter. The novel seems to suggest that despite the twists and turns that a person's life may take, there is a way out once the pattern is discovered. The novel rings true as a saga of the extraordinarily ordinary Larry. [Sally E. Parry]

Knut Hamsun. *Rosa.* Trans. Sverre Lyngstad. Sun & Moon, 1998. 254 pp. Paper: $12.95.

A Nobel laureate, Hamsun is often regarded as Scandinavia's greatest novelist. When he was nine, his family was obliged to surrender him as a laborer to his uncle, who beat and starved him. He escaped five years later and became a nomadic laborer, almost dying of starvation and disease several times. As a result, Hamsun and his protagonists were loners who nonetheless sought others, however passively and hopelessly, for validation. In his earlier work Hamsun thematizes dreams, hallucinations, and the unconscious, using interior monologues and even stream of consciousness. His later work turns to social and environmental concerns.

Rosa, first appearing in 1908, is noteworthy as a transition between the two periods. The protagonist and first-person narrator, Parelius, is another of Hamsun's lonely, insecure artists. Yet Parelius focuses so much on the other characters rather than himself that he almost becomes a participant observer. Accordingly, Hamsun's technique here is far from interior monologue or stream of consciousness. Yet the attention to the villagers does not mark this novel with the quaint regionalism and traditionalism of Hamsun's later work.

Atypical in Hamsun's oeuvre, this text displays a subtle tragicomic humor. The tasteless village capitalist is equal to those of Sinclair Lewis: Hartvigson makes his consumption conspicuous by wearing a diving suit to church; he also changes his company name to Hartwich, thinking it makes him more cosmopolitan. The sea captain, to get even with his wife, runs across a shoal and takes her down with the ship. The Don Juan succeeds because of his two prized commodities, a bathtub and a feather bed.

Rosa is another fine edition from Sun & Moon, a leading source of Scandinavian literature in translation. [Darryl Hattenhauer]

Thomas Bernhard. *The Voice Imitator.* Trans. Kenneth J. Northcott. Univ. of Chicago Press, 1997. 104 pp. $17.95.

Thomas Bernhard's book of extremely short fictions, all less than a page long and some shorter than this review, is not as satisfying as his longer works. Unlike Beckett—whose entire project seems dependent on a sort of distillation and stripping, a voiding and negating—or Kafka—whose concentrated parables and fragments are really similar gestures to his longer, unfinished novels—Bernhard does not seem completely at home in this genre.

In the constricted space of a few sentences or lines, Bernhard does not have the chance to develop adequately the musicality of his prose, a musicality built on repetition of key phrases—such as "so Roithamer" from *Correction* and "Glenn" and "Glenn Gould" from *The Loser*—and accents—all of the italicized words throughout the novels and his autobiography. This quality is hinted at in *The Voice Imitator,* with the repetition of the phrase "in the nature of things," as well as many italicized words, but the book as a whole does not have the space or time to repeat, recombine, and vary the linguistic phrases and motifs. The book never quite attains the fluidity and momentum of the novels, and the language retreats from the resonant and material, almost concrete presence it enjoys in the longer works, to a sort of transparent or anecdotal reportage.

This collection is also only able to suggest some of the humor of Bernhard's novels, and this is perhaps its greatest drawback. *The Woodcutters, The Loser,* even *The Lime Works* and *Correction,* are all brutally funny works. But again, this humor is built on repetition and recombination of linguistic motifs, a technique *The Voice Imitator* simply can't have time for.

Still, this is Thomas Bernhard, and some of the writing is breathtakingly beautiful: he can pack an entire story or lifetime into a single italicized word, as he does with the word *"character"* in a story called "The Prince." For my money, however, and despite the physical beauty of the book and the pristine quality of the prose, *The Voice Imitator* is a minor intermezzo compared to his other work. [Jeffrey DeShell]

Lucy Ellmann. *Man or Mango?: A Lament.* Farrar, Straus & Giroux, 1998. 240 pp. $22.00.

Man or Mango? is a fictional collage composed of many narrative voices interspersed with pictures, drawings, excerpts from a (fictional) student's notebook, quotations from history books, literature, newspapers, the *Guinness Book of World Records,* a variety of nineteenth-century scientific materials on ants and bees, and lists—lots of lists. The characters address the reader directly in the vein of Julian Barnes's *Talking It Over* or Martin Amis's *Success.* Eloïse, a self-described hermit, has a wry sense of humor and a penchant for making lists. George, whose narrative is peppered with phrases in ALL CAPITAL LETTERS, is an American writer living in London trying to finish his EPIC POEM ON ICE HOCKEY. The book includes an assortment of supporting characters, including Ed, a burglar by profession whose true passion is growing huge vegetables and who sends letter bombs to female news reporters as a hobby; Venetia, George's rich, dull, and sexually insatiable patroness; an Evil Doctor; the Earth; and three "Old Biddies" who compose a gang of geriatric shoplifters. The characters' lives don't seem to intersect until the second part of the novel, when we realize that they are each planning a holiday at the same seaside hotel in Ireland.

This disparate group of people all share a similar destiny, and *Man or Mango?* moves from being merely a meditation on burglars and bombs, relationships and gigantic vegetables, to much larger issues of life, death, nature, and human folly in the face of history. Ellmann's postmodern pastiche is full of verve and substance, and reminds me of the best work of Amis, Barnes, Jeanette Winterson, Ian McEwan, and even Ishmael Reed. In spite of sharing similar ingredients with the books of these writers, *Man or Mango?* is thoroughly original, and offers us entertainingly piercing insight into the human predicament. [Michael Reder]

Cris Mazza. *Former Virgin.* FC2, 1997. 145 pp. Paper: $11.95.

As the title suggests, *Former Virgin* is a handful of stories (thirteen) devoted to the sacrifice of innocence. At first glance the characters might seem normal, even typical, but upon closer examination, the creativity involved in their self-destruction becomes readily apparent; without exception, all elements of self are sunk into the overwhelming abyss of the dysfunctional relationship. Though motivated by the insatiable need to be noticed and loved, the characters, some oblivious, some slightly demented, and some eerily aware, are always searching for something *else*, something that might make them happier, something that doesn't seem even to exist at all. Sometimes, as in "Adrenalin," there is no clear-cut reason for their self-imposed downfall. The story concerns a woman, newly married to a man she loves, who commences an obsession with photography of a single subject—her husband. The slow abandonment of everything else in her life still doesn't prompt her to change; she sees only him, but her eyes are replaced by a synthetic lens, creating an immeasurable distance between them. Through this twisted two-dimensional fascination, her husband in the flesh becomes obsolete and without realizing it, she loses interest in him, the adrenalin gone. In "The Cram-It-In-Method" a woman takes almost a frightening deliberation with her life. Like the narrator, we obtain our information by eavesdropping. The story involves two roommates who hardly know one another. One meets a man, and without too much thought and despite obvious differences, she decides to marry him. The narrator observes, "Maybe Annie's father never taught her (like mine drilled into my head) that force doesn't make anything work easier." Consequently, the enormity of the wedding plans replaces the actual reason for the occasion and an ominous future lies ahead for the bride-to-be who makes a shallow, desperate decision. These stories, both darkly funny and serious, seem to raise perplexing issues about postfeminism: the women, who have ceased being the victims, ironically seem to take part in their own degradation. This pertinent collection is an intriguing and worthwhile read. [Kristin Schar]

Neeli Cherkovski. *Bukowski: A Life.* Steerforth, 1997. 352 pp. Paper: $18.00; Jim Christy. *The Buk Book: Musings on Charles Bukowski.* Photos by Claude Powell. ECW Press, 1997. 89 pp. Paper: $12.95.

Writers such as Charles Bukowski or Thomas Wolfe, whose fictions constitute virtual autobiographies, are perhaps the most difficult for biographers to deal with and yet are also the most in need of external investigation. Neeli Cherkovski's book is not the definitive biography of Bukowski, but it is a useful start and written in the clear, direct style of the master. Its strength resides in the soother's close access to the subject during their early friendship, his obvious affection for Bukowski's democratizing work, and the material from interviews that Bukowski eventually consented to. One wishes, on the other hand, that there had been more corroboration, especially of Bukowski's youth, from research. Also, this volume is, as the copyright page admits, only "a slightly different version" of Cherkovski's *Hank, The Life of Charles Bukowski,* published by Random House in 1991. This book purports to include the "wilder stories" which Bukowski regretted were previously omitted, but they are hard to find, as the inadequate index and notes have not been significantly improved. Still, the limited bibliography has been updated. I have made use of *Hank* in my own work and will no doubt be consulting this version. Other accounts of Bukowski's life are reportedly forthcoming. One regrets the omission of the photos by Michael Montfort that appeared in *Hank.*

The Buk Book, although lifting much of this information from other sources, uncited, does provide some of those wilder, hairier anecdotes of the Rabelaisian Buk, but the "musings" seem largely a justification for the publishing of the outlandishly bawdy photos. A young Claude Powell was apparently a carousing buddy of Bukowski's from 1969 into the '70s. Jim Christy corresponded with Bukowski in 1984 and had some contact with a woman upon whom one of the characters in *Women* was allegedly based. *The Buk Book* is brief, rollicking, sensationalistic, and, I suppose, in the worst of taste. But I doubt it would have bothered Bukowski. I found it often hilarious and a mainly credible addition to other such memoirs.

Those who consider Bukowski, as I do, a writer of permanent stature will want both of these books unless perhaps, in the case of the first, they already possess a copy of *Hank.* [Gerald Locklin]

Gordon Lish. *Self-Imitation of Myself.* Four Walls Eight Windows, 1998. 335 pp. $22.00.

Gordon Lish's *Self-Imitation of Myself* is his first entirely new collection of short fiction since *Mourner at the Door.* Clocking in at forty-six stories and 335 pages, it's also his largest and most varied. Although a few of the stories at first seem less strong than others, the volume as a whole shows Lish to be an edgy and capable writer willing to put pressure on fictional convention so as to call the notion of "story" into question.

The stories in *Self-Imitation* range from formal experiments, similar in some respects to those found in *Mourner,* to more sustained narratives. There are narratives that are extended jokes, a story about being in love with a dog named Beatrice, numbered narratives, a fiction modeled after a card game, a fiction based on a recipe, epistolary fiction, a fiction based on permutations of a philosophical statement, short brittle pieces that seem to be extensions of Lish's novels, terse little short shorts (such as the very fine "Konkluding Labor of Herkules"), a fish story, and a story in a subway, just to name a few.

Many of these pieces establish a form and then cause it to collapse or turn against itself in a way not unlike the strangest of Beckett's *Fizzles.* Lish establishes an utterance and then takes it apart, the subject of the fiction shifting to notions of storytelling and aesthetics. A few pieces, however, such as the playful "Fangle or Fire" or the very European "Traveling Man," establish a more sustained narrative and carry a character forward in complex and eloquent fashion. In these self-sabotaging pieces Lish shows himself adept at moving from level to level; in the second he proves he can stay on one level and move forward. In either he remains a quirky and shrewd writer, at once exasperating and effective. [Brian Evenson]

Michel Tournier. *The Mirror of Ideas.* Trans. Jonathan F. Krell. Univ. of Nebraska Press, 1998. 137 pp. $25.00.

One's response to the work of Michel Tournier is likely to fall on either side of a great divide, drawn there by political as much as by literary considerations. For thirty-plus years Tournier has gone his headstrong way, out of step with much of contemporary literature and in direct opposition to virtually every dominant strain in the French novel. Failed philosopher, earnest didact, nonbeliever in human progress, the man's a puzzle. However one feels about Tournier, no one quite knows what to *do* with him.

Much of the force of novels such as *Friday* and *The Ogre* derives from his play with contraries, suspension bridges hung between *sens* and *écriture*, structure and freedom. Tournier ever longs to entrap in the single event, in the single thought or word, both the elemental and cultured, historical and perverse, anarchic and fascistic.

So it is with *The Mirror of Ideas*, fifty-eight brief essays exploring such dualities as "Man and Woman," "The Willow and the Alder," "Act and Potency," "The Absolute and the Relative." Most run a page and a half, the longest just under three. This, for instance, is his one-page summary of all Western philosophy: "In the game of Being and Nothingness, one can state that the Being of Heraclitus is eaten away by Nothingness like a piece of fruit by a host of worms." Speaking of Gaston Bachelard, this book's dedicatee, Tournier has written that "one approaches the absolute by means of laughter." One imagines the two of them tipping hats as they pass one another in the street, this Absolute and this Tournier, both of them laughing. [James Sallis]

Dallas Wiebe. *Our Asian Journey*. Mir Editions Canada (Wilfrid Laurier University, Waterloo, Onterio, N2L 3C3, Canada),1997. 439 pp. Paper: $30.00.

Dallas Wiebe's strange philosophical fiction has been published by small presses since the 1960s. This novel is his most significant work. It is an occult text which deals, in part, with an odd, real journey of Mennonites to the Asian continent to locate the site of the Second Coming, the Apocalypse as described in the Revelation of John. It is obsessed with the "end of things."

The text is a commentary on Revelations (itself a commentary) and, by implications, a commentary by Wiebe on the ultimate meaning of the commentaries. There are three levels, three readings: the structure of *Our Asian Journey* is a juxtaposition of Joseph's diary entries written during the pilgrimage to the Asian city; a commentary by Wiebe on the meaning of this calling; two meditations by Joseph on the significance of the Asian journey (as he waits for his death in, of all places, Aberdeen, Idaho).

The novel is wide in scope, in time and space; its very structure suggests that revelation, interpretation of signs (heavenly and earthly) is often unclear, not centered. Revelation depends on the "correct" response to language. The text makes much of obscure phrases, names, tongues. The text is an ascent and a descent, mirroring the emotions of the pilgrims who discover that their destination is hermetically (un)marked. In a kind of postmodernist turn, the author Wiebe, a relation of the actual historical characters, wonders whether he can find meaning in the diverse texts—diaries, scholarly studies—which are written in various languages. How can he discover meaning in history (if it exists)? How can he "translate" the experiences of a strange cult in a strange land? It is easy to dismiss this text as a perverse, diffuse one. But it suggests that "revelation" is always difficult, that epistemology is convoluted, amusing, sad. The very fact that we are baffled may suggest that "the cloud of unknowing" haunts our longing for ultimate truth and salvation. [Irving Malin]

Jim Krusoe. *Blood Lake and Other Stories.* Boaz, 1997. 158 pp. $18.50.

This is the first collection of stories from the founding editor of the *Santa Monica Review,* publisher of many excellent authors, including Rikki Ducornet, Ron Sukenick, Curtis White, and Gordon Lish. But more than any of these writers, Krusoe resembles Mark Leyner—if he resembles anyone at all. Krusoe bombards the reader with the outrageous in a most consistent and offhanded tone. But make no mistake: Krusoe has his own style, and it is a finely honed and riotous one at that.

Most stories here follow a similar pattern: Krusoe draws the reader in by implying that a "story" is to be told, only to break off into hysterically absurd tangents, leading one to believe that the narrator (usually named Jim, sometimes Mr. Krusoe, one time a bear) is serving as something of a foil after having been rendered hilariously unreliable. In the title story, where the narrator's old friend has suddenly died on the car ride back from their annual fishing trip at Blood Lake (where it's best to get to fishing early before the lake's surface turns into a "clotted crust, impossible to penetrate with all but the heaviest of lures"), our narrator decides it's best for all if he simply buries Marvin and tells his wife he had drowned: "she'd be upset, but would save a lot of money, and I wouldn't have to drive back with him slumping there next to me. I knew that's what Marvin would have wanted."

Before dying, Marvin had related his experiences in the mind mazes at Cornell University, where he tried to duplicate exactly in his mind a just-electrically stimulated memory from his past. These "mazes" are emblematic of the narrator's attempt to re-create the story of "Blood Lake" as he wanders off (taking the reader with him) into the marvelously disparate thoughts he had conjured during the evening of the event that prompted his narrative. "Blood Lake" is representative of this fine collection, which fittingly ends with what I feel to be Krusoe's best piece, "Another Life." But I've saved that one for those who seek out this wryly ingenious book. [Christopher Paddock]

Dennis Barone. *Echoes.* Potes & Poets, 1997. 172 pp. Paper: $14.00.

Echoes collects twenty-eight pieces that can't be called fiction, poetry, essay, biography, or autobiography; between one to fifty pages, the pieces are instead prose assemblages that drift into and out of and in between more familiar genres. "Biography," for one, takes as its subject "you," the reader, while simultaneously telling the story of the writer, who "went to sleep too early and slept restlessly thinking of this page." About the "effacement of the ego," this (auto)biography is nevertheless also absorbed in lyrically haunting personal memories: "The crash on Christmas Eve. At home children waiting for gifts, for you. The glasses shatter in your eyes . . . Resolved: you will learn to see in a new way." A constant throughout *Echoes* is Barone's insistence on making the world, and language, unfamiliar. He says that "where there is no symmetry there can be no rest," and his lines dramatize the tension inherent in insisting upon differences, particularly between what is new and what has been written before. While he is fascinated with the inevitability of repetition, his pieces refuse to surrender to it; they insist on twisting repetition into something else. "Bir-Hakeim is a stop on the Paris Metro, though it could be something else, too . . . Think of the word 'note' because it is between memo and letter . . . Begin then to divide ice with shrill notes, shape ice into continents and where will be the divisions?" In Barone's work "variation will be encouraged"; what he creates and what readers will in turn "study is foreign." The pieces in *Echoes* are difficult, but that is their appeal. They are delirious literary plateaus that ensnare the mind, showing that the "present and necessary function" of literary work today "is transformation" and that "on the slight groundwork of reality, imagination" truly can spin. [Matthew Roberson]

Stephen-Paul Martin. *Not Quite Fiction*. Vatic Hum, 1997. 115 pp. Paper: $8.95.

Don't let the blurbs on the back cover of this extraordinary book fool you: these "essay-fictions" are not cloudy memoirs of a repressed childhood, all-too-clever observations detailing the tiny absurdities of everyday life, or ax-grinding political rants raging against the soulless bureaucratic machine. Instead, these texts, in their wanderings and improvisations, articulate fundamental questions about the relationships between language and representation, while leading the reader on a sort of linguistic joyride, a playful meandering where linguistic indeterminacy, freedom and pleasure are the only constants.

These fictions are about language, about themselves as fiction, about all language as fiction and about all self as language, i.e. as fiction. These are stories that constantly try to describe themselves, with this attempt at description becoming the story that the story is trying to describe. At times, Martin's writing gives the reader the feeling of being trapped inside language, where the only possible escape is more language, which is no escape at all.

Or maybe it is. For in *Not Quite Fiction* Martin makes an all-important connection between the literary and political and shows that those writers who are interested primarily in language can be the most committed of all: "And perhaps most important, if a work of fiction helps readers to think about what self-acceptance is, to see that the self they need to accept is a fiction, an invention, isn't it helping them see themselves as creators, giving them the responsibility to tell stories—interesting stories—as a means of inventing themselves?"

Not Quite Fiction is writing, with all its implications, resonances, and problems, at its best. [Jeffrey DeShell]

Ingmar Bergman. *Private Confessions*. Trans. Joan Tate. Arcade, 1997. 161 pp. $19.95.

Ingmar Bergman has retired from film directing but still directs plays and writes. He has written a two-volume autobiography, plus three novels and their screenplay adaptations for directors such as Bille August and Liv Ullmann. His subject in the theater and in his writing is the family. In *Private Confessions* he writes about how his parents' marriage began at the turn of the century.

Although not a roman à clef, *Private Confessions* renames his parents as Anna and Henrik (they were really Karin and Erik). Extroverted, confident, and sensuous, but also willful, stubborn, and self-centered, Anna is much like Bergman's mother: a child of privilege. Henrik is much like Bergman's father: a disadvantaged and shame-based youth who becomes a Lutheran minister, introverted, insecure, and repressed, but also self-important and passive-aggressive. Bergman once said that his father often humiliated him. In this novel as before, Henrik tries to cope with his insecurity by trying passively to make Anna feel humiliated. In return she does the same to him, only actively.

As one of the last modernists, Bergman uses many different techniques. His character development is largely realistic; for example, his characters often say "forgive me" because Swedes frequently ask for forgiveness (Americans just ask to be excused). Yet the narrative point of view and plotting have a postmodern instability. And although his epistemology is largely deterministic, his worldview seems nonetheless indeterminate.

For his breadth of technical felicity and yet his restraint in using it and for his ability to surprise even as he makes one say, "Yes, that's the way things really are," Bergman dispels any notion that his greatness depends on Sven Nykvist's cinematography and Sweden's inexhaustible supply of gifted actors. This writing is very fine. And it tells the truth.[Darryl Hattenhauer]

Richard Burgin. *Fear of Blue Skies.* Johns Hopkins Univ. Press, 1997. 184 pp. $19.95.

Richard Burgin is the editor of *Conversations with Isaac Bashevis Singer* and *Conversations with Jorge Luis Borges,* as well as the editor of *Boulevard* magazine. These admirable collections helped me greatly by pointing the way to his fictional interest in occult patterns, in odd passions that transform routine perceptions into "fears of blue skies" and force his unbalanced narrators to be trapped in labyrinthine narrations.

The opening sentences of "My Black Rachmaninoff," the first story in this brilliant collection, set the tone for the entire book: "Sooner or later if you stay in a place long enough something odd begins to happen to it. The walls or ceilings start to contort and parts of them may begin to look like tree branches in the wind or fingers trying to caress you." Burgin uses a plain style, strengthening the tone of uncertainty. The familiar becomes strange. The female narrator of the story begins to hear a piano. She creates an elaborate narrative—involving racial and sexual "notes"—to explain the phenomenon. She is wrong but even at the end of the story, she does not admit defeat. The last line refuses to close the matter: "maybe the concert was really the first thought of my new life or at least the first one that made sense."

All of these stories are "detective" stories, but the "detective" is often the "criminal." Thus Burgin suggests the metamorphosis of roles, thoughts, genders. The title of one of the stories captures his uncanny art: these stories are "Ghost Parks." [Irving Malin]

Pierre Jean Jouve. *Hecate* and *Vagadu*. Trans. Lydia Davis. Marlboro/Northwestern Univ. Press, 1997. 145 and 175 pp. $24.95 each.

Known primarily as a poet and essayist, Pierre Jean Jouve (1887-1976) wrote his only novels between 1925 and 1935. In *Hecate* and *Vagadu* Catherine Crachat, a Parisian actress, struggles against violent impulses and fears in order to find unity and meaning in her life. Torn between the twin forces of Eros and Thanatos and surrounded by darkness and shadows like her mythological counterpart Hecate, Catherine brings pain and destruction to herself and others. The first book of her adventures, a haunting tale of desire, hatred, and yearning for spirituality is built around the stormy triangular relationship between Catherine, her lover Pierre Indemini, and the diabolic Baroness Fanny Felicitas Hohenstein. The fragmented, intertwined stories of these three captivating characters draw the reader into the novel, just as Catherine and Pierre are pulled into the destructive web spun by Fanny, whose vitality and unbridled eroticism provide a counterweight to Catherine's strong sense of shame and guilt. As the downward spiral of events approaches its tragic end, the search for redemption intensifies, and Pierre and Catherine strive to transform their desire for each other into a transcendent form of love based on renunciation.

The story takes on a more overtly Freudian slant in *Vagadu*. Here, Catherine achieves liberating self-knowledge through psychoanalysis, and the obsessively recurring symbols of her troubled inner world powerfully convey her fight against her private demons. In particular, the use of doubles and surreal dream sequences gives the novel a strange hallucinatory quality, as figures from Catherine's past return to haunt her.

The two novels provide a fascinating picture of a woman's struggle against the forces of darkness. While the gripping intensity of the path to destruction in *Hecate* may appeal more to some readers, *Vagadu* is of particular interest as a fictional exploration of Freud's theories of the unconscious. [Susan Ireland]

Donald Antrim. *The Hundred Brothers.* Vintage, 1998. 206 pp. Paper: $12.00.

Before the dusk of this short novel's one evening, Doug, the narrator and 1 percent of the novel's hundred brothers, witnesses sufficient evidence of fraternal guerrilla struggles that divide old and young, married and single, and twins and not-twins. All of this before cocktails, dinner, and the Dance of the Corn King, which they're waiting for. Although Doug observes and remarks on many of his brothers' antics, he is a far cry from objective, for Doug is the Corn King and central to the action. As unreliable narrators go, this one is erratically unreliable, at times convincing, but often wildly self-deceived. Doug's narration is frequently knotted as he catalogues the brothers' activities in an epic manner that hasn't been as rousingly employed since Noah begot Shem, Ham, and Japheth six chapters into the Old Testament. While Doug gives every indication of wanting to understand his brothers, his desire exceeds his abilities and the critical tools he has—from primitive myths based on corn harvesting to genealogy and fossilized psychology—to make the task more difficult and finally tangle him in sticky webs of syntax.

It is fitting then that Antrim sets his novel about Western culture's collection of critical tools in the library, where the brothers meet, eat, drink, carouse, and look at eighteenth-century pornography. The stacks meanwhile are a maze, the shelving system's gone to pot, and books are piled on the floor. Antrim's library is both a physical place and a collection of conceptual signposts.

The Hundred Brothers is high-test literary absurdity. Explaining the need for ritual, Doug says, "Modern men had lost touch with ancient rhythms of death and regeneration, but that it was possible—if you took intoxicants and wore the right mask and costume—to regain connection with the primeval aspects of the Self." This is not too far from T. S. Eliot's prescription for Western culture in "The Waste Land," his vegetal myths and regeneration legends. The Fisher King has merely become the Corn King, right? One detail that will distinguish them is that Doug is talking to Gunner here, his brother's Doberman pinscher. [Paul Maliszewski]

Harold Brodkey. *The World Is the Home of Love and Death.* Metropolitan, 1997. 312 pp. $25.00.

Although some critics dislike Brodkey's texts because their style is convoluted, narcissistic, and "imitative"—I think of Proust and James—they do not recognize that he bravely attempts to capture the power of consciousness (or the consciousness of power). He wants to bully us—the first story is appropriately entitled "The Bullies"—and indeed to seduce us.

"Waking" is surely the best story in this collection. It is, perhaps, one of the best stories written by an American since World War II. It violates the norms of family life, the easy role playing we learn to survive. It uncannily demonstrates the wild darkness of Brodkey's art. "Waking" is an exploration of the painful relationship of son and mother, of "slave" and "master." It alerts us to the blurring of boundaries. It is a trancelike presentation of complicit incest. The narrator returns to the primal scene: his mother, Lila, and her inability to care for him—to clean his dirtied body. He realizes, as an adult, that he may be misreading the past. Throughout the text the pronouns are transformed: "I" turns into "he" and, without doubt, "she." (The transgression of "male" and "female" is an obsession of Brodkey's.) The sentences move slowly, tentatively, seductively as do the actions of infant and mother. Here is a representative sentence: "She holds me; she holds me by the shoulders and turns me and lowers me—she is going to stand me and prop me on the edge of the tub—and it is as if her arms were slow, straining wings, my wings." The infant is shaped by his mother-lover to reach angelic bliss. Even as the adult narrator remembers the terrifying embrace of ritual, he tries to relive it again and again. But his consciousness overwhelms him: "This local reality half shared—that is to say, judged and fixed as something other than private hallucination by my mother's being here—becomes strangely blank, elegant in a way, stripped of particularities, and close to a proud madness of making things into a theater of meaning." The common realities—waking, washing, speaking—are the "theater of meaning." And the theater compels the narrator to recognize that his life, his art, is perversely beautiful and painful. [Irving Malin]

Don Webb. *Stealing My Rules.* Cyber-Psychos AOD, 1997. 74 pp. Paper: $5.00.

At the turn of the last century Alfred Jarry invented protopomo "Pataphysics," or "the science of imaginary solutions" as he called it in *Exploits and Opinions of Dr. Faustroll, Pataphysician* (1911). Don Webb, someone we should all be paying a lot more attention to at this point in his career, has kept Jarry's torch of paradox and nonsense burning madly for more than a decade. His latest offering, *Stealing My Rules,* a dozen flash fictions ranging from a haunted piece of slipstream to a wacked-out version of cyberpunk space opera featuring the Great Ubu himself, carries more plot and ideas per paragraph than most fully formed novels and does so through a jagged prose that has little use for commas, subordinate clauses, or other emblems of linear mundaneness. Webb's world makes Julio Cortázar's look a little predictable, Philip K. Dick's a drab shade of mimetic. Every object and person shimmers with mystic mythic mystery at the verge of an epistemological phase transition: people caught in a traffic jam decide to abandon their cars and desert their city for twenty-four hours; a puddle of oil talks; a woman becomes the Welsh banshee she mimics to fool her husband; men wear each other's bodies like fur coats; and today flickers into 1966 or 2637 just like that to feed a Living Dead's time addiction. Rife with sacrifices and spells, split-open viscera and sexual horror shows, green goo and intrabody Ubu-morphing, these fictions don't so much steal as break the rules while proving again that Webb has more electroshock inventiveness in his left toenail than most writers have in their entire cosmos. [Lance Olsen]

Ilma Rakusa. *Steppe.* Trans. Solveig Emerson. Burning Deck, 1997. 77 pp. Paper: $10.00.

In *Novelistic Love in the Platonic Tradition* Jennie Wang argues that "lover's discourse" is a "socially privileged language" postmodernists must disrupt. Why? Because, in Wang's paraphrase of Noam Chomsky, "what enters the mainstream will support the needs of established power." Consequently, love in postmodern fiction is often a means of making political points while evading condemnation or willful neglect.

Something like the above may explain the twelve stories of *Steppe*, the third book of fiction (published originally in German in 1990) by Ilma Rakusa, a Swiss writer also known for her poetry and translations. Yet if these seductive stories make eyes at the reader, they also manage to stay teasingly just out of reach, as this typical passage perhaps suggests: "And then I fell into this state of mind which does without the justification of cause, context, in short, reason. Do you like that, my dear? Not: why do you like that, my dear? Your bass voice is beautiful, and you are called Kasimir and Otto, nobody claims that is tautology, nobody claims the ideal is at hand."

Love—what one narrator calls "a word from a dead language"—functions in Rakusa's postmodern world as focal point for a reappraisal of sexual politics and metaphor for established power of whatever sort: "He who swings the whip may not despair"; "At least behave as though the status quo were the most peaceful of all possibilities"; "made to feel small, smaller, smallest, as gnomes we are controllable."

"The novelist," Wang contends, "sells ideology," and "novelistic love" works as that ideology's "advertisement." I suggest this is what Rakusa may be up to here. But I am also prepared to do what she politely requests: to "please don't trap me in the narrow limits of your imagination." [Brooke Horvath]

Sadi Ranson. *Eels*. Salamanca/Alyscamps (35, rue de L'Espérance, 75013 Paris, France), 1997. 92 pp. No price given.

Eels is a slim, elegantly produced book comprising forty-two selected poems and a novella. The volume's actual physical elegance correlates rather closely to the writing within, and though there's something decidedly dissolute in this *soigné* little book, both in the way it's comprised and in its content, its unfalteringly beautiful writing allows it a seriousness which I think places it at the other extreme from wantonness.

Eels opens with the novella by the same title. Daniel and our narrator Esther, both married to other people, are falling in love, starting an affair. Their relationship to the world is that of lovers: the world and its inhabitants are out there and it goes by. Meanwhile, Daniel and Esther are nature, are smells and sounds and water and squirrels and flowers. "The one cell in my body that retains its primordial mating instinct—that puts its stock, instead—in scent—this part of me, this part of him, made a decision and we recognized each other as 'potential.' "

From the point the affair becomes de facto, the writing rushes thrillingly, and we are swept from office to cafe to study—assignation to assignation—quite as if we too were part of the rarified ocean *à deux* of lovers, these lovers. The poem "Eels" ends with this image: "But rest now in his arms. / Watch the silver fish and eels / Flashing all around you."

Eels can be read in a heartbeat, but the erotic power of that heartbeat is remarkable, and though the poems, all coming after the novella, cool us down, they also deepen the experience of the novella, remind us of the abiding power of risks taken with our hearts. No matter those risks always end disastrously, we dine out on the damage forever. [Michelle Latiolais]

Diamela Eltit. *E. Luminata.* Trans. and Afterword by Ronald Christ, with Gene Bell-Villada, Helen Lane, and Catalina Parra. Lumen, Inc., 1997. 234 pp. Paper: $15.00.

E. Luminata is an active unworking, a vigorous defying of psychological characterization, chronological story, unequivocal occurrences, and limiting or limited signification. It immediately brings to mind Blanchot's *The Madness of the Day* and Beckett's *The Lost Ones,* but refuses the coherence and presence of these equally tenebrous texts. This active unworking makes any sort of metatextual comment, let alone interpretation, difficult: to summarize what "happens" in the novel's ten chapters (just over two hundred pages)—a woman in a gray dress stands looking at a neon sign in the middle of a deserted plaza one night in Santiago—is to say next to nothing. The text agrees to, indeed requires, interrogation and interpretation, while simultaneously refusing and escaping such inquiry.

It is this very act of resisting that the text both "is about" and "is." Eltit sees complicity between critical interpretation and political totalitarianism. She writes, "I am interested in . . . cracking the monolith of completed stories," and is attracted by "the rebellious circulation of strategic fragments oppressed by official cultures." To Eltit, writing is an "act of liberating meanings and of protecting against the ideologizing of literature." In other words, it is literature's resistance to unequivocal meaning, its refusal to be allegorized, its detachment from significance, that gives it its truly revolutionary power.

I did have some trouble with the novel: Eltit's insistence on the substantiality of the book in her introduction—"An experiment may turn out or not; what I make is a work"—as well as Christ's placing it within a tradition of great (instead of minor) literature in his afterword, belies the novel's fugitive quality. I also had some problems making the connections the text requires: I must confess that I left the novel feeling it just eluded my grasp. Still, it is important to realize that *E. Luminata* is a text—in the most extreme sense of the word—and as such is profoundly contentious, discomforting, and unstable. [Jeffrey DeShell]

Johnny Payne. *Kentuckiana.* TriQuarterly/Northwestern Univ. Press, 1997. 255 pp. $24.95.

Kentuckiana is fiction writer and playwright Johnny Payne's second novel, and it is a finely written, completely entertaining work, indeed. Set in Lexington, Kentucky (specifically, in the subdivision of Garden Springs), *Kentuckiana* is the bizarre story of a real-estate developer and his son, Junior, an unlikely pair of storytellers whose weird cast of characters, the Miles family, literally come to life. In fact, the Miles family proves to be so realistic and so powerful that their respective voices quickly seize control of the novel's narrative, and the monologues of the developer and Junior become the bookends, the first and the final chapters of Payne's metafictional tale of family life in suburbia in the 1960s and '70s. Six of the seven Mileses take a turn at telling about their wild, unpredictable, and thoroughly dysfunctional family—the seventh manages to capture the heart of Junior—progressively blurring the line between their own imaginary existence and the reality of the real estate developer's attempt to report on his brainchild, the Garden Springs subdivision. Their respective monologues reveal a family trying hard to avoid the label "redneck," while confronting the evils of alcohol and drug abuse, free love, feuds, self-doubt, picky squabbles, teenage angst, love, duty, and much, much more. *Kentuckiana* is a funny, funny book that scratches at the surface of suburbia . . . and draws blood. Payne's writing is smooth and artful; each chapter is characterized by a distinct prose style and a unique narrative voice that resonates with charm and truth. This fanciful, sometimes hilarious portrait of working-class life in Kentucky is witty, ironic, and completely engaging. *Kentuckiana* deserves to be read. [Robert Headley]

Kathryn Davis. *Hell*. Ecco, 1998. 179 pp. $22.00.

This postmodern novel by Kathryn Davis (*Labrador, The Girl Who Trod on a Leaf*) uses food as the central metaphor for safety and order, a metaphor which fails to sustain two families, one a 1955 Philadelphia family struck by hurricane Hazel, and the other a nineteenth-century house kept in good order by Edwina Moss, an expert at housekeeping and a masterful cook. Both houses contain anorexic daughters, neither of whom can be protected from destructive forces outside their respective houses. The anorexic adolescent girl living in a twentieth-century Philadelphia suburb loses a girlfriend to murder or the hurricane (no conclusions can be drawn about the circumstances of the death), and the nineteenth-century homemaker Edwina has to endure a doctor who tries to make money from her anorexic daughter's condition, and she must also say goodbye to her union-soldier husband, who goes off to war and ends up in the Battle of the Wilderness, perhaps burned to death in the general conflagration which is war.

If food sustains us and the house in which food is prepared protects us, Davis is determined to show us that both houses and food can do little for daughters who refuse to eat. Davis juxtaposes lines from *Little Women,* which give us a glimpse of a loving family, with her Philadelphia household, which seems to offer little love. The nineteenth-century Moss household seems more loving.

Homemakers and chefs spend their lives learning to fix meals expertly, but food is not enough, in either household, to deflect chance and fate. Davis's book becomes a postmodern version of Günter Grass's *The Flounder,* which also chronicles the generations by means of food. Grass's mammoth novel might be the easier of the two to read. [Frank Kooistra]

Ali Smith. *Like*. Virago (London), 1997. 343 pp. £12.99.

The first 150 pages of *Like* are captivating because at their narrative center is an eight-year-old girl by the name of Kate whose bemused and intelligent curiosity about both the natural and civilized world around her commands our respect, even our affection. She is reminiscent in a marvelous way of Colette's Bel-Gazou, and one is happy to inspect figuratively the insides of this child's pockets, to listen in on her taxonomic musings of the world. As we read on we understand that a mystery is also at the center of these pages, one which perhaps doesn't rivet Kate quite so much as it does the reader. Why is Kate's mother, Amy, incapable of reading and why does she upon seeing a picture of an erupting Vesuvius suddenly begin to regain not only her past, but her skills to read?

Narrative convention promises us we will find out the answers to these questions—and others—and in various intriguing movements in the key of flouting conventions we do. In the remaining two hundred pages of the novel the answers come not alongside Kate but rather in the voice of a character heretofore mentioned only teasingly, her mother's would-be inamorata, a young Scottish woman by the name of Aisling, or Ash, who has "made it" as a movie star, perhaps a lesbian porn star.

I can't figure out whether it was a bold move against the conventions of fiction or some failure of nerve on the part of the author to maintain a young girl as the central character in a longish novel ostensibly about the great to-ings and fro-ings of fates which then, by way of trickle-down, inform hers. But I'm not only never distracted from my interest in Kate by the novel's remaining two hundred pages in Ash's voice, my interest is also never satisfied by a return in the narrative to Kate's life.

It's all very sophisticated in a theoretical way, so very modern, and I admire the writing and the abilities of Ali Smith to create tremendous characters. If my interest in the novel eddied solely within the well of the intellect, then I think I'd have few reservations, but Ali Smith writes a better book than that, dramatizes a far more complicated emotional world; I was sorry a certain structural insistence disallowed connections less cerebral. Still, her work certainly deserves reading. [Michelle Latiolais]

Sara Chin. *Below the Line.* City Lights, 1997. 149 pp. Paper: $9.95.

The Chinese-American characters in Sara Chin's collection of short stories and vignettes are trying to fit themselves in: into families, freeways, grocery stores, Chinatowns, or occasionally China itself. But, like the old man who gets lost on Washington, D.C.'s Beltway, most have the sensation of going around and around, unsure of which direction will take them where they want to go. What they have to guide them—exit signs, family legends, translated recipes—is frequently confusing: How can you tell where you're going and what you've passed already?

In "Red Wall" a team of independent filmmakers goes to China to make a documentary about the post-Mao years. The narrator, who is in charge of sound, signs on in order to look "for the heart, the trashy heart of my history." She confronts a jumble of contradictory images and people: ancient peasants marked by torture; an opera singer with a flush toilet; an old family friend and government official who wants to know all about Hollywood. In this as in other stories the characters' journeys through China and America are a constant debunking of the stories they have always believed, and in the end they show the stories to be unimportant. What matters is the human element, the human connection, in spite of individual facts. As the soundwoman finally realizes, "I didn't have to worry about facts or truth. I could ponder other things. Things closer to my heart."

Not all of the pieces are successful—"Fevers," about an elderly woman who enters the world of her favorite television show, has the air of trying too hard. But Chin has an excellent ear; her prose is as rhythmic and condensed as poetry. And like her filmmaker, she has made herself the guardian of memory, so that what is close to the heart of this book is truth, of a transcendent nature. [Susann Cokal]

Martine Bellen, Lee Smith, and Bradford Morrow, eds. *Conjunctions* 29: *Tributes*: *American Writers on American Writers.* Bard College, 1997. 405 pp. Paper: $12.00.

The editors of this special issue of *Conjunctions* describe *Tributes* as "an anthology of personal enthusiasms." As they explain, "a number of contemporary writers were invited to pay homage to an American writer, one who made something possible for them, whether that was the act of writing itself, or writing a certain book, or in a particular manner, or living in a way that was consonant with the work of writing."

The result is forty-five essays running from half of a page (Diane Williams on Emily Dickinson) to twenty-nine pages (Carole Maso on Gertrude Stein) but averaging five to eight pages. Some are self-focussed ("I read a lot as a kid," begins John Sayles's essay on Nelson Algren) or boldly idiosyncratic (Cole Swensen on Marianne Moore), others genially academic (Joanna Scott on Poe) or overflowing with quotations as though in recognition of the fact that to recall approvingly an author's own words is the best tribute (Ntozake Shange on Sterling Brown). Some contributors offer straightforward commentary or defenses of writers felt to be misunderstood or underappreciated (Ellen McLaughin on Lillian Hellman), others impressionistic collages (C. D. Wright on Frank Stanford) or lists of discrete particulars (Peter Straub on Raymond Chandler). Still others tender thanks or gush eloquently. All take their subjects personally, and all are magnanimous.

Filled with good writing and provocative insights, *Tributes* raises any number of questions about the Americanness of American literature, the changing import and constituency of our literary past, and the importance of understanding what one is doing by grasping what others have done. If it is true, as Emerson once wrote, that "sometimes a scream is better than a thesis," many of these brief essays remind us that it is also the case that sometimes a tribute is better than a dissertation. [Brooke Horvath]

Rick Moody and Darcey Steinke, eds. *Joyful Noise: The New Testament Revisited.* Little, Brown, 1997. 250 pp. $23.95.

Joyful Noise is an eclectic collection of essays on religion in general and the New Testament in particular by mostly young, contemporary writers including Madison Smartt Bell, Benjamin Cheever, Barry Hannah, bell hooks, and Joanna Scott. It is a pleasure to see an engagement with spirituality in a less than dogmatic manner, by writers who represent a variety of interpretations and come from backgrounds ranging from white, heterosexual, and Christian to African-American, Hispanic, gay, Jewish, and Buddhist. The editors compare the collection to jazz, hence the name *Joyful Noise*, various riffs on Jesus and the apostles.

Topics in this volume range from personal interpretations of Jesus to how the Gospels can affect the way we live in modern society. Among the most successful are the essays which blend personal narrative with a carefully thought-out reaction to a specific part of the New Testament. Bell hooks's "Love's Alchemy," for example, starts with her experience of attending a class on the Bible as Literature and ends with a beautiful meditation on 1 John, on how perfect love can cast out fear and what the implications of that notion mean.

There is a fascination with the human side of Jesus, as a teenager, as a convict, as a friend to the imperfect apostle Peter, and with his physicality, including his feet. The least successful of these essays are those that seem to be primarily childhood reminiscences of God, Jesus, and the Bible and stay at the anecdotal level rather than transcending these remembrances. *Joyful Noise* will be of interest to those who want to think seriously about their own spirituality and relate it to their concerns about modern society. [Sally E. Parry]

Hugo Claus. *The Swordfish.* Peter Owen, 1997. 104 pp. £14.95.

This novella by Hugo Claus, Belgium's most famous contemporary writer, partly accomplishes what it sets out to do, which is to show the creating and destroying power of an iconoclastic Christ in a rural Belgian town where religious zeal barely exists. Martin, the young son of Sibylle Verhegge, the divorced wife of a manufacturer, learns about the crucifixion from a dying music teacher who wants to convert one impressionable soul before she dies. She teaches Martin about Jesus's crucifixion and resurrection in secret; then Martin does what mature Christians often do, which is to imitate the crucifixion by carrying a wooden cross, which an ex-abortionist turned drunken handyman, Richard Robion, has made for him out of scrap wood.

The interesting side of the novel is that Martin's obsession with Christ precipitates change (secular changes to be sure) in the lives of Martin's mother, the handyman Richard, and Headmaster Goosens, who is Martin's teacher at the local school. Sibylle and Goosens begin an affair, which will be a short-term antidote to the boredom and frustration in their own lives. Richard Robion, the handyman, undergoes a more drastic change, beating to death Julia, his alcoholic wife, who has followed her lover into alcoholism to keep him company in his disgrace. He takes out all the anger of their sexually dysfunctional relationship on her, beating her to death the same day. Julia becomes the Christlike sacrificial figure in the novel, who bleeds like Christ on the cross. The novel ends with a description of her death. Richard is talking with the police inspector, who is interrogating him: (" 'But when you fell unconscious, before that I mean, was she still alive?) "Of course she was still alive! ('was she bleeding?') Of course she was bleeding!' " Martin cannot (nor does he try to) convert the skeptical adults his obsession brushes against briefly, but the changes he affects in their lives go far beyond the ordinary events of one day. A Christlike and sacrificial death occurs in an unlikely place, which is both threatening and astonishing, but in the spirit of the crucified and risen Christ. [Frank Kooistra]

Mark Axelrod. *Cardboard Castles*. Pacific Writers, 1996. 233 pp. Paper: $16.95

Axelrod's novel is a moving and at times hilarious adventure through one writer's life of the imagination, the intellect, and the libido. The novel introduces Brazilian-American novelist Duncan Katz, whose story—told by Katz himself with a self-consciousness that at once acknowledges, expands upon, and satirizes the playful seriousness (serious playfulness?) of much postmodern fiction—moves from the narrator's first encounters with books, wherein as a child he literally "consumes" their pulpy pages, through his frustrations as a burgeoning author, his lawsuit against God for the deity's irresponsible creation of Minnesota winters, and his flight to foreign lands.

The novel is driven by Katz's contradictions. His voice is one that has acquired a contemporary dose of irony and resignation; nonetheless, the narrative betrays the depth of Katz's seemingly indestructible idealism. He is a man defeated not only by American publishing but also by God Himself (in the courtroom encounter); yet he is moved to reveries on love, hunger and responsibility that can spring only from a still vital well of hope that even Katz's most bitter defeats have not dried up. In this he is a hero for our times, ever-aware and willing to push on regardless of the frustrations that inevitably accompany such cursed/blessed awareness. Here lies the triumph of Axelrod's compelling protagonist—that engagement with a world that is in countless ways coercing us to *dis*engage is in itself a rich enough "means" that arriving at one or another particular "end" is finally unimportant.

Cardboard Castles is an important novel and—as it is the first in a trilogy featuring Katz—a promising one as well. [Gordon McAlpine]

Christopher J. Knight. *Hints & Guesses: William Gaddis's Fiction of Longing*. Univ. of Wisconsin Press, 1997. 302 pp. Paper: $24.95.

This is the most complete study of Gaddis's fiction to date, and it provides highly stimulating readings of his four novels. To his credit, Knight avoids enlisting Gaddis in exclusively academic debates that in no way concern him, such as the hermetic cottage industry obsessed with defining what counts as postmodern. Instead, Knight examines themes and topics explicitly developed within Gaddis's fiction: the role of the artist and the aesthetic in contemporary society, along with the question of "what is worth doing" in a socioeconomic system that seems to be running us rather than we it (*The Recognitions* and *JR*); the hope of transcending humankind's chronic stupidity, evil, and violence (*Carpenter's Gothic*); and the possibilities of realizing ideal standards of justice, or at least of following the established procedures of worldly law (*JR* and *A Frolic of His Own*). Knight's readings occasionally launch into excursuses on "extramural" matters like history, philosophy, politics, and economics, but in each case the digression is highly worthwhile. Along with the pioneering studies of Steven Moore and John Kuehl, Knight's book should prove to be a valuable introduction to one of the most important novelists alive today, one who is not only the most talented ventriloquist of various forms of American speech but, as Knight forcefully argues, a profound satirist who always returns, with encyclopedic breadth, to the oldest but still most urgent questions of ethics: How should we live and how might we work against the self-destructive tendencies of human history? [Thomas Hove]

James R. Giles. *Understanding Hubert Selby, Jr.* Univ. of South Carolina Press, 1998. 164 pp. $24.95.

At last a book on Selby, a mere thirty-four years after the publication of his first novel *Last Exit to Brooklyn,* which was followed by the equally brilliant *The Room.* Giles's approach is to place Selby in the naturalist tradition of Crane, Dreiser, and Algren, or more accurately, that in Selby naturalism is coupled with existentialism, which connects Selby with Dreiser, at one end of the spectrum, and with Genet, at the other end. Giles does a very credible job of explicating Selby's work, placing him in a tradition, and providing relevant biographical details. What he is less good at is showing the artistry at work, which is precisely what has baffled critics (especially academics) and continues to leave Selby outside the discussion of postwar American fiction. Selby has nothing whatsoever to do with the "serious," officially sanctioned fiction of the 1960s (Bellow, Updike, Malamud) nor the experimental works of such writers as Hawkes, Barth, and Pynchon. Belonging in neither camp, he had no camp. As such, he occupies the space that a writer like William Carlos Williams continues to occupy in relation to *his* fiction: the academics don't get it, it doesn't have the convenient handles that a Bellow provides nor the highly intellectual foundation that the early Barth offered, it doesn't fit the ready-made modes that make him teachable. Instead, Selby plumbed an American speech, thought, and sensibility that is foreign to almost all of his contemporaries, looking like a naive genius to some and an unsophisticated, foul-mouthed naturalist to others. In the very attempt to give legitimacy to Selby as belonging to a tradition, Giles gives too little attention to what makes Selby unique in American writing. But the attempt to place Selby anywhere at all is long overdue, and Giles's book, I hope, will begin to generate the discussion that Selby's work deserves. [John O'Brien]

Timothy S. Murphy. *Wising Up the Marks: The Amodern William Burroughs.* Univ. of California Press, 1998. 276 pp. $45.00; paper: $17.95.

"Burroughs' work," Timothy S. Murphy declares, "constitutes an exacting critique both of the social organization of late capital and of the logic of representation or textuality that abets it." He substantiates his thesis by taking bearings from Ralph Ellison's *Invisible Man* and by repeatedly drawing comparisons between Burroughs and the theoretical positions of Gilles Deleuze and Félix Guattari. These comparisons work well on the whole and underpin a critical commentary which has many insights to offer into the experience of reading Burroughs. Thus Murphy rejects the simplistic view of Burroughs as a "revolutionary" writer by arguing that the addict in his early work is antiproductive. Murphy also brings out clearly Burroughs's view of the interdependence of police and criminal as personified in the paradoxical figure of the addict-agent. Burroughs emerges from this account as a kind of literary trickster, manipulating media expectations in *Naked Lunch* and combining science fiction with the detective novel in his Nova trilogy. An unusually detailed section explores the significance for Burroughs of Haasan I Sabbah, the founder of the Assassins, who figures as an author-surrogate or subversive opponent of autocracy. Murphy stresses the importance of *The Wild Boys* as introducing a new genre to Burroughs's work (the book of the dead) with the purpose of evoking a fantasy destruction of the world as a prelude to political change. Burroughs's late trilogy, a "paradoxical group fantasy," explores utopian themes and describes the process of writing as a forging of alternate histories. Murphy takes care to stress the performative nature of much of Burroughs's narratives, coining the term *amodernist* to denote the latter's opposition to extreme postmodernism. Murphy accordingly presents in Burroughs a writer who constantly exploits paradoxes, simultaneously scrutinizing the systems of his culture and expressing the desire to destroy those systems. Murphy joins such recent Burroughs critics as Richard Dellamora in presenting Burroughs as a shrewd critic of homophobia as well as political repression. This valuable new study concludes with an examination of Burroughs's collaborations with the British film director Antony Balch, his cut-ups, and his sound recordings. [David Seed].

Lucile C. Charlebois. *Understanding Camilo José Cela*. Univ. of South Carolina Press, 1998. 187 pp. $29.95.

It has been fifty years since Cela published *La familia de Pascual Duarte* (1942; English translation published in 1964 as *The Family of Pascual Duarte*). Yet this remains an important literary event in twentieth-century Spanish literature. It is not so much that *Pascual Duarte* defied various segments of the Franquista ideology at a time when there were few other notable efforts in fiction. Rather, Cela legitimated a form of gritty realism that has remained a hallmark of Spanish writing ever since, as it has moved through various periods of cultural production in the intervening years. The absolute elimination of any form of sentimentalism and the ability to see even the most apparently random form of individual behavior as deeply rooted in implacable social structures served Cela well for the inauguration of a literary career that is still central to contemporary Spanish literature.

While it is true that Cela wandered far and wide from the social realism of *Pascual Duarte,* he never lost his commitment to the imperative for implacable narrativity. Charlebois's study, part of a series devoted to "Understanding Modern European and Latin American Literature," surveys Cela's ten most important novels, and she quite rightly focuses on the implacableness of his narrative scrutiny of the human enterprise. What remains quite singular about Cela, however, is the enormous variety and versatility of the strategies he found for the representation of the human social condition, which explains to a large extent why he has ended up producing more sustainedly intriguing fiction than anyone else of his generation, as well as how he managed never to become like Pío Baroja, in the sense of a body of writing in which all of the novels end up sounding the same.

Charlebois provides an excellent "humanistic" reading of Cela's novels. Her comments are accurate and intelligent, and her study admirably fulfills the goal of providing an understanding of Cela's writings. [David William Foster]

Linden Peach. *Angela Carter.* St. Martin's, 1998. 183 pp. $35.00.

By including Angela Carter in its Modern Novelists series, St. Martin's Press has inducted her into the pantheon of important twentieth-century authors—a well-deserved addition.

Linden Peach's lucid explication of Carter's works provides a useful resource for future scholars. He asserts that Carter contributes to the development of the novel through a cultural critique which renders her own culture as "foreign." The importance of this project for future critics, he says, includes "the need to recognize how her novels deconstruct the processes that produce social structures and shared meaning, evident, for example, in her recurrent demythologizing of the mother figure and in the way in which the manifestation of the female body in her work disrupts the social construction of women as Woman."

By connecting thematic elements from *The Sadean Woman* to his analysis of her novels, Peach weaves a persuasive argument for assessing Carter's oeuvre as a unified and coherent whole. He outlines her skepticism about all mythologies, including our most recent ones, and her exploration of the role of dominant discourses in character formation. However, Carter did not, he says, simply foreground the problems; her novels emphasize the importance of transgression—of breaking things—in overturning old myths and developing self-autonomy, and she insisted that human beings must take control of language if they wish to establish identity. In making his case Peach effortlessly and judiciously employs contemporary theoretical approaches to illuminate Carter's thematic concerns without resorting to the heavy-handed use of obfuscating jargon. He provides us with a useful and interesting addition to a growing body of work on an important, and greatly missed, voice. [Joanne Gass]

Alfred Kazin. *God and the American Writer.* Knopf, 1997. 272 pp. $25.00.

Early on in this informal study, Kazin explains that he is "interested not in the artist's professions of belief but in the imagination he brings to his tale of religion in human affairs." For their exemplary treatments of this tale, Kazin singles out Hawthorne, Emerson, Stowe, Melville, Whitman, Lincoln, Dickinson, William James, Twain, Eliot, Frost, and Faulkner. His critical approach consists mainly of paraphrasing fundamental texts from the American canon and providing biographically informed commentary. Often, he will also interject illuminating literary comparisons or historical anecdotes, and he frequently manages to sum up the most salient features of a writer's thought and style with dazzling economy. In some cases Kazin merely goes over familiar ground, as in his chapters on Hawthorne and Eliot. But in other cases, his paraphrases manage to perform at least two important tasks of criticism: to explain why a writer's works are worth reading and to inspire the reader to experience those works directly, whether for the first or the fiftieth time. Kazin is most inspiring when he discusses the literature of the Civil War, particularly Lincoln's speeches. For varying reasons, his other favorites are the tormented agnostics Melville, Dickinson, and Faulkner. Those looking for a broader and more systematic study of religion and American literature might be more satisfied by Andrew Delbanco's *The Death of Satan.* But Kazin's book should satisfy those who want to see how a particularly sensitive and eloquent reader engages with works he continues to find, in his ninth decade of life, important. [Thomas Hove]

Jan Philipp Reemtsma. *More Than a Champion: The Style of Muhammad Ali.* Trans. John E. Woods. Knopf, 1998. 172 pp. $21.00.

Let's use the cheese tester's method for what goes on in commercial publishing, and here is the piece of cheese: Jan Philipp Reemtsma's *More Than a Champion: The Style of Muhammad Ali,* translated from the German by John E. Woods. The jacket says that Reemtsma is "one of Europe's most prominent intellectuals" (usually when such claims are made, there is at least a hint as to what this is based on, e.g., the names of a few books the person has written: no such information about the author here). Well, let's see. The book's 172 pages are primarily given over to accounts of Ali's fights, written in a prose that resembles the worst of sports writing (Grantland Rice and Alfred E. Knopf must both be turning in their graves). Example: here is the opening line to the Ali-Frazier fight in Manila: "A renewed hail of blows to Frazier's head. But Frazier won't let himself be driven to the ropes." But from this distinguished intellectual (excuse me, "one of Europe's most prominent"), we also wax philosophical: "We do not grow from defeat. We are destroyed by defeat . . . ." Fortunately, these sophomoric remarks are rather limited, but perfectly fit with the book's awful sports writing á la Bob Costas (that is, sports is not just a game, but is the game of life). The bad writing itself is surpassed perhaps only by the incredible strategy of using the "Rocky" films (and, yes, we get very detailed accounts of the movies) to explicate Ali. And all of this from some unknown German! Perhaps most incredible about this as a sports book is that it is all old, old, old news. Who at Knopf read the manuscript and accepted it for an American market? The *Kirkus* review accurately puts it this way: "Very little of this is new, and one wonder[s] exactly why a distinguished European intellectual is so preoccupied with telling us a great deal that any ordinary boxing fan already knows." Why indeed. But the bigger question is who at Knopf decided this was a good book and should be published?

But there is also a disturbing thesis at work in the book (i.e., its "intellectual" side) which champions the isolated, heroic individual as opposed to the masses. Always a dangerous bent from any German. Are we perhaps talking about the "super man"? I suppose that we are to be reassured by Reemtsma's sympathetic portrayal of the black man in America (once again, he tells us nothing that isn't known, but manages to do so in a very condescending way). So here we have a German who understands black men in America? And Knopf thought this, when all rolled together, added up to a book it should publish? Herr Reemtsma should be strongly encouraged to limit himself to writing about Germans and Jews, and perhaps there he might have some knowledge worth sharing. Once again *Kirkus:* "What's good here isn't original, and what's original isn't good." And so why did Knopf publish this? [Rott Krispen]

Books Received

Adéékó, Adélékè. *Proverbs, Texuality, and Nativism in African Literature.* Florida, 1998. $49.95. (NF)

Agosín, Marjorie. *Melodious Women.* Trans. Monica Bruno Galmozzi. Latin American Literary Review, 1997. Paper: $13.95. (P)

Aira, César. *The Hare.* Trans. Nick Caistor. Serpent's Tail, 1998. Paper: $14.99. (F)

Ansay, A. Manette. *River Angel.* William Morrow, 1998. $24.00. (F)

Albahari, David. *Tsing.* Trans. by the author. Northwestern, 1997. Paper: $14.95. (F)

Alighieri, Dante. *Inferno.* Trans. and intro. Elio Zappulla. Illustrations by Gregory Gillespie. Pantheon, 1998. $30.00. (P)

Bagader, Abubaker, Ava M. Heinrichsdorff, and Deborah S. Akers, eds. *Voices of Change: Short Stories by Saudi Arabian Women Writers.* Lynne Reinner, 1997. $28.00; paper: $13.95. (F)

James Baldwin: Collected Essays. Ed. Toni Morrison. Library of America, 1998. $35.00. (NF)

James Baldwin: Early Novels and Stories. Ed. Toni Morrison. Library of America, 1998. $35.00. (F)

Balutansky, Kathleen M., and Marie-Agnès Sourieau. *Caribbean Creolization: Reflections on the Cultural Dynamics of Language, Literature, and Identitiy.* Florida, 1998. $49.95. (NF)

Banks, Russell. *Cloudsplitter.* Harper Flamingo, 1998. $27.50. (F)

Barker, Nicola, et al. *Does the Sun Rise over Dagenham?: New Writing from London.* Foreword by Mark Lawson. Fourth Estate, 1998. Paper: £9.99. (F)

Bayley, John. *The Red Hat.* St. Martin's, 1998. $21.95. (F)

Beattie, Ann. *Park City: New and Selected Stories.* Knopf, 1998. $25.00. (F)

Ben-Ner, Yitzhak. *Rustic Sunset and Other Stories.* Trans. Robert Whitehill. Lynne Rienner, 1997. $29.95. (F)

Blondel, Nathalie. *Mary Butts: Scenes from the Life.* McPherson, 1998. $35.00. (NF)

Bove, Emmanuel. *A Winter's Journal.* Trans. Nathalie Favre-Gilly. Afterword by Keith Botsford. Northwestern, 1998. Paper: $15.95. (F)

Bowman, David. *Bunny Modern.* Little, Brown, 1998. $21.95. (F)

Bradford, Matías Serra. *Studio.* La Carta de Oliver, 1997. No Price Given. (F)

Breeden, David. *Another Number: A Novel of the 70's.* Silver Phoenix, 1998. Paper: $12.95. (F)

Brookner, Anita. *Visitors.* Knopf, 1997. $23.00. (F)

Broughton, James. *Packing Up for Paradise: Selected Poems 1946-1996.* Black Sparrow, 1998. $27.50; paper: $16.00. (P)

Bukowski, Charles. *The Captain Is Out to Lunch and the Sailors Have Taken Over the Ship.* Illustrated by Robert Crumb. Black Sparrow, 1998. $27.50; paper: $14.00. (F)

Bundy, Alison. *Duncecap.* Burning Deck, 1998. Paper: $10.00. (F)
Bush, Peter. *The Voice of the Blue Turtle: An Anthology of Cuban Stories.* Ed. Peter Bush. Grove, 1998. Paper: $14.00. (F)
Butler, Jack. *Dreamer.* Knopf, 1998. $25.00. (F)
Canetti, Elias. *Notes from Hampstead:The Writer's Notes: 1954-1971.* Trans. John Hargraves. Farrar, Straus, & Giroux, 1998. $23.00. (NF)
Carlston, Erin G. *Thinking Fascism: Sapphic Modernism and Fascist Modernity.* Stanford, 1998. $39.50. (NF)
Carson, Anne. *Autobiography of Red.* Knopf, 1998. $23.00. (F)
Carter, Charlotte. *Rhode Island Red.* Serpent's Tail, 1997. Paper: $12.99. (F)
Casey, Calvert. *The Collected Stories.* Trans. John H. R. Polt. Ed. and intro. Ilan Stavans. Duke, 1998. $49.95; paper: $16.95. (F)
Childress, Mark. *Gone for Good.* Knopf, 1998. $25.00. (F)
Claus, Hugo. *Desire.* Trans. Stacey Knecht. Viking, 1997. $24.95. (F)
Coe, Jonathan. *The House of Sleep.* Knopf, 1998. $24.00. (F)
Collins, Warwick. *Computer One.* Marion Boyars, 1998. $24.95. (F)
Condé, Maryse. *The Last of the African Kings.* Nebraska, 1997. $35.00; paper: $12.00. (F)
Constant, Paule. *The Governor's Daughter.* Trans. Betsy Wing. Nebraska, 1998. $35.00; paper: $15.00. (F)
Cooper, Douglas. *Delirium.* Hyperion, 1998. $21.95. (F)
Coover, Robert. *Briar Rose.* Grove, 1998. Paper: $11.00. (F)
——. *Spanking the Maid.* Grove, 1998. Paper: $11.00. (F)
Coupland, Douglas. *Girlfriend in a Coma.* HarperCollins, 1998. $24.00. (F)
Couser, G. Thomas, and Joseph Fichtelberg, eds. *True Relations: Essays on Autobiography and the Postmodern.* Greenwood, 1998. $55.00. (NF)
Crace, Jim. *Quarantine.* Farrar, Straus, & Giroux. $23.00. (F)
Crews, Harry. *Celebration.* Simon & Schuster, 1998. $23.00. (F)
Dilllon, Millicent. *A Little Original Sin: The Life and Work of Jane Bowles.* California, 1998. Paper: $17.95. (NF)
Duncker, Patricia. *Monsieur Shoushana's Lemon Trees.* Ecco, 1997. $22.95. (F)
Dunmore, Helen. *Your Blue-Eyed Boy.* Knopf, 1998. $23.95. (F)
Duras, Marguerite. *Writing.* Trans. Mark Polizzotti. Lumen/Brookline, 1998. $15.95. (NF)
Dutourd, Jean. *A Dog's Head.* Trans. Robin Chancellor. Chicago, 1998. Paper: $12.00. (F)
Early, Gerald, ed. *Body Language: Writers on Sport.* Graywolf, 1998. Paper: $16.00. (NF)
Echenoz, Jean. *Big Blondes.* Trans. Mark Polizzotti. New Press, 1997. Paper: $12.95. (F)
English, Lucy. *Selfish People.* Fourth Estate, 1998. Paper: £6.99. (F)
Esterházy, Peter. *She Loves Me.* Trans. Judith Sollosy. Northwestern, 1997. $26.95. (F)
Everson, William (Brother Antoninus). *The Residual Years: Volume I of the Collected Poems.* Black Sparrow, 1998. $27.50; paper: $17.50. (P)
Fares, Gustavo, and Eliana C. Hermann, eds. *Contemporary Argentinean Woman Writers: A Critcal Anthology.* Trans. Linda Britt. Florida, 1998. $49.95. (F)

Ferré, Rosario. *Eccentric Neighborhoods.* Farrar, Straus & Giroux, 1998. $24.00. (F)

Fishburn, Evelyn, ed. *Short Fiction by Spanish-American Women.* Manchester, 1998. $69.95; paper: $19.95. (NF)

Flood, John. *Bag Men.* Dell, 1997. Paper: $9.95. (F)

ffrench, Patrick, and Roland-Francois Lack, eds. *The Tel Quel Reader.* Routledge, 1998. Paper: $24.99. (NF)

Futterman, Enid. *Bittersweet Journey: A Modestly Erotic Novel of Love, Longing,* and *Chocolate.* Viking, 1998. $22.95. (F)

García Lorca, Federico. *In Search of Duende.* Trans. Christopher Maurer, et al. New Directions, 1998. Paper: $7.00. (NF/P)

Gifford, Barry. *The Sinaloa Story.* Harcourt Brace, 1998. $22.00. (F)

Gille, Elisabeth. *Shadows of a Childhood: A Novel of War and Friendship.* New Press, 1998. $23.00. (F)

Goodis, David. *The Blonde on the Street Corner.* Serpent's Tail, 1997. Paper: $11.99. (F)

Gretlund, Jan Nordby. *Eudora Welty's Aesthetics of Place.* South Carolina, 1997. Paper: $16.95. (NF)

Gurganas, Allan. *Plays Well with Others.* Knopf, 1997. $25.00. (F)

Hamsun, Knut. *Hunger.* Trans. & Afterword by Robert Bly. Intro. Paul Auster. Noonday, 1998. Paper: $13.00. (F)

———. *Mysteries.* Trans. Gerry Bothmer. Afterword by Isaac Bashevis Singer. Noonday, 1998. Paper: $14.00. (F)

Harte, Jack. *Birds and Other Tails.* Dedalus/Dufour Editions, 1997. $23.95. (F)

Hedges, Peter. *An Ocean in Iowa.* Hyperion, 1998. $22.95. (F)

Heller, Joseph. *Now and Then: From Coney Island to Here.* Knopf, 1998. $24.00. (NF)

Herzog, Tobey C. *Tim O'Brien.* Twayne, 1997. $28.95. (NF)

Hilbert, Donna, and Gerald Locklin. *Two Novellas: Waiting for My Baby & The First Time He Saw Paris.* The Event Horizon Group, 1998. Paper: $29.95 (F)

Hirsal, Josef. *A Bohemian Youth.* Trans. Michael Henry Heim. Northwestern, 1998. Paper: $14.95. (F)

Hoban, Russell. *Mr. Rinyo-Clacton's Offer.* Jonathan Cape, 1998. £14.99. (F)

Høeg, Peter. *Tales of the Night.* Trans. Barbara Haveland. Farrar, Straus & Giroux, 1998. $23.00. (F)

Hoisington, Thomas H., ed and trans. *Out Visting and Back Home: Russian Stories on Aging.* Northwestern, 1998. $26.95. (F)

Hollier, Denis. *Absent without Leave: French Literature under the Threat of War.* Harvard, 1997. Paper: $27.95. (NF)

Houston, James D. *The Last Paradise.* Oklahoma, 1997. No price given. (F)

Hoyser, Catherine E. and Lorena Laura Stookey. *Tom Robbins: A Critical Companion.* Greenwood, 1997. $29.95. (NF)

Iyasere, Solomon O., ed. *Understanding* Things Fall Apart: *Selected Essays and Criticisms.* Whitston, 1998. $23.50. (NF)

Ji-moon, Suh, ed. *The Rainy Spell and Other Korean Stories.* Trans. Suh Ji-moon. East Gate/M. E. Sharpe, 1997. $62.95; paper: $21.95. (F)

Jin, Ha. *Under the Red Flag.* Georgia, 1997. $22.95. (F)

Joshi, S. T., ed. *The Annotated H. P. Lovecraft.* Dell, 1997. Paper: $12.95. (F)
Kavanagh, Patrick. *Gaff Topsails.* Viking, 1998. $24.95. (F)
Kleberg, Lars. *Starfall: A Triptych.* Trans. Anselm Hollo. Northwestern, 1998. $22.95.(F)
Klíma, Ivan. *The Ultimate Intimacy.* Trans. A. G. Brain. Grove/Atlantic, 1998. $25.00. (F)
König, Barbara. *Our House.* Trans. Roslyn Theobald in collaboration with the author. Northwestern, 1998. $26.95.(F)
Kramer, Victor A., and Robert A. Russ, eds. *Harlem Renaissance Re-examined.* Whitston, 1997. Paper: $19.95. (NF)
Kravitz, Peter, ed. *The Picador Book of Contemporary Scottish Fiction.* Picador, 1997. £16.99. (F)
Kristal, Efrain. *Temptation of the Word: The Novels of Mario Vargas Llosa.* Vanderbilt, 1998. $34.95. (NF)
Kristeva, Julia. *Possessions.* Trans. Barbara Bray. Columbia, 1998. $27.50. (F)
Kundera, Milan. *Identity.* Trans. Linda Asher. HarperCollins, 1998. $22.00. (F)
Lamantia, Philip. *Bed of Sphinxes: New & Selected Poems, 1943-1993.* City Lights, 1998. Paper: $12.95. (P)
Lambert, Gavin. *The Slide Area.* Midnight Classics/Serpent's Tail, 1998. Paper: $11.99. (F)
LeFanu, Sarah, ed. *Sex, Drugs, Rock N' Roll: Stories to End the Century.* Serpent's Tail, 1998. Paper: $13.99. (NF)
Lipkin, Randie. *Without.* Fugue State Press, 1998. Paper: $7.00. (F)
Little, Jonathan. *Charles Johnson's Spiritual Imagination.* Missouri, 1998. $39.95; paper: $19.95. (NF)
López Ortega, Antonio. *Moonlit.* Trans. Nathan Budoff. Lumen/Brookline, 1998. $15.95. (F)
Maitland, Sara. *Angel Maker.* Owl, 1998. Paper: $12.00. (F)
Manley, Frank. *The Cockfighter.* Coffee House, 1998. $19.95. (F)
Mann, Thomas. *Doctor Faustus.* Trans. John E. Woods. Knopf, 1997. $35.00. (F)
McCarthy, Cormac. *Cities of the Plain.* Knopf, 1998. $24.00. (F)
McDermott, Alice. *Charming Billy.* Farrar, Straus & Giroux, 1998. $22.00. (F)
McEwan, Ian. *Enduring Love.* Doubleday, 1998. $23.95. (F)
McGee, Patrick. *Ishmael Reed and the Ends of Race.* St. Martin's, 1997. No price given. (NF)
McNamee, Eoin. *Resurrection Man.* Picador, 1995. Paper: £5.99. (F)
Mendoza, Rubén. *Lotería and Other Stories.* Buzz/St. Martin's, 1998. Paper: $12.95.(F)
Mokeddem, Malika. *The Forbidden Women.* Trans. K. Melissa Marcus. Nebraska, 1998. $35.00; paper: $15.00. (F)
Mooney, Ted. *Singing into the Piano.* Knopf, 1998. $25.00. (F)
——. *Paradise.* Knopf, 1998. $25.00. (F)
Murdoch, Iris. *Existentialists and Mystics: Writings on Philosophy and Literature.* Allen Lane/Viking, 1998. $37.95. (NF)
Naqvi, Tahira. *Attar of Roses and Other Stories of Pakistan.* Lynne Rienner,

1997. $25.00; paper: $15.95. (F)
Nicol, Mike. *The Ibis Tapestry.* Knopf, 1998. $23.00. (F)
Nothomb, Amélie. *The Stranger Next Door.* Trans. Carol Volk. Henry Holt, 1998. $20.00. (F)
O'Connor, Bridget. *Tell Her You Love Her.* Picador, 1997. £6.99. (F)
Olson, Charles. *Call Me Ishmael.* Afterword by Merton M. Sealts, Jr. Johns Hopkins, 1997. Paper: 13.95. (NF)
Orpheus Grid: A Literary Arts Magazine. Winter 1997. Number 1.
Pacheco, José Emilio. *City of Memory and Other Poems.* Trans. Cynthia Steele and David Lauer. City Lights, 1998. Paper: $10.95. (P).
Parini, Jay. *House of Days.* Owl, 1998. Paper: $13.00. (P)
Patterson, Richard F. *Caribbean Passages: A Critical Perspective on New Fiction from the West Indies.* Lynne Rienner, 1998. $38.00. (NF)
Pavić, Milorad. *Last Love in Constantinople: A Tarot Novel for Divination.* Dufour, 1998. $23.95. (F)
Plimpton, George. *Truman Capote: In Which Various Friends, Enemies, Acquaintances, and Detractors Recall His Turbulent Career.* Doubleday, 1997. $35.00. (NF)
Powell, Padgett. *Aliens of Affection.* Henry Holt, 1998. $22.50. (F)
Powers, Richard. *Gain.* Farrar, Straus, & Giroux, 1998. $25.00. (F)
Prevallet, Kristin. *Perturbation, My Sister.* First Intensity, 1997. Paper: $10.00. (F)
Puértolas, Soledad. *Bordeaux.* Trans. Fransica González-Arias. Nebraska, 1998. $30.00; paper: $15.00. (F)
Pynchon, Thomas. *Slow Learner.* Back Bay/Little, Brown, 1998. Paper: $13.95. (F)
Quirk, Joe. *The Ultimate Rush.* Morrow, 1998. $23.00. (F)
Raz, Hilda, ed. *The Prairie Schooner Anthology of Cotemporary Jewish American Writing.* Bison/Nebraska, 1998. Paper: $15.00. (F, P, NF)
Reed, Kit. *Weird Women, Wired Women.* Foreword by Connie Willis. Wesleyan/New England, 1998. Paper: 16.95. (F)
Robert, Michéle. *Impossible Saints.* Ecco, 1997. $24.00. (F)
Romero, Sophia G. *Always Hiding.* Morrow, 1998. $22.50. (F)
Rouaud, Jean. *The World More or Less.* Trans. Barbara Wright. Arcade, 1998. $22.95. (F)
Russell, Mary Doria. *Children of God.* Villard, 1998. $23.95. (F)
Sawyer-Lauçanno, Christopher. *The Continual Pilgrimage: American Writers in Paris, 1944-1960.* City Lights, 1998. Paper: $18.95. (NF)
Saxton, Alexander. *Bright Web in the Darkness.* California, 1997. Paper: $12.95. (F)
Schneider, Bart. *Blue Bossa.* Viking, 1998. $24.95. (F)
Schwartz, Jason. *A German Picturesque.* Knopf, 1998. $21.00. (F)
Schwarz, Daniel R. *Reconfiguring Modernism: Explorations in the Relationship between Modern Art and Modern Literature.* St. Martin's, 1997. No price given. (NF)
Scott, Joanna. *The Manikin.* Owl, 1998. Paper: $12.00. (F)
Sebald, W. G. *The Rings of Saturn.* Trans. Michael Hulse. New Directions, 1998. $23.95. (F)
Shepard, Jim. *Nosferatu.* Knopf, 1998. $22.00. (F)

Schoenberger, Nancy. *Long Like a River.* New York UP, 1998. $25.00.; paper: $12.95. (P)

Shua, Ana María. *Patient.* Trans. David William Foster. Latin American Literary Review Press, 1997. Paper: $14.95. (F)

Singer, Isaac Bashevis. *Shadows on the Hudson.* Trans. Joseph Sherman. Farrar, Straus & Giroux, 1998. $28.00. (F)

——. *The Slave.*Trans. Isaac Bashevis Singer and Cecil Hemley. Noonday, 1998. $13.00. (F)

Skemer, Arnold. *Momus.* Phrygian, 1997. No Price Given. (F)

Smith, Larry. *Working It Out.* Ridgeway, 1998. Paper: $9.95. (F)

Steele, Meili. *Critical Conversations: Literary Theories in Dialogue.* South Carolina, 1997. $29.95; paper: $12.95. (NF)

Steiner, George. *Errata: An Examined Life.* Yale, 1998. $25.00. (NF)

Stephenson, Richard. *The Insanity of Samuel Beckett's Art.* Paintbrush Press, 1998. No price given. (NF)

Stortoni, Laura. *The Moon and the Island.* Intro. Diane di Prima. Hesperia, 1997. Paper: $13.00. (P)

Stuart, Francis. *King David Dances.* Dufour, 1997. Paper: $12.95. (F)

Teleky, Richard. *The Paris Years of Rosie Kamin.* Steerforth, 1998. $24.00. (F)

Tournier, Michel. *Gemini.* Trans. Anne Carter. Johns Hopkins, 1998. No Price Given. (F)

Travers, Martin. *An Introduction to Modern European Literature from Romanticism to Postmodernism.* St. Martin's, 1998. No price given. (NF)

Tyler, Anne. *A Patchwork Planet.* Knopf, 1998. $24.00. (F)

Vargas Llosa, Mario. *The Notebooks of Don Rigoberto.* Trans. Edith Grossman. Farrar, Straus & Giroux, 1998. $23.00. (F)

Van Delden, Maarten. *Carlos Fuentes, Mexico, and Modernity.* Vanderbilt, 1998. $32.95. (NF)

Vice, Sue. *Introducing Bakhtin.* Manchester, 1997. No price given. (NF)

VOYS: A Journal Exploring Sign in Sound: The Electronic Voice. Jill Battson, et al. Compact Disk. No price given.

——. *The Voice in the Closet.* Raymond Federman. Compact Disk. No price given.

Wakoski, Diane. *Argonaut Rose.* Black Sparrow, 1998. $27.50; paper: $14.00. (P)

Waldrop, Howard. *Going Home Again.* St. Martin's, 1998. $20.95. (F)

Wallace, David Foster. *A Supposedly Fun Thing I'll Never Do Again.* Little, Brown, 1998. Paper: $13.95. (NF)

Wang, Jing, ed. *China's Avant-Garde Fiction.* Duke, 1998. Paper: $17.95. (F)

Watson, Carl, and Shalom. *Belle Catastrophe.* Surge Graphix LLC, 1997. Paper: $14.95. (P)

Wechsler, Robert. *Performing Without a Stage: The Art of Literary Translation.* Catbird, 1998. $21.95. (NF)

Welsh, Irvine. *Ecstasy.* Norton, 1996. Paper: $13.00. (F)

White, Bailey. *Quite a Year for Plums.* Knopf, 1998. $22.00. (F)

Whitt, Margaret Earley. *Understanding Flannery O'Connor.* South Carolina, 1997. Paper: $12.95. (NF)

Williams, John L. *Faithless.* Serpent's Tail, 1998. Paper: $13.99. (F)

Wilson, Robert McLiam. *Ripley Bogle.* Arcade, 1998. $24.95. (F)

Wojdowski, Bogdan. *Bread for the Departed.* Trans. Madeline G. Levine. Foreward by Henryk Grynberg. Northwestern, 1997. Paper: $19.95. (F)

Wolf, Christa. *Medea: A Modern Retelling.* Trans. John Cullen. Intro. Margaret Atwood. Doubleday, 1998. $22.95. (F)

Yared, Nazik Saba. *Improvisations on a Missing String.* Trans. Stuart A. Hancox. Arkansas, 1997. $20.00; paper: $12.00. (F)

Yumiko, Kurahashi. *The Woman with the Flying Head and Other Stories.* Trans. Atsuko Sakaki. East Gate/ M. E. Sharpe, 1997. $43.95; paper: $19.95. (F)

Ziarek, Ewa Plonowska, ed. *Gombrowicz's Grimaces: Modernism, Gender, Nationality.* SUNY, 1998. $21.95. (NF)

Ziesk, Edra. *Acceptable Losses.* SMU, 1996. No price given. (F)

Translators

Ieva S. Celle is a Ph.D. candidiate in the Department of Slavic Languages at Brown University. She has translated Edvins Liepins's novel *Riga and the Automobile* and stories by Vizma Belsevica, Alberts Bels, and Imants Ziedonis.

Franceska Kirke was born in Rīga, Latvia, in 1953. In 1972 she attended Jānis Rozentāls School of Art in Rīga and in 1978 the Latvian Academy of Arts. Her paintings have been exhibited across Europe and America.

Rita Laima Krieviņa (née Rumpeters, 1960) spent the first twenty-two years of her life in the suburbs of New Jersey and New York City. In 1982 Krieviņa moved to Latvia, at that time a Soviet Socialist Republic, and has lived there since. Krieviņa has had three children's books published in Latvia: her translation of and illustrations for Jaime de Angulo's *Indiāņu teikas* (Indian Tales, 1991) and illustrations for Jaan Kaplinski's *Kas ko ēd* (Who Eats What, 1993) and for *Kaķis lēca smēdē* (The Cat Jumped in the Smithy, 1994), a collection of Latvian children's counting rhymes. Krieviņa's illustrations for her ABC book won the VAGA publishing house's Green Tail Award in 1995. Krievina has worked for the *Baltic Observer* and the *Baltic Times* as culture editor, writing about life and people in post-Soviet Latvia. She presently works for the Delegation of the European Commission in Latvia, where she is keeping track of Latvia's EU preaccessions progress.

Iven Lešinska was born in Rīga and studied at the University of Latvia, Ohio State University, the University of Colorado, and the University of Stockholm. She has translated a number of contemporary Latvian poets into English and the poetry of T. S. Eliot, Allen Ginsberg, Ezra Pound, and Seamus Heaney, among others, into Latvian. She is currently the editor of the magazine *Rīgas Laiks*.

Sarma Muižnieks Liepiņš was born in Kalamazoo, Michigan, in 1960. *Izğērbies,* her first collection of poetry, was published in 1980. Subsequently her poems and essays have been published in periodicals in the US, Canada, Australia, Germany, Slovakia, and Latvia. Currently, Liepiņš works at the Harvard University Widener Library in the Baltic collection and as a professional artist. She lives in Boxford, Massachusetts, with her husband and two sons.

Born in Cesis, Latvia, Ilze Kļaviņa, Mueller lived in Germany and Australia before moving to the United States, where she makes her permanenet home. She has also lived in Tanzania and Zaire. A graduate of the University of Chicago and University of Minnesota, with degrees in German literature, she teaches German at Macalester College in St. Paul, Minnesota. A recipient of a Fulbright Fellowship and the Canadian-Latvian Jauna Gaita Translation Prize, Kļaviņa-Mueller has been translating German and Latvian poetry and prose into English since the 1970s. Her translations include *Idleness Is the Root of All Love,* by German poet Christa Reinig (Calyx Books, 1991). Recently she has begun writing poetry and is published in *Looking for Home* (Milkweed, 1990).

Baņuta Rubess is an award-winning playwright and director who writes and directs in English and in Latvian. Her writing ranges from feminist comedies to political satire, from a jazz play to a teen drama. Rubess also devised and produced the highly successful radio series *Adventure Stories for (Big) Girls* for two seasons on CBC, Canada's national radio network. For the past four seasons, she has been an Associate Artist at Theatre Passe Muraille in Toronto.

Rubess's Latvian plays have been both scandalous and popular. Her first play was the Latvian musical, *Varondarbi* (Heroica, 1978). Her next musical, *Tango Lugano,* was produced both in North America and Rīga. In 1991 when Rīga was barricaded against the Soviet army, Rubess was there to co-direct a play by Latvian feminist Aspazija in the tiny independent theater, Kabata. Her translations of Andra Neiburga's stories have been published by *AGNI* review in Boston.

Māra Sīmanis, although not a professional translator of literature, has been translating concepts across cultures for decades. Born in Chicago in 1960 and raised on the Latvian *dainas* (folk songs), she gained her B.A. in International Relations from Knox College in Illinois and M.A. in International Management from the School for International Training in Vermont. She taught English in Japan and was the Program Coordinator for the Institute of Latvian Studies in Münster Germany during *perestroika*. The day after German re-unification she moved to Latvia where she worked at the newspaper *Diena* setting up the Foreign News Desk, the Foreign Ministry initiating foreign aid coordination, the Ministry for State Reform developing public administration reform policy and the Prime Minister's Office improving policy planning.

Contributors

MARK AMERIKA is the author of two novels, *The Kafka Chronicles* and *Sexual Blood* (Black Ice Books). He is the founder and director of the Alt-X Online Network (www.altx.com) and his multimedia hyperfiction GRAMMATRON (www.grammatron.com) was recently praised as "the world's most ambitious cybernovel."

JEFF BAKER holds a Ph. D. in American Literature from Purdue University and works in Los Angeles as a writer for a small nonprofit publisher. He also teaches part-time at Cal State-Northridge and Mount San Antonio Community College. A singer-songwriter, he performs occasionally in and around greater Los Angeles.

DAGMAR BURKHART is Professor of Slavic Languages and Literatures at the University of Mannheim, Germany. She writes on Slavic literatures, the theory of Slavic folklore, and the semiotics of Slavic ethnological phenomena. Her study *Kulturraum Balkan. Studien zur Volkskunde un Literature Sudosteeuropas* was published in 1989.

STEPHEN DAVENPORT is a postdoctoral fellow in American Literature at the University of Illinois at Urbana-Champaign. In addition to creative work that has appeared or will soon appear in such literary magazines as the *Iowa Review*, *Many Mountains Moving*, *Chachalaca Poetry Review*, and *Flyway*, he has an article forthcoming in *Men and Masculinities* about fathers, sons, family and work in Stephen King's *The Shining*, and he is working on a book on Jack Kerouac.

RADMILA J. GORUP teaches in the Department of Slavic Languages and Literatures at Columbia University. She writes on linguistics and Serbian literature. She co-edited an anthology of contemporary Serbian short stories to be published by the University of Pittsburgh Press.

CHARLES B. HARRIS has published numerous articles on contemporary American fiction and the profession of English studies. His books include *Contemporary American Novelists of the Absurd* (1971) and *Passionate Virtuosity: The Fiction of John Barth* (1983). He directs the Unit for Contemporary Literature at Illinois State University.

RACHEL KILBOURN DAVIS received her B.A. from the University of Maryland and her M.A. from the University of Wisconsin—Madison. She interrupted her doctoral program to care for her baby daughter.

ANDREAS LEITNER, Professor at the University of Klagenfurt, Austria, is a slavicist and philosopher. His publications include works on Russian, Serbocroatian, and Slovene literatures as well as Slavic-German comparative studies. In 1991 he published *Milorad Pavić's roman "Das chasarische Worterbuch."*

TOMA LONGINOVIĆ is Professor of Slavic Languages and Literatures at the University of Wisconsin—Madison and a writer of fiction in both Serbian and English. His books include a theory of the modern novel, *Borderline Culture* (1993) and a novel, *Minut cutanja* (A Moment of Silence, 1997).

JASMINA MIHAILOVIĆ is a literary critic, author, and translator. She lives and works in Belgrade. In 1992 she published *A Tale of the Soul and Body: The Layers and Meanings in the Prose of Milorad Pavić*. In 1996 she published an extensive bibliography of Pavić's works, *Bio-Biografija Milorada Pavića 1949-1995*.

CHRISTINA PRIBIĆEVIĆ-ZORIĆ is an American who lived in Belgrade for twenty years. A translator and broadcaster, she now lives in London. She is the award-winning translator of Pavić's *Dictionary of the Khazars*.

ALAN SINGER is the author of three novels, *The Ox-Breadth* (1980), *The Charnel Imp* (1988), and *Memory Wax* (1996). He has also written two works of literary theory, *A Metaphorics of Fiction* (1984) and *The Subject as Action: Transformation and Totality in Narrative Aesthetics* (1994). He is Professor of English and Director of the Graduate Creative Writing Program at Temple University.

CHRISTOPHER SORRENTINO's *Sound on Sound* was published by Dalkey Archive Press in 1995. He lives in Brooklyn.

DAVID WINN teaches fiction writing and contemporary literature at Hunter College, City University of new York. His first novel is *Gangland* (Knopf). He is at work on his second novel, *Cable Comes to Queens*.

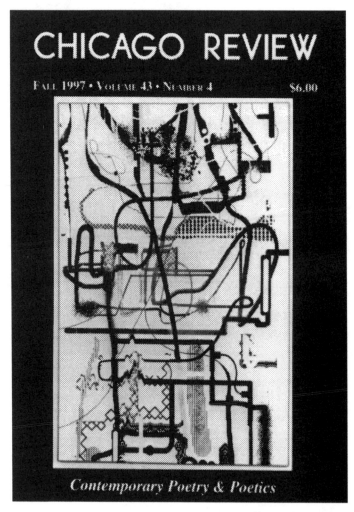

Studies in 20th Century Literature

A journal devoted to literary theory and practical criticism

Volume 22, No. 2 (Summer, 1998)

Special Issue in preparation:

Occupation and Empire in France and the Francophone World
Guest Editors: Anne Donadey, Sarah Farmer, Rosemarie Scullion, Downing Thomas, Steven Ungar

Russian Culture of the 1990s
Guest Editor: Helena Goscilo

Silvia Sauter, Editor
Kansas State University
Eisenhower 104
Manhattan, KS 66506-1003
Submissions in:
Russian and Spanish

Jordan Stump, Editor
University of Nebraska
PO Box 880318
Lincoln, NE 68588-0318
Submissions in:
French and German

Subscriptions

Institutions—\$20 for one year (\$35 for two years)
Individuals—\$15 for one year (\$28 for two years)
Single issues—\$10.00 (add \$5 for Air Mail)

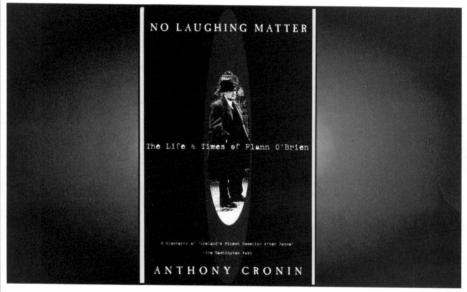

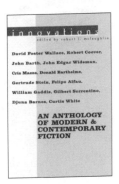

Memories of My Father Watching TV

by Curtis White

$12.50 pb

"Witheringly smart, grotesquely funny, grimly comprehensive, and so moving as to be wrenching—a novel that's 'important' in all senses of the word."—David Foster Wallace

"A bit like Kathy Acker doing Joyce . . . . Hypnotic."—*Booklist*

Monstrous Possibility

by Curtis White

$12.50 pb

"A set of dazzling riffs on literature, theory, cultural politics and mass commercialism, *Monstrous Possibility* is, in the very finest sense, refreshing."—Mark Crispin Miller, author of *Boxed In: The Culture of TV*

"For all of us who persist in thinking that contemporary literature *matters*, these keen and contrarian essays provide many monstrous and wondrous possibilities indeed."
—Michael Bérubé, author of *Public Access: Literary Theory and American Cultural Politics*

Dalkey Archive Press

The Sky Changes

by Gilbert Sorrentino

$11.95 pb

"I have never read a novel more explicitly clear, nor one more relevant, in its statements of contemporary life in this country." —Robert Creeley

"*The Sky Changes* captures the breakup of a marriage with brutal, arresting precision." —*Boston Globe*

"Composed with dazzling and precise verbal dexterity, *The Sky Changes* is replete with sadness for lost love and despair over a cheapened American culture."—*Washington Post*

Time Must Have a Stop

by Aldous Huxley

$13.50 pb

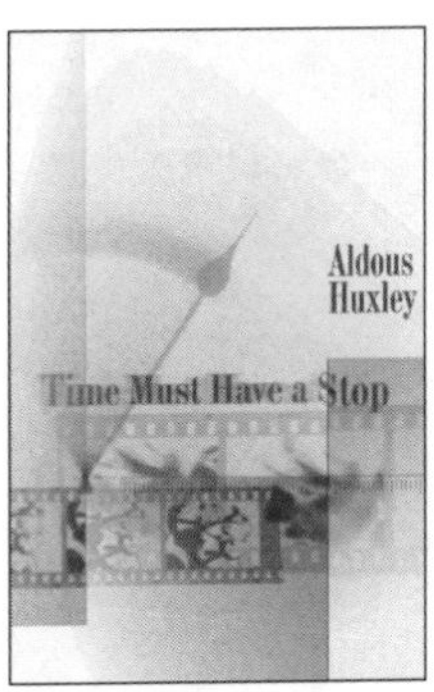

"The book is exciting because it is talented . . . an engagingly advanced accomplishment."—Thomas Mann

"A brilliant performance."—Edmund Wilson

"*Time Must Have a Stop* exhibits Mr. Huxley's learning, his gift for limericks, an acute sense of the craft of poetry and a genuine power of modern poetic phrase, a flow of ribald expression and more than a feast of dark and desperate conclusions about sex."—*Times Literary Supplement*

Giscome Road
by C. S. Giscombe

$10.95 pb

"A book of reckoning, an elliptic, take-no-prisoners tour de force."—Nathaniel Mackey

"A remarkable and surprising book."—Ron Silliman

"This is a work of great originality, authority and verbal beauty, a book that will reward many readings. C.S. Giscombe has attempted much, and realized much, in this long, enthralling poem."—Adrienne Rich

Genii Over Salzburg
by Carl R. Martin

$10.95 pb

"Carl Martin reminds me of certain 'outsider' poets of the past like Gérard de Nerval or Robert Walser—writers whose work one seizes on greedily at moments when one feels like drowning in poetry. This is the right stuff."—John Ashbery

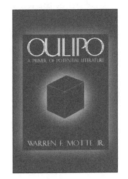

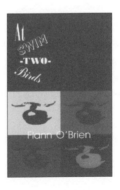

Order Form

Individuals may use this form to subscribe to the *Review of Contemporary Fiction* or to order Dalkey titles or back issues of the *Review* at a 10-20% discount.

Title	*Qty*	*Price*

(10% for one book, 20% for two or more books) Subtotal __________

Less discount __________

Subtotal __________

($4 domestic, $5 foreign) Plus postage __________

1 year subscription ($17 domestic, $20.50 foreign) __________

Total __________

Ship to:

____

____

____

____

____

mail or fax this form to:

Dalkey Archive Press
ISU Campus Box 4241
Normal, IL 61790-4241
fax: 309 438 7422
tel: 309 438 7555

Credit card payment ❑ Visa ❑ Mastercard

Acct # __________ Exp. Date __________

Name on card __________

Phone Number __________

Please make checks (in U. S. dollars only) payable to *Dalkey Archive Press.*

Dalkey Archive Press